DATE DUE

AP 29 '72		
JA 29 '74		
FEB E NF11		
JUN 3 1977		
OCT 30 2012		
DE 15 80		
GAYLORD		PRINTED IN U.S.A.

Time for Stories

of the Past and Present

compiled by May Hill Arbuthnot

and Dorothy M. Broderick

Illustrated by Rainey Bennett

A representative collection of realistic stories for children,
to be used in the classroom, home, or camp; especially
planned for college classes in children's literature; with
section introductions, headnotes for the individual stories, and
a special section entitled "Realistic Literature and Children"

Scott, Foresman and Company

FOREWORD

Time for Stories of the Past and Present introduces another new name to the *Time for* books. It is with pride that I present Professor Dorothy M. Broderick as coauthor of this volume. Miss Broderick is a distinguished colleague from Case Western Reserve University, Cleveland, who is well known for her work in many phases of children's literature. Her knowledge of the field of children's books is incredibly wide and thorough. She has written several books for children and young people. Her classes are popular and provocative, her lectures brilliant, and her book reviews both sound and penetrating. So it is a great satisfaction to have her discriminating judgment in choosing selections for this book and also for the new *Time for Biography.*

May Hill Arbuthnot

Cleveland, 1968

PREFACE

Time for Stories of the Past and Present, like *Time for Biography,* has evolved from *Time for True Tales,* 1961. The development of two volumes from one has come about because of the startling increase in good writing for children in both realistic stories and biographies. It was impossible to include stories from both fields in a one-volume book; hence the need for two separate volumes to represent more fairly the growing emphasis on and demand for sound realistic stories and biographies of today.

This book is intended for use by teachers, librarians, parents, and other adults who work with children both formally and informally. For it, we have endeavored to select excerpts from as wide a range of realistic stories as possible in the hope that each reader will find a nucleus of books with special appeal to him. Each selection has been made on the bases of literary quality and demonstrated appeal to children. The selections should lure many readers and juvenile listeners to read the complete books from which the excerpts were taken. Of course, no single anthology of stories can provide a completely satisfactory selection of books, and so the Bibliography, pp. 243-258, and the section, "On Keeping Up," in Part Two, pp. 240-241, are designed to offer adults further opportunities for good reading in children's realistic literature.

The plan of the book

Part One of the book, the stories, is divided into four categories: Animal Stories, Life in the United States, Life in Other Lands, and Historical Fiction. Each section is prefaced by an introduction which discusses the importance of the type of stories, the criteria for their selection, and their appeal to children. The four introductions provide an overall approach to the categories.

Each selection is prefaced by a headnote designed to make the excerpt meaningful. These headnotes indicate to the adult reader the general tone of the book from which the excerpt is taken and provide an idea as to the value of the book for children.

"Realistic Literature and Children," Part Two of the volume, discusses general criteria for evaluating realistic stories and suggests various ways in which adults can use the anthology section. It covers the values of reading aloud to children and the joys and problems of developing juvenile discussion groups.

The Bibliography comprises Part Three, and the books listed there suggest additional readings for adults and children who wish to pursue further a type of story or an author presented in the anthology section. Besides meeting general literary standards, most of the books in the Bibliography are delightful to read aloud.

Suggestions for using the book

Time for Stories of the Past and Present can be read consecutively from beginning to end, but most adults will prefer to skip and choose selections, as they will best suit the needs of youthful listeners. Thus, when a unit on Indians is introduced early in the school year, the teacher may wish to go directly to William Steele's *Flaming Arrows* (p. 191) as a vivid account of the impact that fear of Indians had on the settlers' lives.

Before reading an excerpt to children, however, adults should be sure that the complete book is obtainable in the school or public library. It would be unfair to both reader and listener to stimulate interest in a book which is unavailable. For that reason, all books included in the anthology and listed in the Bibliography were in print as the volume went to press. We would also remind adults that a growing number of juvenile books are available in paperback editions, which helps ease the problem of providing multiple copies of a popular title.

The selections in each of the four sections are sufficiently contemporary so that they should provoke lively class discussions. Even the historical stories deal with some of our modern problems. In almost every case the excerpt can stand by itself as a unit, and it can also furnish a lead into the book, the author, and his other books. Within each category, the selections have been grouped, as far as possible, to provide a reading-ladder approach to books with common characteristics and appeal. If you read a selection aloud or discuss it with children, you will discover that their interest in it will often send them scurrying to the library to finish the book and read more of the author's other works—for example, Marguerite Henry's books, Beverly Cleary's, William Steele's, or the books of other favorite authors.

About the revision

The purpose of a good anthology is the extension and continuation of interest in the excerpts presented. The best of the old, in-print selections remain—thirty strong; and there are seventeen new selections, which have added richly to the quality and balance of the whole offering. The picture stories for children from ages four to six have been dropped because without their illustrations they seemed sadly crippled and misrepresented.

The seventeen new selections, added to the excellent old selections taken from the 1961 edition of *Time for True Tales*, produce a level of quality which demonstrates the full range and vitality of juvenile publishing. The various changes made for this edition have been strongly influenced by changes in the publishing world. Thus, most of the new selections are in the "Life in the United States" section since that is the area where publishing has made its strongest impact in the last several years. This is especially desirable for children, teachers, librarians, and students of children's literature, because a strong blast of fresh air is blowing through modern realism for today's young people. Here are today's children facing contemporary problems and situations and taking our changing world in their stride.

Stories about people, whether set in the United States or in other lands, are so real that readers can truly see themselves in the characters. Gone are the wishy-washy Elsie Dinsmores, replaced by children who are true to their friends and less than kind to children they don't like. The new breed of author has accepted as fact the idea that children possess a full range of emotions, that they experience despair as well as happiness, and that they develop likes and dislikes for other people. The honesty of such presentations enables the young person to identify with the book characters, and to count them friends as much as if they lived next door or down the block.

Recent stories about animals are often written so realistically as to chill the blood of some readers. *The Frightened Hare* (p. 37) and *The Great White* (p. 54), for example, will not appeal to every reader; and their use with very young children might not prove advisable. However, the new biology being introduced in many school systems is reflected in the honest approach by the authors of both books. By the time children reach the fifth and sixth grades they should have some understanding of the true nature of the natural world and the fight for survival experienced by all animals, including man.

And, to provide a tighter unity within the section on Historical Fiction, all of the selections now pertain to United States history.

In discussing the selections that have been kept and the new additions, we need to insert a word about the economics of publishing an anthology. The fees charged for permission to reprint copyrighted material are set by the publisher (on rare occasions by the author) and are paid by the compilers. In a few cases the fees asked were so high as to make inclusion of the excerpts impossible. When this occurred, no attempt was made to substitute less satisfactory selections for the dropped titles.

Finally, the unity of the book should be mentioned. It has been designed so that each part complements and supplements every other part. We believe that the teachers, librarians, parents, students, and other adults who use the book as a whole will find themselves developing their own criteria for the evaluation of realistic stories while having a marvelous time reading juvenile books, and we believe that their children will have an equally happy time.

Here, then, is your new *Time for Stories of the Past and Present*, a compilation of old and recent realistic stories for children. These are stories to enjoy and mull over—sometimes with laughter, sometimes with sorrow. It is hoped that children will come away from these excerpts and the books from which they were taken with a deeper knowledge of themselves and of the needs, desires, and lives of others; that they will feel that life is preciously valuable. Both you and your children will be richer for having read them.

MHA
DMB

CONTENTS

The following titles were supplied by the compilers for untitled chapters or excerpts: The Beginning of the Journey, Mr. Kildee Makes Friends with Old Grouch, The Wild Rams Find a Friend, New Life on the Mountains, Tragedy, The Rescue, The Thing, Ellen Tells a Story and Hears a Story, Edward Cleans His Room, The School Halloween Parade, Harriet Changes Her Mind, "Checking-In" at the Museum, Everything Is Different, A Hobo Adventure, Kamau Goes Home, A Calm Before the Storm, "That Man Can Stand Up," A Yankee Meets a Young Confederate.

PART TWO: REALISTIC LITERATURE AND CHILDREN

PART THREE: BIBLIOGRAPHY

Story Time

Stories about animals are so popular with modern children that it is sometimes a problem to get them to read anything else. Perhaps the reason is that over half the world's population is now living in urban areas and the city child misses the everyday contact with animals, which is the rural child's heritage.

Although dog and horse stories have been the most popular types of stories over the years, recent times have witnessed an upsurge in books about non-domesticated animals. The traditional dog and horse stories are still with us, but they no longer dominate the field. Current trends take the child reader into the forests, fields, and streams with "biographies" of beavers, bears, foxes, and even that most maligned animal, the skunk.

ANIMAL STORIES

These trends are probably a logical extension of the effects of civilization. Unless there is a mounted police force, the city child rarely sees a horse; and the only dogs he meets are walked on leashes. The chances are that the city child lives in an apartment building that forbids dogs. Thus, if he is interested in dogs and horses, he must turn to books to satisfy his needs.

The environment of the country child, too, has changed in recent times. He no longer lives in a real wilderness; shopping centers and housing developments surround him, even if he lives on a farm. The wild animals have been driven farther and farther away, and the child rarely encounters a fox or a deer in his roamings. This lack of personal encounter with animals increases the fascination of books about them.

Moreover, there has been a change in the attitudes of scientists toward animals. In the early years of this century, anyone attributing human characteristics to animals was looked upon as a hopeless romantic. But recent studies by ethologists like Konrad Lorenz have shown that animals can have a sense of place, can be devoted to each other for life, and can display a full range of emotions and reactions comparable to man's: love, jealousy, aggression toward invaders of their territories, and defense of their young. These new studies of animals have resulted in numerous animal "biographies," the best of which make fascinating reading for young and old alike.

The wide variety and great quantities of animal stories being produced inevitably result in a full range of quality. Many of these books are excellent, most of them are fairly good, but some of them are stereotypes or juvenile thrillers, as sensational as fights and gore can make them. To appraise this offering, it is well to know something about the different types of animal stories, their values and their limitations.

Animals as prototypes of human beings

The animals of folk tales and fables are not, of course, authentic animals at all, but symbols or even caricatures of human beings. "The Three Little Pigs" talk and behave like foolish or wise people, and "The Fox and the Crow" are flatterer and flattered. These traditional stories have their counterparts in such modern picture books as *Finders Keepers* by Will Lipkind. When illustrators add clothes to these creatures, as Beatrix Potter does for the animals in *The Tale of Peter Rabbit*, their similarity to people is even more apparent. Oddly enough, this scientific generation, young and old, thoroughly enjoys animal tales in which the beasts are used as prototypes of human beings. Small children still love "Henny-Penny," their older brothers and sisters weep over "The Ugly Duckling," and both children and adults chuckle at the absurdities of "Donald Duck," "Bugs Bunny," and "Mickey

Mouse." Ourselves in fur or feathers seem irresistibly comic or pathetic, both in stories and in pictures.

Animals as animals but talking

The second type of animal tale is partly make-believe and partly natural science, a hybrid form. The animals in such stories are portrayed with fidelity to the nature and behavior of the species, but they are given the human attributes of thought and speech. To be sure, the beasts don't discuss politics, but they do talk at length about their own affairs. The classic example is not Anna Sewell's *Black Beauty*, in which the horse is much too human for horse nature, but Felix Salten's *Bambi*.[1] In *Bambi*, the deer talk, are puzzled or afraid, warn each other, grieve or rejoice in words, but always in terms of deer life and deer problems. For example, the deer parents do not admonish their fawns to be courteous to their uncles and aunts, but they do warn them to be on the watch for the pale, hairless creature which walks upright and carries a stick that sends out fire and death to animals far away. This type of story is difficult to write with integrity. If the animals are overly humanized, they cease to be authentic animals, and the story tends to become didactic or mawkishly sentimental. Children do not actually object to sentimentality or moralizing; like adults, they will take considerable second-rate reading matter, but they deserve better fare.

Animals objectively reported

The third type of animal story is told from the outside, as if the narrator were able to observe everything the animal does. The best of these stories re-create with scientific accuracy the animal and his environment within the framework of an exciting plot. Whether the animals are household pets, farm animals, or denizens of forest, swamp, or jungle, they speak no words, but the noises they make are subject to general interpretation, such as a cat's purr of contentment, a dog's bark of welcome, a lion's menacing roar, or the loud churr of Mr. Kildee's "Old Grouch,"

[1] Not the altered Disney versions, but the original stories

which marked a full stomach and a dry, warm shelter. Beyond such guesses at meaning, in which all humans seem to indulge, the reader knows nothing about the inside workings of the animal's thoughts and emotions.

The best of these objectively presented books are for older children, but even preschoolers have some realistic animal stories which delight them. The "Blaze" books by C. W. Anderson (see Bibliography, p. 244) are genuine horse stories, and the bear in Lynd Ward's *The Biggest Bear* is all bear and not a disguised human.

Criteria for animal stories

The animal stories in this book belong to this third category—animals objectively reported. They were selected with certain criteria in mind which may serve as standards for evaluating other such animal tales. In addition to the usual criteria for evaluating any story for children—interesting plot, strong theme, memorable characters, and good style (see Part Two, pp. 226–227)—there are also specific standards for judging the merit of this third type of animal tale. The first criterion is, of course, integrity to the species of animal described. Little Bub, Justin Morgan's horse (see p. 21), has the loyalty, stamina, and courage we expect from a champion. The Wahoo Bobcat (see p. 44) saves a boy's life, not from any humanitarian motives, but from sheer blind rage and the instinct to defend a cub. The baby skunk in *Smoke Above the Lane* (see Bibliography, p. 244) makes friends with the tramp because of desperate fear and hunger. The authors of the stories in this section never portray animals functioning from human motives, nor do they sentimentalize them; the creatures run true to their species.

The second criterion applies to the human characters in the stories. If there are people in these animal tales, they should be real people, not stereotypes of cruelty or goodness. Both Marguerite Henry in her horse stories and Jim Kjelgaard in his dog stories give children unique human characters who are as memorable as the animal heroes of the books. So, the old man in that remarkable story *The Defender* (see p. 50) is unlike any other character in children's books. Delightful as the wild mountain rams are, it is the old man, the defender, who gives the story its greatness.

Avoidance of unnecessary cruelty and violence is a third criterion for evaluating animal stories. Because animals are vulnerable and suffer both from man and from other animals, some of the stories in this field go to sensational lengths to achieve a high degree of reading interest. They play up suffering and brutality to a disproportionate degree. The animal stories presented in this book often show animal tragedies and frequently man's injustice or brutality to beasts, but they are written with compassion, and the gory details are kept within bounds. Too much brutality can rouse latent sadism in young readers or develop in them a callous tolerance of suffering. In the field of animal stories, adults who guide children's reading need to distinguish between necessary violence and sensationalism.

Values of animal stories for children

Well-written animal stories have unique values for a young reader. Over and over again, they show him the vulnerability of animals, who are at the mercy of man with his guns and his greedy desire for animal exploitation. An animal's lack of language subjects him to injustice and misunderstanding. A dog can't explain that he did not kill a lamb, nor can he help himself if his master wishes to sell him or to give him away. It is this helplessness of animals which brings out a child's pity and love. And it is quite as important for a child to wish to love and cherish another creature as it is for him to be loved. In many city homes the animal story is vicarious satisfaction for the pets a child is not permitted to own.

Animal stories also give a child vicarious experiences with a variety of wild animals he cannot know in any other way. He learns the habits and needs of a great many beasts, and his admiration for them grows as he understands their problems, their natures, and their hazardous lives.

Books like *Kildee House* (see p. 39) or *My Friend Flicka* (see Bibliography, p. 246) also supply him with considerable information on the biology of mating, birth, and death, which comes in casually and naturally in the midst of an exciting story. Indeed, poor Jerome Kildee's survival in his unique house came to depend upon his ability to cope with the birth of more and more baby animals. The way nature marches on in the animal world takes on meaning for children who read this story.

Finally, animal stories are good for children because they find in their animal heroes the virtues they most admire in human beings and would like to achieve themselves. Look over any first-rate group of animal adventures and see if these virtues are not paramount—courage in the face of danger; fortitude under suffering or injustice; loyalty to cub, mate, or master; and, above all, a shining zest for life that is like a child's own. Colts, cubs, kittens, and children take life gaily with splendid prancings and cavortings. Even mature animals seem to find life good and go proudly and gallantly to meet its challenge. These are some of the reasons why children love good stories about animals and should have them, the soundest and the best to be found.

Animals we know best

from IRISH RED

Jim Kjelgaard

The author said he always had a dog and sometimes "as many as seven at a time." This helps to explain his understanding of and sympathy for dogs. But he knew wild animals too, as his story of a polar bear, Kalak of the Ice, *bears witness. No one who likes dogs should miss* Big Red *and* Irish Red. Snow Dog *is equally popular, and most of the Kjelgaard books are well written and intensely exciting. In* Irish Red, *Big Red's son, Mike, proved to be a self-willed mutt instead of the great bird dog the Picketts had expected. But Danny still believed in the pup. These two chapters tell of the near-tragedy which changed a silly pup into a disciplined hunting dog.*

White Prison

Danny stirred, and fought sluggishly to a bewildered awakening. For a few minutes he lay still, unable to think where he was or what had happened. Bit by bit, like crooked pieces of a jigsaw puzzle, he fitted the picture together.

He was up on Tower Head, he remembered, where he had come to investigate marten sign. Summer had suddenly become winter, and winter had been ushered in by a terrible wind storm which had ripped through the beech trees. Some

From *Irish Red* by Jim Kjelgaard. Copyright, 1951 by Jim Kjelgaard. Reprinted by permission of Holiday House

had broken. Great boughs had been torn like match sticks from their parent trunks, and one had hit him.

Danny lapsed into a numbed slumber and a second time fought to wakefulness. A thousand drums seemed to pound within his aching head and for a moment he felt very sick. The spasm passed, and when it did he could think more clearly. It had, he remembered, been daylight when he decided to return to Budgegummon. Now inky blackness surrounded him. Danny stretched his hand forth and a warm, wet tongue licked it gently. His exploring fingers found Mike's silky coat. At once he felt a tremendous rush of gratitude. Until now he had not remembered bringing Mike.

He sat up, and when he did his head broke through the fresh, fluffy snow that covered him. It had, then, snowed while he lay unconscious and the fact that it had covered him was the reason why he had not been frozen to death. That and Mike, for the red puppy had found him, and was crouching as close as he could get to his injured master. Again Danny gratefully stroked the red puppy's fur.

The snow was still falling fast; even in the darkness Danny felt its soft, deadly caress as he stood erect. He stumbled and almost fell, but by a mighty effort stiffened his legs.

He was aware of Mike pressing closely against his feet, but he could see nothing whatever. Overwhelmed by another spasm of illness, and weighed down by an unbearable burden on his back, Danny crouched in the snow and gave himself over to sheer misery. When he recovered he felt better and could think more clearly.

The burden he bore was only his pack, Danny realized, and forced himself to be calm. What had happened? First, winter had struck with savage fury. There had been no snow at all during the afternoon, but now it was up to Danny's knees and still falling. He was in the forest, and therefore the snow would not have drifted much. However, there was no possible way he could get to Budgegummon without crossing open spaces where there would be deep drifts, and he had no snowshoes. Even with every possible bit of good luck, it would take him days just to get off the mountain.

Then he did his best to forget it and give his thoughts to immediate problems. Falling snow had prevented his freezing to death, but he was numb with cold and ached in every muscle. Before he did anything else he must get a fire going.

Danny plowed forward, a step at a time, groping hands stretched out before him. A few feet from where he had started, he stopped to rest. He was panting, and beads of sweat clung to his forehead. As soon as he stopped, the cold attacked again; he licked frost particles from his upper lip. Starting forward again, he stumbled over a snow-covered limb, and fell on his hands and knees. For a moment he rested where he was, too tired to get up. A delicious, soothing warmth enveloped him. Then Mike's questing nose touched his face.

Danny fought his way to a standing position. Now he must keep going or die. The snow would not save him again for he had started to sweat. Should he relax for more than a few seconds the sweat would freeze, and if it did he was all through. Danny forced his numb body forward.

He jarred his shoulder against a standing tree and stopped, raising cold hands to feel the tree. It was small, scarcely a foot through, and ragged wisps of paper-thin bark hung like shedding fur from it. A great hope leaped in Danny.

Solely by accident he had bumped into a birch. The parchment-like bark covering the trunk was as thin as paper and burned as readily. Keeping hold of the tree with one hand, Danny trampled a hole in the snow.

Carefully feeling his way, he stripped handfuls of bark from the tree and put it in the hole he had trampled. Then he knelt down, holding both hands firmly against Mike's warm fur. When circulation returned to his hands, Danny felt in his pocket for the metal match box he always carried. He unscrewed the top, extracted one match, and carefully tightened the cover down. Striking the match against the box's rough side, Danny held the tiny flame against his pile of birch bark. The match died, and almost went out. Danny's hand trembled, and a cold shiver rippled up his spine. Then a corner of bark curled, smoldered, and burst into flame. Almost instantly the whole pile was alight.

Danny's happy shout vied with the softly ominous sound of falling snow and the whine of the wind that sighed through the beech forest. Guiding himself by the fire's light, he turned back to the tree and feverishly groped for the outer tips of small dry twigs that broke easily. He filled his hands with them and went back to throw them on his dying fire. Hungry flames crackled their way into this stronger nourishment. Turning back to the tree, Danny wrenched off an inch-thick limb, broke it into sections, and heaped them on the flames. The fire climbed higher.

Danny gratefully appreciated his good luck in having an ample supply of wood practically within reach of his fire. Very few trees on Tower Head were dead, and chance alone had guided him to one of them. Fuel awaited only the taking.

He broke off more and bigger branches and carried them to his fire. He laid them the long way, pushing them farther up as the ends burned, and arranged a layer of dead sticks to sit on. There were blankets in his pack, but Danny was too tired to try making a proper bed. Heat from the fire melted an increasing circle of snow, and Danny changed his seat.

Mike, for once subdued, crouched down beside him. Danny put a hand on the red puppy's ruff and drew him close. Mike had already atoned for all his past sins merely by providing company. Danny spoke softly to him.

"Tomorrow we'll see about getting out of here, pup. Sure wish I had a pair of snowshoes."

As soon as he had spoken, Danny wished that he had not even thought about what tomorrow would bring. Certainly there was no immediate hope of rescue for he had told Ross that he was going up Stoney Lonesome. Ross would not worry unduly for a couple of days, and if he did start out, it would not be toward Tower Head. If they were going to be helped, Danny and Mike would have to help themselves.

Danny gazed soberly into the fire. It was ordinarily a few hours' walk back to Budgegummon. Now deep snow covered every inch of the way, and progress would be painfully slow. It would take several days to reach Budgegummon, or even to get down into one of the sheltered valleys where, Danny hoped, the snow would not be so deep.

He knew he was in serious trouble, but bewailing the fact, or worrying about what might happen, would not help at all. Tonight, certainly, he could do nothing except sit here by the fire. He pushed a couple of sticks farther up, bent his head forward so that the collar of his jacket came up around his neck, and dozed fitfully. Creeping cold awakened him when the fire burned low, and Danny built it up again.

He was awakened by Mike's warning bark. He jerked erect, one hand stealing to the grip of his .22, but he could see nothing. Mike touched his hand with a cold nose, and Danny lifted his head to find that dawn had come. He stared around in bewilderment.

The once stately forest on Tower Head had become a shambles. Big trees were piled helter-skelter, a Gargantuan jumble of jackstraws. Boughs and branches had blown down among them in a litter of kindling. As Danny plodded over to get more wood for his fire, he thought of the food in his pack.

Expecting to be away for only two days, he had not packed much food. There was a little slab of bacon, flour, syrup, a chunk of meat, salt and pepper, and coffee. There was not nearly enough of anything. Bucking deep snow would require effort and burn up energy fast. The food that Danny had would have to be conserved to the utmost.

Reluctantly he unbuckled the straps that closed his pack and took out the package of flour. He sliced four strips of bacon from his small chunk and put them into the skillet. Melting snow in the coffee pot, he mixed flapjack batter, and pushed the sizzling bacon to one side of the skillet. He poured a flapjack and let it cook. When it was finished he gave it to Mike, along with two strips of bacon.

The red puppy wagged his appreciation, and gulped his food. He looked on with great interest as Danny fixed the same amount for himself. Mike licked his chops eagerly, and begged with limpid eyes. Danny looked at him.

"Nix," he said. "We're on short rations until we find something else. If one of us eats then both of us will, and there'll be no stealing from each other."

Danny washed the coffee pot with more melted snow and brewed coffee. Letting it cool a little, he drank it directly from the pot. Then he brushed snow over the fire, buckled his pack on, and stood for a moment as he tried to pick out a route through the fallen trees.

Danny plunged his foot into deep snow, and almost collapsed as a red-hot iron seemed to flash across his right side. He felt a momentary dizziness, then eased back into his tracks.

Obviously he was hurt more than he knew. He had not felt it last night either because he was partly dazed or because his injury had not had time to stiffen. Possibly he had a couple of broken ribs or internal injuries. Still, there was no one to help him. What was to be done, he must do alone. Days might elapse before anyone thought of looking for him on Tower Head. Danny tried another experimental step, this time with his left foot.

He stepped into deep snow and brought his right foot up. Danny gritted his teeth. The pain was there, but it was not as intense as when he had tried to walk with his right foot forward. He plowed ahead, favoring his right side as much as possible. He had to keep on.

Mike plodded along in the trail Danny broke, the top of his head four inches below the snow line. The red puppy's eyes were anxious, and he whined at intervals. He was worried, but had every faith in the man he was following.

Danny stopped to rest, leaning against a tree to ease the burden on his back. When he cast his eye over the trail he had made he was panicky. He must have been on the move for half an hour, yet last night's camp was no more than a stone's throw away. He was making very poor time.

It was impossible to go any faster in his condition. He was already panting from exertion. It was turning warmer, too, he noticed. The snow was stopping and the clouds overhead were breaking. A slanting ray of warm sun stole down; the soft snow would soon begin to melt. Danny unbuttoned his jacket, pushed his knitted cap back on his head, and went on.

Two hours later the top of the snow was a soggy mess. Dark wet patches appeared here and there, dips and hollows in what had been a perfectly smooth blanket. Hard to buck before, now the settling snow became doubly difficult to wade through. Danny stopped again to rest.

Hunger that would not be subdued arose within him. Danny licked his lips, and tried not to think of the food in his pack. But he could not help thinking of it, and the very fact that he had food within reach seemed to induce a strange weakness. Danny turned to look at Mike, who was sitting in the snow looking expectantly up at him. Again Danny licked his lips.

The proper course, he had always heard, was to hoard every scrap of food when one had little. But, even though he had come only a short distance, he had burned a terrific amount of energy doing it. It was impossible to continue without eating; he would just have to take a chance of getting some sort of food later on.

Danny stopped and cooked more of his scanty supplies, dividing them equally with Mike. When he had eaten he felt better, but by then it was even more difficult to travel through the wet snow. Every foot he advanced was a foot that had to be fought for, and every step cost pain. He tried counting his steps, then gave it up. The *next* step was the thing. It was all-important, and if he could make that one he could also make the one to follow. Every step he took carried him that much nearer Budgegummon and that much farther away from Tower Head. Distance lost its meaning because of the effort it cost to make that all-important next step.

The sun went down and Danny buttoned his jacket, for with the approach of twilight the cold returned. He stopped to wipe the sweat from his forehead, and considered. He had to rest, for if he tried going on through the darkness he would only exhaust himself and probably fall. Danny glanced at Mike, who sat in the snow, ears erect and tail flat behind him. He whined apprehensively and Danny made up his mind. It was time to camp.

He was very tired, and when he chopped wood for a fire his axe seemed a wooden thing with no edge at all. Danny stopped twice while he was chopping to look at the pile of wood, then wearily turned to cut more. Finally he scooped the snow away, built a fire, laid a mat of twigs, and put one blanket on it. The other he laid on top, and made a pillow with his pack. Mike crowded close to him, and Danny stroked the red puppy's ears.

"Poor pup," he soothed. "You sure got in a fix when you went out with me, didn't you?"

As he comforted Mike, a sudden relief overcame Danny himself. It had been a terrible, endless day. But it had ended, and not until tomorrow must he resume fighting his way through the snow. Tomorrow was a long while away, and they were in camp. At least for the moment their troubles were ended, and within itself that was a relief. The moment was the thing and the future he could work out. Danny prodded the pack with his foot.

"We got this far," he told Mike. "Let's celebrate."

Danny dived recklessly into his store of food and prepared a filling meal for Mike and himself. After eating, he drowsed in front of the fire, then crawled into his blankets. Ordinarily it would have been a hard bed, but not tonight. Danny dropped at once into a deep and untroubled sleep from which he did not awaken until dawn had again come.

He sat up to look at his dead fire. During the night Mike had become cold, and had crawled underneath the blankets to take advantage of the warmth offered by Danny. Now he tumbled unwillingly out of his comfortable sleeping place, stretching and yawning. Danny looked at him and felt comforted just from the puppy's presence.

Yesterday had been a sick day. Still suffering from the effects of the blow when the branch had struck him, Danny had done what he could do. This morning, after a good night's sleep, he could look at their predicament sanely. They were still trapped in a white prison from which there was scant hope of escape, but they must get out if they were to live. It was that simple.

Methodically Danny set about the preparation of a scanty breakfast. He divided the food exactly in half, fed the red puppy and himself. Then he gathered his blankets, shouldered his pack, and started off. After two steps he stopped and looked down at the snow in dismay.

During the night it had turned much colder, and a crust had formed on top of the soggy snow. Mike, climbing up, could run about on it at will. But at every step Danny's foot broke the brittle crust. He shivered, then plodded doggedly ahead.

Mike skipped happily about on the crust, no longer finding it necessary to plod in his master's trail. Danny kept envious eyes on the puppy. If there was some way to make him go there, Mike could reach Budgegummon by nightfall. If Mike came in alone, Ross would set out at once to find Danny. Then he shook his head in despair; it would be hopeless to try to make the obstinate puppy return to the cabin. If only Red were with him!

Mike stopped suddenly, and froze in his tracks. For a moment Danny forgot to breathe; Mike was on partridges! Danny's hand slid to the grip of his .22 revolver.

"Whoa, Mike!" he said tensely. "Whoa!"

Intently he searched the little scattering of evergreens at which Mike was pointing. Partridges were hard to see, but if he could catch one on the ground he had a chance of getting it.

Then Mike went in to flush. There was a thunder of wings and Danny saw five partridges rise. He shot at them, pulling the trigger time after time as he sent the little leaden pellets flying after the grouse. But he knew it was hopeless.

Mike dashed out of sight, and Danny looked after him with sick eyes.

A Rebel's Heart

Trying to keep the partridges in sight, Mike raced happily across the frozen crust. He slipped, went down, and rolled into a small tree. Mike picked himself up and looked about for the birds he had flushed. They were gone, and he could neither see nor smell them. The puppy sat down to puzzle out their probable whereabouts. Then he started toward a copse of evergreens. Halfway there he turned and looked back at Danny. Never before, when partridges were near, had he let anything interfere with their pursuit. But never before had he found himself in a situation such as this one. What should he do?

When the great windstorm had struck, Mike, unlike Danny, had not tried to make his way through it. Instead, the red puppy had curled at the base of a great boulder and waited there, shivering as the mighty beeches trembled and crashed all around him. When the wind died, Mike had started out at once to reach Danny. He had found him before the snow started, lying motionless where he had fallen. The red puppy, sensing something wrong, had tried to awaken Danny by whining, then by pawing, and when he could get no response had curled up beside him. Even though Mike, the rebel, acknowledged no master, the age-old bond between dog and man had instinctively kept him by Danny's side in time of trouble.

So Mike hesitated now, instead of rushing after the partridges, because he knew that Danny was still in trouble. There was an urgency in the way Danny plodded on, and a tense desperation, both of which were entirely foreign to any normal state.

The red puppy turned halfway around to go back. But the will to hunt, as powerful as it had ever been, held him where he was. Mike trembled uncertainly, pulled in two directions at once and wholly undecided as to what he had better do. Then the lure of the hunt prevailed, and he started toward the evergreens.

Because he was certain his game had gone into them, he did not bother to swing downwind where he could get a better scent. He raced full speed toward his objective, then slowed down as he approached it. Wrinkling his nose to clear it, he detected the partridges and stiffened in a point.

He did not rush in at once because there was another faint scent, one he had never smelled before, underlying the odor of partridges. The smell had something of fear in it, and evil, something Mike did not like. He did not know what

it was and because nothing except the porcupine had ever hurt him he eased cautiously forward.

The partridges were in the very center of the thicket, where green branches intertwined so closely that they were almost impenetrable. Mike located the birds exactly and flung himself forward. He heard a partridge's alarmed cluck, and dashed insanely toward the sound. Then his quarry drummed upward and Mike threw himself to one side after it.

A second later and he would have been too late to avoid the beast that had been in the thicket even before the partridges, the thing Mike had smelled and ignored. It was a snowbound puma, a tawny, rippling beast almost invisible in the hemlocks.

The puma had stared with hungry eyes at the partridges when they flew into the thicket, but he had not moved a muscle. They alighted a dozen feet away, too far to let him catch one. But he knew himself unseen; if he did not move one or more of the birds might venture within striking distance.

The hungry puma instantly transferred all his attention to Mike when the red puppy entered the thicket. Here was food in plenty, good food; he had eaten a dog before. He waited until Mike seemed near enough, then launched his lithe spring.

However, the puma did not distinguish between dogs and he had previously caught and eaten only an aging, lost hound. Mike was much younger and infinitely more agile. The puma's outstretched claws missed their target by three inches and Mike dodged out of the thicket.

He ran as fast as he could, with healthy fear lending speed to his legs. Mike had never been hurt by anything except the porcupine, but the law of survival was part of his heritage and he knew that the puma intended to kill him. Furthermore, he knew that it could. Mike raced full speed back toward Danny and found him resting wearily in the snow with his pack braced against a dead stump. Mike slid to a halt beside him and turned around to bristle and bark.

He faced the direction from which he had come, testing the wind with his nose, while the hungry puma lingered behind some brush a few hundred feet away. Having caught man scent, the big cat had no wish to come any nearer. Mike barked again, challenging his enemy, and Danny's hand played around the red puppy's ears.

"What's the matter?" Danny asked. "What's up, Mike? You see your own shadow out there?"

Without understanding the words, Mike sensed the comradeship in the tone of voice.

Danny could not know, nor could Mike himself reason out, that a change had been worked within him. The days when he had been only a senseless puppy, with never a thought except for himself, were definitely in the past. Time, and affection, and now shared trouble, were all combining to work the change. Mike was growing up.

Being a dog, neither the past nor the future mattered to him. The moment was the thing, and now Mike sat on the crusted snow reading the wind that told him of the puma's movements. The big cat had made a circle and gone to one side. Now he lay behind a fallen beech, eyes and ears alert and tail twitching as he studied the situation. The puma had no desire to expose himself to a man, but neither did he have the slightest intention of abandoning the trail until he had caught Mike. Cunning and wise, he would follow the pair until he found an opportunity to catch and kill the dog.

Mike growled low in his throat, and Danny looked questioningly in the direction the red puppy was looking, then turned to go on. Mike stayed behind him, making short little excursions out on the crust to read the wind to better advantage. The puma was coming, slinking along their trail like a tawny shadow. But so woodswise was he that he never once showed himself. Mike knew he was coming only because his nose told him.

With only a mouthful of cold food at noon, they plodded slowly on. The sun started its downward sweep and with its descent the cold became more intense. Accustomed to being outside, and provided by nature with a suitable coat for all seasons, Mike did not feel it. Danny tried to tighten his jacket and shivered as he stopped in a cluster of big beech trees.

A squirrel chattered in one of the beeches. Mike glanced disinterestedly up, not caring about such game. It was fun to chase squirrels, and to watch them leap with panicky haste into the trees. That was all. But now Mike sensed the change in Danny.

Dead-tired and almost apathetic for the past hour, Danny was now tensely alert. The revolver in his hand, he stood in his tracks and looked eagerly into the towering trees. Nothing happened; the squirrel did not even chatter again. Mike knew what Danny did not, that it had gone into a hole in one of the trunks, but long after the squirrel had found safety Danny continued to stare up into the trees.

Then, with a despairing little gesture, he sheathed his gun and set about gathering firewood. Mike crowded anxiously in, staying as close to Danny as he could get and risking a burned nose when Danny lighted a match with which to start his fire. An eddying breeze brought him the puma's scent. It had come in very close, but when smoke started curling from the fire it retreated. The ravenous cat was not so desperately hungry that he would risk getting near a fire. Mike followed the puma's progress with his nose. He also watched Danny's preparation of their meager meal.

The red puppy had never wondered about the source of his food. He knew only that humans had never let him go hungry. When his belly was empty, they gave him something to fill it and he was sure that it would be filled now. Mike gobbled the tiny piece of meat and the bit of bread Danny gave him, and looked questioningly about for more. He whined when Danny ate an equal amount and sat staring dully into the fire. The red puppy scraped his master's arm with an impatient paw. Danny stirred angrily.

"There's no more!" he half shouted. "See?"

Mike sniffed distantly at the pack when Danny opened it for him. He flattened his ears and rolled appeasing eyes, not understanding the fact that food supplies were practically gone and uncomfortable because he was still hungry. Mike knew only that, for some unaccountable reason, Danny was angry with him and he did not like it.

He retreated to the edge of the light circle cast by the fire, then came back within it, for his nose told him that the hungry puma still lingered in the shadows. It was no place for him. In the semi-darkness, he moved confidently closer to Danny. His paws twitched.

He was hungry, but neither exhausted nor terrified. Mike knew that he had been near death when he met the puma, but now that he was again with Danny, that threat was removed. Today, for the first time, he had learned that he was not self-sufficient, but part of a team. He moved softly over to be nearer Danny, and stared steadily into the unfriendly night.

The puma was creeping nearer. A weak moon had risen, casting moving shadows across the snow, and the puma was taking advantage of them to get nearer the camp. He felt bolder now, for the fire sent up only straggling wisps of smoke. Wrapped in his blankets, Danny had surrendered to exhaustion. Mike snuffled again at the creeping puma, then edged in until his rear paws were braced against the sleeping Danny. There fear left him. Alone he could do little, but together he and Danny could face any threat.

The red puppy growled harshly, and the advancing puma stopped. Then he came on, slowly and furtively. Mike growled again, fiercely this time. The numbed Danny stirred fretfully in his blankets.

The puma was very near now; a little more and he would be within leaping distance. Mike snarled again, and again, as he made ready to repel the attacker. Danny stirred, rolled over, and woke up.

He did not make any noise or cry out when he came awake because he had been born to the woods and wild places. He knew the value of silence, and even sick exhaustion could not make him forget it. When Danny rolled out of his blankets he did so carefully and silently. He inched himself to a sitting position and drew the .22 from its holster.

Mike pricked up his ears and stared intently at a motionless shadow. He knew the puma was there for his nose told him, but he could not be certain he saw it. Danny fixed his eyes on the place, like a hundred other shadows but still unlike any of them. Moving ever so slowly, Danny raised the .22 and squeezed the trigger.

When the little revolver snapped, the shadow melted into the night. The puma, taken by surprise, had silently backed away. He was not hurt and he did not run, for to run would be to expose himself. When he knew he could no longer be seen, the puma turned and loped away after easier game. He had gambled and lost.

Knowing the enemy vanquished, Mike relaxed. For a few minutes Danny remained in a sitting position, the little revolver in his hand. What had he shot at? Had he really seen anything? In any event, Mike was now quiet, so Danny put more wood on the fire and returned to his blankets. When he did, Mike lifted a corner with his nose, crawled in beside him, and snuggled up against Danny's back. They did not awaken until dawn had come.

Mike waited hopefully, expectantly, as Danny built up the fire and brewed a pot of coffee. There was nothing else, and Mike tried to stay his rising hunger by licking his chops. He snuffled at the steaming coffee, then turned his nose away.

When Danny resumed his heartbreakingly slow progress toward the distant valleys, Mike climbed out of the trail he broke to run about on the crust. He liked that better, for in the trail the sharp edges of the broken snow were like glass, and hurt his feet. Mike looked back to see if Danny was coming, then gave all his attention to what lay ahead.

They were crossing a small clearing where blackberry brambles barred their path. Tall weeds had found a rooting in the brambles, and their seeded tops still protruded above the snow. Mike caught the scent of partridges that were eating the seeds, and started toward them. Then he heard Danny's tense voice.

"Whoa! Whoa, Mike!"

The red puppy paused, and looked around. Again he swung his head to drink in the entrancing scent of partridges. He froze into a point.

The old urge was there, the driving impulse to rush furiously upon his game and see if he could overwhelm it. But for the first time something in Danny's voice stopped him. The sound of the familiar command had a new meaning, the end of a long chain of occurrences. Mike was no longer the wild, undisciplined puppy who had escaped from the Haggin estate. A thousand wild chases were behind him, and Red's punishment, and the endless patience and affection offered by Danny and Ross. And fresh in his mind was the realization that he and Danny had faced, and overcome, danger and terror—together. He quivered with eagerness, but held his point.

There was motion in the brambles. One of the partridges thrust a curious head straight up, then sat still. Mike drooled, and tensed his muscles. Before he could move, he heard the snap of Danny's .22.

Utterly bewildered, the red puppy paused. Two partridges thundered away. But another one remained in the brambles, an inert heap of brown feathers. Mike felt an overwhelming flood of excitement; at last his dearest wishes were realized. Everything else was forgotten as he bounded toward the partridge. Mike closed his jaws about the bird, then Danny's voice penetrated his delirious haze.

"Mike. Come here, Mike."

The puppy stood still, not knowing in this joyful moment just what he should do. Again he heard Danny's voice.

"Fetch, Mike."

Then, at long last, Mike gave his whole heart to a master. He started back toward Danny.

Two days later, well down in a sheltered valley, Mike pricked up his ears and looked at the snowbound trees ahead of them. He barked, then started happily forward. Danny's incredulous eyes followed him. A moment later Big Red burst out of the trees. A little way behind him was Ross, on snowshoes and pulling a toboggan.

"Danny!" Ross's voice broke. "Boy, I'm right glad to see you!"

"I'm kind of glad to see you," Danny admitted. "What brought you up here?"

"That Red dog," said Ross. "We looked every other place we could think of, and Red wanted to come up here. I figured I might as well follow him. What happened? You hurt bad?"

"Well," Danny said lamely, "I went up Tower Head to look for marten, only there weren't any, and then a big windstorm came, and a limb hit me, and—"

"Save it," Ross commanded. "Climb aboard."

Danny settled gratefully on the toboggan and let Ross wrap him in warm blankets. He fought the drowsiness that overcame him, for he had a very important message. It had nothing to do with marten, or money, or broken ribs. It was something far more important. He fingered the two partridges at his belt.

"We've got a partridge dog, Pappy." Then he fell asleep.

from THE BLIND COLT

Glen Rounds

Raised on a ranch, Glen Rounds can spin a tall tale or a western horse story and illustrate them to perfection. The episode given here from The Blind Colt *is poignant, tender, and true to horse and boy nature. Glen Rounds says perhaps he wrote this story because he was homesick for horses, and he adds that there really was such a colt as the one he tells about, who was blind and smart.*

The Badlands

It was near sundown of an early spring afternoon when the brown mustang mare left the wild horse band where it grazed on the new spring grass and climbed carefully to the top of a nearby hogback.

All afternoon she had been restless and nervous, spending much of her time on high ground watching the country around her. Now she stood and stamped her feet fretfully while she tipped her sharp-pointed ears forward and back as she looked and listened. And her nostrils flared wide as she tested the wind for any smells that might be about.

The rain-gullied buttes and pinnacles of the Badlands threw long black shadows across the soft gray and brown and green of the alkali flats below her. A few jack rabbits had already left their hiding places and were prospecting timidly around in the open, searching out the tender shoots of new grass. They, too, threw long black shadows that were all out of proportion to their size.

A few bull bats boomed overhead, and a meadow lark sang from the top of a sagebrush nearby. Below her the rest of the mustang band grazed quietly except for an occasional squeal and thump of hoofs as some minor dispute was settled. Otherwise everything was quiet.

From *The Blind Colt* by Glen Rounds. Copyright 1941 by Holiday House and used with their permission

But still the little mare didn't leave the ridge. She stood watching while the flats grew darker, and while the darkness crept up the sides of the buttes, until at last the sun touched only the very tip tops of the highest pinnacles. Then after a look back to where the rest of the horses were bedding down for the night, she slipped quietly down the far side of the ridge and was soon hidden in the darkness.

Next morning she was in a grassy hollow at the head of a dry coulee where the rolling prairie and the Badlands meet. And lying at her feet, sound asleep, was her colt, that had been born during the night.

The early sun touched the top of the rim rock behind her, then gradually crept down until it was warming the grass where the little mustang lay. As soon as the ground had begun to steam and the touch of frost was out of the air, she nudged him with her muzzle and waked him. For a little while he lay there, sniffing around in the grass as far as he could reach, and flapping his tail to hear it thump against the ground, while the mare stood relaxed on three legs and watched him.

But after a while she seemed to figure it was time for him to be up and about so she urged him to his feet. And he was as awkward looking a scamp as you'd care to see as he stood with his long, knobby legs braced wide apart and caught his breath after the effort of getting up.

His body was close knit and compact and his back was flat and strong. His muzzle was delicately shaped but his forehead bulged as all colts' do. His neck was so short he couldn't get his nose closer to the ground than his knees, and his legs were so long he seemed to be walking on stilts. His ears were trim and sharply pointed but looked as though they should belong to a horse much larger than he.

The mare saw all this but she knew that all colts were put together so, and that those extra long legs of his were specially made that way so that by the time he was a day or two old he would be able to travel as fast and as far as the grown horses in case of danger. And besides, she thought that his blue-gray coat was especially handsome.

For a few minutes the colt was kept busy trying to balance himself on his legs while he sniffed and snorted at everything in reach. As long as he stood still he was all right but when he tried walking he found he was engaged in a mighty ticklish business, what with his being so high in the air with nothing holding him up but those four knobby legs. They had to be lifted and swung just so or they got all tangled up and started him kiting off in some entirely unexpected direction.

But he was hungry, and the only way he could get anything to eat was to go after it himself, so it wasn't long before he was able to scramble around against the mare's side. After a little nuzzling around he found her teats and settled down to sucking noisily, flapping his tail with excitement.

Before long his sides began to stick out, he was so full of milk, and he was quite ready to enjoy the business of having his coat groomed by the mustang mare. She was fair bursting with pride, as this was her first colt. She whickered softly and caressed him with her muzzle every now and again as she scrubbed him with her rough tongue. When she hit a ticklish spot he'd flap his tail and squirm and snort his tiny snorts. When he did that she'd nip him gently with her big yellow teeth to warn him that wild young ones must learn to obey, and he'd better stand still until she was done or he might get worse.

And not an inch of his hide did she overlook. The white snip on his nose, his speckled blue sides and flanks and his legs that shaded down to black shiny hoofs, all got their share of combing and washing. By the time he had been thoroughly polished the sun was warm in the hollow and he began practising his walking again, and his smelling, and his hearing.

He started taking little exploring trips, a few wobbly steps in one direction, then another, with much snuffing and snorting as the brittle last year's grass crackled under foot. As he got the hang of operating his walking apparatus more smoothly he became bolder and extended the range of his explorations until sometimes he traveled as far as ten or twenty feet from the brown mare's side.

His black-tipped, pointed ears were fixed to turn in all directions, to help him locate the source of sounds he heard. He pointed them forward and back, and the soft wind that springs up on the desert in the morning brushed against them, feeling sweet and clear and smooth. What few sounds he heard at first seemed to float separately through the warm silence as though there was all the time in the world and no need for two noises to be moving at the same time. Meadow larks whistled from nearby sagebrush, and far off he heard the harsh bickering of magpies as they quarreled over a dead rabbit or gopher.

Later on he discovered that down close to the ground there was a thin blanket of bug sounds. Flies buzzed and grasshoppers whirred. And buryer beetles made clicking noises as they busily buried a small dead snake.

Sniffing through his nose, he caught the sharp clean smell of the sagebrush, and the more pungent smell of the greasewood as the sun began to heat it up. Occasionally he got a whiff of wild plum and chokecherry blossoms from the thickets down below the rim of the Badlands.

Of course, these were the big plain smells, easily discovered. Later on he would learn to identify others that had to be searched for with flared nostrils, and carefully and delicately sifted for the story they could tell him of friends, or danger, or the location of water holes in the dry times. But for now the simpler lessons were enough to keep him busy, and the mustang mare was mighty proud of him.

But for all her pride, she was a little troubled, too. For there was something strange about the colt, although she couldn't tell exactly what the matter was. He was as lively as you'd expect any colt only a few hours old to be. He snorted and kicked up his heels when a ground squirrel whistled close by. And he put on a mock battle with a tumble weed when it blew against his legs, rearing up and lashing out with his front feet. When he came back from his trips he'd pinch her with his sharp teeth, and pretend to fight, like any healthy colt should do. But none the less, she felt that something was wrong.

The sun climbed higher, and the colt finally tired himself out and lay down to doze at the mare's feet. She thought about starting back to join the mustang band, but it seemed so safe and peaceful there in the pocket that she hated to leave. And by tomorrow the colt's legs would be stronger and he would be able to follow her with no difficulty.

But before the morning was half gone she heard the sound of danger; an iron shod hoof striking a stone, and looked up to see two cowboys between her and the mouth of the pocket.

It was Uncle Torwal and Whitey out to see how their range stock was getting along. Torwal was a slow speaking fellow with a droopy red moustache, and a good many of the horses running in the Badlands belonged to him. Whitey, who was probably ten years old or thereabouts, had lived with him on the ranch for several years. Almost since he could remember. He wore a cast-off Stetson hat of Torwal's and high-heeled riding boots from the same source. They lived alone like any two old sourdoughs and were a familiar sight at all the roundups, and in town of a Saturday, Torwal on a crop-eared black and Whitey on a pot-bellied old pinto named Spot. Torwal usually spoke of Whitey as his "sawed off" foreman.

The little mare had whirled to face them, keeping the colt behind her. With her teeth bared and her ears laid back, she looked half wolf for sure.

"Spunky crittur, ain't she?" Whitey remarked as they rode carefully around, trying to get a good look at the colt.

"She's a wolf, all right," Torwal agreed. "An' if you ain't careful she's a-goin' t' paste you plumb outta your saddle. Better not crowd her."

They sat on their horses and watched a while and admired the colt. "Purty as a picture, ain't he, Uncle Torwal?" said Whitey. "Reckon we better take him home so the wolves won't get him?"

"Don't reckon we'll take him anywheres," Torwal told him. "Looks like I'm a-goin' to have to shoot him!"

"Shoot him! Why?" squalled Whitey. "Why he's the purtiest colt on the ranch!"

"Better look him over closer, Bub," said Torwal. "See if you notice anything outta the way about him."

"I don't see anything wrong, myself," Whitey told him, after he'd walked Spot in a circle around the mare and colt again. "He looks to me just like the kind of crittur I'd like to have for a 'Sunday' horse."

"Look at his eyes; they're white," Torwal growled. "That colt's blind as a bat!"

"Aw, them's just china eyes, Uncle Torwal," Whitey said. "Lotsa horses has china eyes. Even ol' Spot has one."

"Them ain't no china eyes, not by a long shot," said Torwal. "If you look close you'll see that they're pure white without no center. He's blind, and we gotta shoot him. Otherwise he'll fall in a hole somewheres or get wolf et."

"Well, even if he is blind do we *hafta* shoot him?" Whitey asked. "Couldn't I take him home an' keep him at the ranch?"

"All he'd be is a mess of trouble even if you got him home, and I doubt that he'd go that far without somethin' happening to him anyways," Torwal told him. "An' besides, he wouldn't be good for nothing."

"Well anyway, do we hafta shoot him?" Whitey said. "Couldn't we just let him go loose?"

"Now quit your squallin'," Torwal told him, patiently. "I don't like it any more than you do, but if we leave him he'll either fall in a hole and starve or else he'll get wolf et. Lookit her tracks where she circled during the night. Fighting off an ol' 'gray,' I bet she was."

While Whitey sat with his lip hanging down almost to his collar, Torwal took another chew from his plug and got his rifle out of his saddle scabbard. But whenever he tried to get near the colt the little mare was there, lashing out with her hoofs and showing her teeth to bite either man or horse that got too near. Before long she was covered with lather and her eyes showed white, and the ground was plowed and trampled in a circle. But still the colt was safe.

Then Whitey spoke up again. "Lissen, Uncle Torwal," he said. "Lookit the way she fights. I don't believe any wolf could get to that colt, the way she uses them heels. If you'll let him go I'll watch mighty close to see if he falls in anything. I'll ride out every day to see that he's all right. An' if he does fall in I—I—I'll shoot him myself!"

Uncle Torwal thought the matter over awhile.

"You want that colt mighty bad, don't yuh?" he said at last.

"Yeah, I sure do! He's the purtiest thing I've ever seen!" said Whitey. "I don't think anything will happen to him, really, Uncle Torwal! He's too smart lookin'!"

"Well, I tell yuh," Torwal said, doubtfully. "Since you feel like that about it we'll let him go awhile. We'll be a-ridin' over here every day for a while anyways, so we can always shoot him later."

"But don't go gettin' your hopes up," he added. "The chances are he won't last a week. An' if he does he ain't good for nothing except to eat up good grass an' be a gunny sack full of trouble."

"Nothing is going to happen to him," Whitey exclaimed, "You'll see."

"Maybe," said Uncle Torwal, but Whitey could see that he was glad to have an excuse for not shooting the colt. Uncle Torwal put his rifle back in the scabbard, and they sat for a minute watching the colt, and then rode off to attend to their other affairs.

The little mare watched them until they were out of sight, and finally when she could no longer hear them she turned to the colt. She nuzzled him all over to make sure that nothing had happened to him. Then after letting him suck again she started down the trail toward the place she'd left the mustang band, with the blind colt following close against her flank.

Sounds and Smells

Back with the mustang band, the brown mare and the blind colt settled into the routine of range life. Early mornings they moved to their favorite feeding grounds where they grazed until the sun got hot when they dozed and rested. Late afternoons they grazed slowly towards some nearby water hole for their daily drink.

And the blind colt began learning the thousand and one things that a colt must know before he can take care of himself. Because he was blind he not only had to learn the things all colts must learn, but many others besides. For a week or so he stuck pretty close to the mare's side, and she saw to it that they stayed out where the ground was level with nothing for the colt to run into.

So it was only natural that he soon came to the conclusion that all the world was flat, and that he could travel safely anywhere.

What he did not know was that this Badlands country was criss-crossed and honeycombed with gulleys and washouts of every size, shape and description, and that sooner or later he would have to learn about them.

And sure enough, before long he did. It came about one morning when the horses were grazing on a grassy bench between gray shale bluffs on one side and a deep gulley on the other. The blind colt had wandered off a little farther than usual, when the mare looked up and whinneyed sharply for him to come back. He had learned that she usually punished him with her big teeth when he disobeyed, but he was feeling spooky this morning and figured that a little gallop the way he was going before he turned and came back wouldn't really be disobeying. So he flirted his tail over his back, snorted as loud as he could and made a few buck jumps straight ahead. The third jump sent him over the edge of the gulley and he found there was no more solid ground under his feet!

The sensation was one he never did forget. He turned head over heels and rolled to the bottom unhurt but considerably shaken up, and thoroughly frightened. After he had picked himself up he whinneyed shrilly and stood trembling and snorting until the mare came to the edge of the bank. She made comforting noises to him and with her encouragement he soon found a place where he could scramble back up the bank to where she stood.

For several days after that he stayed almost as close as if he had been glued to the brown mare's side, and carefully felt out the ground ahead at every step. He was afraid it would fall away from under him again.

But after a few days his curiosity got the better of his fear, and he started cautiously exploring again. He soon discovered that it wasn't enough to be careful not to fall over these banks, but that sometimes they stuck up and when he ran into them they were apt to jar the daylights out of him.

However, he learned fast and in a surprisingly short time he developed a sense that warned him of these things in his path even though he could not see them.

Whitey and Uncle Torwal, riding across the range, often saw him as he picked his way cau-tiously over strange ground or traveled with the rest of the horses to water, pressed up close to the brown mare's side.

"Well, he ain't got himself wolf et so far," Uncle Torwal would say.

"Nossir!" Whitey would answer. "An' he ain't a-goin' to, either. He's too smart."

Uncle Torwal would spit and say nothing.

During the late spring and early summer, the band of mustangs didn't travel much. There was plenty of grass on the flats and the water holes were nearly all full. In the cool hours of the mornings the older horses grazed quietly while the colts ran and kicked among themselves. The long middle hours of the day they spent contentedly dozing in the sun.

One or another of the mares usually was to be found a little distance from the rest, where she could keep a watchful eye on the surrounding country. When it was the brown mare who was standing guard the colt stayed close to her side. When she looked he listened, and when she listened, he listened too, and stretched his nostrils wide to smell. This way he learned many things. Things surrounding him were only Sounds and Smells, as far as he could tell. Unable to see them, they of course had no shapes. Bull bats catching bugs overhead in the evening were only Booming Sounds. Coyotes skulking around about their business of catching small rodents and robbing birds' nests were Rank Furry Smells. Jack rabbits were Furry Smells too, but smaller and dustier. The rabbits were also Small Sneezes and Thumping Noises. He learned to recognize the step of every horse in the band, and could spot the step of a strange horse immediately. He learned to tell the difference between the irregular movements of a loose horse and the steady purposeful gait of one ridden by a man.

The blind colt often heard Whitey and Spot go by these days, recognizing them by the lazy clop of Spot's big feet and his habit of blowing imaginary bugs out of his nose every few steps.

By the time summer came on and the band started climbing to the tops of high buttes in the middle of the day to escape the flies, the colt's nose and his ears were giving him almost as good a picture of the things around him as if he'd had eyes.

Now most of these things were friendly and harmless, but the slightest taint of wolf smell, even before he knew what it was, would send him racing to his mother, stamping and snorting with excitement. For the fear of wolves has been born in the bones of horses for centuries. Before long he was to learn of other unfriendly and dangerous things.

On a drowsy afternoon in the middle of the summer, the blind colt was browsing among the broken banks of a black shale butte some distance from the other horses. In little pockets here and there were scattered bunches of grass high enough for him to reach.

He didn't really need the grass, but finding it was a sort of game. He had to work his way carefully along the rainwashed banks, exploring each projecting shelf with delicate sniffings, and when he discovered a green stalk he'd reach out his long upper lip and wrap it around the grass to get it in reach of his biting teeth.

When he succeeded in pulling up a mouthful, he'd stand and grind it busily with his small milk teeth, and flap his tail and nod his head with enjoyment.

After a time he noticed an odd smell. One that was new to him. It was sharp, but not very strong. He lowered his head and snorted his nostrils clear, to catch the new scent better. It didn't have the warmth and body of an animal smell, and yet there was something about it that frightened him a little, he didn't know why.

He stamped and snorted, but nothing happened, and there was nothing moving that he could hear. So after a little he went on with his search for grass. He had worked around a jutting shoulder of the butte when he noticed the smell was suddenly stronger and then he heard a buzzing—something like a grasshopper. But a grasshopper's buzzing had never given his skin the tingly feeling he had now. He was puzzled. He listened in all directions, pointing his ears this way and that, but the sound had stopped. As soon as he stepped forward, he heard the buzz again, and this time it was sharper and louder. It came from somewhere on the ground nearby, but as soon as he stopped to locate it, the sound stopped. He stood motionless for several minutes, waiting for it to come again, and when it didn't he figured that whatever had

made it must be gone, and returned to his search for grass.

But when he stepped forward again the buzz returned, and this time it had a nervous, angry sound. The smell was stronger, too. The colt was frightened, but hadn't been able to figure out where the sound came from so he didn't know which way to run. He stamped his foot, and as he did there was a dry rustling and a sudden movement from under an overhanging ledge at his feet as something struck his foreleg a sharp blow. The colt snorted with terror, whirled and ran for his mother, bumping into things as he went.

He'd been bitten by a rattlesnake that had crawled under the ledge for shade.

The mare fussed over him and worried about him, for in a short time he was a very sick colt indeed. His leg began to swell and he grew sick and feverish all over. Before long he was thirsty. And as he waded around in the nearby water hole he found that the mud cooled and soothed him. By evening his leg had swollen so much he could only hobble around with great difficulty. The rest of the band went away after a time, but for several days the mare and the blind colt stayed by the edge of the water hole. The colt

spent the greater part of his time standing deep in the churned-up mud while the mare grazed nearby, coming back to nuzzle him and to groom his hide with her tongue every few minutes.

In a few days the swelling began to go down and before long he was able to travel slowly, by favoring the sore leg, and they set out to find the rest of the horses. A couple weeks more and he was about as well as ever. But after that, the slightest smell of rattlesnake was enough to set him to snorting and plunging with fear.

The Water Hole

As the summer advanced the hot dry winds blew up from the south with the heat from a thousand miles of desert, and the country turned dry and brown. The small springs with their trickles of clear water were the first to dry up. Then the smaller water holes began to show wider and wider bands of dried and trampled mud around their edges, and finally they too were completely dry.

By late August the only water to be found was in the few large sinks and behind the scattered earth dams thrown up by the ranchers to hold snow water in the spring.

Old trails that had lain hard and untracked all summer now were inches deep in dust, ground up by the hoofs of the wild horse bands and the herds of cattle on their trips to water.

With so many bands coming into the few big water holes, the grass near them was soon gone, so the horses had to travel farther and farther from water to feeding grounds. When the weather was cool and overcast, they sometimes went to water only once in three days. But when the hot winds blew they had to drink every day.

Before long the blind colt's band was traveling so far that the trip to water and back left little time for rest or grazing.

The blind colt was still fat and sassy, growing like a weed, but the heat and traveling were beginning to show on the brown mustang mare. Her coat had begun to look rough, and her hip bones and ribs to show.

The trips in to water were full of excitement for the colt. Early in the afternoon the band would start slowly grazing in that direction. The nearer they came to the water the shorter the grass was, having been eaten down by the stock

that had passed before. After a time they'd fall into one of the well-worn paths and follow it. Before long they'd see the dust of other bunches moving in the same direction. And the last mile or so there would be flocks of sage hens plodding along in single file, also on the way for their evening drink.

When they finally reached the rim overlooking the water hole, the whole band stopped while the leader looked the country over carefully. If there was another band of horses ahead of them they waited until they'd finished and gone away, for two strange bands will not drink at the same time. And, too, there was always a certain amount of danger connected with these isolated water holes. Wild horse hunters sometimes waited there, and the big gray wolves skulked about looking for a chance to pull down any animal that got trapped in the deep mud.

The blind colt enjoyed these trips, however. His ears picked up the disgruntled cluckings of the waddling sage hens, and he smelled the fresh scent of the sagebrush and any number of other pungent desert weeds drying in the hot wind. And while still a long way from the water hole all the horses would smell the water and hurry a little faster.

When they reached the ridge he stood with the others examining the country for danger, throwing his head high and distending his nostrils as far as he could. When the stallion bugled through his nose, the colt tried to do the same.

When they finally started down the trail he'd kick and squeal with excitement, nipping the flanks and hocks of whatever horse was nearest and generally stirring up confusion.

But the water hole itself always frightened him a little, for it was surrounded by a wide band of mud, dried and cracked on top, and thick and gummy under the crust. It wasn't like the nice squishy stuff he'd waded in earlier in the summer. This mud made strange sucking noises around the horses' feet and seemed to be trying to pull them down.

At first he always stayed on firm ground while the brown mare drank, waiting for her. But as the summer got drier and the colt older the mare's supply of milk grew less and less. By this time the colt was able to graze a little so he wasn't troubled by lack of food, but he did begin to get thirsty. So one day he ventured out across the mud himself, being careful to pick a place that had been packed firmer than the rest. Except for the sucking noises around his feet, nothing happened, so after that he always drank with the others.

But one day he accidently shoved up against a short-tempered old mare and she whacked him in the ribs with her heels. The colt was startled and plunged away, landing in a boggy spot the others had been avoiding.

His hoofs, being small and sharp, didn't give him the support that flatter ones of an older horse would have, and he felt himself sinking. The harder he tried to pull his feet loose the deeper he sank. He whinneyed in terror and lunged with all his power, but all he could do was work himself deeper and deeper into the sticky mud.

The brown mare had left her drinking as soon as she heard him squall, but there was nothing she could do but nuzzle him and whicker encouragingly. By the time he was exhausted he had thrown himself partly on his side and was trapped beyond any chance of escape without help. He lay there, covered with mud, his sides heaving and his nostrils showing their red inner side.

The horses milled round, excited by his struggles and his frightened whinneying, but after a time they all went away except for the brown mare standing guard.

She stood over him and nuzzled him with her nose and wiped mud off with her tongue, comforting him as much as possible. By spells he struggled, trying to get to his feet. But after a

time he wore himself out completely and just lay and shivered.

That night was the longest he'd ever known. He heard the sound of other horses coming to drink, and the squeals and thump of hoofs on ribs as the brown mare drove them off.

Somewhere in the night there was the smell of a big gray wolf prowling near, and the snorting and stamping of the mare as she circled between the blind colt and the danger.

In the morning he heard the small sounds of sage chickens and little animals drinking, but nothing else. He and the brown mare were alone. She grazed nearby, returning to the trapped colt whenever he moved or made a sound.

It was late in the morning when the mare threw up her head to listen for a sound the colt had heard some time before. The sound of a shod horse, and from his steady gait it was plain there was a cowboy on his back. In a little while Whitey showed up on old Spot. There was much to be done these days, what with riding out to check the water holes and the like, so Torwal quite often sent him out to ride alone. And when Whitey saw the colt bogged down he was mighty glad that Torwal was not along this particular morning, because he felt sure Torwal would have argued that the colt had best be shot.

He rode up and sat a minute in his saddle while the mare watched him. This time she didn't show fight. Perhaps somehow she knew there was no need. Whitey talked soothingly to her and to the colt while he took down his rope. Shaking out a noose as he'd seen Uncle Torwal do in such cases, he rode carefully out across the mud as close as possible to the colt. The mare

followed anxiously, but still not interfering. After a few unsuccessful attempts he got the loop around the colt's neck and took a dally around the saddle horn. Then, working carefully, he edged Spot towards solid ground. As the noose tightened on the colt's neck he began to struggle again. But now with the pull of the rope to help him, he was soon dragged out to firm ground.

He was a messy looking sight, with all that mud caked on him, as he lay there getting his breath. But luckily he wasn't chilled as he would have been later in the year. The brown mare trotted around like an old hen with a bunch of ducks, snorting and whinneying to herself and smelling and nudging the colt. Working very carefully and without getting out of his saddle, Whitey shook the muddy noose from the colt's neck and rode off a few yards to watch.

For a while the colt was content to lay on the grass and rest while the mare nosed him over to see if he was all right, and licked the mud off his coat. But after being in the mud all night he was mighty hungry, so it wasn't long before he struggled to his feet. His legs were pretty wobbly under him, but beyond that he didn't seem to be damaged any. And by the time the mare had nursed him and polished him from head to foot he looked and felt about as good as new, so they started slowly up the trail the way the other horses had gone.

All this time Whitey had quietly watched them from a distance with his chest thrown out and as near strutting as is possible for a fellow sitting on a sleepy old pinto horse to be. He'd been busting for some time to get a chance to pull a bogged crittur out of the mud by himself. And for it to be his blind colt was almost more excitement than he could hold!

After the mare and colt had disappeared over the ridge he managed to get his attention back on his business and climbed down to clean the mud off his rope before he coiled it back on the saddle.

When that was finished he cocked his handme-down Stetson as far on one side as it would go and rode away, admiring his shadow more than a little. He kind of hoped he'd get a chance to rope a wolf or some such thing to sort of finish his day out right.

from JUSTIN MORGAN HAD A HORSE

Marguerite Henry

No one has written more thrilling tales of different breeds of horses than has Mrs. Henry. King of the Wind, the story of the ancestor of the famous race horse, Man o' War, won the Newbery Medal in 1949. The episodes given here come from a book about the ancestor of a special breed of horses, the sturdy and willing Morgan horse. Little Bub, the horse hero, is given to the schoolmaster Justin Morgan in payment of a debt. Young Joel Goss, who has been apprenticed to Miller Chase and who is also a friend of the schoolmaster, loves the colt from the time he first sets eyes on him and undertakes to gentle him. The excerpts presented herein are taken from chapters seven and eight of the revised edition of *Justin Morgan Had a Horse.*

Little Bub Is Rented Out

Never was a creature more willing to be gentled. After but two lessons, he wore a halter as if it were a part of him. Like his forelock. Or his tail. Fastening two ropes to the halter, Joel drove him around and around in a circle, teaching him to "git up" and to "whoa."

Next Joel slipped a bit in the colt's mouth. At first Bub's ears went back in displeasure. He did not mind rope or leather things, but iron felt cold and hard to his tongue. One night Joel warmed the bit in his hands and coated it with maple syrup. From then on Little Bub accepted it each time, actually reaching out for it, jaws open wide.

Whenever the colt learned a new lesson, Joel told him what a fine, smart fellow he was. "Soon you'll be *big* for your size!" he would say. "And then you've got to be so smart and willing that even an ornery man won't have reason to whop ye. I couldn't abide that!" he added in dread.

Some nights Joel fastened a lantern to an old two-wheeled cart borrowed from Mister Jenks. Then, filling the cart with stones for weight, he drove Bub over the rolling hills. He practiced

pulling him up short. He practiced walking him, trotting him, stopping and backing him.

The moon waned and became full again. By now Joel was galloping Little Bub, galloping him bareback across the fields. And Bub wanted to go! It was as if the clean, cold air felt good in his lungs, as if he liked the night and the wind and the boy.

One evening when Master Morgan remained late at school, Joel burst in on him so full of laughter he could scarcely talk. The other apprentice boys had gone long ago, and Joel's laughter rang out so heartily in the empty room that the schoolmaster joined in without knowing why.

Between spasms the boy managed to gasp, "You should've seed that little hound-dog run!"

"What little hound-dog?"

"Why, Mister Jenks's yellow one," giggled Joel, bursting into fresh laughter. "He come a-tearin' out the house, yammering at Little Bub, trying to nip his legs. Oh, ho, ho, ho!"

"What did Bub do?"

"What did he *do*?" shrieked Joel. "Why, he sprung forward like a cat outen a bag. And that idiot hound was too addled to go home. He streaked down the road with Bub after him."

Joel had to wipe away his tears before he could go on. "By and by," he chuckled, "the hound got so beat out I took pity on him and reined in."

Master Morgan's eyes twinkled. "I reckon Farmer Beane was right," he said. "Seems as if Little Bub and dogs just don't cotton to each other."

When Mister Goss first heard that Joel was training the schoolmaster's colt, he was furious.

But later, when neighbors marveled at the boy's skill, he boasted and bragged about it: "All that boy knows about horses he got from me!"

The truth of the matter was that in watching his father train a colt Joel had learned what not to do, as well as what to do. While his father could break and train in a matter of hours, his horses often seemed broken in spirit, too. The boy was determined that this should not happen to his colt. And it had not. Little Bub's eyes were still dancy. He still tossed his mane and nosed the sky. He still had a frisky look about him. No, he had lost none of his spirit.

Even in the rough winds of winter, the colt's schooling went right on, night after night. And about the time when Joel began to think Little Bub might be his forever, a stranger came knocking at the schoolhouse door.

School was in full session. A dozen apprentice boys were bent over their copybooks. As if on one stem, a dozen heads turned around.

Master Morgan pushed his spectacles up on his forehead, brushed the chalk off his vest, and went to the door. "Come in, sir," he said.

A tall, gaunt man entered and sat down on the splint-bottomed chair which the schoolmaster offered. "Good evening," he said in a voice that rolled out strong. "I'm Ezra Fisk, a new settler, and word has come to my ear that you have a horse to rent."

Eleven pens stopped scratching and eleven pairs of eyes looked up with interest. Joel's pen skated wildly across the page as if his arm had been jolted out of its socket.

"You will continue with your work," the schoolmaster nodded to the boys. He could not bring himself to answer the man's question at once.

Mister Fisk filled in the silence that followed. "I've been watching a lad ride a smallish horse in the moonlight," he said in his trumpet of a voice, "and by inquiring at the inn, I understand the horse belongs to you, sir."

Justin Morgan made a steeple out of his fingers. His Yes was spoken through tight lips.

"You see," the newcomer explained, "I have a piece of wooded land along the White River. And Robert Evans, my hired hand, will need a horse to help clear it. This fellow, Evans, is a brawny man, and I figure he and a horse with some get-up-and-git could clear the land in a year's time."

Master Morgan hesitated a long moment before he spoke. "You would like to buy the horse, sir?"

"Tsk, tsk, Morgan. No, indeed! Who would buy such a *little* animal? As I said, I merely wish to rent him."

The schoolmaster stood up and looked questioningly at Joel. Ezra Fisk followed his glance. "That the boy who's been riding the colt?"

"Aye," Master Morgan said very softly. "And for his sake I am loathe to part with the animal."

The visitor now lowered his voice, too. "I understand," he said, leaning one arm on the desk, "that you are paid sometimes in Indian corn and sometimes the full sum of two dollars per week. Yet even the latter amount," he added knowingly, "covers no such extras as horses and harpsichords."

Joel sat forward, holding his breath, trying to hear the next words.

"But I, my good man," and now the voice waxed strong again, "stand ready to pay fifteen dollars a year, and the animal's keep, of course."

He said no more.

The noise of the scratching pens faded away. A stray flutter of smoke went up the chimney with a faint hiss. Joel was afraid he was going to cry. He wanted to run to Little Bub and hide him away somewhere deep in the woods. Perhaps this was all a bad dream. It *must* be a bad dream! Why else would his head drop forward in a nod, answering Yes to the schoolmaster's unspoken question?

The next afternoon Joel was setting a log in the sawmill when he heard the creaking of a wagon wheel and the cloppety-clop of hoofs coming down the road. This in itself was nothing to make him stop work, but from the uneven beat of the hoofs he could tell that the animals were not traveling in a team. And then, without looking up, he knew. He knew that the lighter hoofbeats were those of Little Bub. He started the saw, and then he turned and faced the road.

It *was* Little Bub, all right, not five rods away. He was tied to the back of a wagon pulled by a team of oxen. His reddish coat glinted in the sunlight, and he held his head high, as if he found nothing at all disgraceful in being tied to an oxcart.

The blood hammered in Joel's head. He might have called out, "Hi, Little Bub!" and felt the hot pride of having him nicker in reply. Instead, he kept hearing the schoolmaster's words: "I've got to pay off my debts before I die. Will you gentle the colt for me, lad?"

Well, Bub had been gentled, all right. Anyone could see that. With a heavy heart, Joel watched the procession as it passed him by, and then clattered over the log bridge and climbed up and up the steep hill. At last it disappeared over the brow, and nothing was left of it. Nothing, but a wisp of dust.

The Pulling Bee

In the weeks that followed, it was hard for Joel to pay attention to his work. He kept seeing Little Bub in the back of his mind, seeing him go lickety-split after the hound-dog or just capering for the fun of it. And in the sound of the millwheel he kept hearing the high, bugling neigh. And often, when no one was looking, he would sniff his jacket to smell the very essence of Little Bub!

In whatever Joel was doing—gathering stones for fences, wielding a mattock on stumps in the highway, working inside or outside—the little horse nudged into his thoughts.

One day, when Joel was up inside the chimney sweeping away the soot, his ears picked out three names from the talk going on in the room below: Ezra Fisk, Robert Evans, Justin Morgan. Precariously his fingers clung to the bricks like a bird. If he made the least noise or if his bare feet slid into view, the talk might stop or take a new tack altogether. His toes found a narrow ledge of brick and caught a foothold. His whole body tensed with listening.

"Yup," a voice was saying, "the schoolmaster's little horse is turning out to be a crack puller. Already he's made a nice clearing of about five acres."

Another voice said, "So the little horse can pull, eh?"

"Yup," the first voice replied. "Evans brags that the critter can jerk a log right out of its bark!"

A loud guffaw greeted the remark.

In the dark of the chimney Joel smiled in pride. But what if—the smile faded, and worry crept in—what if Evans was working Little Bub too hard? What if he became swaybacked and old before his time?

Joel had to know. Quickly he slid down the chimney and dropped to the hearth. But he was too late. All he saw was the whisk of a coattail and the door to the public room swinging shut, and at the same time Mistress Chase coming at him with a broken lock to be mended.

As the days went by, Joel heard more and more about Little Bub's labors, and his worry sharpened. At last he talked things over with Miller Chase.

"Why, work don't hurt horses," Mister Chase said reassuringly. "It's t'other way around. Idleness is what really hurts 'em. Their muscles git soft and their lungs git so small they can't even run without wheezing."

And so Joel's mind was eased.

By the time spring came on, Joel and the miller were the best of friends. In the late afternoon while Mistress Chase napped, he often waved Joel away with a smile. "Be off with you now. Have a mite of fun," he would say.

Joel took delight in these free afternoon hours. At this time of day Chase's Mill was the liveliest spot on the White River. Farmers would congregate to chat as they waited for the big saw to cut their logs. And often they tested the strength of their horses with a log-pulling contest. Surely, Joel thought, Little Bub must show up some day.

It was on a late afternoon in April that his hopes were realized. The millstream had grown swollen with spring rains, and Mister Chase had taken on a helper to keep the mill sawing logs both night and day.

On this afternoon, when the yard was crowded with farmers, the miller called to Joel. "See the man studying that-there pine log? That's Nathan Nye. And if Nathan Nye is about, acting mighty important and bossy, you can be expecting most anything to happen. He was ever good at fixing pulling contests."

Joel watched the jerky-legged man hop from one group to another, like a puppet on a string.

"If I was a boy, now, with no chores to do," the miller smiled, "it seems like I'd skedaddle right out there and be in the center of things."

In no time at all Joel was helping Mister Nye wrap tug chains about the huge pine log. A big dappled mare stood waiting to have the chains hooked to her harness.

The mare's owner, Abel Hooper from Buttonwood Flats, was too busy bragging to be of any help. "A mighty lucky thing I'm first," he was saying. "Big Lucy and me'll pull this-here piece o' kindling onto the logway in one pull. Then you can all hyper on home afore lantern time."

Abel Hooper had to eat his words. Big Lucy tried hard. She dug her forefeet into the earth and tugged and tugged, but the log barely trembled. Even when he poked her with the prodding stick, she only looked around as if to tell him it was useless.

One after another the work horses had their turn. Yet no matter how whips cracked or masters yelled, the log seemed rooted to earth.

Nathan Nye made a megaphone of his hands. "Folks!" he shouted. "Guess it's just too hefty for a horse. You men with oxen can have a try now."

Just then a bearded farmer came riding up on a chunky young stallion. Joel's heart missed a beat. Could this be Little Bub? This unkempt, mud-coated horse? Why, small as he was, he looked to be a six- or even a seven-year-old! Then Joel grinned as the little stallion let out a high bugle and a rumbling snort.

"Wait!" called the big man astride the little horse. "Here's a critter wants to try."

A smile, half scorn, half amusement, crossed Nathan Nye's face. "Evans," he said, "ye're crazy as if ye'd burnt yer shirt. Look at Big Lucy. She's still blowin' from the try. And Biggle's Belgian—his muscles are still a-hitchin' and a-twitchin'.

Even Wiggins' beast failed. Can't none of 'em budge that log."

"None exceptin' my one-horse team!" crowed Evans.

Fear caught at Joel as a silence fell upon the crowd.

And then came the rain of words, mingled with laughter.

"*That* little sample of a horse!"

"Why, his tail is long as a kite's!"

"Yeah, he's liable to get all tangled up and break a leg."

"Morgan's horse," Evans said slowly, "ain't exactly what you'd call a drafter, but whatever he's hitched to generally has to come."

Joel heard the sharp voice of Mistress Chase calling: "Boy! You come here!"

"Oh, rats!" he muttered under his breath. On the way to the inn he stopped long enough to put his cheek against Little Bub's. "I'll be back," he whispered. "I'll be right back."

Mistress Chase met him just inside the door with a kettle of hasty pudding. "Hang the kettle over the fire," she commanded, "and stir and stir until I tell you to quit."

He hung the kettle on the crane and set to work. "*Hasty* pudding!" Joel cried to himself. "It beats me how it got its name! Nothing quick about this!" Suddenly he heard the clump of boots and looked around to see Evans, followed by a little company of men, strut into the inn.

"Madam Innkeeper!" Evans called. "I'm wagering a barrel o' cider that my horse can move the pine log. But now, pour me a mugful. I'm dying of thirst."

Joel was stirring so vigorously he almost upset the pudding. Mistress Chase let out a shriek. "Boy! Mind what you're doing! Hasty pudding's not meant to feed the fire!"

For once he paid no heed. He tore across the room and grabbed Mister Evans by the sleeve. "Sir!" he cried. "Little Bub's been working hard all day. Please don't ask him to pull that big log."

Evans gulped his drink. "Go 'way," he snapped in annoyance. "When I want advice, I'll not ask it of a whipper-snapper. I know that horse!" He stomped out of doors, the others joking and laughing behind him.

While Joel stirred the pudding, he kept look-ing out the window. He could see Little Bub nib-bling all the fresh green shoots within his range. And he could see the men sizing him up, feeling of his legs, then making their wagers.

One by one, the stars dusted the sky. Nathan Nye brought out a lantern so that Evans could see to fasten the tug chains to the log.

"I just *got* to go out there now!" Joel pleaded. "Ma'am, if you please, could I?"

Mistress Chase nodded. "You're stirring so strong that hasty pudding's heaving like a sea. Go on! Git out, afore ye upset it."

"Oh, thanks, ma'am," Joel murmured as he bolted for the door, vaulted over a barrel of cider, and ran to the mill, where Evans was stepping off ten rods.

"Aye, fellers!" he was saying. "Bub can do it—in two pulls." He turned around, almost stumbling over the boy. "A nettle hain't half as pesky as you," he growled. "Out of my way or I'll clout you!"

Nathan Nye shouted to Evans. "Mebbe you'd oughter listen to the lad. Want to give up afore you start?"

"No such-a-thing! Why, I'm actually ashamed to ask Morgan's horse to pull a splinter like this. Now, if you'll find me three stout men to sit astride the log, why, then I'll ask him."

Joel ran to Little Bub. "Oh, my poor little feller," he choked. "None of the big critters could do it, and now with three men besides!—Oh, Bub, Bub . . ."

Laughter was ringing up and down the valley. "Ho-ho-ho—that pint-sized cob to pull such a big log! Ho-ho . . ."

Nathan Nye had no trouble at all in finding three brawny volunteers. As the men straddled the log, they joked and laughed and poked one another in the ribs.

"Look to your feet, men!" warned Evans. "This horse means business. Something's got to give."

Nye held the lantern aloft. It lighted the hud-dle of faces. They were tense with excitement. Some of the men were placing last-minute bets. Some were chewing madly on wisps of hay. Others twirled their hats and wrung them ner-vously. Joel felt as if he were going to be sick.

Evans repeated his warning. "Look to your feet, men!"

Someone tittered.

Then the silence exploded as Evans roared, "Git up!"

The sharp word of command galvanized the little horse into action. His muscles swelled and grew firm. He backed ever so slightly. He lowered his head, doubling down into the harness. He lunged, half falling to his knees, straining forward, throwing his whole weight into the collar.

A hush closed around the gathering. It hung heavy and ominous. Suddenly the very earth seemed to shake. The chains were groaning, the log itself trembling as if it had come alive. It began to skid. It was moving! The stout man aboard laughed hysterically, then sobered, trying to balance himself, clutching onto the others. The log kept on moving. It was halfway to the mill!

The horse's breath whistled in his lungs. His nostrils flared red in exertion. Sweat broke out on his body, lathering at the collar and traces. Joel, too, was drenched in sweat. He was struggling, straining, panting as if he were yoked alongside Little Bub.

Now the terrible silence again as the horse stood to catch his wind. There was no sound at all from the crowd. Overhead a robin, trying to get settled for the night, chirped insistently.

Now Evans commanded again. And again the horse backed slightly, then snatched the log into motion. Again the log was sliding, sliding, sliding. This time it did not stop until it reached the sawmill!

Still none of the onlookers made a sound. The three men astride were as silent as the log they sat upon. Only the horse's breathing pierced the quiet.

Then as if a dike had opened, there was a torrent of noise. Everyone began shouting at once. "Hooray for Little Bub! Hooray for Evans and Justin Morgan! Hooray for the big-little horse!"

Joel rushed over and threw his arms around Bub's neck. His whole body ached, as if he had moved the log himself. "It's over! It's over! You did it, Bub! You did it!" he kept repeating, sobbing a little from exhaustion and relief.

The horse lipped Joel's cheek and neck. He almost tried to say, "It's all right, boy; don't be taking it so hard." He was winded and leg-weary, but it was good to be near the boy again. It was good.

He nickered softly.

from SMOKY

Will James

Will James was a cowboy, and he wrote in the cowboy vernacular. But don't be deceived by the bad grammar. The story of Smoky the cowhorse is told with consummate skill and feeling. It sets a high standard for telling stories about animals of any sort because it is told with complete fidelity to the species. Smoky lives, enjoys, and suffers as a horse, never as a human being. This book won the Newbery Medal in 1927, and its popularity has never waned.

A Range Colt

It seemed like Mother Nature was sure agreeable that day when the little black colt came to the range world, and tried to get a footing with his long wobblety legs on the brown prairie sod. Short stems of new green grass was trying to make their way up thru the last year's faded growth, and reaching for the sun's warm rays. Taking in all that could be seen, felt, and inhaled, there was no day, time, nor place that could beat that spring morning on the sunny side of the low prairie butte where Smoky the colt was foaled.

"Smoky" wouldn't have fitted the colt as a name just then on account he was jet black, but that name wasn't attached onto him till he was a four-year-old, which was when he first started being useful as a saddle horse. He didn't see the first light of day thru no box-stall window, and there was no human around to make a fuss over him and try to steady him on his feet for them first few steps. Smoky was just a little range colt, and all the company he had that first morning of his life was his watchful mammy.

Smoky wasn't quite an hour old when he begin to take interest in things. The warm spring sun was doing its work and kept a-pouring warmth all over that slick little black hide, and right on thru his little body, till pretty soon his head come up kinda shaky and he begin nosing around them long front legs that was stretched out in front of him. His mammy was close by him, and at the first move the colt made she run her nose along his short neck and nickered. Smoky's head went up another two inches at the sound, and his first little answering nicker was heard. Of course a person would of had to listen mighty close to hear it, but then if you'd a-watched his nostrils quivering you could tell that's just what he was trying to do.

That was the starting of Smoky. Pretty soon his ears begin to work back and forth towards the sound his mammy would make as she moved. He was trying to locate just where she was. Then

something moved right in front of his nose about a foot; it'd been there quite a good spell but he'd never realized it before; besides his vision was a little dim yet and he wasn't interested much till that something moved again and planted itself still closer.

Being it was right close he took a sniff at it. That sniff recorded itself into his brain and as much as told him that all was well. It was one of his mammy's legs. His ears perked up and he tried nickering again with a heap better result than the first time.

One good thing called for another and natural like he made a sudden scramble to get up, but his legs wouldn't work right, and just about when he'd got his belly clear of the ground, and as he was resting there for another try at the rest of the way up, one of his front legs quivered and buckled at the elbow, and the whole works went down.

He layed there flat on his side and breathing hard. His mammy nickered encouragement, and it wasn't long when his head was up again and his legs spraddled out all around him the same as before. He was going to try again, but next time he was going to be more sure of his *ground*. He was studying, it seemed like, and sniffing of his legs and then the earth, like he was trying to figger out how he was going to get one to stand up on the other. His mammy kept a-circling around and a-talking to him in horse language; she'd give him a shove with her nose, then walk away and watch him.

The spring air, which I think is most for the benefit of all that's young, had a lot to do to keep Smoky from laying still for very long. His vision was getting clearer fast, and his strength was coming in just as fast. Not far away, but still too far for Smoky to see, was little calves, little white-faced fellers a-playing and bucking around and letting out wall-eyed bellers at their mammies, running out a ways and then running back, tails up, at a speed that'd make a greyhound blush for shame.

There was other little colts too all a-cavorting around and tearing up good sod, but with all them calves and colts that was with the bunches of cattle or horses scattered out on the range, the same experience of helplessness that Smoky was going thru had been theirs for a spell, and a few hadn't been as lucky as Smoky in their first squint at daylight. Them few had come to the range world when the ground was still covered with snow, or else cold spring rains was a-pouring down to wet 'em to the bone.

Smoky's mother had sneaked out of the bunch a few days before Smoky came, and hid in a lonely spot where she'd be sure that no cattle nor horses or even riders would be around. In a few days, and when Smoky would be strong enough to lope out, she'd go back again; but in the meantime she wanted to be alone with her colt and put all her attention on him, without having to contend with chasing off big inquisitive geldings or jealous fillies.

She was of range blood, which means mostly mustang with strains of Steeldust or Coach throwed in. If hard winters come and the range was covered with heavy snows, she knowed of high ridges where the strong winds kept a few spots bare and where feed could be got. If droughts came to dry up the grass and water holes, she sniffed the air for moisture and drifted out across the plain which was her home range, to the high mountains where things was more normal. There was cougars and wolves in that high country, but her mustang instinct made her the "fittest." She circled around and never went under where the lion was perched a-waiting for her, and the wolf never found her where she could be cornered.

Smoky had inherited that same instinct of his mammy's, but on that quiet spring morning he wasn't at all worried about enemies. His mammy was there, and besides he had a hard job ahead that was taking all of his mind to figger out: that was to stand on them long things which was fastened to his body and which kept a-spraddling out in all directions.

The first thing to do was to gather 'em under him and try again. He did that easy enough, and then he waited and gathered up all the strength that was in him. He sniffed at the ground to make sure it was there and then his head went up, his front feet stretched out in front of him, and with his hind legs all under him, he used all that strength he'd been storing up and pushed himself up on his front feet, his hind legs straightened up to steady him; and as luck would have it there was just enough distance

between each leg to keep him up there. All he had to do was to keep them legs stiff and from buckling up under him, which wasn't at all easy, cause getting up to where he was had used up a lot of his strength, and them long legs of his was doing a heap of shaking.

All would have been well maybe, only his mammy nickered "that's a good boy," and that's what queered Smoky. His head went up proud as a peacock and he forgot all about keeping his props stiff and under him. Down he went the whole length of his legs, and there he layed the same as before.

But he didn't lay long this time. He either liked the sport of going up and coming down or else he was getting peeved; he was up again, mighty shaky, but he was up sure enough. His mammy came to him. She sniffed at him and he sniffed back. Then nature played another hand and he nursed, the first nourishment was took in, his tummy warmed up and strength came fast. Smoky was an hour and a half old and up to stay.

The rest of that day was full of events for Smoky. He explored the whole country, went up big mountains two feet high, wide valleys six or eight feet acrost, and at one time was as far as twelve feet away from his mammy all by himself. He shied at a rock once; it was a dangerous-looking rock, and he kicked at it as he went past. All that action being put on at once come pretty near being too much for him and he come close to measuring his whole length on Mother Earth once again. But luck was with him, and taking it all he had a mighty good time. When the sun went to sinking over the blue ridges in the west, Smoky, he missed all the beauty of the first sunset in his life—he was stretched out full length, of his own accord this time, and sound asleep.

The night was a mighty good rival of what the day had been. All the stars was out and showing off, and the braves was a-chasing the buffalo plum around the Big Dipper, the water hole of The Happy Hunting Grounds. But all that was lost to Smoky; he was still asleep and recuperating from his first day's adventures, and most likely he'd kept on sleeping for a good long spell, only his mammy who was standing guard over him happened to get a little too close and stepped on his tail.

Smoky must have been in the middle of some bad dream. His natural instinct might of pictured some enemy to his mind, and something that looked like a wolf or a bear must of had him cornered for sure. Anyway, when he felt his tail pinched that way he figgered that when a feller begins to *feel* it's sure time to act, and he did. He shot up right under his mammy's chin, let out a squeal, and stood there ready to fight. He took in the country for *feet* and *feet* around and looking for the enemy that'd nipped him, and finally in his scouting around that way he run acrost the shadow of his mammy. That meant but one thing, safety; and that accounted for and put away as past left room for a craving he'd never noticed in his excitement. He was hungry, and proceeded right then and there to take on a feed of his mammy's warm, rich milk.

The sky was beginning to get light in the east, the stars was fading away and the buffalo hunters had went to rest. A few hours had passed since Smoky had been woke up out of his bad dream and there he was, asleep again. He'd missed his first sunset and now he was sleeping thru his first sunrise, but he was going to be prepared for that new day's run, and the strength he was accumulating through them sleeps and between feeds would sure make him fit to cover a lot of territory.

There wasn't a move out of him till the sun was well up and beginning to throw a good heat. He stacked up on a lot of that heat, and pretty soon one of his ears moved, then the other. He took a long breath and stretched. Smoky was coming to life. His mammy nickered, and that done the trick; Smoky raised his head, looked around, and proceeded to get up. After a little time that was done and bowing his neck he stretched again. Smoky was ready for another day.

The big day started right after Smoky had his feed; then his mother went to grazing and moving away straight to the direction of some trees a mile or so to the south. A clear spring was by them trees, and water is what Smoky's mammy wanted the most right then. She was craving for a drink of that cold water, but you'd never thought it by the way she traveled. She'd nose around at the grass and wait for spells, so as little Smoky could keep up with her and still find time to investigate everything what throwed a shadow.

A baby cottontail had jumped up once right under his nose, stood there a second too scared to move, and pretty soon made a high dive between the colt's long legs and hit for his hole; Smoky never seen the rabbit or even knowed he was there or he might of been running yet, cause that's what he'd been looking for, an excuse to run. But he finally made up an excuse, and a while later as he brushed past a long dry weed and it tickled his belly, he let out a squeal and went from there.

His long legs tangled and untangled themselves as he run, and he was sure making speed. Around and around he went and finally lined out straight away from where his mammy was headed. She nickered for him and waited, all patience. He turned after a spell and headed for his mammy again the same as tho he'd run acrost another enemy at the other end; and as he got close to his mammy he let out a buck, a squeal, a snort, and stopped—he was sure some little wild horse.

It took a couple of hours for them two to make that mile to the spring. The mother drank a lot of that good water, a few long breaths and drank some more till the thirst was all gone. Smoky came over and nosed at the pool, but he didn't take on any of the fluid, it looked just like so much thin air to him, the same with the tender green grass that was beginning to grow in bunches everywhere; it was just growing for him to run on.

The rest of that day was pretty well used up around that one spot; adventures of all kinds was numerous for Smoky, and when he wasn't stretched out and asleep there was plenty of big stumps in the cottonwood grove that could be depended on to give him the scare he'd be looking for.

But there was other things and more threatening than stumps which Smoky hadn't as yet spotted, like for instance,—a big cayote had squatted and been watching him thru dead willow branches. He wasn't at all interested in the action Smoky was putting into his play, and only wished the colt's mammy would move away a little further when he would then take a chance and try to get him down—colt meat was his favorite dish and he sure wasn't going to let no chance slip by even if it took a whole day's waiting for one to show itself.

A couple of chances had come his way but they was queered by Smoky's mammy being too close, and he knowed better than show himself and get run down by them hoofs of hers. Finally, and when he seen his appetite wouldn't win anything by sticking around that spot any longer, he took a last sniff and came out of his hiding place. Keeping the willows between him and the horses, he loped out till he was at a safe running distance and where he could see all around him, and there he squatted again, in plain sight this time. He hadn't quite made up his mind as yet whether to go or stick around a while longer. Just about then Smoky spots him.

To him, the cayote was just another stump, but more interesting than the others he'd kicked at, on account that this stump moved, and that promised a lot of excitement. With a bowed neck and kinked tail Smoky trotted up towards the cayote. The cayote just set there and waited and when the colt got to within a few feet from him, he started away and just fast enough so as the colt's curiosity would make him follow. If he could only get the colt over the ridge and out of his mammy's sight.

It all was only a lot of fun to Smoky, and besides he was bound to find out what was that gray and yellow object that could move and run and didn't at all look like his mammy. His instinct was warning him steady as he went, but curiosity had the best of him, and it wasn't till he was over the hill before his instinct got above his curiosity and he seen that all wasn't well.

The cayote had turned and quicker than a flash made a jump for Smoky's throat. The generations of mustang blood that'd fought the lobo and cougar, and which was the same blood that flowed in Smoky's veins, is all that saved the colt. That inherited instinct made him do the right thing at the right time, he whirled quicker than lightning and let fly with both hind feet with the result that the cayote's teeth just pinched the skin under his jaws. But even at that, he wasn't going to get rid of his enemy (it was a sure enough enemy this time) that easy, and as he kicked he felt the weight of the cayote, and then a sharp pain on his hamstrings.

Smoky was scared, and he let out a squeal that sure made every living thing in that neighborhood set up and wonder; it was a plain and loud distress signal, and it was answered. His mammy shot up the hill, took in the goings on at a glance, and ears back, teeth a-shining, tore up the earth and lit into the battle like a ton of dynamite.

The battle was over in a second, and with hunks of yellow fur a-flying all directions it wound up in a chase. The cayote was in the lead and he stayed in the lead till a second hill took him out of sight.

Smoky was glad to follow his mammy back to the spring and on to the other side a ways. He didn't shy at the stumps he passed on the way, and the twig that tickled his tummy didn't bring no play. He was hungry and tired, and when the first was tended to and his appetite called for no more he lost no time to picking out a place to rest his weary bones. A thin stream of blood was drying on one of his hind legs, but there was no pain, and when the sun set and the shadow of his mammy spread out over him he was sound asleep, and maybe dreaming of stumps, of stumps that moved.

When the sun came up the next morning, Smoky was up too, and eyes half closed was standing still as the big boulder next to him and sunned himself. A stiff hind leg was a reminder of what happened the day before, but the experience was forgotten far as dampening his spirits was concerned, even the stiffness wouldn't hold him back from whatever the new day would hold. He'd always remember the cayote, and from then on never mistake him for a stump, but that sure wasn't going to take any play out of him.

He was two days old now and strength had piled up fast, he felt there was no trail too long for him and when the sun was a couple of hours high that morning and his mother showed indications that she wanted to drift he sure wasn't dragging along behind. The stiffness gradually went out of his hind leg as he traveled, and by the afternoon of that day he was again shying at everything and sometimes even shying at nothing at all.

They kept a-traveling and traveling, and it seemed like to Smoky that the trail was getting pretty long after all. They skirted the flat along the foot of the mountains, crossed one high ridge, and many creeks, and still his mother was drifting on. She wouldn't hardly even stop for him to nurse, and Smoky was getting cranky, and tired.

The pace kept up till the sun was well on its way down, when it slackened some and finally the mother went to grazing. A short while later Smoky was layed out full length and dead to the world.

Smoky didn't know and didn't care much just then, but his mammy was headed back to her home range, where there was lots of horses and other little colts for him to play with; and when late that night she lined out again traveling steady he wasn't in any too good a humor.

Finally it seemed like they'd got there, for his mammy after watering at a creek went to grazing at the edge of some big cottonwoods; she showed no indications of wanting to go any further. Right there Smoky was willing to take advantage of the chance and recuperate for all he was worth. The sun came up, but Smoky was in the shade of the cottonwoods what was beginning to leaf out. He slept on and a twitching ear once in long spells is all that showed he was still alive.

That day never seen much of him; once in a while he'd get up and nurse but right away after he'd disappear again and stretch out flat on the warm earth.

He kept that up till way in the middle of the next night, and it was well towards morning before he felt like he was all horse again.

He come out of it in fine shape though, and he was stronger than ever. His vision was taking more territory too, and he was getting so he could see near half as far as his mammy could. She was the first to see the bunch of range horses trailing in to water early that morning. Smoky heard her nicker as she recognized the bunch and it drawed a heap of interest as to what she nickering about, for he was right there alongside of her and he couldn't see nothing for her to nicker at, but pretty soon he could hear the horses as they trailed towards him. His ears straightened towards the sound and a while later he could make out the shapes of 'em. Smoky just kind of quivered at the sight of so many that looked like his mammy. He was all interested, but at the same time, and even tho his instinct told him that all was well, he had no hankering to leave his mammy's side till he knowed for sure just what was up.

The mother watched the bunch coming closer with ears pointed straight ahead, but soon as some of the leaders discovered little Smoky there was a commotion and they all begin crowding in to get a look at and greet the newcomer, about which time the mother layed her ears back. It was a warning that none of 'em come too close.

Little Smoky's knees was a-shaking under him at the sight of so many of his kind; he leaned against his mammy half afraid, but his head was up far as he could get it and facing 'em and showed by the shine in his eyes that he liked the whole proceeding mighty well at that. He rubbed nostrils with a strange gelding which was braver than the rest and dared come close, and when that gelding was nipped at by his mammy he had a mighty strong hankering to help her along just for fun, and nip him himself.

The preliminary introduction took a good hour, and the mother stood guard; not for fear that any of 'em would harm Smoky, but she wanted it understood from the start that he was her little colt and she had the say over him. It finally *was* understood, but it took all that day and part of the next for the bunch to get used in having the new little feller around and quit making a fuss over him.

They was all jealous of one another and fought amongst themselves to be the only one near him, and his mother, of course she'd declared herself from the start, and it was took for granted from all around that her place in Smoky's heart couldn't be considered, and all knowed better than try and chase her away from him. Fillies and old mares, young geldings and old ponies and all, had it out as to which was the most fit to tag along and play with Smoky and keep a watchful eye over him along with his mammy. All wanted the job, but a big buckskin saddle horse who all the time had been the boss of the herd took it to hand to show them that *he* would be the all around guardeen for Smoky, and second only to his mammy. He delivered a few swift kicks, pounded on some ribs, left teeth marks on shiny hides, and after taking one last look and making sure that all was persuaded, grazed out towards Smoky who by his mammy had watched the whole proceeding with a heap of interest.

There was three other little colts in the bunch besides Smoky, and each time one of them little fellers came the buckskin horse had to whip the bunch so as he'd have the say over the newest one. Now Smoky was the newest one, and the buckskin horse had first rights as an outsider once again. He was an old horse full of scars showing where he'd had many a scrap; there was saddle marks on his back and at one time he had been a mighty fine cowhorse. Now he was pensioned; he'd more than earned a rest and all he had to do for the rest of his life was to pick out good feed grounds for the winter, shady places and tenderest green grass for the summer, and his other interest in life was them little colts that came in springtime.

Smoky's mother was young, at least ten years younger than the buckskin horse, but the buckskin was like a colt compared to her when it come to be playful. She had the responsibility of Smoky and while she let him play with her, kick or bite at her, she never played with him and once in a while if he'd get too rough she'd let him know about it. She loved little Smoky with all her heart and would of died for him any time, and her main interest was to see that she kept in condition so that Smoky would never be stunted by lacking of rich milk. She had no time for play.

And that's where the old buckskin came in. Him and Smoky was soon acquainted, in a short while they was playing, Smoky would kick at him while the big buckskin nipped him easy and careful along the flank, then he'd run away from him, and the little colt had a lot of fun chasing that big hunk of horseflesh all over the country. The rest of the bunch would watch the two play and with no effort to hide how jealous they felt.

Smoky's mother kept her eye on the buckskin, but never interfered, she knowed, and it was only when Smoky came back to her, tired and hungry, that she put her ears back and warned him to keep away.

It took a few days before the buckskin would allow any of the other horses to get near Smoky, and then he had no say about it for he found that Smoky had his own ideas about things, and if he wanted to mingle in with the other horses that was his business, and all the buckskin could do then was to try and keep the other horses away. That was quite a job, specially if Smoky wanted to be with them. So the buckskin finally had to give it up and do the best he could which was to see that none of 'em done him any harm. But none of 'em had any intentions of doing the little colt any harm, and as it was it looked like Smoky had 'em all buffaloed. He'd tear in after some big horse like he was going to eat him up and all that big horse would do was to scatter out like the devil was after him.

Smoky was the boss and pet of the herd for a good two weeks and then one day, here comes another little feller, a little bay colt just two days old and trailing in alongside his mammy. Smoky was left in the background and witnessed the same fuss and commotion that was done over him that morning by the creek. The buckskin horse once again fought his way in that new little feller's heart, and right away he forgot Smoky.

But Smoky never seen anything wrong to that, he went on to playing with every horse that would have him and it wasn't long till he picked up with a young filly and afterwards went to mingling with other young colts.

From then on Smoky had more freedom, he could go out a ways without having some big overgrowed horse tagging along, but he never went far and if he did he always came back a heap faster than when he started out. But them spring days was great for Smoky; he found out a lot of things amongst which was, that grass was good to eat, and water mighty fine to drink when the day was hot. He seen cayotes again and the bigger he got the less he was afraid of 'em till he finally went to chasing every one of 'em he'd see.

Then one day he run acrost another yellow animal. That animal didn't look dangerous, and what's more it was hard for Smoky to make out just what it was, and he was bound to find out. He followed that animal plum to the edge of some willows, and the queer part of it was that animal didn't seem at all in a hurry to get away, it was mumbling along and just taking its time

and Smoky was mighty tempted to plant one front foot right in the middle of it and do some pawing, but as luck would have it he didn't have the chance, it'd got in under some willows and all that was sticking out was part of the animal's tail. Smoky took a sniff at it without learning anything outside that it shook a little. There didn't seem to be no danger, so the next sniff he took was a little closer, and that done the trick. Smoky let out a squeal and a snort as he felt his nostrils punctured in half a dozen places with four-inch porcupine quills.

But Smoky was lucky, for if he'd been a couple of inches closer there'd been quills rammed into his nose plum up to his eyes, which would've caused a swelling in such size that he couldn't of been able to eat and most likely starve to death. As it was there was just a few of them quills in his nostrils, and compared to the real dose he might of got, it was just a mild warning to him. Another lesson.

It was a few days later when he met another strange animal, or strange animals, for there was many of 'em. He didn't get much interest out of them somehow, but while they was handy maybe it was just as well for him to have a close look at one. Besides he had nothing else to do, and mammy wasn't far away.

His instinct had no warning to give as he strutted towards the smallest one of the strangers which he'd picked to investigate. He wasn't afraid of this animal and this animal didn't seem afraid of him so Smoky kept a-getting closer till one was within a couple of feet of the other. Both Smoky and this stranger was young, and mighty inquisitive, and neither as yet knowed that they'd sure be seeing plenty of each other's kind as they get older, that they'll be meeting thru the round-ups at the "cutting grounds," on "day herd" and on "night guard," on the long, hot, dusty trails. A cowboy will be riding Smoky then and keeping a whole herd on the move, a whole herd of the kind that little Smoky was so busy investigating that day. They'll be full grown then, and there'll be other young ones to take the place of them that's trailed in to the shipping point.

But Smoky wasn't as yet worried or even thought on what was to come, neither was the little white-faced calf he was exchanging squints with; and when the critter called her long-eared, split-hoofed baby to her side, Smoky just kicked up his heels, put his head down, and bucked and crowhopped all the way to where his mammy and the rest of the bunch was grazing.

from THE INCREDIBLE JOURNEY

Sheila Burnford

This is Chapter 2 of the story of three heroic animals—a young Labrador retriever, a Siamese cat, and an old bull terrier—who travel through two hundred and fifty miles of Canadian wilderness to the place and people that mean home and love to them. Young children will listen enraptured to its being read aloud, while older children and adults will find pleasure in reading it to themselves.

[The Beginning of the Journey]

There was a slight mist when John Longridge rose early the following morning, having fought a losing battle for the middle of the bed with his uninvited bedfellow. He shaved and dressed quickly, watching the mist roll back over the fields and the early morning sun break through. It would be a perfect fall day, an Indian summer day, warm and mellow. Downstairs he found the animals waiting patiently by the door for their early morning run. He let them out, then cooked and ate his solitary breakfast. He was out in the driveway, loading up his car when the dogs and cat returned from the fields. He fetched some biscuits for them and they lay by the wall of the house in the early sun, watching him. He threw the last item into the back of the car, thankful that he had already packed the guns and hunting equipment before the Labrador had seen them, then walked over and patted the heads of his audience, one by one.

"Be good," he said. "Mrs. Oakes will be here soon. Good-by, Luath," he said to the Labrador, "I wish I could have taken you with me, but there wouldn't be room in the canoe for three of us." He put his hand under the young dog's soft muzzle. The golden-brown eyes looked steadily into his, and then the dog did an unexpected thing: he lifted his right paw and placed it in the man's hand. Longridge had seen him do this many a time to his own master and he was curiously touched and affected by the trust it conveyed, almost wishing he did not have to leave immediately just after the dog had shown his first responsive gesture.

He looked at his watch and realized he was already late. He had no worries about leaving the animals alone outside, as they had never attempted to stray beyond the large garden and the adjacent fields; and they could return inside the house if they wished, for the kitchen door was the kind that closed slowly on a spring. All that he had to do was shoot the inside bolt while the door was open, and after that it did not close properly and could be pushed open from the outside. They looked contented enough, too—the cat was washing methodically behind his ears—the old dog sat on his haunches, panting after his run, his long pink tongue lolling out of his grinning mouth; and the Labrador lay quietly by his side.

Longridge started the car and waved to them out of the window as he drove slowly down the drive, feeling rather foolish as he did so. "What do I expect them to do in return?" he asked himself with a smile, "Wave back? Or shout

'Good-by'? The trouble is I've lived too long alone with them and I'm becoming far too attached to them."

The car turned around the bend at the end of the long tree-lined drive and the animals heard the sound of the engine receding in the distance. The cat transferred his attention to a hind leg; the old dog stopped panting and lay down; the young dog remained stretched out, only his eyes moving and an occasional twitch of his nose.

Twenty minutes passed by and no move was made; then suddenly the young dog rose, stretched himself, and stood looking intently down the drive. He remained like this for several minutes, while the cat watched closely, one leg still pointing upwards; then slowly the Labrador walked down the driveway and stood at the curve, looking back as though inviting the others to come. The old dog rose too, now, somewhat stiffly, and followed. Together they turned the corner, out of sight.

The cat remained utterly still for a full minute, blue eyes blazing in the dark mask. Then, with a curious hesitating run, he set off in pursuit. The dogs were waiting by the gate when he turned the corner, the old dog peering wistfully back, as though he hoped to see his friend Mrs. Oakes materialize with a juicy bone; but when the Labrador started up the road he followed. The cat still paused by the gate, one paw lifted delicately in the air—undecided, questioning, hesitant; until suddenly, some inner decision reached, he followed the dogs. Presently all three disappeared from sight down the dusty road, trotting briskly and with purpose.

About an hour later Mrs. Oakes walked up the driveway from her cottage, carrying a string bag with her working shoes and apron, and a little parcel of tidbits for the animals. Her placid, gentle face wore a rather disappointed look, because the dogs usually spied her long before she got to the house and would rush to greet her.

"I expect Mr. Longridge left them shut inside the house if he was leaving early," she consoled herself. But when she pushed open the kitchen door and walked inside, everything seemed very silent and still. She stood at the foot of the stairs and called them, but there was no answering patter of running feet, only the steady tick-tock of the old clock in the hallway. She walked through the silent house and out into the front garden and stood there calling with a puzzled frown.

"Oh, well," she spoke her thoughts aloud to the empty, sunny garden, "perhaps they've gone up to the school. . . . It's a funny thing, though," she continued, sitting on a kitchen chair a few minutes later and tying her shoelaces, "that Puss isn't here—he's usually sitting on the window sill at this time of the day. Oh, well, he's probably out hunting—I've never known a cat like that for hunting, doesn't seem natural somehow!"

She washed and put away the few dishes, then took her cleaning materials into the sitting room. There her eye was caught by a sparkle on the floor by the desk, and she found the glass paperweight, and after that the remaining sheet of the note on the desk. She read it through to where it said: "I will be taking the dogs (and Tao too of course!) . . .", then looked for the remainder. "That's odd," she thought, "now where would he take them? That cat must have knocked the paperweight off last night—the rest of the note must be somewhere in the room."

She searched the room but it was not until she was emptying an ash tray into the fireplace that she noticed the charred curl of paper in the hearth. She bent down and picked it up carefully, for it was obviously very brittle, but even then most of it crumbled away and she was left with a fragment which bore the initials J. R. L.

"Now, isn't that the queerest thing," she said to the fireplace, rubbing vigorously at the black marks on the tiles. "He must mean he's taking them all to Heron Lake with him. But why would he suddenly do that, after all the arrangements we made? He never said a word about it on the telephone—but wait a minute, I remember now—he was just going to say something about them when the line went dead; perhaps he was just going to tell me."

While Mrs. Oakes was amazed that Longridge would take the animals on his vacation, it did not occur to her to be astonished that a cat should go along too, for she was aware that the cat loved the car and always went with the dogs when Longridge drove them anywhere or took them farther afield for walks. Like many Siamese cats, he was as obedient and as trained to go on

walks as most dogs, and would always return to a whistle.

Mrs. Oakes swept and dusted and talked to the house, locked it and returned home to her cottage. She would have been horrified to the depths of her kindly, well-ordered soul if she had known the truth. Far from sitting sedately in the back of a car traveling north with John Longridge, as she so fondly visualized, the animals were by now many miles away on a deserted country road that ran westward.

They had kept a fairly steady pace for the first hour or so, falling into an order which was not to vary for many miles or days; the Labrador ran always by the left shoulder of the old dog, for the bull terrier was very nearly blind in the left eye, and they jogged along fairly steadily together—the bull terrier with his odd, rolling, sailorlike gait, and the Labrador in a slow lope. Some ten yards behind came the cat, whose attention was frequently distracted, when he would stop for a few minutes and then catch up again. But, in between these halts, he ran swiftly and steadily, his long slim body and tail low to the ground.

When it was obvious that the old dog was flagging, the Labrador turned off the quiet, graveled road and into the shade of a pinewood beside a clear, fast-running creek. The old dog drank deeply, standing up to his chest in the cold water; the cat picked his way delicately to the edge of an overhanging rock. Afterwards they rested in the deep pine needles under the trees, the terrier panting heavily with his eyes half closed, and the cat busy with his eternal washing. They lay there for nearly an hour, until the sun struck through the branches above them. The young dog rose and stretched, then walked towards the road. The old dog rose too, stiff-legged, his head low. He walked toward the waiting Labrador, limping slightly and wagging his tail at the cat, who suddenly danced into a patch of sunlight, struck at a drifting leaf, then ran straight at the dogs, swerving at the last moment, and as suddenly sitting down again.

They trotted steadily on, all that afternoon— mostly traveling on the grassy verge at the side of the country road; sometimes in the low over-grown ditch that ran alongside, if the acute hear-

ing of the young dog warned them of an approaching car.

By the time the afternoon sun lay in long, barred shadows across the road, the cat was still traveling in smooth, swift bursts, and the young dog was comparatively fresh. But the old dog was very weary, and his pace had dropped to a limping walk. They turned off the road into the bush at the side, and walked slowly through a clearing in the trees, pushing their way through the tangled undergrowth at the far end. They came out upon a small open place where a giant spruce had crashed to the ground and left a hollow where the roots had been, filled now with drifted dry leaves and spruce needles.

The late afternoon sun slanted through the branches overhead, and it looked invitingly snug and secure. The old dog stood for a minute, his heavy head hanging, and his tired body swaying slightly, then lay down on his side in the hollow. The cat, after a good deal of wary observation, made a little hollow among the spruce needles and curled around in it, purring softly. The young dog disappeared into the undergrowth and reappeared presently, his smooth coat dripping water, to lie down a little away apart from the others.

The old dog continued to pant exhaustedly for a long time, one hind leg shaking badly, until his eyes closed at last, the labored breaths came further and further apart, and he was sleeping— still, save for an occasional long shudder.

Later on, when darkness fell, the young dog moved over and stretched out closely at his side and the cat stalked over to lie between his paws; and so, warmed and comforted by their closeness, the old dog slept, momentarily unconscious of his aching, tired body or his hunger.

In the nearby hills a timber wolf howled mournfully; owls called and answered and glided silently by with great outspread wings; and there were faint whispers of movement and small rustling noises around all through the night. Once an eerie wail like a baby's crying woke the old dog and brought him shivering and whining to his feet; but it was only a porcupine, who scrambled noisily and clumsily down a nearby tree trunk and waddled away, still crying softly. When he lay down again the cat was gone from his side—another small night hunter slipping through the unquiet shadows that froze to stillness at his passing.

The young dog slept in fitful, uneasy starts, his muscles twitching, constantly lifting his head and growling softly. Once he sprang to his feet with a full-throated roar which brought a sudden splash in the distance, then silence—and who knows what else unknown, unseen or unheard passed through his mind to disturb him further? Only one thing was clear and certain—that at all costs he was going home, home to his own beloved master. Home lay to the west, his instinct told him; but he could not leave the other two—so somehow he must take them with him, all the way.

Animals of field, forest, and jungle

from **THE FRIGHTENED HARE**

Franklin Russell

In the world of nature, each animal has its special traits which enable it to survive against its particular enemies. Franklin Russell captures the qualities of the hare, its fleetness of foot and its wariness, which keep this small animal alive in a dangerous world.

A Season of Young Animals

The moon rose and the chill forest air held the first exciting smell of spring. From the spidery shadow of a young red oak came the thump of a hare's foot. From a thicket came an answering thump and then a double thump from some hemlocks. An old hare hopped three times, stood erect in the moonlight and wiggled his nose frantically.

Around him, in the forest and along its edge, were other hares. All had recently shed their white winter coats and were now brown with summer fur. They were greatly excited. One of them raced off through the trees at full speed. The old hare followed. He turned and doubled and twisted, as if to urge the other hares to close in behind him.

Suddenly, all was still. A dozen hares stood erect in the moonlight. Then they were running crazily again. The breeding season of the hares was about to begin.

The playful chasing concealed a more deadly game among the animals. During this mad moonlit night, some of the hares would fight. Fur and blood would fly when the strongest and most aggressive animals attempted to choose females for mating. The young hares fought first. The battles were vicious. Then, as if to rest from their combat, the group of hares would turn to another mad frolicsome race through the forest.

"A Season of Young Animals" is the first chapter of *The Frightened Hare* by Franklin Russell, with illustrations by Fredric Sweney, a *Wise Owl Book* edited by Bill Martin, Jr., copyright © 1963, 1965, and published by Holt, Rinehart and Winston, Inc. Reprinted by special permission of the publishers

The alternate fighting and racing continued night after night for almost a week. The old hare did not shrink from the fighting, but he sensed that he could not beat the younger animals. He stayed on the fringe of the fighting as long as possible.

One night a young hare challenged him with a thump of his foot and the two creatures stood in a forest clearing, facing each other. The young hare ran forward and the two animals grappled violently, biting and kicking. The old hare fell, and his body jerked with the impact of back legs kicking at his belly. He bit the young hare's ear and the animal squealed and leaped away.

Eventually the old hare was exhausted. He bled from rips and cuts. One ear was torn. As the young hare was rising for another attack, the old animal quietly disappeared through the trees and crept to the river where he would drink and rest.

Later, at the river, the old hare found his mate. She was a young female that never ventured from a small area running along the bank of the river. Forty days after they had mated, she hollowed out a nest under a fallen tree near the water and lined it with fur from her body. She bore four young hares. All were born with their eyes open and their tiny bodies covered with dark brown hair. One of them was larger and more vigorous than the others. When he was hungry, he pushed and jostled his way to his mother's milk. The young hares' coats grew sleek and acquired the fragrance of the grass in the nest. They snuggled close together and fearfully watched grasses waving in the wind. From the moment of their birth the young hares sensed that their world was filled with danger. Every movement and sound near the nest caused them to freeze into fearful watching.

It was a time of birth throughout the forest. As the old hare roamed at night, chipmunks were being born in deep burrows beneath his feet. Skunks came into the world in burrows along the river banks. Gray squirrels were born in bulky nests set high in trees. Female raccoons waddled clumsily out of hollow trees where they fed their noisy youngsters.

Once the old hare paused suspiciously, scenting a living thing close to him. He sniffed in every direction. Then he leaned forward. Almost at his nose, hidden in thick grass, was a mat of fur. As he peered at it, a dark brown eye looked back at him. It belonged to a young cottontail, which with three brothers and sisters, was lying frozen into stillness waiting for the intruder to go away.

When the old hare came loping along the river bank, he found his four young offspring venturing from the nest. They froze with fear; then they raced to safety. The young hares were gaining strength. Although they were still wobbly on their uncertain feet, they were developing into runners like their parents. Unlike young skunks, foxes and raccoons, very young hares rarely play. Their survival depends on a continual balance of boldness and caution, fear and fleetness. Above all, their safety depends on the speed of their flying feet.

The largest young hare was also the fastest, the strongest, and the most vigorous. He was the least frightened of the four youngsters. This young hare was the Runner. His strength and speed gave him a better chance for survival than most hares had in the forest.

As the young hares grew, their confidence increased and they ranged through the forest in search of food. Their mother's care for them lessened quickly. Now she often left the youngsters alone. She mated again with the old hare, and, long before the young hares were full grown, she bore another nestful of youngsters.

The Runner roamed farthest from the nest. One night he found himself alone in a strange territory, a new world teeming with enemies.

He saw a shadowy weasel speeding towards him across a moonlit clearing. He ran instinctively, ran with all the strength of his young limbs. Then, exhausted, he stopped by the tinkling river. Another shadow, another weasel, came speeding down the river bank towards him. The Runner leaped away, fleeing with the panic of despair. The weasels were far more intelligent than he. They knew that terror-stricken hares always ran in wide circles through the forest. One weasel chased the hare while the other waited for the victim elsewhere in the forest.

But the weasels could never equal the Runner's tremendous speed. He lost them that night by sheer speed and endurance.

In this way, the Runner learned about weasels. He was lucky to learn so early and survive. His brothers and sisters, now separated from him in the forest, were less fortunate. They all had an instinctive fear of flying creatures, but there was nothing to warn them against a creature which might spot them from the air and then stalk them on the ground. A hawk saw one of them on a misty wet morning. He dropped quickly out of sight into the trees and flew until he saw the hare again. Then he dropped to the ground and continued his approach on foot. When he came within a few paces of the young animal, he suddenly burst through the tall grasses and seized his victim.

Many times the Runner did not know whether he was in danger or not. But when in doubt, he usually ran. Shortly before dawn one day, he stopped by the bank of a stream and looked into the gray light of early morning. Suddenly he became aware of a tiny buzzing creature almost at his feet. It was flying quickly towards him. He sensed it was dangerous and with a great leap, he bounded away. He had disturbed a female wasp digging a burrow in the ground.

The Runner witnessed the death of one of his sisters. She had been nibbling grass, unaware that she was being watched by an owl. The owl floated silently down toward her. Suddenly the forest echoed with her screams, a series of ghastly cries. Irresistibly, the Runner felt himself drawn through the forest toward the cries. He saw other hares running with him. A scrabbling of leaves, a rustling of undergrowth, a pattering of flying feet, and six hares suddenly appeared at the edge of the forest where the owl held down his screaming victim. The hares stood tall and still in the dim moonlight. The cries died away. The owl, bent intently over the silent body, was disconcerted by the six animals standing so close to him. He puffed out his feathers and curved his wings menacingly so that he looked twice his normal size. Then he flew to a nearby tree.

One by one, the hares dissolved into the darkness among the trees. Then the owl glided down again to where his victim lay.

from **KILDEE HOUSE**

Rutherford Montgomery

This opening chapter of Kildee House *should lead straight into the book. It is a tender and amusing story about Jerome Kildee's problems in preventing the animals from taking over his house entirely and in resolving the enmity between two strong-minded young neighbors.*

[Mr. Kildee Makes Friends with Old Grouch]

Jerome Kildee had built himself a house on the mountainside. It was an odd house because Jerome Kildee was an odd man. He built his house under a giant redwood tree on Windy Point. Since the days of Julius Caesar creatures had been building homes at the foot of the redwood or in its branches. At the time Jerome built his house most folks did not build on knobs

From *Kildee House,* by Rutherford Montgomery. Copyright 1949 by Rutherford Montgomery. Reprinted by permission of Doubleday & Company, Inc. and Barthold Fles, literary agent

high on a mountainside, even the round-topped, wooded mountains of the Pacific Coast Range.

What the neighbors said or what they thought was of no concern to Jerome. The day he walked out on Windy Point, and looked up at the giant redwood towering into the sky, and stood savoring the deep silence, he knew he was going to stay. When he turned from the great tree and looked down over the green ridges, the smoky valley, into the gray-white haze of the Pacific, he smiled. This was a land of silence, the place for a silent man.

The house Jerome built was not as wide as the redwood; to have made it so wide would have been a waste of space, because Jerome did not need that much room. He toted the biggest window he could buy to the cabin, and set it in the wall which faced a panorama of ridges and valleys. The window was as high as the wall; it was one wall as far across as the door. It had been rolled out as a plate-glass window for a store.

The back wall was the redwood trunk. It made an odd house, one wall curved inward, and finished with shaggy redwood bark. Jerome rented a horse and packed Monterey stone up for a fireplace. The fireplace was a thing of beauty. It filled one end of the room. The cream Monterey stone, traced through with threads of red, was carefully fitted and matched for grain; the hearth was wide, and the mantel was inlaid with chips of abalone shell. It was the last piece of stonework Jerome planned to make, and he made it a masterpiece. In a recess back of the last slab of stone he tucked away the tools of his trade and sealed them into the wall. Jerome Kildee, maker of fine monuments, was no more. There remained only Jerome Kildee, philosopher, a silent little man, seeking to become a part of a silent mountain.

Jerome Kildee did not work. He owned the hundred acres of woods and hillside around him, but he did not clear any of it. He bought all of his food, and he had stove and fireplace wood hauled up and stacked outside his door. Jerome hired the Eppys to haul the wood to the bottom of the hill, then up the hill with their tractor because there was only a winding footpath up from his mailbox. The Eppys laughed and made quite a bit of it. Jerome had hundreds of cords of oak and madroña close to his cabin.

The farmer and his sons would have cut it and sawed it for a tenth of what Jerome paid for the wood and the hauling.

Jerome had no near neighbors, nor would he ever have any, because he had built in the exact center of his hundred acres. He had gone through life silent, unable to talk to people, expecting them to leave him to his own thoughts. He had never visited the Eppy family after they hauled his wood, although they lived at the foot of his hill on the north side. They put him down as a queer one. The nine Eppys, as they were known locally, were robust folks. The six sons were all over six feet tall. Emma Lou would someday be almost as tall as her brothers. The Cabot place, at the foot of the mountain on the other side of the hill, was certainly not a place where Jerome would care to go. It was a fine estate with landscaped gardens and a swimming pool. The Cabots had one son, Donald Roger, who had never given Jerome more than a brief look.

But Jerome Kildee found he was not without friends. He had a host of friends and he didn't have to talk to them to keep their friendship. In fact, his silence helped to keep them friendly. They were all interested in him, a new experience for Jerome, and he was interested in them. Jerome found that they were not unlike the people back where he had operated his monument shop. They were willing to take advantage of him, they were selfish, and some of them were thieves, like the trade rats who packed off anything they could carry, regardless of whether or not they could use it. He soon learned that none of the raccoons could be trusted inside the cabin. They unscrewed the caps off ketchup bottles as easily as he could do it; they unlatched cupboard doors or opened them if there was a knob on them. One old raccoon, who was the neighborhood grouch, lived in a hole in the trunk of his redwood tree. Old Grouch had refused to move when Jerome built his house. He considered the redwood tree his tree. He made it clear to Jerome that he was trespassing.

The pair of spotted skunks who set up housekeeping under his floor were folks of a different sort from the raccoons. They were not dullwitted stinkers of the sort Jerome had known in his boyhood, dumb fellows who for ages had been de-pending upon poison gas instead of their wits for protection. They carried guns but seldom used them. The little spotted skunks were as smart as the raccoons, and about as curious. They had a real sense of humor and were always playing pranks on the raccoons. With them around, Jerome always had to get down on his hands and knees and explore the chimney of his fireplace before he built a fire. The skunks liked the fireplace and would gladly have traded it for their nest under the floor. They were not big stinkers like the swamp skunks, so Jerome could always fish them out of the chimney with his broom.

Jerome would probably have been crowded out of his house by the assortment of mice that found his house and the fine bark wall of the redwood to their liking if it had not been for the spotted skunks. The skunks had large appetites, so they kept the mouse population on an even keel. Two big wood mice lived in a bark nest back of a knot in the tree trunk. They furnished dinners for the spotted skunks with a regularity which should have become monotonous. How they could go on having big families, nursing them to a size to go out into the world, only to have them gobbled up one at a time as they left the nest, was more than Jerome could understand.

There was another pair of mice who lived under his bed in a box of old letters, which they made good use of without snooping into the contents, or trying to figure out why Jerome had tied them in bundles. They chewed up all of the letters except those written in indelible pencil. This removed from Jerome's life any desire to brood over the past. The spotted skunks could not get into the box. The mice went in through a knothole in the end. But their families suffered the same fate as the wood mice. And they went on having big families.

Jerome's wooded acres harbored many black-tailed deer and many gray foxes and possums. The foxes never made friends, and the possums ignored him because he never kept chickens. They had no bump of curiosity to draw them to his house. He saw them often and had a nodding acquaintance with them, so to speak. The black-tails visited his garbage pit regularly. The does often brought their fawns into his yard. But they did not bother much with him because he did not grow a garden or set out young fruit trees. He was about like any other dweller on the wooded mountain: he just lived there.

It was during the second year that Old Grouch turned the head of a dainty little miss. She was just sixteen months old, and like many another lass before her, she fell in love with a good-for-nothing. Old Grouch brought her to his nest in the redwood. It was high up on the tree where a burl formed a deep pocket. Old Grouch had learned that a redwood tree was a safe haven. When coon dogs chased him, followed by yelling humans, all he had to do was shinny up the giant tree. The hunters could not shake him out or climb the tree. Of course after Jerome came, the coon dogs and the hunters stayed away.

Old Grouch brought his bride home in January during the heavy rains. In April she presented him with a family. Like many another good-for-nothing, Old Grouch failed to provide for his family, though he did share the nest with them, taking the dry side and grabbing any of the food she rustled which suited his taste. Jerome couldn't climb the tree to look into the nest, but he heard the babies and listened to the family chitchat over them.

Old Grouch mildly irritated Jerome. He was smug and fat, always ready to march into the cabin and demand part of Jerome's fried egg or lamb chop, but never thanking his host for anything, and always staying outside unless there was food. Any friendly advance was always met with a snarl or a snapping of white fangs. He was a surly fellow, but Jerome admired the way he had with the ladies.

His wife was of a different sort. She was friendly and thankful to Jerome for bits of food he gave her. She visited the cabin while he was in it, and not just when it was mealtime. She would have taken over his larder if he had allowed it. Her willingness to shift Old Grouch's responsibility for the family to him gave Jerome a problem. He was forced to invent new catches for his cupboard doors, and to fashion latches for his pull drawers.

Outwitting the slim little bride was no easy matter. With feminine wile she made up to Jerome, letting him stroke her head and scratch around her ears, smiling coyly up at him as he sat in his padded chair, but raiding his cupboard as sure as he went for a walk. Jerome fixed inside catches for the doors worked by wires which went up through the inside of the cupboard and were pulled by strings dangling from the ceiling, well out of reach of a raccoon. The pull drawers became pop-out drawers worked by wires with dangling strings attached to them. Jerome's house was well decorated with strings hanging from the ceiling. A large button dangled at the end of each string like a black spider.

When Jerome wanted an egg for breakfast he pulled a string, and open popped a drawer exposing the egg carton. Then Jerome always had to take out two eggs because the minute the door popped open in popped Mrs. Grouch, and Jerome had to split fifty-fifty with her. He could have closed and barred the door, but then he would have had to sit by the big window eating his egg with Mrs. Grouch's furry bangs pressed against the plate glass, her bright eyes watching every bite he took, her little tongue dripping hungrily.

The rains lasted a long time that spring, keeping on until June. Mrs. Grouch stood the home her old man had provided for her as long as she could. The babies were growing and taking up more room, the roof leaked, and Old Grouch always took the dry side. When the wind blew from the north there might as well have been no roof at all. One afternoon while Jerome was tramping in the woods, snug in oilskins and rubber boots, she moved her babies into the house. Helping herself to the stuffing in his mattress, she made a nest in the oven. She had long ago learned how to open the oven door. The smell of the oven pleased her. It had a faint food smell which was elegant. She could feed her babies and lick the oven walls, nibbling bits of burned meat as she came to them.

Jerome discovered the family at once because the oven door was open. He did not scold about the mattress when she showed him her brood of silky raccoons. But he was hungry and this was Saturday afternoon. Jerome always fixed a beef roast for Saturday supper. Once a week the mailman left the meat in his mailbox at the foot of the hill. Jerome got a wooden box and put it in a corner, then he moved the family. Mrs. Grouch was miffed, but she accepted the change with a sly smile. Later she would slip her family back into the oven.

Old Grouch stamped up on the porch and seated himself in the open doorway. He scolded his wife in proper style; he glared at Jerome and tossed a few nasty cracks at him. Between growls he kept sniffing the roast cooking in the oven, and shaking his fur to get the raindrops off it. With a final warning to his wife he turned about, climbed the redwood trunk, and got into his nest. The wind was from the north, and his wife was not there to keep the rain off his back. He stayed in the nest for half an hour, then he climbed back down the tree trunk and walked to the door. Jerome grinned at him. He was cutting the roast. He sliced off a piece and laid it on a saucer. He set the saucer on the floor.

Old Grouch looked at the saucer. This was dangerous business. Going into a cabin was like stepping into a box trap. But he was wet and cold; his wife had walked out on him. He needed food and warmth. Ruffling his scruff, he walked into the house. He paused at the saucer and sniffed the good smell of the roast. He took a bite. When Mrs. Grouch scurried across the floor to share with him, he caught up the piece of meat in his forepaws. He sat up and glowered at her. Then he began munching the roast. His wife sniffed eagerly. She looked up at Jerome. He handed her a slice of meat. She took it and seated herself beside her husband. They sat there eating very much like humans, using their small hands to tear bits of meat from the large pieces, then stuffing the bits into their mouths.

By the time Jerome had finished his supper Old Grouch had made up his mind. He had marched to the door three times, and each time the cold rain had spattered into his face. He knew his wife and babies were going to sleep warm and dry inside the cabin. She had already returned to the box, where she sat with her small black eyes just above the edge. Old Grouch felt he could do with some more roast, too. He was still a bit hungry. He would stay in the cabin.

After the dishes were washed Jerome lighted his pipe. He was faced with a new problem. He had been trying for weeks to get Old Grouch into the cabin. Now that the old fellow and his family had moved in he dared not close the door. If he closed the door it was hard to say what Old Grouch would do. Jerome was sure it would be pretty wild.

But the night air was growing chilly. The wind was blowing into the room, wet and cold. Even if he did chase Old Grouch out into the rain he couldn't put Mrs. Grouch and the babies out. Jerome got to his feet. Old Grouch took one look at Jerome towering above him, then scuttled out into the night.

Jerome set the gasoline mantel lamp on the table so the white light would flood the door. He got his tool chest from under the bed. Mrs. Grouch kept her eyes just above the edge of the box. Jerome cut a small door in the bottom of his big door. He swung the small door by a pair of butterfly hinges and bored three holes in it.

As he gathered up his saw and auger and screw driver Jerome realized that the little door would offer welcome to any and all who roamed. It would mean keeping open house to all, except, of course, those neighbors too big to squeeze through the little door. He had never been able to make friends; it might be that the little door would change everything. He took the lamp and examined the chimney of his fireplace. The little skunks were not sleeping on the damper, so he lighted the fire he had laid earlier in the day. Pulling his padded chair up to the fireplace, he set his tobacco jar on the chair arm. As an afterthought he got a saucer and stacked a few squares of roast on it. He set the saucer on the floor beside the chair.

Jerome puffed slowly on his pipe. He watched the red tongues of flame lick around the oak and madroña logs in the fireplace. The beating warmth made him feel drowsy. He was on his second pipe when Old Grouch solved the mystery of the little door. He had peeped in through the three holes and discovered that Jerome had turned out the gasoline lamp, that his wife was snug and dry in the box with the babies. He sniffed and caught the rich smell of roast beef. He was wet and cold. He eased through the little door just as his wife hopped from the box, carrying one of the babies. She had her teeth set in the scruff. Shaking the water from his fur, he watched her put the youngster into the oven. He scowled at her, but he didn't make a sound. The warmth of the fireplace and the smell of the roast in the saucer drew him. He moved warily toward the fire. His experience with men had made him wary. But he was cold and he had an idea he could eat some more. Seating himself in the deep shadows near the chair, he stretched his snout toward the dish. He kept his eyes on Jerome. When Jerome did not move Old Grouch eased forward and picked up a piece of meat. He sat up and began munching it.

Mrs. Grouch had finished transferring her babies to the oven. She sat on the door for a while, watching the two males at the fireplace. Shaking her head, she turned her back upon them and curled up with her brood.

Jerome had never been able to talk with people. He had always known he was missing a great deal, but he had never been able to say the weather was nice or that the weather was bad when people came into his shop. He set his pipe on the arm of the chair and tossed another log on the fire. Old Grouch ducked into a patch of deep shadow, but he came out again and got another piece of meat. The warmth of the fire was beating against his fur. He felt contented and happy. Jerome leaned back and spoke out loud. When he spoke the sound of his voice startled even himself. Old Grouch, now gorged with roast and sleepy from the heat, toppled off the hearth and had to make quite an effort to right himself. Mrs. Grouch thrust her head out of the oven and stared at Jerome wildly. If it had not been for her babies she would have fled into the night.

"When I came up here I was licked," Jerome had said. It was as though a stranger had spoken to him; he heard his own voice so seldom. He felt called upon to answer the stranger.

"And were you licked?"

Old Grouch batted his eyes fearfully. He looked all around the room but saw no human being except Jerome, whom he had ceased to consider a man, because Jerome never shouted or whistled or talked at all.

"I've spent a lifetime carving cherubs and angels on tombstones. I've cut many a nice sentiment on a gravestone, but never was able to recite a single line before company." Jerome pointed his pipestem toward the fire. "It's a sad business, dealing with sad people, and not being able to say a word to comfort them."

Old Grouch braced himself and let his stomach ease down until he was resting comfortably. He had room for a bite or two more, and the fire

was very nice. Jerome smiled down at him. Old Grouch looked like a small bandit with the black patches which circled his eyes and extended along his cheeks like black bands, making a perfect mask against the lighter coloring of his fur. He cocked his head. He was in a mellow mood. His stomach was full to bursting; his furry hide was warm. He felt like singing.

He started out with a soft "Shur-r-r-r," then went into a deeper note, a long-drawn, tremulous "Whoo-oo-oo," not unlike the call of a screech owl, only softer and sweeter, much more mellow. Jerome's smile widened. He had never dared venture a note himself. In all of the hundreds of times he had sat alone in his pew in church he had never dared open his mouth and sing.

"I have missed much," he said.

"Whoo-oo-oo," Old Grouch sang, his head swaying sleepily.

From the oven door came an answering trill. Never had Mrs. Grouch heard her husband put so much tenderness, so much romance into his song. It touched her deeply, so deeply she closed her eyes and sang back to him. Jerome laid down his pipe.

Turning to catch the high soprano from the oven, Jerome noticed that the little door was bobbing back and forth. He fixed his attention upon it. A small head with black shoe-button eyes appeared. The head moved into the room, followed by a slim body. A moment later another slim body moved through the door. Two tall white plumes lifted. The little spotted skunks had come visiting. Papa waved his plume and stamped his feet; Mama waved her plume and stamped her feet. Like a good host, Jerome arose from his chair. Instantly the two little skunks vanished through the door. Jerome filled a saucer with canned milk and set it near the door, then he went back to his chair before the fire.

Almost at once the little door opened and the skunks marched in. They sat down and began lapping eagerly. When Mrs. Grouch hopped off the oven door and started toward the saucer, Papa elevated his plume and stamped his forefeet. He rushed at her, did a handstand, flipped his hind feet down again, then stamped some more. Mrs. Grouch knew what that meant, as did every other living thing in the woods. She hastily retreated to the oven door. Papa went back to his milk.

Jerome leaned back in his chair. Old Grouch was in full voice now; his whoo-oo-oo was deep and bell-like. Jerome tried an experimental note himself. He was amazed at its quality. It was a baritone note with feeling and depth in it. But it sent Mrs. Grouch scrambling back into the oven; Papa and Mama left without waiting to stamp their feet. Only Old Grouch was not startled at all. He just sat and swayed back and forth and sang. He seemed to have caught the fine flavor of Jerome's baritone. Jerome tried a few more notes. Mrs. Grouch stayed in the oven; the spotted skunks stayed under the floor. Old Grouch picked up the last square of roast and ate it slowly. When he swallowed it his stomach bulged bigger. He cocked an eye at Jerome. Jerome tried a few hymns he remembered. Old Grouch joined in. He had only one song, but it blended well with any hymn.

After a bit Jerome began to feel sleepy. He was sleepy and he was happy. He leaned back and closed his eyes. Old Grouch yawned. He ambled toward the oven door. After two tries he managed to hop up on the door. Easing into the oven, he curled up with his family. Jerome sighed deeply. Here among friends he could talk about things he had always wanted to talk about, and he could sing when he felt like it. He got to his feet and took his flannel nightgown from its hook. He smiled as he got ready for bed.

from THE WAHOO BOBCAT

Joseph Wharton Lippincott

An animal story by Mr. Lippincott, publisher as well as author, is invariably exciting. In this first episode from the book, the bobcat has been discovered by a hound, and begins the adventures that are going to lead to his strange friendship with a boy.

Fight with a Hog

The Tiger, completely taken by surprise, waited to see what the big dog would do, and the dog,

"Fight with a Hog" and "Sammy and the Wildcat" from *The Wahoo Bobcat* by Joseph Wharton Lippincott. Copyright 1950 by Joseph Wharton Lippincott. Published by J. B. Lippincott Company

a hound, just stood there looking at him in the dim light. The hound was trying hard to understand the weird combination of a wildcat's body and a skunk's smell which made his eyes mistrust his nose. At length, the hair began to rise on his back, and with a bellow of combined glee and fury he sprang at the fence, forcing the cat to leap back to the protection of the bushes. Over the fence then came the hound with a clatter of rails, and after the cat he dashed with bellow after bellow fairly bursting from his chest.

Shrill yaps of delight now sounded behind him as the three other dogs heard the row and could not resist running from the house to join in the chase. Down the hog path went the Tiger in long, easy bounds, toward the Prairie and the swamps that he knew so well, the briar thickets in which he could hide and the deep mud holes over which he could leap. He drew away from the bellows and the thumping feet and sprang out of the path into the thick bushes to confuse his followers and give himself more time to elude them, for instinct told him that a hound like this one would trail him as long as his scented tracks could be followed.

The four dogs were all together now, thrashing about in the bushes to find where he had dodged. Occasionally they yelped with excitement, occasionally too there were distant shouts indicating that a man had joined the hunt. Fiercely the Tiger fought his way through the swamp growth, reached the Prairie and dashed along its edge among the tussocks of heavy grass and the tricky holes that had no bottom, places where snakes lurked and the barbed briars would rip any creature that did not understand their tangles.

Bellows from the black hound began again; he was once more on the trail and coming fast. The cat stopped for a moment to listen and make sure he was not too close, then deliberately turned back and followed his own tracks until he came to a tree whose limbs hung low. With a mighty leap the Tiger reached one of these stout limbs, climbed along it to the tree's trunk and crouched there, twenty feet from the ground, so high that his scent would be caught by the rising currents of night air and kept away from pursuers below. If they discovered him he would jump into the bushes and run again.

He was not afraid now. His pounding heart slowed down and he rested. As presently the dogs came bounding single file along the Prairie's edge on the trail he had left, he stood up to watch them flounder in the mud and fight the tangles. They passed him and reached the place where he had doubled back, but then their glad tonguing ceased and they searched in all directions for more tracks. It did not occur to them to turn back on the trail and look up the tree. Once a circle made by the black hound in his hunting brought him directly under the cat, but there was no scent on the ground and he did not guess that he was so close to the Tiger.

Gradually the dogs worked their way farther into the swamp and far from the cat, the crashing and splashing sounds they made dying out and the shouts of the man growing dim as he tired of the fruitless hunt in the musk-laden air and returned to his house. The moon was rising and filling the swamp with remarkable shadows; the Prairie shimmered wherever there were grassless pools and the frogs were yelling as if their lives depended on the noise, but no creature appeared to notice the Tiger as he climbed down the tree, backwards like a bear, sniffed at his fur, rolled a few times in a sandy spot and once more hungrily began his search for food.

Everywhere was the smell of musk. It had bothered almost all the little furry creatures and made them hide or travel beyond the reach of the fumes; this meant that some had to go into the pine woods or far down the Prairie's edge, others into holes in the ground or in hollow trees; even the hum produced by the countless insects of the swamp seemed to have changed.

Like a ghost in the deserted swamp the cat wandered, ever on the alert but more and more discouraged. He did not want to go near the home of the dogs, so at length he trotted to the second-best field, arriving at its edge just as dawn grayed the sky and the birds of day began to awake and give their first morning cries. Soon they would sing and play and feed on all sides and the creatures of the night would vanish into hiding. Hunger, however, kept the Tiger on the move. Even more stealthy now, he crept along the fence, looking well ahead for gray squirrels and unwary birds of any kind, ears cocked at every sound and muscles ready for instant leaps.

He belonged to the creatures of the night and therefore was too easily spotted now by his intended prey; the birds scattered before him in alarm and the squirrels barked derisively from safe perches over his head, advertising his presence wherever he went. The Tiger, however, was resourceful; he knew that if he found a good hiding place he could crouch there unseen and spring upon unwary creatures that came near him in their own feeding. Such a place was inside the fenced area, in an unplowed corner where tall briars gave perfect cover. So, after leaping the worm fence to this corner he sneaked, and under the green cover of the thorny tangle he hid himself.

A hundred yards across the field stood the house where humans lived and already were clattering about. Their breakfast was finished and the two children, a boy of nine and a girl somewhat smaller, were out on the back porch playing. But the Tiger was not afraid of children.

The grunt of a hog sounded some distance to the right and presently a lean, brown-black sow grubbed her way under the fence and led six very young black piglets into the forbidden area. She was nearer to him than to the house and at the edge of a strawberry patch where her rooting could do much harm. Under some of the plants went her powerful snout and contentedly she munched the roots and grunted while the piglets clustered around her legs.

The half wild sow was having a very happy time until the little boy happened to see her. He knew that hogs had to be chased out of the field whenever they came under the fence, so he shouted to his parents and, seizing a stick, bravely jumped from the porch and ran at the hogs, waving the stick and still yelling.

The old sow looked up, realized at once that this was an attack on her for trespassing, and, with a grunt of alarm led the piglets towards the hole through which they had come. The little ones toddled after her with might and main but were held back by a stretch of soft, ploughed ground and were continually falling into the furrows and having to climb out. The smallest, a mere runt with tiny legs and a very wrinkled snout, was having the worst time of all and suddenly got into a furrow from which he could not climb.

The runt kept very quiet for a few moments, but when the others left him and the boy came running, he gave a shrill squeal of fear and struggled anew with the crumbling furrow. The boy's first instinct was to help him out, so he stooped and put his hands under the runt, whereupon the tiny pig thought his doom was sealed and let out piercing squeals which went to his mother's heart and brought her back on the run to his rescue.

She charged across the soft ground in wild mother rage, reached the boy, knocked him head over heels with her snout and began to rip at him with her toothed mouth, furiously grunting amid the squeals of the piglet and the sudden howls of the boy who was pummeling her as best he could with his fists. The noise reached every corner of the field and brought the father out of the house in his bare feet, running so fast that he tripped on a bush and fell full length in the sand. Behind him came the yelling mother, brandishing a saucepan, her face white with fear as she ran toward her son. The squeals, grunts, shrieks and yells continued unabated as the sow furiously rolled the boy over and over, biting and rooting at him and trampling him into the sand.

Strangest of all was the action of the wildcat. A sudden fury took possession of his brain and blotted out all else. He rushed along the fence, then cut across the ploughed ground and coming close to the battling mass of screaming bodies, threw himself on top of the sow and hurled her to the ground. Buffeting her head with his two forepaws, he raked at her snout and clawed her sides, bit with all his strength into her thick neck and in spite of her kicks held on and rolled about with her in the heavy sand, now on top now underneath, his screams and growls joining the high pitched voices of the others as he ripped and tore and tried to batter the black, fighting body locked in his embrace.

Suddenly the big sow, with a great heave of her snout, threw him away from her, rose to her feet and stood facing him with mouth open, little eyes sparkling and wicked. The cat got his paws under him and crouched, when suddenly he seemed to awaken. He looked this way and that in a daze. He saw the man and the woman standing over him holding the boy between them in their arms, saw the bare, sandy field around him all white in the sun that was rising over the trees. Gone was the old sow in a whirl of dust and gone all of a sudden was his fury and his courage.

He got shakily to his feet, looked for an instant at the man and woman standing there so oddly quiet, then started for the fence, slowly at first until his legs unlimbered and he could take the furrows in his great, graceful bounds. He

scarcely touched the top of the fence as he went over it and he did not stop until he was far in the cool, shadowed swamp, among the silent places, away from all signs and sounds of the strange, wild fight. Throwing himself flat on the ground under the green tangles he lay with heaving sides pulling himself together and getting back his normal balance. Forever in his memory, however, would be the very strange adventure of this day.

Small birds sang as if nothing at all had happened. The gray moss swayed and the leaves rustled in the growing breeze; ants ran up and down the tree trunks; buzzards circled like kites, with flattened wings and tails spread. Gradually the Tiger relaxed, dozed a little, licked his rumpled fur, tested his bitten legs a few times and arranged himself into a ball that could lie snugly among the dead leaves. Night would come again and with it the hunting time, the magic hour, when the rabbits and mice would appear from their hiding places and again the chance would come for him to still his hunger pains. Yes, night would come and night was really cat time; then he would hunt again and eat frogs if nothing better came his way.

Sammy and the Wildcat

The day dawned like any other day. The swamp, never entirely asleep, teemed with life and pleasant sounds as birds and beasts went about their usual pursuits. Cattle lowed and hogs grunted as if to show that man was nearby, and far away a railroad engine tooted mournfully as though tired of sticking to the same old track.

Stretched on a low limb of a moss-festooned live oak, with his four feet under him, the Tiger dozed and dreamed. Occasionally his claws moved and often his ears wiggled to ward off flies, but otherwise he was as motionless as the limb itself. The hours passed until the August sun overhead marked high noon and soon began to sink toward the western horizon, its heat growing slowly less as the rays slanted more and more.

The cat was becoming restless. He stretched his legs and yawned, and he began to look around and listen attentively to the sounds in the swamp. An unusual noise came faintly from

the direction of the clearings and at once caught his attention. It was whistling, for Sammy liked to whistle whenever he was alone, and now he was making his way to the Prairie, taking what he thought was a short cut to the boat that his father kept moored at the water's edge. He should have stayed on the little path that led there from the house, but Sammy had ideas of his own and wanted to explore. In his bare feet he found it easier to walk under the oaks where the briars were not so tangled, and he was heading in almost a straight line for the tree in which the Tiger rested.

It was not difficult for the cat to tell by the sounds that only one person was approaching, and this a youngster with no evil intentions. A hunter would keep as quiet as possible and sneak along the paths, instead of whistling loudly and padding carelessly over the dry leaves.

Presently he sighted Sammy's head above the palmettos, then his thin body; there seemed nothing dangerous about this little human and, besides, the cat felt that if he kept still he would not be seen on his limb. As he watched, his memory brought him back to the time when he had seen this boy before, running across the field, and he felt curiosity about this small edition of dangerous man.

Sammy came whistling past the tree and then stopped. The vague feeling that he was being watched had come to him as it comes to many creatures more sensitive than the average. He stood quite still and looked around him. The swamp seemed deserted to his eyes, but he continued to turn them this way and that until suddenly they met the stare of the big cat crouching on the limb not twenty feet away. Sammy wasn't scared, but he was mightily surprised. He could not remember ever having seen a cat one quarter as large as this one, which must be the daddy of them all, the kind he had heard his parents speaking about. They liked cats and so did he.

"Kitty, Kitty! Here Kitty!" said Sammy; but as the cat did not stir and continued to gaze at him he grew disconcerted and took several steps backward. He decided something must be wrong with it because it did not move, and he was troubled by the fixed stare of its round, yellow eyes.

He walked farther, still looking back and calling "Kitty," and when it was out of sight he thought about it and wondered whether it was hungry, out here in the swamp all by itself.

He found the boat, pulled a bait can from under the seat and put a white worm on the hook which dangled from a fishing pole he had hidden in the bushes at his last visit. The worm was one of a number he had found under the bark of a fallen and partly decayed pine. The nose of the boat was stuck in the mud and the stern projected into the Prairie to the edge of a little pool surrounded by grass. In this pool he dropped his hook and waited expectantly until the line began to move and he felt a nibble. He gave the fish time enough to swallow the worm, then jerked and brought out a flopping bream the size of a pancake.

The bream flopped about on the bottom of the boat but was soon unhooked. Another worm, then another bream. In all, he landed four before they stopped biting. To carry them he strung them on a little forked stick, one end of which he passed through their gills. Now he was ready to go home, so he hid his pole and started up the path, whistling as before and holding the stick on his shoulder so that the fish dangled behind him. He was feeling happy and carefree until all at once he remembered the cat and again wondered whether it was hungry.

He decided then to leave the path and have another look at the big animal, if it was still in the same place; and this time, when he came near the tree, he saw the yellow eyes immediately.

"Here Kitty," he called. "Here Kitty." The cat did not move, and Sammy went quite close, until he was almost directly under it. This was too close for the Tiger, who immediately leaped noiselessly to the ground and vanished in the bushes, leaving the boy surprised and disappointed by its lack of friendliness. He thought of the fish and, acting on a generous impulse, pulled one off the stick and laid it on the ground. Again he called, but getting no response, decided he would leave the fish for the cat to find, because he was sure all cats were hungry like his cat at home. Now he began to whistle again and continued his walk through the swamp to the field and then to the house, where he gave the three remaining bream to his mother to clean and cook for supper.

"Did you have a nice time?" asked Eliza.

"Oh, yes, and I caught another bream, but I gave that one to a great big cat."

"What?" gasped his mother. "What kind of a cat?"

"An awful big one. It looked hungry."

His mother dropped her dish cloth and sat down in a chair beside him.

"Tell me all about it," she demanded. And Sammy, excited by her interest, gave a very good description of the cat in the tree and how it had jumped down and run away, although he had left the bream for it to find because he knew it was hungry.

For once Eliza was speechless, but when Bill returned from a trip into the woods to feed his wandering hogs a little corn and keep them gentle and tame, she gave him Sammy's story word for word.

"I wonder if it was the Tiger?" mused Bill.

"Aren't you worried about the boy walking in the swamp and running into catamounts like that?"

"Not one bit," he answered. "I was like him when I was a little feller and the swamp was swarming with varmints. Nothing ever happened to me."

"Well, I don't feel it's safe. Suppose that critter had jumped on him?"

"It wouldn't. He's safer with the cats around

than if they were all dead; that fuss with the old sow proved it."

Eliza calmed down after that.

"At least, it's better, I guess, for him not to be made timid," she said. And so Sammy was not prevented from continuing his walks to the Prairie.

The Tiger found the bream and ate it. He had gone only a few yards into the bushes and had waited there until Sammy was out of sight; then he returned to the tree to look around and at once saw the fish as well as scented it. Fearing a trap, he walked around it very carefully before daring to pick it up and swallow it with a few guarded chews before the gulp that took down head, bones and all. The good-tasting tidbit was definitely associated in his mind with the tree and Sammy, which led to his resting on the same limb during the next day and listening for the whistling which heralded the boy's approach. And since Sammy had been greatly interested in his experience with the cat, the two met again in the same place. This time Sammy lingered longer and talked to him.

"Why you stay up there?" he wanted to know. "You come down here or maybe I won't bring you a bream. You're bad; when I call you, you got to mind!" He did bring a bream, however, and this time had the luck to look back just as the Tiger jumped from the tree and picked up the fish.

At the house he told his mother that the poor cat had only half a tail as if it had been run over by a wagon. He wanted to know who owned it.

"You own it as much as anyone," his mother told him. "That cat's wild. It stays in the swamp and never goes near anyone's house."

"It's my cat?" he asked just to make sure.

"Yes, it's yours just as I said, as much as it's anyone's."

"It's my cat!" he repeated several times. After that he never caught bream without leaving one and sometimes two of them under the tree. If the Tiger was not on his favorite limb, the fish were left anyway with much calling of "Kitty." And never was a fish wasted because sooner or later the Tiger always came to look for it and to follow Sammy's trail as far as the field as if hoping he would drop others. There came the day when he jumped from his limb to take the

fish as soon as the boy left it, and later the day when he circled the boy on the ground, waiting for him to drop the fish.

Sammy now accepted his timidity as he accepted everything when he got used to it, and so gradual was the cat's growth of confidence that the boy was not at all surprised when the big, beautiful animal at last followed him to the boat and sat on its haunches watching him fish. Sammy talked to the Tiger as he would to a companion, and if the cat did not understand the words, at least he knew that they indicated good feeling between them. The Tiger, indeed, while in awe of the boy as a superior being, had no longer any real fear; he knew that Sammy was a very friendly benefactor, and he liked Sammy. He was restless and nervous whenever the boy did not come on time or was kept in the house on account of rainy weather.

Bill and Eliza knew what was going on and never ceased to marvel. They would see the boy and the bobcat come out of the swamp together, the cat trotting ahead of the lad or directly behind him until the field was reached, whereupon the cat would stop and the boy would turn around to talk to him and say goodby.

"I can't understand it," Eliza would exclaim again and again. "It isn't human; maybe we ought to stop it."

"What for?" Bill would ask. "The boy is healthy and happy and keeps up his work. He's got a way with animals that seems to make them trust him. It's a sign of character. Let him develop it."

"But we're not raising a son of ours to be a wild animal trainer in a circus!"

"That's true, but he's nearly ten and there are no boy companions his age around here. That's hard on him, and certainly he won't play with doll babies like Mary does."

"Well, keep your eye on them and don't let anything happen to Sammy," was Eliza's final word. "A catamount is always a catamount even if he gets tame."

Those were warm days, when the black hound did not feel like going into the swamp to hunt cats or anything else. They were beautiful days that made the acorns fatten and the berries and seeds develop over all the land as if in preparation for the autumn chills that were sure to come. The young birds and animals grew large and strong and learned to shift for themselves in the big world, and the snakes began to grow lazy with all the food they could hold, and the fish swarmed in the tepid water of Wahoo Prairie.

from THE DEFENDER

Nicholas Kalashnikoff

The mountain rams, ruthlessly hunted by greedy men, are a noble and pathetic herd, struggling for survival in the remote vastness of the mountains. The man Turgen has been cruelly misjudged by his fellows, and he too has taken refuge in the mountain tops. How he becomes the defender of the mountain rams and of an unfortunate family and finds himself, in the process, is a moving story. "Everywhere there is life and everywhere are warm human hearts" is the theme of the book.

[The Wild Rams Find a Friend]

By stepping on to a ledge outside his door, Turgen on a clear day had a wonderful view of the valley below and the mountains above him. When he tired of watching the tiny figures of men and women scurrying about at the foot of his hill, he had only to turn his eyes upward to see a different and fascinating sight. For there, dodging among the crags, were specks which he knew to be wild rams.

"How do they live?" he asked himself one evening. The hills were barren except for sparse tufts of moss, an occasional thin clump of grass, and now and then a tough, hardy shrub that could not contain much nourishment.

His curiosity and pity aroused, Turgen watched the rams intently all that season and the next. He could make out nine individuals of what he assumed to be a family—or, as he called it, a tribe. In summer one lamb—or it might be two—were added to the number, but they disappeared with cold weather.

Then Turgen began to worry. For with the cold weather came snow to cover the moss and

grass and dry up the meagre shrubs. Even at a distance he could sense the animals' despair as they searched avidly beneath the snow for any poor morsel to chew upon. Their grey-brown wool hung loosely on them now, and they moved indifferently, without spirit. Unless there was a hint of danger. Then they would lift their heads proudly and take themselves into the distance with incredible lightness and speed.

"Poor things." Turgen spoke his thoughts aloud. "To think that I used to hunt you to kill you! What harm are you to anyone? You who ask only for freedom."

But pity could not help them. He must find a way to give them practical aid. He considered one thing, then another. At last he fixed upon a plan.

First he built a light sleigh which he loaded with hay. Then, putting on skis, he pulled the sleigh to the ridge of the next mountain, dumped the hay, and returned home. Not a ram was in sight, but he could feel their inquisitive and fearful eyes upon him from behind the boulders farther up the hill.

From his own door he watched them approach

the hay warily, circle it and trample it, and stoop to nibble at it. They seemed to fear a trap. But when he went back to the spot the hay was gone. After that he took frequent offerings of food to them, and gradually the rams came to accept his gifts without hesitation. Although they never approached him when he visited the feeding ground, he caught glimpses of them in hiding, awaiting his coming. In order to gain their greater confidence, he made it a point never to carry a gun. He even gave up his habit of carrying an iron-tipped stick which helped him in climbing. For he knew that all animals fear the rod which gives forth noise and fire.

It was not easy to conquer the fear of these wild creatures. It needed patience as well as understanding. But Turgen had both. Season after season he gave them care and attention, and was rewarded by knowing that they accepted him and depended upon him even though they did not fully trust him. A time came when they no longer hid from him but stood watching from a safe distance as if to determine what sort of being this was from whom they received nothing but good. And he had another satisfaction. The food he gave them worked a miracle in their appearance. They were no longer the sad, dishevelled animals of former days.

His heart leaped for joy one day when he went to the feeding ground and discovered the entire ram family gathered in a group on a little mound near by.

"Eh!" Turgen declared with pleasure. "You are truly a good-looking band—strong and healthy. And you eat now as if you enjoyed it."

The rams eyed him gravely, with an expression that might have been gratitude on their long homely faces.

"Yes," they seemed to be saying. "Perhaps your pampered cattle down below would not thrive on this fare, but for savages like us it is nourishing. You see, we are not looking to put on fat, merely to survive."

With these friends, who had become like his own children, Turgen knew that he would never again be lonely as before.

[New Life on the Mountains]

"A good man greets each new day as if it were a holiday." Turgen thought of this proverb upon waking every morning now, because it described exactly the way he felt. By becoming the protector of these defenseless animals, he had found a mission which used all the warmth of his lonely heart. He only regretted that the idea of feeding the rams had occurred to him so late. "But why waste time in regret?" he reflected. "Better rejoice that the idea came to me at last."

In order not to give the rams occasion for fright, it was necessary to change certain of his habits. For one thing, he did no hunting at all in the neighborhood of his yurta and the rams' feeding ground, but travelled some distance before permitting himself to fire a shot. He was gratified to discover before long that with the coming of spring, birds and small animals, especially squirrels, flocked to his mountain side in great numbers. It was as if a rumor had spread that his place was their assurance of safety. The next spring and the next it was the same. Gay and charming visitors he had never known before came to delight him with their presence, and he felt himself being drawn into another world. How wonderful to be looked upon as a friend rather than as an enemy of these creatures.

In three years the rams, too, showed growing confidence in him. He fed them regularly, even when the snow melted and the crevices of the rocky hills revealed young grass and tender new shoots on the shrubs.

One sunny day he had gone as usual to the Rams' Mountain and was standing on a ledge near the feeding ground waiting for them to appear. Soon he saw three coming cautiously toward him. Quickly he stepped out of sight. By their watchful movements he judged that they had been sent to reconnoitre, and he was more sure of this a moment later when they bleated a piercing "Ma-a! Ma-a!"

He could not doubt that this was a signal to inform hidden companions that all was well, for the entire ram family now appeared, led by a huge powerful fellow who held his head with its sharp spiralling horns proudly. "What strength! What assurance!" Turgen thought, enchanted. The long beard and tail indicated that the leader ram was not young, but his legs were slender and built to endure. He had a reddish-brown coat flecked here and there with white. By his extraordinary size and confident attitude he impressed his authority on the herd.

When the leader after a brief survey had satisfied himself that there was no danger he spoke calmly to his charges. "Ma-a!" he said. Whereupon all the rams fell to eating.

Turgen counted them: six females and three males—with two lambs not more than three weeks old, which he had not seen before. Unlike the lambs he had noticed briefly in previous seasons, these were gay and frisky and seemed prepared to enjoy a long life. Two lambs to six females was not a large increase. Still they were promise of new generations. Turgen was overjoyed. Surely the smaller one must be a girl, the larger one a boy. He watched them drink greedily of their mothers' milk, then pick at some grass only to reject it disdainfully and return to their mothers. Clearly they preferred milk to the food of grown-ups.

Turgen could not take his eyes from the rams, his wild mountaineers. In his imagination he saw this little family grow into a great herd. . . .

[Tragedy]

September came, bringing its customary changeable weather. One damp and windy day when all the furies seemed loose, Turgen went as usual to take food to his charges and stand watch.

"Though why anyone should come out in this weather I don't know," he thought. "Even the rams will surely keep under shelter."

But no. He had time only to drop the hay and retreat to his watching post when there they were in full strength—the whole family. The rain annoyed them and they shook themselves from time to time. Otherwise they showed no discomfiture. While the leader and two other males circled the clearing on the alert for danger, the rest stood quietly in the lee of the cliff waiting for the rain to abate. Looking for the lambs, Turgen saw them lying snugly under their mothers' bellies.

At the first sign of the weather's clearing Turgen's favorite jumped up and ran to urge the second lamb to romp with him. She refused, preferring her comfort.

He then advanced on the older rams, trying by all the wiles he could command to get their attention. Turgen almost laughed aloud watching his antics.

"What a show-off!" Then he worried. "It is cold and wet for one so young. He will get sick. —But that's an absurd idea. He is not made of clay that he will melt."

Soon after this the rain stopped and Turgen started for home. He had gone only a few steps when a shot rang out. There were hunters somewhere in the hills nearby—too far away to menace the herd of rams but the sound of gunfire alone was enough to cause panic. While the echo was still curling around the mountains the rams crowded around the leader as he stood irresolute, his head raised, his nostrils distended to test the air. It was he who must say what they should do.

In a minute the old ram turned and came at a light trot across a narrow stone abutment that formed a natural bridge between the clearing and the adjoining hill where Turgen stood. Without hesitation the other rams followed him in single file, males and females alternating. Turgen's lamb was behind his mother and just in front of the male ram who brought up the rear. The bridge led to a labyrinth of caves where escape was easy. That it led past Turgen seemed a matter of no concern to the rams in the face of great danger.

The bridge was no doubt slippery but the rams were sure-footed and they did not give way to panic. They were moving in a direction away from the gunfire. But Turgen had another plan. He would go toward the place from which the shot came. Should he meet the hunter, the hunter would understand that he was trespassing and leave the neighborhood—for such was the custom. Only one hunter was allowed to a region.

But before Turgen could act on his resolve, there was another shot. The ram at the rear of the line, hearing it, jumped, made an incautious step, and knocked against the lamb, who fell from the bridge.

[The Rescue]

Turgen's heart turned in him as he watched the small body hurtle down the crevasse. Then, peering over, he saw the lamb lying motionless on the mountain slope. Quickly, he made his way to the spot, fearing that wild animals would get there first.

The lamb's eyes, raised to his, were black with

terror. It tried convulsively to rise but could not.

"Thank God, he's alive," was Turgen's first thought. "There's a chance I can save him."

With that he stooped and lifted the lamb gently.

"Ma-a," said the lamb in a weak, childish whimper. And from a distance came a mournful answering bleat. "Ma-a! Ma-a!" that might have been the old leader. Then fog enveloped the mountain.

The lamb was surprisingly heavy, but Turgen hardly noticed the burden in his anxiety and excitement. Carefully he made his way to the yurta through the darkness, and as he went he murmured reassurance to his patient, who made no further effort to escape.

"It is not far to go. Be quiet. Rest. Do not fear—I'll do you no harm." Over and over Turgen said it, like a chant.

At the yurta Turgen laid the lamb on some soft pelts to examine him. Noticing fresh blood stains, he looked for a wound and found a flesh cut under the right front leg. It took but a minute to wash it clean and cover it with a poultice of plantain leaves to stop the bleeding.

The lamb's fright returned now and he struggled to gain his feet. But his hind legs would not obey him.

"There, there, lad," Turgen soothed him with tender strokes and pats. "What are you afraid of? I will soon make you well and take you back to your family. Who am I but an old man? There is no harm in me. Besides, who would dare to lift a hand against such a splendid fellow? Lie still. Trust me."

Pain, weariness, and the strange but unterrifying sound made by a human voice finally had their effect. The lamb rested while Turgen explored more thoroughly for possible injuries. There were scratches and bruises, none of them serious. And one hind leg was plainly swollen.

"God forbid that it should be broken," Turgen thought in dismay. For he was expert with animals and he knew the difficulty of keeping a wild young thing quiet while bone mended.

Fortunately, he found that the injury was no more than a dislocation, but extremely painful to the touch. With practiced skill, while the patient bleated piteously, he swathed the whole body to keep it immobile except for the head. Then, quickly and deftly, he set the bone, bandaged the leg and hoof between splints and satisfied himself that the lamb could do no harm to the injury should he get on his feet. As he worked the lamb regarded him with fixed and startled eyes. It was breathing heavily and clearly would have liked to offer resistance.

The bandaging operation finished, the lamb grew calm, fright gave way to weariness.

"Why," Turgen thought. "There is the same look in his eyes that I saw in Tim's when I set his arm. Children are alike. They suffer more from fright than pain." To the lamb he said: "That other little fellow drank some milk and fell asleep when I had doctored him. And so should you."

Fortunately, Turgen had only the day before brought milk from Marfa's cow. It stood untouched in the cellar. He poured some into a large wooden bowl and offered it to the lamb. At first the lamb turned his head away in distaste, but when by accident a few drops found their way into his mouth he smacked his lips with enjoyment. After that he drank willingly, with relish, looking at Turgen as if to say: "Really, this isn't bad at all."

Turgen was beside himself with joy as his charge finished his meal and promptly went to sleep.

"Food and attention—that's all anyone wants," Turgen reflected. "Just food and attention."

It was late when he himself was ready for bed, and after the agitating events of the day he slept fitfully. Whenever he wakened, as he did frequently, his first thought was for the lamb—and this stranger in his yurta seemed not a wild ram but a person close and dear to him. By going to his rescue, Turgen had found someone to share his yurta.

It is true, he marvelled, what our people say: "Misfortune can sometimes bring happiness."

from THE GREAT WHITE

Jane and Paul Annixter

In The Great White, *the Annixters have written a small but powerful book about the conflict between man and beast. The story tells of Iskwao, a monstrous polar bear, from the time of his birth through his violent adulthood until "The Last Hunt." It tells also of Nunku, the young Eskimo crippled by Iskwao's mother, who stalks the Great White. The reader is filled with mixed emotions: admiration for Iskwao's ability to survive and concern for Nunku's need to triumph. Only one of the combatants can succeed, but each is triumphant in different ways.*

Iskwao

It was a dim ghostland of one endless horizon. As far as the eye could sweep on every side stretched a limitless snow expanse, and there was only a slight rise in the levelness to show where the tundra merged into the ice fields of the unnamed Arctic bay. Seaward showed a tongue of dark water where the restless floes heaved and split against the fixed ice of the shoreline. Splatted shapeless against the ice at the edge of the open water crouched the spirit of the region. The huge polar bear might have been taken for one of the tossed-up hummocks of pressure ice that rose about her.

Moveless she waited, her narrow black-tipped muzzle pointed out across the swirling waters. On the edge of a big floe the dark form of a ringed seal stood out against the white. It was nearly a quarter of a mile away, but as usual the bear's keen wet nose told the story.

The bull seal was dim of sight. He trusted mainly to his acute hearing and to submarine vibrations for safety and for prey. In his element under water his microphone eardrums and the whole of his sensitized body were like a radar system, and he could track and swim down the fastest fish. It was on land or ice that he was handicapped.

Out in the open water to leeward of the seal's floe many big ice pans and small ice cakes were floating. The smallest of these kept to the line of whitecaps breaking against the far side of the floe. Strangely, it was scarcely tossed by the waves but seemed to have a will of its own. When it was just abreast of the seal's floe, it suddenly sank. A few moments later, from out of the white smother of spray almost beneath the bull seal's nose, there rose the startling head and shoulders of a second polar bear.

The great floe rocked as the bear kicked his ten-foot mass up on the ice. Cut off from the nearest water, the terrified seal wheeled and scuttled across the ice on spasmodic flippers. Doubling and releasing himself in two incredible lunges, the bear was upon the seal before he gained the farther edge of the floe. A great darting paw scooped the prize over on its back, and powerful jaws with an eighteen-inch gape met in the seal's neck. Then half-risen, with his forefeet on the kill, the male polar sent a hoarse coughing call across the water to his mate.

Already she had slid forward and was swimming toward him through the dark heaving water. Together on the rocking floe the pair feasted on the kill. There was a perceptible difference in size between the two; also, the coat of the male was a bit shaggier, and his was the greater length of head and jaw.

It was the she-bear that devoured most, and when the kill was torn open, she appropriated the choicest portions, bunting her mate aside while he, as if by tacit agreement, drew back. It was she too that first withdrew from the feast.

The wind had been rapidly increasing to a gale out of the northwest. Daily the stretch of open water offshore had been narrowing. Soon the white world would be utterly ice-locked. Out on the bay a driving scud veiled the yellowish light from the south, so that strange shadows lay crimson across the snow. From underneath the ice fields came a dull rumbling sound, and the whole expanse of ice quivered restlessly, expectantly. This was the first of the October gales from the Arctic, and already a fine sleet was in the air.

Something of the heaving uneasiness of the ice fields was tossing within the great she-bear. To the edge of the floe she shambled and stood looking off across the angry waters, her gaunt black-muzzled head rocking up and down and swinging slightly at each descent, making a U in the air. The call had come to her down the wind. The great snows were at hand. From down shore the high wild screaming of the glaucous gulls and dovekies, among the last birds to leave for the south, told of the massing and drilling for the Labrador flight.

Pivoting on her ungainly hind legs, the bear moved back to her mate and laid her muzzle on his shoulder. Low communion passed between them, almost inaudible, like the sounds a dog makes when it yawns. Turning with one accord they slid into the water and swam to the stationary ice of the shoreline. There the she-bear again tested the wind, while the old male sat on his haunches and approved.

It was settled in a few minutes. Loathe to leave the rich hunting of the seal grounds, the female had stayed on week after week. Now the rising storm admonished her to move south for the good of her cubs yet unborn. Shoulder to shoulder the two stood for another short interval, ruffing each other's necks and shoulders. Gently the male bunted his mate's side, and for a space each rested a muzzle across the other's back. Then, as with one thought, they wheeled about and shambled off, the female taking the south bend of the shore, the male turning northward, where he would spend a more-or-less sleepless winter stalking seal among the bergs and ice fields at the top of the world.

Southward along the west shore of the bay the she-bear held her course at a loose, shambling gait that knew no fatigue. The oily, downy inner nap of her coat shed moisture and had scarcely been affected by her swim. The water in her shaggy outer coat had mixed with the driving snow and had frozen, forming an armor of ice-crust about her body. She utilized this as a means of locomotion, sliding down icy slopes and hum-

mocks on her haunches and the underpart of her forelegs with comical, ungainly pleasure. There was speed in that lumbering pace in spite of the loafing ease of the movements.

All that day she stopped for neither food nor sleep, all her energies bent on reaching a region she knew. All her life this huge padded creature had eaten meat that still quivered with life. Incredible stores of vitality were acrawl in her great sliding muscles.

The second day found her turning inshore. By now the permanent slate-black clouds of winter darkened the sky to the north and east. They were far away and mackereled, like banks of corrugated metal, and told of a winter of more than ordinary severity. At last, in the low-lying valley of the Anninuik at the edge of the Barren Grounds her journey ended.

Here in a snowdrift between jagged rocks she dug in and curled up for the long winter sleep, letting the snow cover her as it would. Three days later in a temperature of 40 below zero the ceaseless Arctic storms were raging over the Barrens, and the she-bear was sleeping in a cave under three feet of snow.

In the next months, storm after storm swept down from the north, but only once was her rest broken; then it was to give birth to two whimpering cubs, a male and a female. For all the size of the mother the cubs were hairless ten-inch little creatures that weighed less than two pounds and lived only by snuggling for warmth into the shaggy fur of the mother's coat. Two hours in all she was awake licking and cleansing the cubs and schooling them in the baffling process of nursing in the dark.

Then the she-bear slept again, conserving all her vitality for the young. In usual course, they would sleep and feed the winter months away, growing fast and growing fat while she fell gaunt and lean. Food was all she need supply. The rising heat from her great body had already melted a sizable cave about them. The snow, topped now with an iron crust, was a natural protection.

But nothing about this whelping was usual. It so happened that the splayed hoof of a young bull caribou broke through the icy roof of the bear's cave, leaving an eight-inch hole open to the deathly cold and winds of the Barrens. The warmth of the she-bear's body could no longer properly warm the cave, and her sleep became troubled and fitful as the cubs whined and squirmed, seeking vainly to burrow to warmth beneath the mother's fur. For several days the three occupants of the cave touched only the restless edge of sleep. Then another snowstorm partially covered the hole, and the cubs huddled down within the curve of the mother's legs and slept.

The larger of the cubs, the male, had been growing fast, preempting by his superior size and strength the warmest places and best feeding fount at his mother's dugs. By February he was crawling over sister and mother in his restless search for more warmth, more sustenance.

It was now that one of the worst enemies of the helpless young discovered the den. An old male wolverine had wandered northward from tree line as was sometimes his habit in dead of winter. Known to hunters and trappers as *Carcajou* and to the Indians as "Bad Dog," the wolverine was too savage and ill-tempered to associate even with his own kind. Some three feet long with a heavy bear-like body and a coat of incredible thickness, he was practically immune to cold. When the long winter came to the tundra and the constant gales raided down from the Polar Sea, he roamed the frozen wastes of the Arctic, depending upon his predatory skill to carry him through.

This was one of his lucky times. The chance hole made by the caribou's hoof told the tale of a hibernating bear with cubs. The warm scent upwind turned the old wolverine in his tracks and brought him unerringly to the hole in the snow. He knew just what lay below and set to work ripping and tearing with his fierce oversize claws. Thick chunks of ice and snow broke away round the hole as he heaved and tore, and soon the den was open to the sky. The despoiler hung in the opening, glaring downward with his grim flat-pupiled eyes.

The cubs were his prize, but what he did must be done quickly, before the she-bear turned into an avenging demon roused by the cold and his rank scent. Without hesitation he slithered down into the dark hole.

The little female crouched trembling while the male backed into a crevice, his new hair risen in a roach, eyes aglow, small snarls rattling in his throat. The teeth of the marauder met in the female cub's neck and tore out her life. He had turned upon the male cub when the she-bear woke abruptly, in full and wrathful possession of her senses.

A low sound between a growl and a moan came from the mother as the wolverine, with the dead cub in his jaws, clawed his way up and out of the den. Thrusting the male cub behind her, she tore her way out into the open and went raging across the snow no more than twenty yards behind the robber. The wolverine knew well the terrible rage of a she-bear with a slaughtered cub. His back humped and doubled like a measuring worm as he fled, but his speed was nothing compared to the polar's. Drop his kill he would not, and it was as he struggled to climb a big rock that the mother caught him up and snuffed out his savage life, with a mighty paw that could have broken the back of a stallion with a single blow.

Slowly, wrath drained out of the she-bear. But she stood over the body of her dead cub, sunk in deep primeval grief. Only the appearance of her other cub, staggering toward her over the snow, pulled her out of her misery. The strength it had taken to climb out of the den and the instinct—it could scarcely have been scent—that had led him along his mother's trail were unusual in a cub so young, and foretold the craft, strength, and prowess that would accrue to the little male as he matured.

Another storm was brewing, and as the she-bear nudged and bunted the cub before her, back to the den among the rocks, snow began pelting down the wind. A few hours later it had covered the opening once more, and soon there was a cap of snow-ice that would last till the warm winds of spring.

By mid-March the she-bear's sleep was definitely over. Longer and longer stretches of daylight were seeping through the snow above her. In usual course she would have remained denned another two or three weeks, tossing restlessly and dozing at times while she waited for her cubs to grow to proper size and strength for the long trip north to the floes. But this spring it was her single cub that tossed and mumbled restlessly, crawling and clambering over his mother as he waited for her to rouse and be on her way.

Though the worst of the winter storms were over, it was still early for a sow polar to be abroad with her young. She knew this, but the churning of the cub precluded all rest or peace. So on the blustery last day of the month she broke free of the cave, and headed north with the cub.

The cub, Iskwao as he was to be known later by the Eskimos—a name meaning "Great White" —showed no disgruntlement at icy wind or driving sleet. It was as if he had been born for snow and cold and tireless trekking, as indeed he had been, though the she-bear at times had to slow her pace to his. Sated on milk enough for two ordinary cubs, he was as rugged and almost as large as a cub twice his age.

Toward nightfall of the first day a small pack of wolves came sweeping up on the polars' trail. There were six of them, the big white wolves of the Barrens, taller and fiercer than the timber wolves to the south. They were not desperate enough to attack the she-bear herself; it was the cub they sought. The mother clapped him close and moved toward a vantage point among distant rocks, the cub moving almost beneath her. Once the wolves made a concerted rush, but the she-bear whirled, slapping two wolves from her as though they were flies. A lightning swipe of her paw caught another wolf fairly, and it landed, disemboweled, some five yards away.

Throughout the encounter Iskwao squatted down and watched. He did not quail, but met the wolves' green glares with his little button eyes and echoed his mother's growls with small fierce growls of his own. Once the she-bear had gained a protected spot among the rocks and turned about, the remaining wolves melted away. Contrary to many tales, they left their fallen companion in the snow, making no attempt to devour him. It was the polars who feasted on the slain wolf, Iskwao ripping and growling beside his mother at his first solid meal. In usual course, the cub would have nursed for many months to come, but Iskwao was initiated at once into the mystery of a blood and meat diet. Never had the she-polar known a cub the like of this one.

Because of the slower pace of the cub, the journey back to the ice fields took more than four days. The she-bear made another kill along the way, a ringed seal she scented on the ice some three hundred yards from shore. She slipped into the icy water, Iskwao close behind her, swimming as easily and naturally as if he had been born there. Far out to leeward of the floe the she-bear swam, then floated craftily close with only the tip of her snout showing above the surface. Before the seal was aware of danger the bear had heaved herself onto the ice, cutting him off from the water. One swift rush and she flattened the seal to the ice; and there was Iskwao beside her, helping at the kill, as if he already knew that seal meat was to be his chief sustenance for life. The two moved on then, well fed and well contented with each other.

Needs of children remain essentially the same throughout the centuries,[1] but the way such needs are met varies with the particular society in which the child finds himself. In the early days of our nation when there was a wilderness to be conquered, the need to belong was more easily satisfied than it is in today's society. Most children were important to the welfare of the family; they were needed to milk the cows, feed the chickens, and harvest the crops. They might have even been called upon to defend the family homestead as Edward was in *The Matchlock Gun* (see Bibliography, p. 255). They also knew almost to the minute when they ceased being

LIFE IN THE UNITED STATES

children and became adults. Although white society in America never had quite the rigid training period most Indian youths went through, it did have a firm idea of when a child could have his first gun, when he was ready to go hunting on his own, and when he could be counted a full-fledged member of society. While individual children differed according to the rapidity with which they progressed toward the goal of becoming adults, the basic standards existed.

[1] May Hill Arbuthnot, *Children and Books*, Scott, Foresman, rev. ed., 1964, Chapter 1

Many of these basic standards have changed with the coming of the technological age. Is a young person in graduate school, being supported by his parents, a child or an adult? Does becoming economically self-sufficient make one an adult? If so, does this mean that the high-school dropout with a job is an adult and that the doctoral student is still a youth? Silly as these questions may sound to some, they are not silly to the youths concerned. The difference between physical maturity and the time at which one enters the adult world today presents serious problems.

How does a young person "grow up" in our current society? The answers differ according to the class of people and the area of the country in which a child lives. In the sheepherding country of Joseph E. Krumgold's *. . . and now Miguel* (see Bibliography, p. 250), it is clear to Miguel that he is a child until the day comes when he is allowed to go with the sheep to the summer pasture on the mountains. His life structure is that simple. In Krumgold's second book, *Onion John* (see Bibliography, p. 248), Andy Rusch, Jr., has a much harder time in his struggle to attain adulthood because his desires are in conflict with his father's and his society's.

In his third book, *Henry 3* (see Bibliography, p. 248), Krumgold again tries to cope with the problem of what goals a boy sets for himself to achieve in manhood, only this time within the structure of upper-middle-class suburbia and the power elite. In almost every way it is a less satisfying book than the first two, not because Krumgold is no longer a good writer, but because the more complex society becomes, the less sure it is of its values. The end result is that *Henry 3* often strikes the reader as a mixed-up book. But it is not the book that is mixed up; it is the society it depicts that is mixed up.

Miguel wants to be just like his father and his older brother, and the society in which he lives approves of his goal. Andy Rusch, Jr., wants to be just like his father but is being pushed to be "better," which Andy correctly discerns as meaning richer, but not necessarily happier. Henry discovers that his father consciously hides the best part of himself in order to survive in the business world; and thus Henry is faced with the conflict of wanting to be like the best of his father while rejecting the surface person.

The three Krumgold books, taken together, depict as clearly as any sociological study the impact of a child's environment on his values and development. This means that all of us who work with children must understand not only the children, but also the society surrounding them, if we are to help satisfy their needs in any meaningful way.

Books alone cannot solve problems. But those of us who grew up as devoted readers do know from our own experiences that books can be of great help. On occasion, books can help us, quite literally, to survive; they can help us turn chaos into order. Well-written, thoroughly honest books provide the youthful reader with insights into his own and other people's problems. Books can recount both the joys and sorrows of life, and can offer ideas about how one copes with the world in which he lives. Such books are often called "realistic," a label which means nothing more or less than that the author has tried to the best of his ability to depict the world as it is, not as he wishes it were.

Characteristics of realistic stories

Because so many adult novels which are termed realistic deal with sordid and unhappy events, some adults assume that misery is a necessary feature in a book labeled "realistic." But this is not the case. It is true that all the characters must resolve a problem, but in books, as in life, problems vary in degree. Going to dancing school is a problem for both little Eddie (see p. 68) and Harriet (see p. 123), but because *Eddie and the Fire Engine* was written for young children and *Harriet the Spy* was written for upper elementary and junior high school readers, the responses of the characters differ, as do the authors' styles and vocabularies. For Eddie and Harriet, dancing school is a problem, but it cannot be compared with Skinny's concern (see p. 77) with going to an orphanage or with Dave Mitchell's problem of getting along with his father in *It's Like This, Cat* (see Bibliography, p. 248).

The range of problems in realistic stories reflects the authors' understanding of the need to present material appropriate to a wide range of age levels. What is a problem to a five-year-old has little meaning for a ten-year-old; this is as it should be if the child is maturing normally.

Examination of realistic stories shows that the authors pose a problem for the central character and allow the character to solve or resolve it in a thoroughly plausible way. There are no fairy godmothers in realistic stories; their place is taken by hard work and reasonable action on the part of the main characters.

Such stories can be as exciting as fairy tales and as full of humor, adventure, or romance as "non-realistic" stories. The difference lies only in their plausibility and the absence of magical forces. The plot may turn simply upon a child's need to stoop down and tie his shoelace (see *Wait for William* by Marjorie Flack, Bibliography, p. 247), or it may be as important as the search for a home by a boy so deprived that he lacks even a name of his own (see *The Loner* by Ester Wier, Bibliography, p. 249). But whatever the action of the realistic story, it must carry the conviction of complete plausibility so that the reader can identify himself with the hero and believe in the hero's mistakes and triumphs as if they were his own.

There is considerable dissension in the world of children's books today about the subject matter being handled in realistic books. A number of adults reject out of hand the idea that juvenile literature can—or should—cope with such things as menstruation (*The Long Secret* by Louise Fitzhugh), or a child murderer (*The Egypt Game* by Zilpha K. Snyder). These same adults would also reject children's books that cope with problems of divorce, alcoholism, and all social problems, whether they are brought about because of race, nationality, or religion.

The adult's role in choosing realistic stories

Such adults think of themselves as protectors of youth. They are, in reality, merely protecting themselves from acknowledging the world around them as it exists today. They are also lacking in historical perspective, for many of the books they most cherish were highly controversial when they were first published. *The Adventures of Tom Sawyer* and *Adventures of Huckleberry Finn*

were banned from libraries; even *Little Women* was considered unsuitable for children.

All of us have not only the right but the responsibility to reject any book which is badly written, but we should not confuse the author's ability to write with his choice of subject matter. It is how he handles the subject, not the subject matter *per se,* which is the crux of literary judgment. Thus, we should not ask, first, "What is the book about?" but rather, "How well written is the book?" Only after we have determined that a book meets literary standards do we then discuss it in terms of "values," for if there is one thing we do know, it is that all well-written books make some important statement about life.

The trouble is that the moment we begin to talk about a book's having values, we are accused of approving of didacticism. Perhaps we can put this controversy into perspective by analyzing the differences between the didactic book and the well-written book, which possesses values and makes important points pertinent to helping children grow.

Didacticism versus realism

A didactic book is one which is written to teach children a lesson, a type of book which has its roots in eighteenth- and nineteenth-century tracts. These tracts were written in story form with children as the central characters, and they were designed to teach the young to be pious, industrious, or honest.[2] One of the recurring religious lessons in these early tracts was that it was a great blessing to die young before one had time to sin, thus assuring oneself of a place in heaven. Over and over in the early books for children, one encounters painful death scenes followed by pious moralizing about the joys of dying. All character development and plot action were twisted in order that the author might make his —or more often, her—point.

As the harsh religiosity of the Puritans eased, it was followed by books which preached to the little daughter of the manor that it was wrong for her to play with the young son of the gardener, that she must learn her place and role in a rigidly constructed society. The action in such

[2] May Hill Arbuthnot, *Children and Books,* Scott, Foresman, rev. ed., 1964, pp. 41–43

books was constantly interrupted by long lectures delivered in the most dogmatic tones.

We must not think that children were singled out for such writings. Juvenile literature parallels adult literature, and the redemption of Robinson Crusoe was far more important to its writer and readers than the survival story aspect of that book. Adults who today object to some of the coincidences in Jean George's *My Side of the Mountain* (see p. 131) might do well to compare it with *Robinson Crusoe* to see which is the more likely tale.

For over two hundred years, didacticism dominated juvenile literature. Then came *Hans Brinker, Heidi, The Adventures of Tom Sawyer,* and *Little Women,* bringing a fresh wind to the field. These remarkable books were thoroughly entertaining, moral but not moralizing, and so popular that their success would seem to have been sufficient to wipe out forever the juvenile tract type of story. But not so.

Unhappily, didacticism in children's books seems to rise in one form or another in every generation. The theological didacticism of the Puritans hung grimly over the heads of their children. And the intellectual didacticism of the eighteenth century and the moralistic didacticism of Maria Edgeworth in the early nineteenth century were almost equally oppressive. In our own time didacticism has risen again, cloaked in educational jargon as "developmental values."

When psychologists use the phrase, "developmental values" represents a sound concept of mental health: behavior is appropriate or inappropriate according to the age of the child. When this phrase invades the literary field, it becomes old-fashioned didacticism thinly disguised by a new label.

Books with emphasis on developmental values set out to teach children how to behave. Thus, we have picture books about abused toys that leave home to teach their young owners to appreciate them; books which teach children to pick up their clothes and brush their teeth. There are books which are designed to help a child adjust to being smaller or larger than his classmates; others stress the need to overcome sibling rivalry or to cope with the problem of being an only child. No subject, big or small, escapes these authors' attention.

When reading such books, one can almost hear the author saying, "Pay attention to this point. Learn the lesson. This is important." Such books are dull books, and what devotees of didacticism have yet to learn is that an unread book does no good no matter how many lessons it is designed to teach.

Criteria for realistic stories

Goods books are concerned not so much with teaching the child reader as they are with offering him a new way of seeing the world, helping him discover the way things are, and making him realize the way things might be if we were all better people. So white children who enjoy *Roosevelt Grady* (see p. 93) may discover, on their own, that Negro migrant workers have dreams and aspirations like anyone else. What child has not wondered what happens to the "leftover number" when his long division problem does not come out evenly? And in our mobile society, even middle-class children can sympathize with Roosevelt and his mother and their yearning for a place "to stay put." There is no preaching in *Roosevelt Grady;* it is just a good story about human beings and their search for the good life.

In the area of race relations we have had some of our worst books in recent years, not because of faulty intentions, but because it takes a really good writer to depict the similarities while also showing the uniqueness of people. Being a Negro in America is different from being a white person, not because of internal differences, but because of external pressures; the author who writes a book which states that race doesn't count is fooling himself, not his readers. Hopefully, race someday will not matter, but it does today and the author writes a dishonest book if he shows it otherwise.

Aside from an obvious difference in talent, the difference between a didactic author and one who writes good realistic books might be expressed in these terms: the didactic author writes glibly and dully about broad subjects (race relations, sibling rivalry), while the author of good realistic stories explores the growth and development of a few characters in a specific situation. He draws no great conclusions, but he offers enough insight within the book so that the sensitive, thoughtful reader can draw his own conclusions.

In his attempt to portray the world as it is and thus make it recognizable to the young reader, the author of today's realistic stories must move into previously uncharted areas. He must listen to children when they do not know that they are being observed so that he can capture the full flavor of the language they use, complete with its titillating use of profanity and its careful exploring of sex. He must see the ambivalent relationships among children and between children and parents. He must absorb what the psychologists and child psychiatrists can tell him. And finally, he must retain the ability to remember what it feels like to be a child. He must remember with as much honesty as an adult can master, not yielding to the deceptive adult myth that childhood is the happiest time of our lives.

If he does all this and has the ability to write, someday he will sit down and begin a story. The mysterious process of creative writing is at work—a process neither writer nor reader can describe or completely understand. All that he is and has been, all that he has seen and heard and read blend together, and out of this totality of one person's being comes a book which makes others feel more alive. Whether the book is happy or sad, whether it deals with people like ourselves or those different from us, becomes irrelevant. We recognize a part of ourselves in the author's characters, and yet we also come to understand that no person is exactly like another. That is what books are all about: being able to see that "People" consists of a multitude of individuals, each one searching for his own particular way of life.

DOWN DOWN THE MOUNTAIN

Ellis Credle

It is especially good for city children to encounter stories about mountaineer children whose environment is less complex and more challenging than their own. The ingenuity and self-reliance of Hetty and Hank in solving their problems and in achieving their hearts' desire are admirable.

Once upon a time, in a little log cabin away up in the Blue Ridge Mountains, there lived a little girl named Hetty and her brother Hank.

Although their home was a small one, it was a cozy place to live. There was a big stone fireplace at one end. That was where Mammy cooked beans and cornmeal mush and fried pork in a big, black, frying pan.

There was a big bed in one corner and a little bed in the other corner, and in the middle of the room there was a long table made of planks. That was where Mammy and Pappy and Hetty and Hank ate their dinner every day.

All kinds of things hung from the rafters, strings of shucky beans, bunches of bright red peppers, ears of popcorn all tied together, hams, and sausages, and baskets full of this and that.

Never in all their lives had Hetty or Hank had a pair of shoes. In the summer it was fun to run around barefoot, but when winter came, and the snow lay on the mountains like a chilly white blanket, their little feet were blue with cold and they longed for a pair of shoes.

They each wanted a beautiful shining pair that sang, "Creaky—squeaky—creaky—squeaky," every time they walked.

They begged their mammy to buy them some shoes, but she said, "You can't find shoes like that in these hills! Such shining shoes come from the town, away down down at the foot of the mountain."

So they asked their Pappy, but he said, "There's not a cent of money in this household. We've everything we need right here in these hills."

Hetty and Hank felt very sad, but they did not give up.

"Let's ask our Granny," said Hetty. And they did.

"Some shining shoes?" chirped Granny. "I'll tell you how you can get them yourselves."

"How? How?" cried Hetty and Hank.

"Plant some turnip seeds," said Granny, "and when they have grown into fine big turnips, you can take them all the way down to town and trade them off for some shining, creaky, squeaky shoes."

"Thanky' Ma'am, that's what we'll do," cried Hetty and Hank.

They raced away and planted some turnip seeds in a tilted field right next to Pappy's corn patch.

Home they went singing,

"Our fields are high up in the air,
  We wouldn't dare plant pumpkins there,
  For pumpkins grow so big and round,
  They'd break right off and tumble down.
  But turnips grow on hills or vales,
  Because they twist their little tails
  Around the rocks and hold on tight
  And don't let go for day or night!"

When Hetty and Hank got home it was dark. The whippoorwills were calling sadly from the deep woods, "Whip-poor-will! Whip-poor-will!" and a little owl was asking "Who? Who-o-o?"

Mammy was waiting for them. She gave them a nice supper of corn bread and butter and yellow honey. Then she tucked them snugly into bed. They dreamed all night about shining shoes that played a creaky, squeaky tune, just like Pappy's fiddle.

The next day they climbed up the steep, steep mountain-side to see if the turnip seeds had come up. But they had not, and Hetty and Hank had to wait and wait and wait, before they spied the baby turnip leaves peeping out of the ground.

Then there was plenty of work for Hetty and Hank! They had to chop away the weeds each day, and chase away the worms and the bugs and the grasshoppers that come for a taste of nice green turnip leaves.

When there was no rain and the little turnips felt dry and thirsty, Hetty and Hank had to bring big buckets of water to make them fresh and green again.

The little turnips were very grateful. They grew and grew until they were the finest and the biggest turnips to be found any where in the hill country.

Then Hetty and Hank brought Granny and Mammy and Pappy up to see them.

"Sakes alive!" cried Mammy, "I never saw such big turnips!"

"Yes siree!" smiled Granny, "These are mighty juicy turnips."

"And they'll fetch a fine price in the town," said Pappy. "Hetty and Hank shall have the old gray horse to take them down the mountain."

So Hank quickly brought the gray horse. Then they pulled up all the beautiful turnips and packed them into a big bag.

Pappy laid the bag proudly across the gray horse's back, then he gave Hetty and Hank a boost and settled them safely right behind the turnips. Now they were ready to go.

"It's no trouble to find the town," said Granny. "Just you keep to the road and it will lead you down. Sometimes it's steep—just like the stair. Sometimes it's narrow—like a hair. It turns and twists and winds around, but at the end you'll find the town!"

"We'll keep to the road," promised Hetty and Hank. Hank pulled on the reins. Hetty gave the gray horse a slap on the side, and they were off.

"Goodby!" cried Granny and Mammy and Pappy.

"Goodby!" waved Hetty and Hank. And away they went, clippity, cloppity, down the road to town.

They had not gone very far before they came to an old man cutting sugar cane in a field beside the road.

"Howdy young ones!" he called. "What have you in that big bag?"

"Some turnips we're taking to sell in the town," said Hank proudly.

"Oh, my! Turnips!" cried the old man. "How I'd love some nice juicy turnips for my dinner. Couldn't you spare me just a few?"

"I suppose we wouldn't miss just a few," said Hetty, and she gave him some.

On they jogged between great bushes of pink mountain laurel, and after awhile they came to an old woman who was making soap in a big black kettle.

"Howdy, children!" she called. "What have you in that big bag?"

"Some turnips we're taking down to town," said Hank.

"Turnips!" cried the old woman. "Mercy me! How I'd love just a taste of turnip for my dinner. Couldn't you spare me just two, one for my old man and one for me?"

"I suppose we wouldn't miss just two," said Hetty and she gave her two big ones.

Down, down, down they went between the rows of tall blue mountains, down, down, down until they came to a little stream flowing over the rocks. There the little road ended. They looked here, they looked there they looked everywhere but it was nowhere to be seen.

But just then along came a woman on horseback, splishing and splashing right down the middle of the stream.

"What's the matter young ones?" she called.

"We've lost the little road to town," said Hank.

"Follow the creek," said the woman. "That's all the road there is in these parts."

So Hetty and Hank went splashing along and along and pretty soon they spied the little road leading up from the water.

They said goodby to the kind woman and gave her a bunch of turnips for her dinner.

On they went along the little road beneath the tall pine trees. After awhile they overtook a man who was driving a flock of turkeys down to town. "Howdy," greeted the man. "What have you in that big bag?"

"Some turnips we're taking to sell in the town," said Hank.

"Oh my stars!" said the man. "Turnips! and I've had nary a bit to eat since break of dawn. A nice, juicy turnip would taste mighty good now, for I've been running after these turkeys 'til I'm nigh worn out."

"We'll have to give him a handful of turnips," said Hetty. And she did.

"Thanky, thanky," said the man, "you're kind and generous young ones!"

Now they were very near to town. They could look down and see the roof tops in the valley.

The little road became so smooth and straight that the gray horse broke into a gallop.

"Here's the town!" cried Hank.

Along they went, clippity clop, clippity clop, past the schoolhouse, past the church, past the courthouse, and suddenly there was the little red store.

"Whoa!" cried Hank, pulling on the reins. "Here's the place to trade our turnips off for some shining shoes!"

They climbed down and lifted off the sack. Somehow it felt very light and very, very empty. Had they given all their turnips away?

Hetty put her hand into the bag and brought out one large, fat, lonesome turnip. It was the only one left.

And there—shining through the store window were those beautiful, creaky, squeaky, shining shoes!

Hetty and Hank gazed at them longingly. But one turnip would not buy a pair of shoes.

Two big tears began to roll down Hetty's cheeks.

"There! There!" said Hank. "No use crying. We'll just walk around and see the sights. Come on."

So they walked along the little road looking this way and that way. They saw the big covered wagons, all loaded with apples, come rumbling down from the hills. They saw the men trading horses in the courthouse square. Then a train went thundering past and they watched it with round eyes.

Along and along they went and after awhile they came to a field where there were many, many people. A big sign over the gate said "COUNTY FAIR."

Hetty and Hank went hustling and bustling about in the crowd. Pretty soon they came to a long row of tables, each one groaning with a different kind of vegetable. There were tomatoes on this one, and beans on that one, and pumpkins on the other one.

"Oh, here are some turnips!" cried Hetty.

"Are they as big as ours?" asked Hank.

Hetty held up her turnip. It seemed larger and juicier than the rest.

"Howdy, young ones," said the old man who was looking at the turnips. "Do you want to enter that turnip in the contest?"

"What contest?" asked Hank.

"Why there's a prize offered for the finest turnip at the fair," replied the old man.

"Mercy me!" said Hetty. "Let's try it."

"You bet your life!" said Hank.

So the old man wrote their names on a tag and tied it to the fat turnip. Then he laid it carefully among all the other turnips.

"You are just in the nick of time," he said, "for I was just a-getting ready to do the judging."

He began to examine the turnips. He weighed each one to see how heavy it was. He felt each one to see how firm it was. And when he had tried them all he held one large turnip high above his head.

"Folks!" he cried. "Here's the finest turnip at the fair. It belongs to a little girl and a little boy!"

Hetty and Hank listened with all their ears.

"Come forward, young ones and receive the prize!"

Hetty held out her hand and there shining up at her was a bright five-dollar gold piece.

"Oh thank you sir!" cried Hetty and Hank. "Now we can buy our shining shoes!"

They dashed along past the beans and tomatoes. They ran past the squash and skipped past

the potatoes. They dodged through the hustle and the bustle on the fair grounds. They raced along the street until they came to the little, red store.

The storekeeper was standing behind the counter.

"We want to buy some beautiful, creaky, squeaky shoes!" said Hank all out of breath.

The storekeeper got down his brightest shoes,

and Hetty and Hank each chose a pair that played a creaky, squeaky tune.

Then they bought some gifts to take home with them. A yellow hat for Pappy, a bright sash for Mammy and a big, red handkerchief and a package of needles for Granny.

And off they started on the long trip home. Up, up, up they wound, round and round the mountain, past the pink laurel flowers, along the little stream and underneath the tall pine trees.

After a long, long climb they reached their own little cabin. There sat Mammy and Pappy and Granny waiting on the porch. How pleased they were to see Hetty and Hank and all the new things they had brought!

The next day was Sunday, so they put on their beautiful things and went to preaching.

Hetty and Hank walked proudly into the meeting-house. Their shoes were playing such a creaky, squeaky tune that all the people craned their necks to see who could be wearing such beautiful shoes.

from DID YOU CARRY THE FLAG TODAY, CHARLEY?

Rebecca Caudill

The honor of carrying the flag of the Little School goes to the boy or girl who has been "specially good that day." Charley is sure from the beginning of his school career that he will carry the flag, but it is many a day before he can answer "Yes" when his family asks, "Did you carry the flag today, Charley?" In Charley, Rebecca Caudill has created one of the most delightful characters of recent times, a boy who will appeal to all age groups.

[The Thing]

Of all the rooms at Little School, the one Charley liked best was Mr. Sizemore's. Charley's group went there the last half hour of every Wednesday.

In Mr. Sizemore's room the children made things of clay. They colored with crayons. They painted pictures with their fingers on big sheets of paper. They built houses and fences and calf pens with blocks. One day a boy built a mountain with blocks. On the mountain top he put a little flag.

The blocks were in a small room just off Mr. Sizemore's classroom. On a low shelf in that room stood big jars of clay of many colors.

One Wednesday afternoon, Mr. Sizemore said, "Suppose we paint today."

All the boys and girls liked to paint with their fingers. Whenever they sat at the tables to paint, Mr. Sizemore placed a piece of drawing paper in front of each of them. Then he took a large jar from a shelf, and went around the room pouring a blob of starch on each piece of paper.

Charley was sitting at the end of his table. He laid both hands flat in the blob of starch and smeared, and smeared, around and around. "It feels slick, like ice," he said, and he smeared some more.

"Ready for the blue stuff, Mr. Sizemore," he called.

"Is everyone ready?" asked Mr. Sizemore.

Around the room Mr. Sizemore went from table to table, sprinkling a few drops of tempera paint on each paper. He sprinkled blue paint on some papers, red paint on some, and yellow paint on some.

"I want some of every color, Mr. Sizemore," said Charley.

Mr. Sizemore sprinkled blue and red and yellow on Charley's paper.

"You know what I'm painting?" Charley said to Vinnie who sat next to him.

"No. What?" asked Vinnie.

"A rainbow," said Charley.

"I saw a rainbow one time," said Vinnie.

"Where was it?" asked Charley.

"In the sky, of course," said Vinnie. "Where'd you think it would be?"

"I saw a rainbow on the ground one time," said Charley.

"Mr. Sizemore," said Vinnie, "you know what Charley said? He said he saw a rainbow on the ground one time. He didn't, did he?"

"I did, too," said Charley.

"Where was it, Charley?" asked Mr. Sizemore.

"In a puddle," said Charley. "At a filling station."

"You could have seen one there," said Mr. Sizemore. "In an oil puddle. It wouldn't have been exactly like the rainbow you see in the sky, but it could have had some of the same colors."

"See?" Charley said to Vinnie.

Charley smeared and smeared.

"Done, Mr. Sizemore," he called.

Mr. Sizemore wrote on one corner of Charley's paper in big black letters, CHARLEY.

"It's name is Rainbow in a Puddle at a Filling Station," said Charley.

Mr. Sizemore wrote on one edge of the paper, RAINBOW IN A PUDDLE AT A FILLING STATION. With two clothespins he fastened Charley's picture on a cord stretched along the wall. When it was dry he would put it in a big folder labeled CHARLEY with all the other pictures Charley had painted. On the last day of school, Charley could take the folder home and show his mother all his pictures.

"Now I want to make something out of clay," Charley said.

"All right," said Mr. Sizemore. "You may get some clay off the shelf."

Charley went to the block room and chose some pink clay. Back at the table he pinched off a piece of the clay and rolled it in his hands till it was as thin as a toothpick. He took another piece and rolled it as thin as a pencil, and pinched one end of each of the two together to make a straight line. He rolled another piece just a bit thicker, and pinched one end of it to the end of the second piece. To keep it in a straight line, he had to move Vinnie's paper.

"Quit that, Charley!" scolded Vinnie.

Charley rolled another piece of clay, a little thicker still. To pinch the end of it to the third piece, he had to move Carl's paper.

"Mr. Sizemore, make Charley quit!" complained Carl.

"What's Charley doing?" asked Mr. Sizemore as he walked over to the table.

"He thinks the whole table belongs to him," said Carl and Vinnie.

"What are you making, Charley?" asked Mr. Sizemore.

"A Thing," said Charley as he rolled another piece.

"You come with me," Mr. Sizemore said. "Bring your clay."

Mr. Sizemore led the way to the room where the blocks were kept. The other children went on painting.

"Since the Thing is so long, why don't you work in here by yourself?" asked Mr. Sizemore. "We'll spread a newspaper on the floor, and you can make your Thing on the paper."

"It'll have to be a long newspaper, Mr. Sizemore," Charley told him. "Because this sure is a long Thing I'm making."

Together Mr. Sizemore and Charley spread newspaper on the floor from the middle of the room up to the door. Then Mr. Sizemore went back into the classroom where the other boys and girls were painting.

Alone in the room, Charley looked at the row of jars of clay standing on the shelf. He took down the jar containing the pink clay and went to work, rolling and rolling, each piece a little thicker than the one before, and pinching the ends together.

Soon Charley had used up all the pink clay there was, and the Thing was not finished. He took down the jar of black clay and went to work again, rolling and rolling, each piece thicker than the one before. He used all the black clay there was. Then he took down the jar of yellow clay and began rolling.

The Thing was finally as big around as Charley's arm. It had reached almost to the door when the bell rang for the end of the school day.

Charley heard the children in the next room putting away their papers. He heard them getting in line in the hall. He heard Miss Amburgey say, "If you're going to meet that three o'clock bus at Elkhorn, Mr. Sizemore, you'll have to leave right away. I'll take care of your group."

Charley heard more talking and more shuffling of feet down the hall. Then everything grew still.

It was the best day he'd had at Little School. Here he was, all alone, with nobody to tell him "Do this" and "Do that." And the Thing was growing longer and thicker. It was now as thick as a baseball bat, its front end yellow, its middle black, its tail pink.

Charley heard footsteps in Mr. Sizemore's room. For a few seconds everything was quiet. Charley listened. Then he heard the footsteps go away down the hall. He heard Mr. Webb's voice. "Charley! Charley Cornett!"

He'd have to hurry, thought Charley to himself.

He took one more piece of yellow clay, shaped it broad and flat, and fastened it to the piece as thick as a baseball bat. That was the Thing's head. The Thing's head lay across the doorsill into Mr. Sizemore's classroom.

Charley stood up and looked at the Thing. He laughed as he thought how scared Mr. Sizemore would be when he walked into his room the next morning and saw the Thing looking at him over the doorsill.

The Thing ought to have a tongue, decided Charley. He took from the jar of red clay one tiny piece. He shaped it thin and short and flat, and fastened it to the Thing's head. The tongue curved upward. Charley stood up to admire it.

He heard steps coming along the hall toward Mr. Sizemore's room. He looked around. There stood Miss Amburgey in the doorway.

"Charley," she scolded, "where have you been?"

"Here," said Charley.

"All the time since the bell rang?"

"Yes'm."

"Why didn't you come with the other children?"

"I wasn't with the other children," said Charley. "They were out here and I was in there."

"But you heard the bell, didn't you?"

"Yes'm."

"Don't you know that when the bell rings it says you must come?" asked Miss Amburgey.

"Yes'm."

"Why didn't you come then?"

"I hadn't finished."

"What hadn't you finished?"

"A Thing I was making."

"Whether you've finished or not, when the bell rings you're to put everything away and come at once. You can finish the next day. Do you know the bus left fifteen minutes ago?"

Charley's face grew serious.

"But I wasn't done," he said.

"What were you doing," asked Miss Amburgey, "that you couldn't leave till tomorrow?"

"I told you, Miss Amburgey, I was making a Thing."

"What kind of thing?"

"Miss Amburgey," said Charley, "shut your eyes and I'll take your hand and lead you to see it. But you won't tell Mr. Sizemore, will you?"

"Charley," said Miss Amburgey sternly, "you know very well—"

She stopped and looked down at Charley.

"All right," she said, and she shut her eyes. Charley took her hand and led her to the door of the room where the blocks stayed.

"Open!" said Charley.

Miss Amburgey opened her eyes.

"Charley! What a snake!" she gasped. "It looks like a real one, except, of course, it is an odd color."

"You know what kind of snake it is?" asked Charley. "It's a yellowblackpink snake and it bites. I'm going to leave it here to scare Mr. Sizemore in the morning."

"Well," said Miss Amburgey, "since you've taken such pains to make the Thing, I guess you may leave it. But come along now. Since the bus has left you, I'll have to take you home myself."

Charley followed her out of the schoolhouse and climbed into her jeep beside her.

What a place school was! thought Charley. He had made the Thing to scare Mr. Sizemore and now he was going to go jeeping home along the blacktop.

As Miss Amburgey turned the key and stepped on the gas pedal, Charley braced himself and ordered, "Now, Miss Amburgey, let 'er tear!"

"You really ought to have to walk home," said Miss Amburgey.

Charley was silent.

"I told Mr. Mullins to stop and tell your mother we couldn't find you, but that, as soon as we did, I'd bring you home. If she weren't worried, I'd let you out right here and start you walking."

They drove along in silence for another minute.

"Miss Amburgey," asked Charley, "how can snakes run so fast when they don't have legs?"

"They're made that way," said Miss Amburgey.

"A rope's made that way too," said Charley, "but it can't run."

They drove another minute in silence.

"You want me to name all the snakes I know?" asked Charley.

"Let's hear them," said Miss Amburgey.

"Rattlesnake. Copperhead snake. Black snake.

Chicken snake. Blue racer snake. Garter snake. Water moccasin snake."

"There are books in the library that tell all about snakes," Miss Amburgey said. "And all kinds of snakes that you don't know about, like boa constrictors, and king cobras, and sidewinders. I suspect they even tell how a snake can run fast when it hasn't any legs."

"Sure enough, Miss Amburgey? Books tell you that?"

"They do," said Miss Amburgey. "That's what books are written for."

"Is that what books really do?" asked Charley. "Tell you about things?"

"Books tell you almost anything you will ever want to know," said Miss Amburgey. "Some things, of course, you'll have to find out for yourself."

"When do I go to the library again?" asked Charley.

"This is Wednesday," said Miss Amburgey. "You go to the library day after tomorrow. On Friday."

Miss Amburgey stopped the jeep in front of the Cornetts' mailbox. All the Cornetts were waiting anxiously.

"No need asking," said Claude as Charley climbed out. "You didn't carry the flag today, Charley."

"No," said Charley. "But I made a Thing. Boy, you ought to see it!"

from EDDIE AND THE FIRE ENGINE
Carolyn Haywood

Once children discover Eddie, they will want to read all the Eddie *books and the* Betsy *books too. No one writes about pleasant family life and the mild adventures of children 4 to 7 more happily than Carolyn Haywood.*

Eddie Goes to Dancing School

One day when Eddie came home from school his mother said, "Eddie, Mrs. Wallace was here this afternoon."

"You mean Toothless's mother?" Eddie asked.

"Eddie, that's a dreadful way to speak of Anna Patricia," said Mrs. Wilson.

"Well, it's true!" said Eddie. "She hasn't had any front teeth for such a long time that I guess she's never going to get any. And anyway, Anna Patricia is a silly name. Why don't they call her Anna or Patricia? Or just Pat? If I had a name like that I'd make everybody call me Pat."

"I guess Anna Patricia likes to be called by her full name," said Eddie's mother.

"Well, in school we all call her Toothless," said Eddie.

"Mrs. Wallace is forming a dancing class," said his mother. "She came to invite you to join."

Eddie looked at his mother with a face filled with horror. "A dancing class!" he cried. "What would I want to do that for?"

"Now, Eddie," said Mrs. Wilson, "it will be very nice for you to learn to dance. Dancing school is fun."

"Fun for the girls maybe, but not for boys. Are Rudy and the twins going?"

"It's just for the children in your room in school," said his mother.

"That's tough," said Eddie. Then his face brightened. "I know, Mama! You tell her Papa can't afford to send me to dancing school."

"But it's free, Eddie," said his mother. "Only the girls have to pay."

"That's a mean trick," said Eddie. "And I bet I'll have to dance with Toothless. And she lisps!"

"Of course you'll dance with Anna Patricia," said Mrs. Wilson. "The dancing class is going to be held at her home."

Eddie sat down and held his head. "Ugh!" he said. "When?"

"Friday afternoon, at half past four," replied Mrs. Wilson.

"Friday afternoon!" wailed Eddie. "That's when we practice for the Saturday ball game."

"Eddie," said his mother, "you wouldn't want it to be on Saturday, would you?"

"Of course not," Eddie moaned. "But why does it have to be at all? Why do I have to learn to dance? Rudy and the twins don't have to learn to dance. Why do you pick on me?"

"Eddie, you will have a very nice time," said his mother. "Don't raise such a fuss. Go and see."

"If I don't like it can I stop?" Eddie asked.

"Yes, if you don't like it you can stop," his mother replied.

"O.K.!" said Eddie. "But don't tell Rudy and the twins that I have to go to dancing school."

"O.K.!" said Mrs. Wilson.

On Friday, when Eddie came home from school, his mother said, "Eddie, put on your best suit for dancing class."

"You mean my best Sunday suit?" said Eddie.

"Yes, dear," replied Mrs. Wilson.

"Golly! This dancing school business gets worse all the time," said Eddie.

Eddie washed his face and hands and soaked his hair with water. Then he took off his blue jeans and put on his best suit. "What will I do if I meet Rudy and the twins, all dressed up in my Sunday suit on Friday?" Eddie shrieked from his bedroom.

When he came downstairs his mother handed him a package. "These are your pumps, dear," she said.

"My what, Mama?" said Eddie, screwing up his nose.

"Your pumps," replied Mother, "your dancing pumps."

"What do I do with 'em?" Eddie asked.

"You wear them on your feet," said Mrs. Wilson.

"You mean I can't dance in my shoes?" Eddie cried.

"You would step on the little girls' feet, Eddie, in those clumsy shoes," said his mother.

"Serves 'em right!" said Eddie. "I'll walk all over Toothless's feet. Just let me at 'em."

"Eddie, do stop dawdling and get off," said his mother. "Have you money for bus fare? And don't forget to ask for a transfer."

Eddie pulled some change out of his pocket and looked at it. "O.K.," he said.

Just then he heard the twins coming in the front door. Eddie leaped like a deer and was out of the back door in a flash. He did not stop running until he reached his bus stop.

When the bus arrived Eddie stepped in. He knew the bus driver. He often rode with him. His name was Mike.

"Hi!" said Mike. "You look like a movie actor.

All you need is a carnation in your buttonhole. Where you going, all dressed up?"

"Don't ask me," Eddie moaned. He flopped into the seat nearest the door.

"Come on, tell me. You'll feel better if you tell me," said Mike.

"You promise you won't tell anybody?" said Eddie.

"On my honor," said Mike.

Eddie got up and whispered in Mike's ear. "I'm going to dancing school. Isn't that horrible?"

"Oh! Cheer up!" said Mike. "I went to dancing school once. And look at me now."

"You did?" said Eddie, with a brighter face. He leaned over and whispered, "And did you have pumps?"

"Sure! Sure!" said Mike. "I was the best pumper in the crowd. You'll learn to pump. It's easy."

"No, Mike," said Eddie. "They're some kind of shoes. They're in this package."

"Oh, I thought that was your supper," said Mike. "Oh, sure! Pumps. Sure, you gotta have pumps."

"I have to change buses at Brewster Road," said Eddie.

"Righto!" said Mike. "Three more stops before we get there."

When the bus reached Brewster Road, Mike drew up to the curb. As Eddie stepped out he said, "So long, Mike."

"So long, pal!" said Mike. "I'll wait for you to cross the street."

Eddie crossed the street in front of the bus. When he reached the opposite corner, he heard Mike calling, "Hey, Eddie!"

Eddie looked back and saw a package flying toward him. It landed at his feet. "Your pumps," Mike called out, as he started the bus.

Eddie picked up the parcel and put it under his arm. He stood on the corner and waited for the other bus. Across the street there was a used car lot. It belonged to Mr. Ward, a friend of Eddie's father. Eddie looked over the cars while he waited. Suddenly, he caught sight of something bright red. Eddie's heart began to beat faster. He ran across the street and over to the lot. Sure enough! It was just what he thought. There was the fire engine he had ridden on at the Fair. A man was lying under it, working with a hammer.

Eddie stooped down and looked under. There was Mr. Ward. "Hello, Mr. Ward!" said Eddie. "I rode on this fire engine once. It was super!"

"You did, Eddie?" said Mr. Ward, pushing himself out from between the wheels. "Well, how would you like to ride on it again?"

"Now?" said Eddie, his eyes shining.

"I want to see how it runs," said Mr. Ward. "I just put in a new part."

"Swell!" said Eddie, climbing right up into the front seat. "This is great!" he added, as the fire engine started.

Then Mr. Ward looked down on the ground. "Does that bundle belong to you?" he asked.

"Oh, golly! Yes," said Eddie. "Stop."

The fire engine stopped and Eddie got down. He ran back and picked up his package. Then

he climbed up again. He put the package on the seat beside him and they started off. "I sure like this fire engine," he said.

"You going anywhere special?" Mr. Ward asked.

"Oh, not very special," Eddie replied.

"Got plenty of time?" said Mr. Ward.

"Oh sure!" said Eddie.

"Very well! She's going good. We'll take a spin around," said Mr. Ward.

Eddie held onto the seat and swung his legs. This was wonderful! "Can I pull the bell?" he asked.

"No, we can't ring the bell," said Mr. Ward. "The fire company would object. Might look like a false alarm."

Mr. Ward drove Eddie way out into the country before he said, "I guess I had better get back. Where can I drop you?"

Eddie thought of dancing school for the first time since he had been on the bus. "Oh! I have to go to Beech Tree Road," he said.

"Beech Tree Road?" said Mr. Ward. "What's going on there? By the way, you look all slicked up."

"Yeah," said Eddie. "I forgot all about it. I'm going to dancing school."

"You don't say!" said Mr. Ward. "What have you got in the package?"

Eddie looked sheepish. "Aw, pumps," he said.

"Pumps!" said Mr. Ward. "What the heck are pumps?"

"I don't know," said Eddie. "Something you wear on your feet."

"Well, suppose I take you right over to the place," said Mr. Ward.

"Oh, that would be great!" said Eddie.

Mrs. Wallace was standing at the front door when Eddie drove up in the fire engine. As he jumped down she said, "Why, Eddie! You're very late. I've been wondering why you didn't get here."

"I guess I am a little late," said Eddie. "Mr. Ward gave me a lift."

Eddie could hear the boys and girls laughing. They were all in the dining room.

"It's too bad you missed the dancing class," said Mrs. Wallace. "The children are having their ice cream now."

Eddie's face shone. "Ice cream?" he said. "Gee, that's great!"

"Hello, Eddie!" the children called out when Eddie walked into the dining room.

"Hello!" said Eddie, sitting down at the table.

Mrs. Wallace handed him a large plate of ice cream and Eddie lost no time in eating it. Just as he swallowed the last spoonful, the doorbell rang. Mrs. Wallace went to the front door and opened it. Eddie heard Mr. Ward's voice say, "Is Eddie Wilson still here?"

"Yes, he is," said Mrs. Wallace.

"Well, here are his pumps," said Mr. Ward.

The children had caught a glimpse of the fire engine through the open door. They rushed to the door to look at it. "Oh, here's the fire engine that was at the Fair!" they cried.

"I had a ride on it this afternoon," said Eddie.

"Oh, can we have a ride?" the children shouted. "Can we have a ride?"

"You have on your best clothes," said Mrs. Wallace. "You can't go riding on a fire engine in your best clothes, in your dancing clothes."

"We won't hurt them," the children cried.

"I didn't hurt mine, did I?" said Eddie.

"I'll take them all home," said Mr. Ward.

The children rushed to the fire engine, the little girls in their ruffled dresses and the boys in their Sunday suits.

"Now, everybody sit still," said Mr. Ward. "You have to keep your clothes clean."

Just as everyone was settled Eddie jumped down. "Wait a minute," he said.

He ran into the house and came back with his package. He looked up at Mr. Ward and grinned. "Forgot my pumps," he said.

Mr. Ward dropped the children off, one by one. Eddie was the last. When he drove up to the house, the twins were looking out of the window. When they saw Eddie, they rushed to the front door.

"What's the idea," cried Joe, "riding on the fire engine?"

"Where have you been?" cried Frank.

"I've been to dancing school," said Eddie.

"Dancing school!" cried the twins in chorus.

"Gee, it's swell!" said Eddie, as he waved good-by to Mr. Ward.

When dinner was almost over, the doorbell rang. Mr. Wilson went to the door and opened it and everyone around the dining-room table heard Mr. Ward's voice say, "Here are Eddie's pumps. He left them on the fire engine."

When Mr. Wilson came back to the dining room, he was carrying a package. He put it on the window sill. "Here are your pumps, Eddie," he said.

"Pumps!" cried Rudy and the twins together. "What are pumps?"

"I don't know," said Eddie. "I haven't had time to look at 'em. But dancing school was swell, Mama. Dancing school was swell!"

from ELLEN TEBBITS

Beverly Cleary

Beverly Cleary's first book, Henry Huggins, *was an instantaneous success. There are now several other books about Henry, all of them equally funny and popular. Ellen in* Ellen Tebbits *is the feminine counterpart of Henry. This book about Ellen's adventures is just as hilarious as the other books and is especially popular with girls. As American as supermarkets and completely true to child nature, Mrs. Cleary's stories are humorous commentaries on modern life.*

Ellen Rides Again

The arrival of spring meant different things to different people. To Mrs. Tebbits it meant spring cleaning. To Mrs. Allen it meant planting seeds and setting out new flowers. To Ellen and Austine spring meant something much more important. It meant no more winter underwear.

The two girls were walking home from the library one warm spring afternoon. They felt light and carefree in their summer underwear. It was a wonderful feeling. It made them want to do something exciting.

At the library Austine had been lucky enough to find two horse books. "I wish I could ride a horse sometime," she said.

"Haven't you ever ridden a horse?" asked Ellen.

"No. Have you?" Austine sounded impressed.

"Oh, yes," said Ellen casually. "Several times."

It was true. She had ridden several times. If she had ridden twice she would have said a couple of times. Three was several times, so she had told the truth.

"Where? What was it like? Tell me about it," begged Austine.

"Oh, different places." That was also true. She had ridden at the beach. Her father had rented a horse for an hour and had let Ellen ride behind

him with her arms around his waist. The horse's back had been slippery and she had bounced harder than was comfortable, but she had managed to hang on.

And she had ridden at Uncle Fred's farm. Uncle Fred had lifted her up onto the back of his old plow horse, Lady, and led her twice around the barnyard. Lady didn't bounce her at all.

And then there was that other time when her father had paid a dime so she could ride a pony around in a circle inside a fence. It hadn't been very exciting. The pony seemed tired, but Ellen had pretended it was galloping madly. Yes, it all added up to several times.

"Why haven't you told me you could ride?" Austine demanded. "What kind of saddle do you use?" Austine knew all about different kinds of saddles, because she read so many horse books.

"Oh, any kind," said Ellen, who did not know one saddle from another. "Once I rode bareback." That was true, because Lady had no saddle.

"Golly," said Austine. "Bareback!"

Ellen was beginning to feel uncomfortable. She had not meant to mislead Austine. She really did not know how it all started.

"Oh, Ellen, you have all the luck," exclaimed Austine. "Imagine being able to ride horseback. And even bareback, too."

"Oh, it's nothing," said Ellen, wishing Austine would forget the whole thing.

But the next day at school Austine did not forget about Ellen's horseback riding. She told Linda and Amelia about it. They told Barbara and George. Barbara and George told other boys and girls. Each time the story was told, it grew.

Even Otis was impressed and he was a difficult boy to impress. When the girls started home after school, he was waiting on the edge of the school grounds. He had a piece of chalk and was busy changing a sign from "Bicycle riding forbidden at all times" to "Bicycle riding bidden at all times." Otis crossed out "for" every time he had a chance, but the rain always washed away the chalk marks.

"Hello, Ellen," he said, walking along beside her in his cowboy boots. Since Christmas Otis had worn boots instead of Oxfords. He was not wearing spurs today. Miss Joyce had asked him not to wear them to school.

Ellen and Austine ignored him.

Otis kicked at the grass along the edge of the sidewalk. "Say, Ellen, is it true you ride a lot? Even bareback?"

"Of course it's true," said Austine.

"I wish people would stop talking about it," said Ellen crossly. "What's so wonderful about riding a horse, for goodness' sake?"

"Gee whiz," said Otis enviously. "Some people have all the luck."

The girls continued to ignore him. He followed them for a while, kicking at the grass, and then turned down another street.

When the girls came to Austine's house, they found Mrs. Allen on her knees beside a flat box of pansy plants. She was taking them out of the box and setting them into a border along the driveway.

"Hello there," she said. "Since tomorrow is Memorial Day and there isn't any school, how would you like to go on a picnic?"

Ellen did not say anything. She thought Mrs. Allen meant her, too, but she was not sure. She hoped so. That was the trouble with the word *you.* Sometimes it meant one person and sometimes it meant a lot of people. Maybe Mrs. Allen was talking to Austine and not to both of them.

Mrs. Allen said, "Ellen, I have already asked your mother and she says you may go."

"Thank you. I'd love to go." Maybe a picnic would make Austine forget about horses. And if they went on a picnic, Austine couldn't come to Ellen's house to play and perhaps say something about horseback riding in front of Mrs. Tebbits. Ellen was worried about what her mother would say if she found out how Ellen had exaggerated.

"Where are we going?" asked Austine.

"We're going to drive out toward Mount Hood. The rhododendrons are beginning to bloom, and I thought it would be nice to see them blooming in the woods."

The next morning at ten o'clock Ellen ran down Tillamook Street and around the corner to Austine's house. For her share of the picnic she carried eight deviled eggs carefully packed in a cardboard box. Mr. Allen was backing out the car. Mrs. Allen sat in the front seat and Austine in the back.

"Hop in," said Mr. Allen. "Bruce isn't going with us. The boy scouts are marching in a parade."

Ellen was glad she and Austine could each sit by a window. That made it easier to look for white horses and to play the alphabet game. The first one to see a white horse got to make a wish. Ellen was going to wish Austine would forget about her horseback riding.

The girls always played the alphabet game when they rode in a car. Each watched the signs on her own side of the road for the letters of the alphabet. Each letter had to be found in order or it did not count. The *k* in a Sky Chief Gasoline sign could not be used unless a *j* had already been seen. The girl who had a Burma Shave sign on her side of the road at the right time was lucky because it contained in the right order both *u* and *v,* two hard letters to find. The game went quickly at first, because there were lots of signs, but as they neared the mountains the signs became more scarce.

Ellen was looking for a Texaco filling station for an *x* when Austine shouted, "Look, a white horse! I've got dibs on it." She shut her eyes to wish.

Ellen was sorry she had not seen the horse first. She needed a wish. Finally both girls were down to *z.* By then the car was winding along the mountain roads.

"Z!" shouted Ellen. "I win. There was a sign by that bridge that said 'Zigzag River.'"

"That's all right," said Austine generously. "I'm going to get my wish."

It was a few more miles along the highway that Austine saw the horses. "Look, Daddy! Horses for rent, fifty cents an hour! Please stop," she begged.

Mr. Allen drew over to the side of the road near some horses in a makeshift corral. Austine scrambled out of the car and ran to the horses, while the others followed.

"Daddy, please let us go horseback riding. All my life I've wanted to ride a horse. Please, Daddy. You and Mother could go on and look at the rhododendrons and come back for us."

"Would it be safe for the girls to ride alone?" Mrs. Allen asked the man with the horses.

"Please, Mother," begged Austine. "Make my wish come true."

"Sure. Kids do it all the time," answered the man. "They ride up that dirt road as far as the old sawmill and turn around and come back.

The horses know the way. Takes about half an hour. Road runs right along the highway."

"They won't be thrown from the horses?" asked Mrs. Allen.

"From these horses?" said the man. "No, lady. These horses worked at a riding academy for years."

"You're sure they're gentle?"

"Yes, ma'am. Gentle as kittens."

"The girls could hang onto the saddle horns," suggested Mr. Allen.

"Oh, Daddy, you aren't supposed to hang onto the saddle horns. Only tenderfoots, I mean tenderfeet, do that. We'll be safe, because Ellen has ridden a lot and I know all about riding from books."

Ellen wished Austine would keep still. She was not at all sure she wanted to ride, especially without a grownup along.

"I suppose it would be safe to let the girls ride for half an hour," said Mrs. Allen. "We could walk along the dirt road and look at the rhododendrons while they rode. That way they would be within shouting distance."

"All right, girls, which horses do you want to ride?" asked Mr. Allen, taking a handful of change out of his pocket.

Ellen thought she had better act brave even if she didn't feel that way. "The spotted horse is nice, but I think I'd rather have the brown one over in the corner of the pen." She thought the brown horse looked gentle.

"I'll take the pinto on this side of the corral," said Austine, glancing at Ellen.

Oh dear, thought Ellen. I've said the wrong thing. I wish I'd read some horse books.

Austine watched eagerly and Ellen watched uneasily while the man saddled and bridled the two horses. "O.K., kids," he said.

Ellen walked over to the brown horse and patted him gingerly. He seemed awfully big when she stood beside him. But he looked down at her with large gentle eyes, and Ellen felt braver.

The man held out his hand, palm up.

Oh, I wonder if he wants me to give him some money, thought Ellen. It must be that, but I'm sure Austine's father paid him. Or maybe he wants to shake hands. A sort of farewell.

"Come on, girlie. Step up," said the man.

"Don't be scared. Brownie isn't going to hurt you."

My goodness, thought Ellen. I guess he expects me to step in his hand. I suppose it's all right. His hand is dirty anyway.

She put her foot into his hand and he boosted her onto the horse. The ground seemed a long way below her. And Ellen had forgotten how wide a horse was. The man shortened her stirrups and then helped Austine onto the pinto. Ellen patted Brownie on the neck. She was anxious to have him like her. If only she had a lump of sugar in her pocket.

"Look," cried Austine. "I'm really on a horse."

Ellen knew she was expected to take the lead. "Giddap," she said uncertainly. Brownie did not move.

The man gave each horse a light slap on the rump. They walked out of the corral and ambled down the dirt road as if they were used to going that way. Austine's mother and father followed on foot.

Ellen carefully held one rein in each hand. As she looked at the ground so far below, she hoped Brownie wouldn't decide to run.

"I'm going to call my horse Old Paint like in the song," said Austine, who never missed the Montana Wranglers on the radio and knew all about cowboy songs. "I wish I'd worn my cowboy neckerchief."

"Yes," said Ellen briefly. She didn't feel like making conversation.

When Austine's horse moved in front, Ellen took hold of the saddle horn. It wasn't so much that she was scared, she told herself. She just didn't want to take unnecessary chances.

"I wish we'd worn our pedal pushers," said Austine. "It's sort of hard to feel like a cowgirl in a dress."

"I wish we had, too."

Maybe this wasn't going to be so bad after all. The horses seemed to know the way, and Ellen found the rocking motion and the squeak of the saddle rather pleasant. She was even able to look around at the trees and enjoy the woodsy smell.

Then when they had gone around a bend in the road, Brownie decided it was time to go back to the corral. He turned around and started walking in the direction from which they had come.

"Hey," said Ellen anxiously. She pulled on the right rein, but Brownie kept on going. "Stop!" she ordered, more loudly this time.

"What are you going that way for?" asked Austine, turning in her saddle.

"Because the horse wants to," said Ellen crossly.

"Well, turn him around."

"I can't," said Ellen. "He won't steer."

Austine turned Old Paint and drew up beside Ellen. "Don't you know you're supposed to hold both reins in one hand?" Austine was scornful.

Ellen didn't know. "I just held them this way to try to turn him," she said. She took them in her left hand. They were so long she wound them around her hand.

Austine leaned over and took hold of Brownie's bridle with one hand. "Come on, Old Paint," she said, and turned her horse forward again. Brownie followed.

"Thanks," said Ellen. "My, you're brave."

"Oh, that's nothing," said Austine modestly. "You don't steer a horse," she added gently. "You guide him."

"Oh . . . I forgot." Ellen wondered how she would ever explain her ignorance to Austine. What would her best friend think when she found out how Ellen had misled her?

The horses plodded on down the woodsy road. Through the trees the girls could see the highway and hear cars passing. Austine's mother and father appeared around the bend, and Ellen began to feel brave again.

"Let's gallop," suggested Austine.

Ellen's legs were beginning to ache. "How do you make them gallop?"

"Dig your heels in," said Austine.

"Oh, I wouldn't want to hurt the horse," said Ellen.

"You won't hurt him, silly. Cowboys wear spurs, don't they?"

Ellen timidly prodded Brownie with her heels. Brownie ambled on.

Austine dug in her heels. Old Paint began to trot. At first Austine bounced, but soon she rode smoothly. Then her horse began to gallop.

When Old Paint galloped, Brownie began to trot. Ellen began to bounce. She hung onto the saddle horn as hard as she could. Still she bounced. Slap-slap-slap. Her bare legs began to hurt from rubbing against the leather of the saddle flap. Slap-slap-slap. Goodness, I sound awful, she thought. I hope Austine doesn't hear me slapping this way.

Austine's horse, after galloping a few yards, slowed down to a walk. "Whoa, Old Paint," cried Austine anyway, and pulled on the reins. Old Paint stopped and Austine panted a minute.

"I did it, Ellen!" she called. "It was just a few steps, but I really, truly galloped. I hung on with my knees and galloped just like in the movies."

"Wh-wh-oa-oa!" Ellen's voice was jarred out between bounces. Brownie trotted on. Slap-slap-slap.

Austine began to laugh. "I can see trees between you and the saddle every time you go up. Oh, Ellen, you look so funny!"

Slap-slap-slap. Ellen didn't think she could stand much more bouncing. It was worse than being spanked.

"Ellen Tebbits! I don't think you know a thing about horseback riding."

"Wh-wh-oa-oa!" When Brownie reached Old Paint he stopped. After Ellen got her breath, she gasped, "I do, too. It's just that the other horses I rode were tamer."

The horses walked on until the road curved down to the edge of a stream.

"Oh, look. There's a bridge," exclaimed Ellen, looking up.

"I guess the highway crosses to the other side of the stream," said Austine. "I wonder if the poor horses are thirsty."

There was no doubt about Brownie's wanting a drink. He left the road and picked his way down the rocky bank to the water.

"Poor horsie, you were thirsty," said Ellen, patting his neck.

But Brownie did not stop at the edge of the stream. He waded out into it.

"Whoa," yelled Ellen, above the rush of the water. "Austine, help!"

Brownie waded on.

"Austine! What'll I do? He's going swimming!"

"Here, Brownie! Here, Brownie!" called Austine from the bank. Her voice sounded faint across the surging water.

When Brownie had picked his way around the boulders to the middle of the stream, he stopped and looked around.

"Look, he's in over his knees!" Ellen looked down at the swirling water. "Giddap, Brownie!"

"Kick him in the ribs," yelled Austine from across the stream.

"I don't want to hurt him," called Ellen, but she did kick him gently. Brownie did not appear to notice.

"Slap him on the behind with the ends of the reins," directed Austine from the bank.

Ellen slapped. Brownie turned his head and looked at her reproachfully.

By this time some hikers had stopped on the bridge. Looking down at Ellen, they laughed and pointed. Ellen wished they would go away.

Brownie lowered his head to drink. Because Ellen had the reins wound around her hand, she could not let go. As she was pulled forward, the saddle horn poked her in the stomach.

"Oof," she said. Hanging over the horse's neck, she clung to his mane with one hand while she unwound her other hand.

Brownie looked at her with water dripping

from his chin. Ellen thought it was his chin. Maybe on a horse it was called something else.

Austine broke a branch from a huckleberry bush that grew out of an old log at the edge of the stream. She waved it toward Brownie. "Here, horsie. Nice horsie."

Brownie glanced at her with mild interest.

"Oh, go on, Brownie," said Ellen in disgust. She kicked him hard this time. Brownie looked at her sadly and swished his tail.

A couple of cars stopped on the bridge and the occupants looked down at Ellen and laughed. "Yippie!" yelled one of the hikers and everyone laughed. "Ride 'em, cowboy!"

"Do something, Austine," Ellen called across the water. "Our half hour must be nearly up."

"Maybe I could ride back and get the man who owns the horses," Austine yelled back.

"No, Austine. Don't leave me here alone," begged Ellen. "Maybe I could get off and wade. I don't think the water would come up to my shoulders."

"The current's too strong," called Austine. "And anyway, we're supposed to bring the horses back. You can't go off and leave Brownie."

Austine was right. Ellen knew that she couldn't leave Brownie. She might lose him, and the man would probably make her pay for him. At least, she thought he would. She had never heard of anyone losing a horse, so she wasn't sure. "I can't stay here forever," she called.

"Mother and Daddy should catch up with us in a minute," Austine called. "They'll know what to do."

That was just what was worrying Ellen. She didn't want the Allens to see her in such a predicament. What would they think after Austine had told them she had ridden before? Maybe they had wandered off to look at rhododendrons and were lost in the woods by now.

Still Brownie did not move. Ellen wondered what it would be like to try to sleep on a horse. Again she wished she had brought some lumps of sugar. She could have eaten them herself when she became hungry.

One of the hikers climbed down the bank to the edge of the water. "Need some help, little girl?" he called.

"Oh yes, please," answered Ellen gratefully.

Jumping from boulder to boulder, the man

drew near her, but he could not get close enough to reach Brownie's bridle. "Throw me the reins, little girl," he directed.

Ellen threw them as hard as she could. They fell into the water, but the man grabbed them as the current carried them toward him.

"Come on, old fellow," he said, pulling at the reins. Meekly Brownie began to pick his way around the boulders toward the bank.

"Oh, thank you," said Ellen, when they reached dry ground. "I guess I would have had to stay out there all day if you hadn't come for me."

"That's all right," said the man. "The trouble is, you let the horse know you were afraid of him. Let the old nag know you're boss and you won't have any trouble."

"Thank you, I'll try," said Ellen, taking a firm grip on the reins. "Good-by."

Just then Austine's mother and father appeared around the bend in the road. "Enjoying your ride, girls?" asked Mr. Allen.

"Oh, yes," said Austine. "We just stopped to give the horses a drink."

"It's time to turn back now," said Mrs. Allen.

"All right, Mother," said Austine.

The girls headed their horses toward the corral. Ellen was so embarrassed she didn't know quite what to say to Austine. What would Austine think of her after this? What would she tell the kids at school?

Finally, when Austine's mother and father were a safe distance behind, Ellen said in a low voice, "I guess I didn't know quite as much about horseback riding as I thought I did."

"Your horse was just hard to manage, that's all," said Austine generously.

"Austine?" said Ellen timidly.

"What?"

"You won't tell anybody, will you? You won't tell that Otis Spofford what happened, will you?"

Austine smiled at her. "Of course I won't tell. We're best friends, aren't we? It'll be a secret like the underwear. Giddap, Old Paint."

"Thank you, Austine," said Ellen gratefully. "You're a wonderful friend. And you know what? I'm going to look for some horse books the next time we go to the library."

The horses, knowing they were headed to-ward hay, showed more spirit. Ellen held the reins firmly. That Brownie was going to know who was boss. She began to enjoy herself. She pretended she was returning to a ranch after a hard day riding the range.

"I didn't know horses had such long hair," she remarked.

"It's their winter coat," explained Austine. "They'll shed it this summer."

Ellen laughed. "Just like winter underwear," she said.

from SKINNY

Robert Burch

Although he is a child of the Depression, Skinny's special way of looking at the world makes him one of the most delightful characters in recent children's literature. For a time it looks as if Miss Bessie will be getting married and will be able to adopt Skinny, but that was not to be. When his going to the orphanage becomes a certainty, he takes it with good grace and the reader is sure that Skinny will continue to enjoy the good things in life and to accept those which he can't change.

The Hotel

"You mean you're eleven years old and don't know how to read?" asked the man, propping one foot against the banister.

Skinny continued sweeping the hotel porch. "I'm going on twelve," he said.

"But why can't you read?"

"I just ain't never took it up," said Skinny, thinking it was an aggravation the way some folks promoted book-learning. All he had done was ask the man, one of the highway engineers staying at the hotel, if he would mind reading the weather forecast out loud. "Have a look for yourself," the man had said, offering him the newspaper.

Any other time Skinny would have taken it and pretended to read. But he was so anxious to know about the weather for tonight that he had admitted his one little failing. And the man carried on as if it were a serious matter. "Don't you go to school?" he was asking now.

"Sure," said Skinny, pushing straggly hair away from his forehead, "two or three weeks every year. But that's not long enough to get the hang of reading."

The man wanted to know why he had never stayed longer. Skinny explained. "Cotton was always ready to be picked not long after school got under way, and Pa would keep me home to help out. And by the time I'd get back to that ol' first grade, everybody would be so far ahead of me, I'd give up till the next year. But comes September, if I'm anywhere near a school, I'll try again. Miss Bessie's convinced me it's worth while."

"Didn't anybody try to make you stay before?"

"They tried. But Pa didn't believe in it either." Then he laughed. "Want to hear something? One time an ol' man from the county office came out to the farm and asked how come I didn't go to school. And Pa brought out the shotgun and asked what business it was of anybody's whether I ever went to school." Skinny laughed so much he could hardly finish the story. "That ol' man took off like he'd been sent for," he concluded. "Pa was funny. Too bad he's dead."

"What about your mother?"

"She died a long time ago," answered Skinny. "I just barely remember her." He moved a rocker and swept behind it. "And that makes me an orphan," he continued. "Did you know that? I'm supposed to go and live in an orphans' home if they find one that'll have me."

One of the other highway men had come onto the porch. He patted Skinny on the head. "Why, this hotel would close up if you went chasing off to an orphans' home. Don't you run the place?"

"No," Skinny answered, "I just help out. I'd like to stay, but Miss Bessie only took me in so I'd have a place to live till something else comes along."

Two more highway workers came out of the hotel, and one of them said, "Back to work, men!"

The one who had been there longest complained, "There ought to be a law against working in July." He folded his newspaper and tossed it into the swing.

Skinny asked, "What about the weather forecast?"

The man pointed a finger at him. "Miss Bessie's right: schooling is worth while," he said, and followed the other men from the porch.

Skinny took his broom and started inside. "I hope it don't rain," he said under his breath. "I sure hope it don't rain tonight."

In the kitchen, Peachy was grumbling. "I wishes those highway men would take to coming to lunch on time. I got enough to do without cleaning up this kitchen twice."

"Have you seen a can of patching tar?" Skinny asked.

"I got enough to do without looking for a can of tar," said Peachy. "And besides, you're supposed to be bringing me them dirty dishes."

"That's where I'm headed," said Skinny, picking up a large tray and going into the dining room. He filled the tray with plates and glasses and returned to the kitchen.

Roman, the Negro man who worked at the hotel, came in from the garden with a basket of tomatoes. Skinny asked, "Don't either one of you know where that can of tar is?"

Peachy stopped her dishwashing. "Child, why's you so worried about tar?"

"Because I can finish patching the front porch roof when I find it. Reckon you got it mixed up with a bucket of syrup and put it in the pantry?" He started into the storage room.

"Don't go messing around that pantry," said Peachy. "If I don't know the difference 'twixt a bucket of syrup and a can of tar, I got no business being head cook in this establishment."

Roman, busy spreading out the tomatoes on a shelf near the window, looked up. "I didn't realize you were the head cook, Peachy-gal," he said, winking at Skinny. "I been thinking all this time you were the *only* cook here."

Peachy said, "That makes me the head one," and went on with her work.

Skinny was always glad when Roman was around; things were apt to be livelier. And besides, Roman was his friend. Sometimes he felt closer to him than to 'most anybody alive. In a way, Miss Bessie had rescued both of them from trouble. She had bailed Roman out of the chain gang, freeing him to work for her as long as he didn't get in a scrape with the law. And Skinny had been taken in until there was space for him at the orphanage. They both had rooms off the hotel's back porch, and sometimes at night when the work was done the two of them would sit out in the yard and talk. Roman would tell of his adventures before he had gone to jail, and Skinny would tell about how things used to be when he and his Pa were sharecropping.

Peachy finished washing the dishes and began to hang up her dishrag and towels. Roman emptied the last tomato from his basket and started toward the back door. "You better go ahead and check in the pantry," he said to Skinny. "Otherwise Peachy's liable to feed us hot biscuits some morning with patching tar poured over them." He closed the screen door behind him, and Peachy muttered that she had enough to do without worrying about sassy ex-convicts.

Skinny went to the front of the hotel and climbed to the roof by way of a trellis at the end of the porch. The roll of roofing was still there from the afternoon before, but he couldn't remember where he had put that worrisome can of tar. He was scratching his head to help him think, just as the doorbell rang.

Instead of climbing down to answer it, he crossed the roof to the edge nearest the front door. Lying on his stomach, he leaned his head over to see who was there. "Howdy," he called to the man and woman who stood nearby.

The couple looked around but did not see him. They glanced at each other. "I thought somebody spoke to us," said the man.

"It was me," said Skinny, pushing his head a little farther through the wisteria vine that ran along the top of the porch. He smiled at the couple and said, "Welcome to this-here hotel. Is there something I can do for you?" Before they could answer, Skinny pointed toward the trunk of a sweet gum tree. "Say," he said, "there's that can of tar I've been looking all over for." He asked the man, "Would you mind handing it up to me?"

The man went into the yard, took the can to the top step, and held it over his head. "Thank you," said Skinny, reaching for the tar. "Now I'll come down and see what you're wanting."

He crossed the roof to the far end, climbed down the trellis, and jumped onto the porch. Instead of going across it he went into an end door and hurried to the back hall. He lifted his white jacket from the nail near the broom closet and put it on carefully, making certain the sleeves were turned back far enough for his hands to stick out. The bottom of the jacket struck him just above his knees, and his overalls were rolled up to just below them. Barefooted still, he walked to the front door.

He greeted the couple as if he were seeing them for the first time. "Howdy," he said, smiling hospitably. "Welcome to this-here hotel." Noticing the man looking at his coat, he explained, "It's my uniform. Somebody left it in one of the rooms and never did come back for it." He took a step or two across the porch and turned around, showing off the jacket from all sides.

The woman asked crossly, "May we see the manager?"

"The manager?"

"That's right."

"Oh," Skinny said, "we don't have a manager. This hotel ain't all that big."

"Somebody must run it," said the woman.

"Sure. Miss Bessie runs it. Would you care to see her?"

"Yes, please."

"She's not here," Skinny said. "But if you'll just take a seat, she'll be back before long." He motioned toward two rocking chairs for them, and he sat down in the swing. "Hot today, ain't it?" he said, when everyone was settled. The couple said nothing, and after a brief silence Skinny held out the newspaper. "Do you go in for reading?" he asked.

"We've read it," said the man.

Skinny flipped through a few of the pages, stopping from time to time as if he had come across an article of special interest. Then he put the paper down and said, "I was patching the roof when I heard the doorbell."

The man said, "You don't look big enough to be patching a roof."

Skinny stopped swinging and held his shoulders back and puffed out his chest as best he could. "I'm older than I look," he said. The couple didn't comment, and he went back to swinging, saying softly, "It's just that I'm not filled out good yet."

The woman asked, "Do you know if this Miss Bessie whatever-her-name-is will have a room to rent when she gets back?"

Skinny jumped to his feet. "Is that all you want? Why, I can rent you a room." He sat back down and asked solemnly, "Have you got two dollars and twenty-five cents?"

"Of course," said the man and reached for his wallet.

"Pay when you leave," said Skinny, leading the way into the hotel. "I just wanted to make sure you understood about that part." He explained as they followed him up the stairs that the price included supper and breakfast for both of them, and that they were in luck on account of this was chicken night. "Tuesdays are nice too," he said. "That's when we have pork chops." He pushed one door open as they went past. "This is the bathroom, but wait till nearer suppertime if you plan to bathe. There'll be hot water then."

The woman groaned. "None earlier?"

"The tank's hooked up to the cookstove," Skinny said. "But we start a fire about four-thirty." He led them into a room at the end of the hall, walked across it, and pulled up the shades to give more light. "It's pretty, ain't it?"

"Looks clean," said the woman, and the man agreed. "It's all right."

"Well," said Skinny, "have a seat"—motioning toward the chairs, while he sat down on the edge of the bed.

The couple looked at him, and the woman said, "That will be all, thank you."

"You're welcome," said Skinny, crossing his legs.

The man reached in his pocket. "I suppose you're waiting for a tip."

"No, sir," said Skinny. "We don't go in much for that. I just thought I'd catch you up on what's going on around here."

"We're not interested," the woman said. "Our car broke down and we're forced to spend the night. So if you would just—"

The man interrupted her. "Take this for your trouble," he told Skinny and held out a dime.

"I couldn't do that," said Skinny, reaching into his own pocket. "But I reckon I could accept a nickel." He took the dime that was offered him and counted out five pennies from his own change and gave them to the man.

He left then and went out to the chicken yard and gathered the eggs. That was one of his chores. Next he returned to the job of patching

the roof. As he was pouring tar along a seam of it, he came near the window of the room the couple had rented. The man was saying, "That boy was going to tell us what was going on around here." After a sigh, he added, "What could be going on in this dried-up town?"

Skinny called out cheerily, "A watermelon-cutting."

The man stepped to the window and asked, "What'd you say?"

"The Baptists are having a watermelon-cutting tonight," Skinny said. "All you can eat for fifteen cents." He took the can of patching tar and continued along the seam. "I ain't never been turned loose with all the watermelon I could eat," he called from across the roof. "Yes siree, this is going to be my big night!"

The Watermelon-cutting

Skinny took the big bell from the dining room and went upstairs. He rang it as he walked along, calling, "Suppertime! Come to supper!" Downstairs he rang it as he passed the parlor, and the guests there began to rise. He opened the screen door that led to the front porch, clanged the bell once more, and announced loudly, "SUPPER'S SERVED!"

Two of the highway engineers and Miss Clydie Essex, the town's beauty-parlor operator, were seated at the end of the porch. Miss Clydie didn't board at the hotel but ate supper there one night a week when she kept evening hours at her shop. One of the men said to Skinny, "Were you talking to us or to somebody across the street?"

The other one asked, "What'd you say, anyhow?"

"I said, 'Supper's served,'" Skinny explained. "It means supper's ready, that's all it means. I've heard tell that's the way they say it in city hotels."

The group walked across the porch. One man said, "In city hotels the dining room is open 'most all the time, and folks go in and out and order whatever they please."

Skinny sniffed. "Seems like a poor arrangement," he said, holding the door open for the trio to enter. "How do they know how many to fix for?"

Miss Clydie Essex said, "Pay him no mind, Skinny. I've been in some of those big hotels and the food's not near as good as it is here."

"Why, thank you, Miss Clydie," said Skinny. He started to bow to her as she walked inside, but one of the men gave a friendly poke at his stomach and he had to jump back.

After the blessing Roman passed hot biscuits and brought out extra platters of food, and Skinny began asking guests what they would like to drink. "Buttermilk, sweet milk, or iced tea?" When he received orders for as many glasses as he could handle, he would go to the kitchen. When he came to the couple who had arrived that day, he asked, "Buttermilk, sweet milk, or iced tea?" and the woman answered, "Coffee."

"Oh, we don't have coffee in the summertime," Skinny said. "Most folks like something cold."

"Well, I don't."

"We have coffee for breakfast," Skinny said proudly. "Every morning we have it."

The woman said, "Well, I'd like some now."

Miss Bessie, who had been chatting with the people at her table, looked across and asked, "Is something wrong?"

Skinny said, "I was just explaining that we don't have coffee at night."

Miss Bessie smiled at the woman. "That's right," she said. Then she added, "Except when we have fish. I think fish calls for coffee, no matter how hot the weather gets."

A man sitting near her said that he thought so too, and Miss Bessie turned back to her table. A discussion was soon under way about all the fish caught recently at Shallow Creek by local men.

Skinny stood very straight, holding his shoulders back so far that his white coat almost fell off. He said to the woman who was displeased about the choice of drinks, "Buttermilk, sweet milk, or iced tea?"

"Water," the woman answered, and Skinny quickly brought her a large glass of it filled with chunks of ice.

When supper was over he hurried along with his chores. "Ain't the knives and forks scrubbed yet?" he asked, agitating for Peachy to get on with the dishwashing. "How can I set the tables for tomorrow without knives and forks?" Most nights he wasn't in a rush to be finished with the after-supper chores. But most nights he wasn't going to a watermelon-cutting afterward.

Peachy sighed. "It's too hot a night to rush, child."

Roman, who was stacking away clean saucers, said, "Ain't no hotter than it was during your Revival Week." He was reminding her that the dishwashing was not likely to be as drawn-out when she was in a hurry to get away.

"One of these times you're gonna say the wrong thing," said Peachy, lowering her voice. "And I'll take this butcher knife and you'll wish you were back in the chain gang."

Roman and Skinny laughed. Miss Bessie, at the icebox rearranging shelves, asked, "What's so funny?"—but nobody could remember.

At last the dishwashing picked up to almost Revival Week speed, and the work was soon finished. Peachy took off her apron and went home; Roman went to the back porch, saying he would stay awake and listen out for guests who might need anything; and Miss Bessie and Skinny walked across town to the watermelon-cutting.

At the entrance to the long walkway in front of the Baptist church, they paid their admission fee to Mrs. Spunky Edison. She put the money into a cigar box she held in her lap. Miss Bessie looked toward the people gathered farther up the walk and in the pine grove to one side of it. "Seems like a good turnout," she said.

"All the Baptists," replied Mrs. Edison, "and half the Methodists."

Miss Trudy Boylan, who was assisting in taking up the money, added, "And we expect the other half of them when their choir practice lets out."

Skinny and Miss Bessie went on up the walk. "Reckon they planned for this big a crowd?" asked Skinny, sounding worried. "What if they run out of watermelons?"

Miss Bessie assured him there would be plenty. On a hot summer night, with nothing else going on in the community except the choir practice at the church across town, the Baptists naturally expected a lot of people.

"I hope so," Skinny said, "because my system sure is craving watermelon."

"I think it would be all right if you just said you were hungry for watermelon," suggested Miss Bessie.

"That's a good idea," Skinny agreed as they reached the edge of the crowd. "Goodness me!"

he said. "It's as light as day out here." And he stopped to admire the extension lights that were swung from branches of the trees.

Miss Bessie told him to walk around and have himself a good time; she said she believed she would go over and visit with the ladies.

Mr. Barton Grice, the superintendent of the Sunday school, saw Skinny and asked if he wouldn't like to go across the yard and join in the games.

"No, sir," said Skinny, "I don't care too much for games."

Mr. Grice smiled. "All the children are there. Wouldn't you like to play with them?"

"No, sir," said Skinny. "I don't care too much for children." He didn't explain that he had never known other children very well and had seldom played with them.

A moment later one of the teachers he knew from Sunday school came over. "Come on, Skinny," she said. "Join in the fun."

"Thank you," said Skinny, "but I think I'll just stand around."

"Of course you won't," said the woman good-naturedly. She put her hand on his neck and urged him forward to where the children were playing.

He recognized members of his Sunday-school class and soon was enjoying the game. It was "'Tis but a Simpleton," and he was first to figure it out. He guessed right off what was required in order not to be a simpleton.

Next a game of "Cross Questions and Crooked Answers" got under way. One of the teachers from the Junior Department handed out questions on slips of paper to all the boys, and the girls were given answers. The boys stood on one side and the girls on the other.

The player at the head of each line stepped to the center, and the game began. The boy's question was: "Who was the first President of the United States?" The girl read her answer, which turned out to be: "I prefer pumpkin pie." They went through it three times. The boy remained solemn, but the girl giggled, so they both had to go to the ends of their lines.

The next question read was: "Shall I sing you a song?" and the answer was: "Underneath a washpot." Everybody laughed, including the two who were having their turn. They were sent to the ends of the lines, and the game continued.

Skinny was having a good time, and it would soon be his turn in the center. Then he realized that there he was, with his slip of paper—and not able to read what was on it. He thought of asking somebody to tell him what it said. But after he had won the last game himself, and everybody had said how smart he was to figure it out, this was no time to admit a weakness—even something as unimportant as not knowing how to read.

He kept his place in line and, when his turn came, stepped to the center to meet the girl across from him. He looked down at the paper and, pretending to read, said, "Who was the *second* President of the United States?"

The girl snickered. Skinny wondered if it had been a mistake for him to make up a question. The girl then began to giggle hysterically.

The teacher said, "Why, Cloris, you laughed before you even read your answer. Scoot to the end of the line." Then she added, "But I don't think it was quite fair to Skinny. Shouldn't he have another chance?"

The players agreed, and the woman handed him a piece of paper. "Here's another question," she said.

"Thank you," said Skinny, smiling as he accepted it.

"Now just stay in the center," continued the woman. "And, let's see, it's Lora's turn from the girls' side."

At that a pretty thin-faced girl came forward, and everyone waited quietly for Skinny to read the question. Suddenly his face turned red and beads of perspiration appeared at the top of his forehead. He clenched his fists and cleared his throat but said nothing.

The teacher asked, "Is something wrong?"

"No, ma'am," said Skinny. He hesitated. "It's just that—I mean—" And then his eyes brightened and he pointed toward the walkline. "There's a boy over yonder who got here late," he said. "I don't feel right about reading so many questions when he hasn't had a one." He called out, "Howdy, over there! You can take my place if you want to."

The boy quickly accepted, asking as he took the question, "Are you tired of playing?"

"Yes," said Skinny, walking away, "I'd rather

stand around." He went near a gathering of grown people and stood by himself.

Mr. Grice walked across to him. "You look worried, young man. What's on your mind?"

Skinny didn't like to talk about not knowing how to read and write. "I was just thinking," he said. "I mean I was sort of concerned about where the watermelons are. I don't see any here."

"Oh," said Mr. Grice, "they're at the icehouse —a truckload of 'em. They'll be brought over now directly."

Before Skinny could reply, Mr. Murray Huff came to speak to them. He owned the land where Skinny and his father had been sharecroppers until the old man died. "Well, Skinny-boy!" said Mr. Huff, sort of half chuckling, "with your face washed and clean clothes on I almost didn't know you. You're looking better."

"Yes, sir," said Skinny. "I think I do very well."

The men laughed, and Mr. Huff said, "I was out at the old place today."

"Who lives there now?" Skinny asked.

"Nobody. I can't find anybody worth a cuss, so I'm gonna store corn in the house. That's about all it's fit for."

"Why, it's a fine place," said Skinny, shocked to hear such a comment about the house that had been his home until two months ago. Then he smiled, as a thought occurred to him. "I'll make a crop for you," he said.

Mr. Huff laughed, but Skinny continued, "I could do it. I ain't awful big, but I'm strong." He rushed on as if he were sure the plan would work out if he put it in words soon enough. "If you'd just get me up a mule and stake me to a few supplies, you'd be plumb surprised at what all I can do."

When he stopped, Mr. Huff laughed more and didn't even comment on the idea. Instead he asked, "Remember that little rat-terrier-looking dog you used to have?"

"Sure," said Skinny. "That was R.F.D."

This time it was Mr. Grice who laughed. "How'd a dog get a name like that?"

"On account of the mailman gave him to me. R.F.D. stands for Rural Free Delivery. Did you know that?"

"I'd heard it," said Mr. Grice, and Skinny continued, "Pa wasn't feeling well one night and ran him off. Threw rocks at that poor dog and chased him into the woods. I tried to find him but couldn't."

"Your pa was a mite cantankerous at times," said Mr. Huff, "especially when he was drunked-up."

"No, sir," said Skinny, "he wasn't cantankerous. He just didn't feel well sometimes. But I genuinely hated for him to chase off R.F.D."

"Well," said Mr. Huff, "what I set out to tell you was that the dog has turned up again. He was sitting on the back steps when I drove up today. I didn't throw a rock at him, but he lit out for the woods so fast you'd have thought I did."

"What?" Skinny said. "He's back? I always figured Pa hurt him worse than he meant to and drove him to take up with somebody else."

"He better take up with somebody else," said Mr. Huff, " 'cause there sho ain't nobody out there now."

"No, sir," agreed Skinny, "there sho ain't. And I'm obliged to you for telling me you saw him." He started away from the two men then but, instead of going toward the crowd, turned and walked in the opposite direction.

At the end of the walkway Mrs. Edison was collecting admission money from latecomers. She noticed Skinny and asked, "Aren't you staying for the cutting?"

"No, ma'am," answered Skinny, heading into the dark. "I don't crave watermelon as much as I thought I did."

from COTTON IN MY SACK

Lois Lenski

Lois Lenski has given children a wonderful picture of life in the United States and of its diverse people. Among her regional stories are Strawberry Girl *(Florida), the 1946 Newbery Medal winner,* Boom Town Boy *(Oklahoma),* Bayou Suzette *(Louisiana),* Blue Ridge Billy *(North Carolina),* Judy's Journey *(migrant workers),* Prairie School *(Dakota prairies), and* Cotton in My Sack *(Arkan-*

sas), from which this excerpt is taken. Every one of these is a lively, enjoyable story. What the people in the stories lack in money and education, they make up for in pride and family loyalties. Young readers who share the problems, hardships, and occasional fun of the children in these books will have a deeper understanding of people and of what Albert Schweitzer calls "reverence for life." Joanda in Cotton in My Sack is one of the most appealing little girls in the series. This excerpt, other chapters in the book, and many of Lois Lenski's stories will prove admirable for dramatization.

Home

"Sun up in the mornin'
Hot upon my back,
Got to go start pickin'
Cotton in my sack . . ."

Joanda's voice rang out clearly over the cotton field. She had made up the song herself and its simple tune wavered uncertainly. Then it stopped.

"Oh!" she cried. "Don't you put that worm on me."

"I will so!" answered Ricky.

She ducked to get out of her brother's way.

"There it is on you," said Ricky.

"Git it off! Git it off!" screamed Joanda, shaking herself. "If there's one thing I can't stand about cotton pickin', it's worms. Where'd it go? What kind was it—a fuzzy one, or one that's speckeldy-like with lots of feet?"

"I don't know," said Ricky. "You lost it. It's gone now."

"You better git busy and pick," said Joanda.

Five-year-old Ricky sat down in the cotton row. "I *can't* pick and I *won't* pick," he said.

"When you take a notion to pick, you *can* pick," said Joanda.

"What we got to pick for?" asked Ricky.

"This is Daddy's cotton," explained Joanda. "We're pickin' for Big Charley, Daddy's boss-man."

"Is Daddy gonna pay me?" asked Ricky.

"Daddy's s'posed to pay *me* for pickin', but sometimes he don't," said Joanda.

"When I git my money, I'm gonna git me a new coat," said Ricky.

"You'll be an old man before you git it," said Joanda.

Ricky slung his tow sack over his shoulder and began to pick. "I'm gonna git my sack full."

Joanda started a game she had made up: "Do you chew tobacco?"

"No," said Ricky, shaking his head.

"Do you dip snuff?"

"NO!" answered Ricky.

"Do you smoke a pipe?"

"NO, NO, NO!" shouted Ricky.

"Do you eat popcorn?"

"No—oh yes! YES!"

"Do you chew gum?"

"YES MA'M, when I can git it!" laughed Ricky.

The small boy held out both hands filled with cotton. "Look how much cotton I got!" He had a sweet smile. His face was plump, but it was very dirty. "For Christmas I want a tractor. I'm gonna be a farmer."

"It's a long time 'fore Christmas comes," said his sister. She stopped in her row and lifted the middle of her seven-foot pick sack to shake the cotton down to the end. Her face was pretty, but had a wistful, sad expression. Dark brown eyes looked out from under her floppy checked sun-bonnet. Tangled brown hair hung beside her cheeks. She wore baggy patched blue jeans and a faded red plaid shirt.

"After it's shook down it's not half full," she said. "If I could only git it full once, I'd be happy. Daddy says I won't be even half-a-hand till I git it full."

"Am I a full hand?" asked Ricky.

Joanda laughed. "You? Course not. Mavis is fourteen—she's a full hand, only she can't pick now 'cause she's got a boil on her neck. Steve's twelve, but he's not half-a-hand 'cause he stands and looks around so much. You have to be eleven or twelve to be a full hand."

"Oh!" said Ricky.

"Bless Pat!" cried Joanda suddenly. "That's our baby crying."

"Maybe it's Mr. Burgess's cotton pickers singin'," said Ricky. "I hear our dog barking. *Here, Trouble, here, Trouble!*" He called, but the dog did not come.

The children looked down to the far end of the rows, where three bent figures were picking.

"Listen how the baby's hollerin'," Joanda went on. "Bet she's cryin' to come over here to me. Bet she'd be quiet if she was here with me. Mama won't git her sack full if Lolly keeps on yellin'."

"I'm gonna pull my shoes off," announced Ricky.

"Mama'll whoop you. Daddy'll whoop you," said Joanda.

"No, they won't," answered Ricky.

"Big Charley, the boss-man will whoop you."

"No, he won't!"

"Miz Shands will whoop you."

"She jest better not try it," laughed Ricky. "She'd have to ketch me first."

"You'll git sandburrs in your feet," warned Joanda.

Ricky walked around in the dirt. "I ain't got no cuckleburrs," he said.

"Pick some more, sugar," said Joanda. "Pick four more pounds, then you can rest."

"I'm tard of pickin'," said Ricky. "I ain't never gonna pick no more cotton as long as I live."

Joanda laughed. The children had picked to the end of their row and now came out on the turn-row between two cotton fields. Here stood the trailer, three-quarters full of cotton. It was an old rickety cotton wagon, with high board sides. Ricky started to climb up the ladder at the back.

"Daddy don't want you to git on the cotton," warned Joanda. "Git down, Ricky." He kept on climbing.

"Cotton feels good on my bare feet, so soft and squnchy," said the boy. He jumped and came down *plop*. He rolled over and over, the fuzzy cotton sticking to his clothes. "I like to go bare-footed. It feels good on my toes!"

"We don't have to go barefooted now," said Joanda. "We got shoes to wear. We used to go barefooted when we didn't have money to buy any."

"My shoes hurt my feet," said Ricky. "One time I had some money and I spent it."

"I got $3.45 now, I had $5.00," said Joanda proudly. "I spent it for groceries. I got baloney and bread and two cans of fish and two candy bars. Steve owes me a quarter. He better pick cotton and pay it back. If he don't, I'll make

him. He says he's goin' to, but if he don't, I'll take my switch after him."

The Negro pickers in the next field were singing. Joanda stood still to listen:

"Oh, the cotton needs pickin' so bad!
Cotton needs pickin' so bad,
Cotton needs pickin' so bad,
Gonna pick all over dis field" . . .

"Mama and Daddy's pickin' fast," said Ricky. The children looked at the three figures who were coming closer and closer.

"Why is Steve so far behind the others?" asked Ricky.

"He's lookin' at every bird and wishin' it was an airplane," said Joanda. "He's lookin' at the cars along the road." She pointed to the highway off on the right.

"Where's all the cars a-goin'?" asked Ricky.

"To town," said Joanda.

"I don't want to live in town," said Ricky. "You can't make any money in town."

"I do," said Joanda. "You can spend all your money in town. Let's ask Daddy to go to the gin this evenin', when he takes the cotton in."

"Goody, goody!" cried Ricky, jumping up and down.

All the time she had been talking, the girl's nimble fingers had been putting cotton in her sack, as she started on the next row. Her bent back moved from plant to plant, and her thin arms moved in a steady rhythm.

"Why don't you rest a while?" asked Ricky.

"I don't rest, I have to keep on workin'," said Joanda. "I picked twenty-seven pounds one evenin'. Maybe if I try hard, I'll git my pick sack *full.*"

"Here, Trouble, here, Trouble!" called Ricky.

A little gray dog came tearing down the cotton middle, barking. Then Daddy came, carrying his bulging sack over his shoulder. He was a thin man with a weathered face, and he wore a slouchy felt hat. Mama came more slowly, dragging her heavy load. Joanda ran to meet her. Mama's load was not all cotton, for there on her pick sack rode the baby, Lolly, as comfortable as a bird in a nest.

"Lolly rolled off back down there," said Mama, "and how she did yell. When I looked around, there was Trouble sittin' in her place as smart as you please, expectin' a ride."

Cotton in My Sack

The song *Cotton in My Sack*. Copyright by Lois Lenski and Clyde Robert Bulla; used by permission of author and composer.

"Betcha he pushed her off," said Joanda. "Can I take her, Mama?"

"Land sakes, yes, git her off," said Mama. "My back's nigh broke. She's as heavy as a ton o' bricks."

"Betcha she was hollerin' for me," said the girl. "Betcha she missed me all right."

Mama had so many clothes on, it was hard to tell whether she was a large or small woman. She wore pants to cover her legs, her cotton dress came to her knees, and over it she wore one of Daddy's old shirts to cover her arms. Brown eyes peered out from under her large slat bonnet. Hot, tired and dirty, she slipped down on her cotton sack to rest.

Joanda took Lolly on her lap, her thin arms squeezed tightly around the heavy two-year-old. The baby was plump and had curly red hair. She was dressed in a khaki coverall suit with red buttons down the front. Joanda looked down at her, adoration in her eyes.

"Lolly pick cotton? Lolly like to pick cotton?" she asked.

Lolly reached over and pulled off a fluffy boll. She began to make a humming sound.

"You singin', Lolly? You singin' *Cotton in My Sack?*" Joanda turned to Mama. "Lolly makes out like she's singin', Mama."

"Only time that young un's quiet is when she's eatin' or sleepin'," said Mama. "She's the noisiest little somebody."

Joanda gave the baby a tight hug.

Daddy began weighing. He tied the two ends of his long pick sack together and hooked them over the scales. "Fifty-two pounds," he said. "Git off that sack, you two."

Mama and Joanda stood up and watched as he weighed the others. Mama had forty-four pounds, Joanda eighteen and Ricky seven. Daddy marked all the weights down in a little green record book. Steve came up, and he had thirty pounds. Daddy shook his head. "We'd a had more if Mavis coulda picked today. Cotton's light. It don't weigh much when it's plumb dry."

Each sack, after being weighed, was thrown up on top of the load. Mama took the baby and Joanda climbed up to help. Ricky and Joanda and Steve and Daddy jumped up and down, emptying the sacks and tramping the cotton. Trouble jumped and bounced and barked.

Mama looked down at Lolly and said, "They're havin' a time, ain't they?" Lolly clapped her hands and laughed.

"Can we go to the gin?" "Oh, Daddy, can we?" "Mama, can we ride to the gin?" begged the children.

Mama looked at Daddy who nodded his head.

"I reckon so," answered Mama. "Come, Trouble. We'll go see if Mavis has got supper cooked." She started across the field, baby in arms and dog at her heels.

Daddy's truck, already full of cotton, had been left parked in the turn-row. He backed it up, hitched the trailer on, and drove out of the cotton field. Joanda threw off her sunbonnet to cool her face in the breeze. The children sat down on the cotton. Their bright faces and figures, seated on the white cotton, made a colorful pattern against the blue of the sky. A radiant sunset threw out flames of red and gold, casting changing shadows across the level Arkansas fields. The truck bumped along the dirt road until it came to the crossroads center, where beside a garage and a country store, stood the White Top cotton gin.

Daddy drove up under the shed until the trailer was on the scales.

A man hurried out. "Hi there, Dave Hutley!"

The children hopped down and the man weighed the cotton. He went in the building to mark down the weight, came out and hooked a tag on the trailer. Then Daddy backed up and he weighed the cotton in the truck.

"O.K., Hutley," the man called out.

Daddy drove the trailer under a large round pipe which came down from the main part of the gin. The man jumped on the load and began to move the pipe about. A loud noise was heard as the motor was turned on and the fan began to operate. The suction pulled the cotton up into the pipe.

"That's the suck!" Joanda explained to Ricky. "See how it sucks up all the cotton?" She turned to Steve. "What do they do with the cotton after they git it in the gin?"

"Don't *you* know?" answered Steve. "They've got big machinery in there. It separates the seeds from the cotton and blows the hulls out in a big pile at the back. The seeds go out in another place. And the cotton goes round and round till it gits clean of leaves and trash, then it's pressed in a bale."

"They put a tow sack around it and tie it with wires," said Joanda. "I know that much."

"Big Charley, our boss-man, took me in and showed me all over one time," said Steve.

"Oh look, what's that up there in our cotton?" cried Joanda. "It's something blue . . . it's . . . whish! There, it's gone. *It was my sunbonnet!*"

"It went so quick!" cried Ricky, laughing. "I saw it go."

"You left it on the cotton," said Steve. "Wasn't it funny to see it go up?"

Joanda didn't know whether to laugh or cry. She started for the door of the gin.

"Where you a-goin'?" called Steve. "Kids are not allowed in there."

"Gonna git my sunbonnet," said Joanda, "before anything happens to it."

Daddy came up and the children explained.

"You're too late, sugar," said Daddy. "It's all chawed up to bits by this time."

"Chawed up?" Joanda blinked. She was used to sudden losses and things she could not help.

After the cotton was unloaded, the man said, "Goin' home now? You live in that shotgun house out on the by-o road, don't you?"

The children climbed into the cab of the truck with Daddy. As they rode along the dusty dirt road, Ricky asked, "Daddy, what's a shotgun house?"

Daddy laughed. "Where'd you hear that, son?"

"The man at the gin said we lived in one," answered Ricky.

"That's right," said Daddy. Now they were close enough to see the house, which was painted red. "It has three rooms in a row. I can take my shotgun and shoot through the front door and the bullet will go out the back door. It will go plumb through all four doors in a straight line."

The children laughed.

"But you won't do it, will you, Daddy?" asked Ricky.

"I got better use for my gun than any sech fool doin's," said Daddy. "Might better go squirrel huntin' over in them woods along the Mississippi River, eh, boys?"

"You bet!" agreed Steve.

The small yard around the house was bare of grass and untidy with trash. Near the back door was a pile of coal and beyond were several rickety sheds. Cotton grew close on all sides. There was just room for Daddy to park the truck and trailer close to the front porch.

The children ran around and went in at the back door. Mama was bent over the stove, putting coal in. Hot bacon fat sizzled angrily and sent up an appetizing odor. A few dishes were set on the oilcloth table.

"I lost my sunbonnet, Mama," said Joanda. "I left it on top of the cotton. It went up in the suck and got chawed to bits."

"Why didn't you keep it on your head where it belongs?" said Mama. "You'll have to find another old one to wear. Mavis didn't even git the fire started. She's still in bed in there. And Lolly's been cryin' so . . . Take her, Nannie."

Joanda picked up the baby and went through to the front part of the house. Mavis lay on one of the two double beds that nearly filled the middle room. Joanda was hot and tired after her all-day picking. A gentle breeze came in at the open front door. Joanda sat on the floor and played with the baby. Then Lolly crawled off to explore. Joanda stretched out full length.

Her tired back felt better when she lay flat on the floor. She rested, not moving, her head placed near the wall. Then she looked up. There on the wall old newspapers were pasted, in place of plaster. They were stained and dirty, but she could still read the words and study the pictures and advertisements. The papers were pasted on upside-down. She could read them better lying on the floor.

Joanda loved to read. There were no books or magazines in the house, only the newspapers on the wall. The words—strange words she did not know the meaning of—had a fascination for her. She used to ask Daddy to explain what they meant. But he couldn't—he only went to the third grade, he said. Joanda could pronounce them, if she took one syllable at a time and tried to say them slowly.

" 'Perm—a—nent, permanent—lasts forever.' They do something to the hair, I reckon. $5.00 —that's too much," Joanda said to herself. "But it sure does look purty." She must save up all the hard words she did not know and ask the teacher when she went back to school.

"Supper's ready!" called Mama from the kitchen.

Mama knew how to cook supper, but she did not know the magic of words.

from CHI-WEÉ AND LOKI

Grace Moon

Mr. and Mrs. Moon spent many years in the Indian country of our Southwest. Mrs. Moon's stories, which her husband illustrated, are exciting and also authentic.

Chi-Weé Runs a Race

Here is a tale of the desert wide,
A tale of the Mesa high,
With sage and sand on every side,
And the blue of a cloudless sky.

Here is a tale of a little maid,
And a boy of a desert band;
Of the things they did and the games
    they played,
In far-off Indianland!

Chi-weé wriggled! Chi-weé squirmed! Out there in the sunlight the call of the little hoot-owl had sounded three times. In the broad day when there were no hoot-owls. That meant that Loki was waiting for her, outside in the dancing sunlight where he could hear all the sounds of the desert and see the thousand play places that called louder than voices. And here, in the dark house, she must sit and listen to the words of old Mah-pee-ti while he talked and talked endlessly to her mother.

Her mother had told her she must sit quietly, and the *outside* of her was as quiet as possible, but no little girl could be quiet *inside* while old Mah-pee-ti talked, and the hoot-owl called, and on the very end of her tongue was a secret so big she had to close her lips *tight* to keep from shouting it out loud to the whole world.

How could big people sit so quietly, and talk and talk when there were such wonderful things to do, and all outdoors called with tongues that would not be still?

Chi-weé belonged to the outdoors. She was a little Pueblo Indian girl and lived in a town built like an eagle's nest high on the top of a mesa. For all the eight years of her life she had lived in this little town overlooking the desert— this queer little town built stone, that had houses whose flat roofs were the front-door yards of other houses built above them and whose crooked little streets led nowhere in particular except that sometimes they ran to the edge of the mesa so that they too might look out over the desert.

The houses had ladders for stairways and often no doorways at all in the first story. That was because long, long ago when many other tribes were at war with them, each house was really a fort, and to keep the enemies from surprising them at night they would pull up their ladders and then go to sleep in peace knowing that no one could get into the house. But no one came to fight now, as their enemies were not so brave as they used to be and would only steal in secret. There were many children in the little town, and dogs and wild turkeys playing all together in the streets, and women sitting on the roof-tops painting jars and bowls of pottery and stringing long strands of red chili peppers to dry in the sun. They had always many smiles and nods for Chi-weé, who, with her shy little ways, was well loved in the town. Chi-weé was small for her age, with a great mop of black hair and a serious manner, but she was not serious *inside,* and those who knew her well could see in her black eyes a little fairy of mischief ever dancing, and in her heart she said there were wings— wings like those of the little bird for which she was named.

It did not seem that old Mah-pee-ti *ever* would stop—but *now*—he was slowly rising—and at a little nod from her mother Chi-weé was through the door and out to the head of the mesa trail like a tumbleweed blown by a strong wind.

There was Loki waiting as she knew he would be waiting, at the top of the trail that led down the mesa side to the spring below—Loki, who kept sheep in the desert and was Navajo, but who was her very best friend. Better than all else she liked to play with him in the desert, to see the strange places he would find and hear the wonderful tales he would tell. Loki was not very much older than Chi-weé, but he liked to have her *think* that he was very old and wise. Oh, yes—better than with the little chubby baby brother who gurgled, and better than with Ba-ba, her little goat, Chi-weé liked to play with Loki. And now, when she saw him, she called aloud before she came very near.

"Three times must you guess the great surprise secret I have to tell!" she cried, and she jumped up and down in her excitement. "Three times, like *this*—" and she held up three fingers, wiggling them in front of Loki—"and *never* will you guess it!"

"But, how can I guess," he said, with a little pretend-frown. "How can I guess when I do not know what you speak about?"

"W-e-e-ll," said Chi-weé slowly, "I will tell this much—it is about the Trader—a *little* of it is about him. Did you know," she asked excitedly then, "that he had brought a lady wife to the Cañon—a lady with a white face—and she wears shiny clothes?"

"Yes, I know," said Loki. "One time I saw her."

"She knows magic," said Chi-weé with much impressiveness. "*Great* magic she knows—I have seen how she knows it."

"What kind of magic?" asked Loki, and he tried not to appear too interested.

"Listen, and I will tell you," said Chi-weé, and she felt very important, to know more than Loki. Usually *he* was the one who knew everything. "One day—it was yesterday, I think—I found a little flower in the desert. It was one I have not seen before—and, as it was the day when we rode to the trading store, I took the little flower with me and gave it to the white lady. She has a smile that is nice, and she said, 'Oh, but that is a pretty flower, it is one I have wanted to see.' 'Did someone tell you about this flower?' I said, and she said, 'No, I saw it in a book.' Now, that is great magic, to see a flower in a book."

"Pooh!" laughed Loki. "That is nothing—in school places they teach about *everything, all* from books."

"I know about school places," said Chi-weé eagerly. "Once, the mission lady asked me to come in and sit down. It is a very, very bad place."

"Why is it a bad place? I think it is good to know about things," said Loki.

"Oh, but it is bad to sit very still all day in a house, and if you say one *word* the lady says, 'S-S-S-SH!' and waggles her finger at you, and if you move your foot she goes, 'Bang—Bang!' with a little stick on a table, and when the very, very little ones come in with no clothes on she says, 'Shame—shame! Run home to your mama and get a dress!' No, that school place is a bad place. I do not have to look in a book or ask a teacher lady to know things. If I want to know about a little flower I run out and find it; *then* I know —and how can a book or a teacher lady show to me the sunshine and the little dawn wind and the song of the night hawk? But the magic of the white lady of the trader was different from the books in the school, for she said it had a long, long name, that little flower, and she told me what it was—and she told me——"

"But what is that great surprise?" interrupted Loki. "Listen, I will guess one time—that you go to some place soon?"

"No—no!" cried Chi-weé, all excitement again. "It is a *big* surprise, and maybe a part is for you."

"Then it is seed cakes your mother has made."

"Oh, no!" cried Chi-weé, dancing around him, "and two times you have guessed. Look! Two fingers are gone. Now, one more time——"

Loki grinned. "It is that you can come down in the desert and play with me. Is that the great secret—is it, mesa girl?"

Chi-weé laughed in answer to his grin and made a little face at him. "*That* would be no great secret—many times I come down to the desert to play with you. This is a very different thing. Listen——" and she waited just a little to see if she could make Loki eager to listen, but he made a great show of indifference, and when she waited, he looked across the desert as if he saw something there.

"Well," continued Chi-weé, after a very little, for she was too excited to wait long herself, "listen, Loki—we are to have races and games and prizes"—she was dancing again, up and down—"a whole day—and dances and good things, *many* good things to eat—and——"

Loki too, was excited now, and his eyes sparkled.

"Where will it be—and who will race—and when is this to be?"

Chi-weé laughed joyously.

"I *told* you how it was a great secret. It is that the Trader is very happy to bring the white lady to the Cañon, and in three days from now everyone is to come to the ranch where he lives, and it will be a great day—and *you* will come, Loki— and will play in the games?" she questioned eagerly.

"I will put the sheep in corral that day and I will come," answered Loki joyously, and it was hard to keep his feet from dancing a little jig as the feet of Chi-weé were dancing, but it would not do for him to jump up and down like a little girl.

Those were long days, those three days in between, but at last came the big one. Bright and clear it dawned, and from every direction came people riding to the dance.

"It is like the 'Chicken-pull'!" shouted Loki, when he saw Chi-weé coming down from the mesa; Chi-weé all dressed in her very best, with a green waist and long, brown skirt, and a woven red belt with bobby tassels hanging down. She wore white boots too, and silver bracelets, and

a string of silver beads at her throat, and she was very conscious of all this splendor.

"It is like the time at Ganado," called Loki. "*Now* you will see how that was like. I could not tell you much—it is a *see* thing, not a *tell* thing. But now you will know."

"Yes, I will know," shouted Chi-weé in answer, though she was so near she did not need to shout. "And see how I have wings in my feet," and she jumped high with no effort at all. "To-day I could run faster than the wind—to-day the little hares in the desert could not run so fast as I can run. I will be the one that will win in those races—you shall see!"

"If you will talk so much, Chi-weé," called her mother, laughing, "you will have no breath to win races."

But Chi-weé and Loki gave little heed to words. They climbed into the back of the wagon, for Loki was to ride with them this day, and Loki, too, was dressed as Chi-weé had never seen him; with a plum-colored velvet waist with silver buttons and soft buckskin pants, and a

woven red belt around his waist and a red band about his black hair, and in his ears bits of turquoise as blue as the deepest blue of the sky. Chi-weé's father drove the wagon and the mother sat beside him holding the fat baby brother, and in the back, on a pile of blankets sat Loki and Chi-weé, and they all felt that they looked very fine in their best bright clothes.

After this they spoke but little, for the eyes of each were big with thoughts of what was to come this day.

Over the glowing desert they drove, down sandy washes and up again—the steep other side —over rocky stretches and past rocks and buttes of the strangest shape and color. Past clumps of pinyon trees, mesquite and cactus, and always, everywhere, were tumbleweed and sagebrush and the little scurrying animals of the wild places. Other wagons, many of them, were driving in the same direction, and people on horses and burros, and many walking. It was the sort of excitement that Chi-weé and Loki loved, and their hearts sang within them.

Finally, they came to the place. It was at the mouth of a broad cañon, and in this sheltered place were the ranch and the store of the Trader.

Now, it was filled with many people and the noise and wagons and confusion made it seem almost like a town, but a town on a holiday, and there was an air of happy excitement over everything.

After a little while, the Trader came out of his store and he told them all that this was a very happy time for him, and that he wanted everybody else to be happy, and so he started the games and said there would be many fine prizes, and especially he said there would be a prize of a big piece of beautiful cloth stuff for the little girl who won in the race. Chi-weé's eyes sparkled at that—and then he said there would be a great feast and everyone was to eat more than they had ever eaten before. The men laughed then, but Chi-weé did not laugh, for it was a serious matter. If she obeyed the Trader she was not just certain what would happen, for there had been times—at other feasts, when good things had tempted very, very strongly—that she had eaten until she had been very sure that she had heard the sewed places of her little dress stretching, and if she ate *more* than that—she

wondered if she had better *see* what would happen—and her eyes grew thoughtful for a moment—and then—!

"Look—look!" cried someone. "There go the pony races!" and she ran to where the crowd was thickest, to see. Young men and boys were mounted on ponies and were to race down a place cleared for them. Buried in the sand near one end of the cleared place was a bag with money in it, and just a piece of the neck of the bag stuck out of the sand so the men could reach down and grab for it as they rode past. It was a very exciting race, and many times they grabbed for the bag before one man got it. There were many games that followed the race, some played with balls and some with arrows, and there were other races and tests of strength, and so many things that Chi-weé grew dizzy with trying to see them all. Loki won a game with arrows, and he came running to show how they had given him a beautiful belt with silver buttons on it. And then, at last, came the race for little girls.

When they stood in line for the race, Chi-weé was so excited that at first she could hardly think; and then, very suddenly, she grew quiet and looked around her at the other little girls. Two or three she knew and the others she did not know. They were all as eager and excited as herself and she knew they thought longingly of that beautiful piece of cloth stuff that would make such a lovely warm dress for a little girl. One little girl looked as if the dress she had on could not last much longer than this day. It was very thin and worn and Chi-weé saw that the little girl was thin too. Two red spots were burning in her cheeks and she looked at Chi-weé with eyes that were very bright.

"If I win this race," she almost whispered to Chi-weé, "my mother will be very glad, and I will be glad. I can run fast—I—I think that I will win."

Chi-weé did not answer, for she thought how fast she too could run. And then came the word to be ready, and then—BANG!—they were off!

At first, they ran all together. But very soon first one and then another dropped behind, and then Chi-weé saw that the little thin girl had told true, for just they two together led all the rest and quickly got a great way ahead. They were running very fast now, but Chi-weé could breathe

TIME FOR STORIES **92** LIFE IN THE UNITED STATES

easily, and she heard the breath of the other girl coming quickly in little short sounds.

"I can win," thought Chi-weé, with fast-beating heart. "Something has said that I could win and it told true. That is very beautiful cloth stuff they will give for a prize—and, look—there is the line that makes the race to end, and I am a great way ahead."

It was true—the other little girl had run slower and slower as they came near to the winning place—and then—such a strange thing happened! As she came almost to the line, Chi-weé dug her little toe into the earth and dropped down in a little bunch on the ground.

"Oh!" cried the other girl, panting as she came close, and she would have stopped, but then *another* strange thing happened, for Chi-weé, without speaking, reached up and gave her a push that sent her stumbling across the winning line, and then she got up and walked slowly across the line herself.

"I stumbled my foot on a little stone," said Chi-weé then to the other girl. "I am glad that you won the race. You run very fast."

At first the thin little girl did not know what to do, but the others crowded around her and told her that she had won the race.

"Often people fall when they race," they said, "and that makes them to lose. Look how you have won this beautiful cloth stuff."

"And for *you*," said the Trader, then turning to Chi-weé with a twinkle in his eye that spoke of understanding, "for you there is *this*," and he shook out of a little bundle a beautiful shawl, the most beautiful shawl Chi-weé had ever seen, with flowers along the border and a fringe as soft as baby hair. Her eyes flew wide and her little mouth dropped open as she saw it, but longingly her arms reached wide to receive it.

"I—I—do not understand," she said tremblingly. "I did not win a prize."

"You did not *think* you won a prize," said the Trader smilingly, "but for *this* race there are *two* prizes—and this one is for you," and he placed the shawl in her arms.

That night, when they were back in the home place, after a long, long happy day, and Chi-weé was tucked safely in her blankety bed, she held her shawl close to her cheek and remembered the smile of the thin little girl. "How nice to win *two* prizes," she whispered into the soft folds, and settled down to sleep with a great content.

from ROOSEVELT GRADY

Louisa R. Shotwell

There are two things in life Roosevelt Grady wants: to find a place to "stay put," and to learn what happens to the leftover number when "putting into" doesn't come out evenly. Neither dream seems so much to ask from life, unless you are a child in a migrant worker's family and have to follow the crops: beans today, tomatoes tomorrow, going wherever the season of picking offers employment. It is a tiring life, and Roosevelt's need to stay in one place, to belong, is told with heart-warming empathy that never degenerates into sentimentality.

Putting Into

Roosevelt bunched his sweater underneath him to soften the jouncing floor of the moving truck. He leaned his head back against his mother's arm. If the air got any chillier, he'd have to take his sweater out from under him and put it on to keep warm, but it wasn't quite that cold. Not yet.

Along with three other families, the Gradys rode in the back of the truck. All but Papa, who sat up front to spell Cap Jackson. Cap was the regular driver and he was the crew leader, too. He owned the truck and in it he carried the people to places where crops were ready for picking.

"We're heading for beans and cucumbers," Cap Jackson said.

Roosevelt's mother sat straight up on the flat side of the family suitcase. It was made of metal and it was slippery, so she had her feet planted wide apart and flat on the floor to brace herself. On her lap she held Princess Anne, sleeping.

Between Mamma's feet lay Sister. She was seven years old and dainty, with dimples. Her smile, Papa always said, could charm a snake out of a tree.

"Honest, could it?" Roosevelt asked him once.

"Well, I tell you, Roosevelt," Papa said, "the first time we find a snake in a tree, we'll get Sister to smile at him and we'll see what happens." So far they hadn't found a tree with a snake in it.

On the other side of Mamma slumped Matthew, who was only five and chubby. Matthew had a lame foot, but that didn't keep him from enjoying life. He was great on making jokes, and he didn't miss a thing.

The truck had a canvas roof. The roof sloped up on each side to a peak like the top of a barn, and it kept you from seeing the sky. Anyway, it was dark outside. It was the middle of the night, but the truck kept right on going.

Between sleeping and waking, Roosevelt thought about putting into. He thought about that special thing he wanted to know. The question kept running around his head the way a mosquito teases you in the dark.

This was his question: When you put something into something else and it doesn't come out even, what do you do with what's left over?

What happened yesterday was exactly what had happened at the school where he'd first heard about putting into. The teacher came to where it seemed she must explain it the very next day. And then what? That time it wasn't beans that ran out. It was celery, but it didn't matter what the crop was. If it ran out, it ran out, and that was the end. The whole family packed up and piled into Cap Jackson's sputtery old truck and away they went to find a place where onions or tomatoes or some old thing was coming along ready to harvest. And same as yesterday, Roosevelt never got back to school to hear what the teacher had to say.

Some places there wouldn't be any school at all. Or else there'd be a school and the bean-picker boys and girls didn't get to go to it. The school would be for residents, and bean-picker families weren't residents. They didn't belong.

Once there was a school and it was closed when they got there. It was closed because the crop was ripe. A crop vacation, folks called this, and everybody picked, young ones and grown-ups and old people. Everybody except, of course, Princess Anne. Over in Louisiana she sat by herself in a fruit crate at the end of the strawberry rows and sucked her thumb, cute as a bug.

Roosevelt rubbed his eyes, leaned his head against Mamma's knee, and tried hard to go to sleep. He'd almost made it when buzz went that old mosquito again, nagging at him about putting into. Like 3 into 17. You can't say 17's got six 3's in it, because six 3's need 18. So the answer has to be five 3's. But that's only 15. So what do you do with the poor little 2 that gets left over?

Roosevelt liked to have things come out even. He liked to have a place to put every piece of whatever it was he had. He liked to pick all the ripe beans quick and clean off one plant and then move along that row to the next. He liked to fill his basket just full enough so it was even across the top. If one bean stuck up in the air, he'd pull it out and make a little hole among the other beans and poke it carefully down in. He liked to make a pan of corn bread and cut it into exactly enough squares to make one piece for everybody in the family. Except Princess Anne. Her teeth hadn't come through far enough yet to chew anything crusty. Sometimes Mamma would break off a little of her piece of corn bread and dunk it in her coffee to soften it. Then she gave that to Princess Anne.

Bouncing along through the dark, Roosevelt got to thinking some more about numbers. Take nine. Right now nine was an important number in his life. He was nine years old. His birthday was the ninth day of September, and if you began to count the months with January one and February two and so on, what did September turn out to be? Why, nine!

To be perfectly sure, he whispered the months over to himself, counting on his fingers. Sure enough, nine came out to be September.

How many different schools had he been to in his lifetime? He counted to himself. Six, seven, eight . . . and nine. There was that nine again. Different schools, that is. If you counted twice the schools he'd been to and then gone back to, they made thirteen, but Roosevelt didn't want to count that way. He didn't like the number thirteen. Papa said thirteen was unlucky. Mamma said she didn't believe in lucky or unlucky, but there was no use tempting fate.

"What's tempting fate?" Roosevelt asked her.

"It means trying to outsmart the devil," Mamma said. "And he's really smart. You're best off to stay clean away from thirteen this and thirteen that. You can just as easy make it twelve or fourteen and not take any chances."

One day a while back, Roosevelt had asked Papa about putting into and the poor little left-over number. He had laughed and said: "Just throw it away."

But Roosevelt couldn't feel right doing that. What would become of it?

Another day he had asked Mamma. She said: "Save it till you need it."

"What do you do with it," Roosevelt wanted to know, "while you're waiting to need it?"

Mamma didn't laugh nearly so often as Papa did, but she laughed that time.

"Put it in your pocket," she said, "and go fetch me a bucket of water."

The Secret

The truck jerked to a stop, and the motor coughed and went still. From the driver's seat, Cap Jackson called out:

"Anybody want a drink? There's a spring here at the edge of the woods."

The people stirred. Cap came around and let down the tailgate and put up the ladder. Roosevelt experimented with a swallow and his mouth felt dry, so he clambered down. The stars were bright. The air was cold and it had a piney smell, clean and fresh. He waited his turn in line in front of a pipe with water bubbling out of it. In the starlight the pipe looked rusty. The men had to stoop over to reach it, but it was exactly the right height for Roosevelt. He didn't have to bend down or stand on his toes, either one.

When his turn came, the water was cool and he took a big gulp, but it didn't taste good. Not good at all. It tasted like a bad egg.

"Sulphur water," said one of the men.

Roosevelt spit his mouthful out on the ground. He shivered. When he climbed back into the truck, he put his sweater on and sat right flat down on the boards.

As the motor wheezed and the truck began to move, Sister and Matthew both woke up and wiggled. Roosevelt was glad they'd waked up. He felt like having company.

"Talk to us, Mamma," said Matthew. "Tell us a story."

"Hush," said Mamma. "Other folks want to go to sleep."

"Talk to us soft-like," begged Matthew. "Whisper to us about . . . you know . . ."

Roosevelt knew what was coming. Matthew always asked for the same story. It was Roosevelt's favorite story, too.

". . . about the olden days. And the dog run."

"All right," said Mamma. "Lean close and I'll tell it to you short. Then you go to sleep."

And she did. She didn't make it too short either. About the little house in the cotton field in Georgia, how it sat up on stilts and was a house in two parts like, with this comfortable sitting-out place in between and a roof over the whole thing. The sitting-out place was the dog run, and it had a rocking chair like President Kennedy's.

The Gradys had a dog there too, a hound, sort of. Named Nellie. She had short tan hair and floppy ears and brown eyes. Her eyes were wistful.

"What's wistful?" Matthew demanded.

"Wistful is you want something and you don't know what," said Mamma.

They had chickens, too, and two big pigs and a litter of little pigs. And a goat. And growing out back they had sweet potatoes and collards and mustard greens.

Roosevelt moved his tongue around to see if he could make himself remember the taste of a sweet potato. He couldn't.

Now it was Sister's turn. Was she still awake? She was.

"Take us back to your wedding day, Mamma," she said. "Tell us about your white dress and what Papa said."

"There was this magnolia tree," said Mamma, "right ouside the Pink Lily Baptist Church. And it was brim full of waxy white blossoms. I wore a shiny white dress with a green sash and long streamers and I had a veil, all cloudy, made of net. Your papa told me I was almost the prettiest thing in the whole county.

"'*Almost* the prettiest? Why *almost?*' I said, kind of sniffy and jealous."

"Jealous," said Sister. "Tell us what's jealous."

"Jealous is you're scared somebody you like likes somebody else better than you," Mamma explained. "Now don't interrupt me any more. And your papa said, 'You or that magnolia tree.

I can't make up my mind which one is prettier. But I'll pick you.' So off we went to live in the little house in the cotton field."

"Now tell us why we left the little house in the cotton field," insisted Matthew. "Why did we go away and leave our dog Nellie and the little pigs and the dog run all behind us?"

"Why we left? Why, honey, the machines came along. The tractors got bigger and bigger and they did more and more of the work the people used to do. Mr. Wilson let us stay on a while and your papa got some work in the sawmill six miles off. But pretty soon Mr. Wilson plain had to tear down our house to plant more cotton. So that's when we went on the season, looking for work wherever we could find it."

She stopped a minute. When she went on, her voice sounded different. Angry, almost.

"Some folks say now they've even got a machine that knows how to pick cotton. A big red monster. With fingers."

Sister sighed, a long whishy sigh that meant she was on her way to sleep again. Roosevelt waited. When Matthew breathed so even it seemed certain he must be asleep too, Roosevelt sat up close to Mamma's ear.

"Now let's you and me talk about our secret," he whispered.

"Hush," said Mamma.

"Please," said Roosevelt.

Mamma didn't say anything right away, and Roosevelt sat stiff and still. Then she spoke, not whispering but still so low he could hardly hear. She said just what he knew she'd say.

"Someday we'll find ourselves a house in a place where there's work for your papa every one of all twelve months in the year. Maybe the house won't have a dog run, but it'll sure enough be a home. And you and Sister and Matthew will go to school, the same school right along, day in, day out, fall and winter and right on to the end of spring."

"And Princess Anne?" asked Roosevelt.

"Princess Anne, too, soon as she's big enough. You'll all go right along with the children that belong. Because we'll be in a place where we'll all belong. We'll be right out of this bean-picking rat race and we'll stay put."

"How will we find this place?" asked Roosevelt anxiously, even though he'd asked this before and knew what the answer would be.

"I don't know how," said Mamma, "but we'll know it when we see it. There'll be something about it so we'll know it. And don't you forget. This is our secret."

"It's our secret," said Roosevelt, and he dropped his head in the crook of Mamma's elbow and fell sound asleep.

HATSUNO'S GREAT-GRANDMOTHER

Florence Crannell Means

Told Under the Stars and Stripes, *from which this story is taken, is one of several collections compiled by the Association for Childhood Education International. The stories in* Told Under the Stars and Stripes *reflect the many racial and ethnic groups which live together under the flag of the United States.*

Hatsuno Noda walked alone in the crowd of girls and boys pouring out of school. She held her head so straight that her chubby black braids spatted her trim shoulders, and her step was so brisk that you would have thought she enjoyed walking by herself. Hatsuno could not bear to let anyone guess how lonesome she felt in the gay throng.

Brother Harry and six-year-old brother Teddy were deep in clumps of their schoolmates, but the girls from Hattie's class streamed by her without pausing. Behind her Patty White, whom she liked best of all, skipped along between Sue and Phyllis, giggling and talking. Hattie wondered what they were talking about. Often they were chattering about Hattie's secret dream; but today it sounded as if they were discussing the Mother's Day tea next month. This morning the teacher had appointed Patty chairman of the decorating committee.

Hattie could have helped decorate. Her slim fingers knew how to fold amazing Japanese paper birds, flowers, dolls. And at the old school the teacher would have had her do colored drawings on the blackboard, along with Tommy Lin, who was Chinese, and Consuelo, who was Mexican. The three drew better than any of the "plain Americans." But in this new school, where almost all were "plain Americans," no one knew what Hattie's fingers could do.

No, the girls were not talking about the tea.

"If you join now," Patty was saying, "you can go up to camp this summer—"

Oh, if only Patty were saying it to Hatsuno! But she wasn't. She broke off as she danced past with the others.

"Hi, Hattie!" she called, wrinkling her uptilted nose in a smile and tossing back her thistledown curls.

Hattie smiled a small, stiff smile, though she ached to shout "Hi!" and fall in step with Patty. Then maybe Patty would think to ask her.

"Join"—"camp": those words were the keys to one of Hattie's dearest dreams.

Hatsuno had never been in the mountains. All her life she had lived where she could see them, stretching like a purple wall across the end of the dingy downtown street. They were beautiful, with snow-capped peaks shining pink and lavender and gold in the sunrise, and Hatsuno had always longed to explore them; but though they looked so near, they were miles and miles away.

The new school had given her hope. In the new school there was a Camp Fire group; and every summer it spent a few days at a camp far up in the mountains. Hattie had seen pictures of its bark-covered lodges climbing steeply among the tall evergreens beside a sparkling stream. She had heard Patty tell of the campfires and the horse-back rides. For Patty was a Camp Fire girl, and Patty's mother was the guardian of the group. Yet, friendly though Patty was, she never spoke of Hattie's joining. And Hattie was far too shy to bring up the subject.

In her old home she had not been so shy; but the old house had grown too small, and they had had to move to a larger one. Hattie, the first Noda baby, had been followed by five boys, and, as Harry said, each child shrunk the house a little bit more. This spring brought not only a new baby but a new grandmother, and the house was as small as Hattie's year-before-last coat. Even

Mother couldn't let out its hems enough to make it do.

Mother could manage almost anything. During the depression, when Father was out of work, Mother had kept the children neat as wax and even stylish. She was always up, working, when Hattie woke in the morning, always up, mending and making over, when Hattie went to sleep at night. Mother was proud that even in the bad years Denver had few Japanese Americans "on relief": almost as few as in jail.

Even Mother could not stretch the house enough for the new baby and Great-Grandmother. So the Nodas had moved, uprooting the children from neighborhood and school. The new school was pleasant; Hattie's teacher, Miss Bender, was lovely; Patty White was the gayest, prettiest girl Hattie had ever met. But Hattie didn't fit in.

So here she was, walking home alone, with Camp Fire and the mountains as far away as ever. Teddy overtook her, making noises like a machine gun—like a railway train—like an airplane. Teddy's face was as round as a button, his eyes as black as coal, his teeth as white as rice.

"Last one home's a lame duck!" he chirped at her.

She did not hurry as once she would have done. Home was a changed place now; changed by Grandmother as well as by the new house.

Though Great-Grandmother had come from Japan ten years ago, Hattie had never seen her till this month. Great-Grandmother had lived with Aunt Kiku in San Francisco, until Aunt Kiku's death had left Grandmother alone.

She was not at all what Hattie had expected; not at all like grandmothers in books, comfortable, plump people who loved to spoil their grandchildren. No, Grandmother was not that kind.

Hattie slowly opened the door, which still quivered from Teddy's banging it. Little gray Grandmother sat stiffly erect, only her head bent toward the sock she was darning, her small feet dangling.

"How do you do, Grandmother?" said Hattie.

"How do you do, Elder Daughter?" Grandmother responded. There is no easy way to say "granddaughter" in Japanese.

Under their folded lids Grandmother's eyes

traveled down Hattie. Hattie, feeling prickly, smoothed her hair, straightened her collar, twitched her checked skirt, and finally shifted her weight to one knee as Grandmother reached her feet.

"A cold day for bare legs," Grandmother observed. Hattie thought her look added, *And a great girl twelve years old should wear long stockings.*

Self-consciously Hattie's eyes pulled free from Grandmother's. "Oh," she cried, "Dicky's climbed on the piano again." She ran over and replaced the box of satiny white wood in which her latest—and last—doll always stood on view, fairly safe from the six boys. It was an enchanting doll, with glossy black hair and a silk kimono. "The other boys at least keep off the piano," Hattie scolded, "but not Dicky."

Grandmother's cool eyes seemed to say, *Boys have to be excused, since they're so much more important than girls. And why should a great girl of twelve care about dolls?*

Hattie hurried on into the good-smelling kitchen. "Mother," she complained, "Grandmother doesn't understand that we're Americans, not Japanese. I bet she'd like me to flop down on my knees and bump my head on the floor the way you used to have to, and say, 'Honorable Grandmother, I have returned.'"

"Wash your hands," said Mother, "and help me get dinner on the table."

Hattie slapped her shoes down hard, as she went to the sink to wash. She wished her heels weren't rubber; they didn't make enough noise to express her feelings.

"Of course you will give proper courtesy to the old," Mother said quietly.

"Why? She doesn't even like me." The question was useless. Hattie had grown up knowing that politeness to the old was as much a law as honesty, industry, self-control—and minding parents.

Mother only said, "Stop and buy grapefruit on your way from school. Be sure to pick out heavy ones."

"Of course," Hattie grumbled. Hadn't she known how to choose good fruit and vegetables since she was nine?

Dinner was Japanese American. Seven Nodas —and Grandmother—crowded around an ordi-nary American table; but the utensils were chopsticks instead of knives and forks. The fish soup and the pickled radish were Japanese; the *pakkai* were American spareribs and the fluffy white rice was international. Bread and butter were pure American, and the dessert was Japanese gelatin, too firm to quiver. "It's not so nervous as American jelly," Harry said, and made Teddy laugh till his eyes went shut.

Only Grandmother seemed all Japanese; in the way she sipped her soup and tea, with a noise that was polite in Japan but not in America; in the way she refused bread and butter; in the way she greeted an old neighbor of the Nodas', who came in as they were finishing the meal.

Grandmother shuffled across the room, toeing in, because for sixty-five of her seventy-five years she had worn clogs; and she bowed the deep bow of old Japan, her withered hands sliding down to her knees. Why couldn't Grandmother be more American?

The neighbor had come to remind them that tonight was the festival called Buddha's Birthday. Grandmother's eyes brightened at the news. But Mother apologized: she could not go with Grandmother, for Saburo the new baby was feverish, and she could never bear to leave her babies when they were sick. Father? He had to work tonight. Thoughtfully Grandmother looked at Hattie. Hattie excused herself and hurried back to school.

Right up to the time school opened, she kept seeing Grandmother's eyes brighten and grow dull. If Hattie had been with Patty and the others on the schoolground, as she longed to be, she might have forgotten Grandmother. But sitting lonesomely at her desk, pretending to read, she could not forget.

Maybe it was good, after all, to have a rule about being kind to old people whether they like you or not. Hattie thought of Mother, taking care of her and her brothers when they were young and helpless. How dreadful if, when Mother grew old and helpless, they did not take turn about and care for her! Hattie frowned at her book, thinking.

"Mad, Hattie? My, but you're scowling!" teased Patty, pausing as she came in from the schoolground.

Hattie shook her head and smiled. If only Patty would sit down beside her and say the thrilling words, "Oh, Hattie, wouldn't you like to join Camp Fire?" If she would even say, "Can't you come over after school?"

But after school Hattie walked home alone, as usual, stopping for the grapefruit on her way. When she had put them in the home cooler, she hunted up Grandmother, and ducked her head in a shy bow. "Grandmother," she said, "if you want to go to Buddha's Birthday tonight, I'm sure Mother will let Harry and me go with you."

The Nodas were Methodists, so the Buddhist church was strange to Hattie and Harry. Tonight it was crowded, and all through the program small children trotted in and out and climbed over people's feet, with nobody minding. There were songs and dances and pantomimes, graceful kimonos, stately poses, dignified steps; and voices in the high falsetto which was the proper tone for Japanese actors, but which gave Hattie a funny, embarrassed feeling. "Such squeaky doors!" Harry whispered comically.

Coming home by street-car and bus, the three arrived so late that the house was all sleeping. Harry bade Grandmother good-night and stumbled drowsily to his room, but Grandmother lingered, eyes bright and cheeks flushed.

Hattie hunted for something to say. "The dancing was lovely," she said. "And the kimonos."

"I have one old kimono," Grandmother said, turning toward her door. With Hattie at her heels, she opened a dresser drawer and took out a silken bundle which she unfolded and held out, smiling faintly at Hattie's gasp of admiration.

"Chrysanthemums, for your aunt's name, Kiku, Chrysanthemum," said Grandmother. Gorgeous blossoms in many rich colors grew across the heavy blue crepe. "It was the only one saved from the great San Francisco fire. She wrapped it round one of her doll boxes." Grandmother motioned toward the drawer and a white wood box that lay there.

"Could I see?" Hattie stuttered.

"You may," Grandmother answered.

When Hattie slid open the box the breath of the Orient puffed out into her nostrils. She lifted the bag that protected the doll's hair and face,

and gazed at the miniature lady, exquisitely moulded, and robed in brocades, padded, corded, embroidered. Clasping the box to her breast with one hand, Hattie pulled out a chair for Grandmother. "I don't know much about the doll festival," she coaxed shyly. "Here in Denver we don't."

She curled up on the floor at Grandmother's feet. "O Kiku San brought her doll set with her," Grandmother said, "when she married and came to America. This one is more than a hundred years old. We were taught to take care of things. The girls' festival—O Hina Matsuri—was a great day. It was play, but it taught us history and manners."

Looking from the doll to Grandmother, Hattie listened with all her might. She missed some words, for the Japanese the Nodas used at home was simple, and, to Hattie's relief, there had been no Japanese Language School for some years now. Still, she could follow the story, and it made pictures for her in the quiet night: little-girl-Grandmother wearing enchanting kimonos, in charming rooms carpeted with cushiony mats; spending long hours learning to serve tea just so, to arrange flowers just so, to paint the difficult Japanese letters just so; learning to hold her face and voice calm no matter how she felt. Girl-Grandmother, writing poems with her friends and going to view the full moon, valuing beauty above riches. Grandmother, hearing about America, and longing to go where life was free for women. Grandmother, never able to come until she was too old to fit herself into this new land.

When the parlor clock struck one, Grandmother stopped short. "A girl of twelve should be asleep!" she said severely.

Next morning Hattie wondered if she had dreamed that companionable midnight visit, for Grandmother looked coldly at Hattie's bare knees and said, "Since you must run and jump like a boy, I suppose those ugly short clothes are necessary." But even while Hattie was biting her lip uncomfortably, Grandmother added, "Hatsuno, the chrysanthemum kimono and the doll are to be yours. After all, you are our only girl."

Home was beginning to seem homelike again.

That was fortunate for Hattie, since neighborhood and school were still strange. It was a relief to go back to their old district on Sundays, to the Japanese Methodist Church. And once Mother took the older children to an evening carnival at their old school. On the way they stopped at the store where they used to buy Japanese food, dishes, cloth. Clean and bright itself, it was jammed in among grimy second-hand stores and pawn shops. It was queer, Hattie thought, but no matter how clean people were, or what good citizens, if they happened to be born Chinese or Japanese or Mexican, they were expected to live down on these dirty, crowded streets, with the trucks roaring past. Yes, the new neighborhood and school were far pleasanter than the old—if only Hatsuno could fit in.

As Mother's Day approached, Hattie felt lonelier than ever. When she came into school two days before the tea, Patty, Sue and Phyllis were huddled round the teacher's desk. Miss Bender smiled approvingly at Hattie, who was already top student in Seventh Grade. Patty smiled, too, and looked at her expectantly. Hattie's heart thumped with the wish to push herself in amongst them. But how could she? She smoothed her starched skirt under her, sat down, and pretended to clean out her desk.

"It's such a late spring," Miss Bender was saying, "the lilacs aren't out. But I'll bring sprays of cherry-blossoms. And we must find out how many mothers to expect. I hope your mother is coming, Hattie."

"No, ma'am," Hattie said soberly. "The baby has chickenpox, and Mother just won't leave a sick baby."

"Haven't you an aunt or grandmother who could come in her place?"

Oh, dear! Grandmother would be so different from the rest. What would Patty think of her? Then Hattie's head came up. "I'll ask Great-Grandmother," she said.

She thought Grandmother would refuse. She hoped Grandmother would refuse. Instead, Grandmother asked, "Every girl should have mother or grandmother at this tea?"

"Yes, Grandmother."

"And your mother will not leave the baby. Elder daughter, you went with me to Buddha's Birthday. I go with you to school."

Hattie swallowed a lump in her throat. Grandmother was doing this because she thought Hattie wished it. Tea—Grandmother would sip it in Japanese fashion. Would she notice if the girls giggled? She would hide the fact if she did. Hattie thought of Grandmother's long training in the concealment of pain or disappointment. Well, that was a good heritage for anybody. Hattie would use it now. "Thank you, Grandmother was doing this because she you Friday, after school."

When the two came into the schoolroom that afternoon, the mothers were all there and having their tea, and it seemed to Hattie that everyone stopped talking and turned to gaze. Well, she and Grandmother must look pretty funny, Hattie thought.

Hattie was dressed like the other girls, in white sweater and short white skirt, her white anklets folded neatly above her oxfords, and her black hair out of its braids and done in another favorite style of the season. Grandmother, as short and slim as Hattie, wore a dress nicely made over from a kimono, but looking a little strange; and her gray hair was combed straight back from the withered little face with its slanting eyes.

Politely Hattie introduced Miss Bender to Grandmother, and pulled up one of the visitor's chairs, since Grandmother had never been to a tea where people stood up and balanced the dishes on their hands. Patty brought her a plate, Phyllis the sandwiches, Sue a cup of tea. Then Patty returned, pulling her mother after her.

"Mom," she said, "here's Hattie. And here's her great-grandma." Patty dropped her mother's hand and stood beaming.

Hattie looked anxiously at Grandmother. She could not speak a word of English, nor the others a word of Japanese. But, instead of words, Seventh Grade and its mothers were bringing sandwiches and cakes till Grandmother's plate was heaped. And Grandmother sat there, as stately and self-possessed and smiling as if she went to seven teas a week.

Hattie studied her more closely. Others might think Grandmother's little face a mask, but Hattie saw that the eyes were bright again, and that the wrinkled cheeks were pink. Grandmother liked it! Grandmother felt happy and at home!

Maybe even a great-grandmother could be lonesome, especially when she was too old to learn the ways of a new land. Thinking so happily of Grandmother that she forgot all about her own shyness, Hattie squeezed Patty's arm, just as she might have squeezed Teddy's on some rare occasion when he was sweet instead of maddening.

Patty squeezed back—quickly, as if she had been waiting for the chance. "Mother!" she stuttered, in a voice that matched her gay fluff of curls. "Mother, I think maybe I was mistaken. I think Hattie might like to—" She looked eagerly up into her mother's questioning eyes—"You ask her, Mother!" she begged.

"About Camp Fire? Hattie, would you like to join our Camp Fire group?"

Hattie was silent from pure joy and astonishment.

"If I got your name in this week," Mrs. White continued, "you could go to camp with us. A camp in the mountains; do you know about it?"

"Oh, yes, ma'am, *I know,*" Hattie said with shining eyes. "Oh, yes, ma'am!"

from ELLEN GRAE

Vera and Bill Cleaver

Few readers who meet Ellen Grae are likely to forget her. Ellen is a real creative artist, and her story leaves readers with much to think and talk about. How much of what she says is true? Every-one recognizes that the tale of Fortis Alonzo Gridley is a story, but what about Ira's account of his parents' death? Around that question the authors have written a short but provocative book that is humorous and at the same time seriously explores the question of moral responsibility.

[Ellen Tells a Story and Hears a Story]

Mrs. McGruder isn't a religious person especially, although she and Mr. McGruder attend the Methodist Church every Sunday and when I live with her I have to leave off being a Pantheist and turn Methodist too. But she likes to have people talk to her about religion.

So, wanting to please her, I told her that I had learned to be most truly, humbly grateful for all the benevolences God had seen fit to bestow upon me.

She turned a light green gaze upon me and asked, "Oh? What brought that on?"

From *Ellen Grae* by Vera and Bill Cleaver. Copyright © 1967 by Vera and William J. Cleaver. Published by J. B. Lippincott Company. Reprinted by permission of J. B. Lippincott Company and Paul R. Reynolds Inc.

"Nothing brought it on," I explained. "I just started feeling grateful toward Him. I feel grateful toward you too, Mrs. McGruder. For letting me come back down here and stay with you while I go to school. I vow that I've changed since last year and won't be as much trouble to you this year as I was last."

She said, "Well, if that's true it'll be my turn to be grateful. Like what, for instance, have you changed?"

"Well, for one thing I take a bath every night now without anybody hollering at me to do it and for another I've stopped swearing. I don't even say hell any more. I think that the use of profanity is a vocabulary deficiency, don't you?"

"At the moment I can't think," Mrs. McGruder said, handing me a freshly sugared doughnut. "I'm too busy counting my blessings."

"I know a girl whose father, they said, dropped dead from swearing. Her name's Opal Gridley. Her father's name was Fortis Alonzo and I think that's what killed him."

"I'm really trying but I don't get the connection," Mrs. McGruder said.

"You will in a minute. Well, anyway, he was a meter reader for the gas company and I guess that and his having a name like Fortis Alonzo burdened him heavily and made him feel unimportant."

"I think Fortis Alonzo is rather a pretty name," Mrs. McGruder murmured.

"Do you? Well, that's what it was. Fortis Alonzo Gridley. He used to drive around with all the windows in his car rolled up. Even when everybody else was standing around pouring sweat and with their tongues hanging out having trouble breathing because it was so hot, Mr. Gridley would get in his car and roll up all the windows and drive around and wave to people."

"I'm still trying," Mrs. McGruder said.

"His wife was fat and could sing Italian. She practiced every night after supper. If you listened it was sadly pretty but nobody did. They'd all come out on their porches and stand around and laugh and this made Mr. Gridley mad. He'd run out of his house and shake his fist at them and swear. When he died everybody said that's what caused it. They said God struck him dead for swearing so much. But do you know something?"

"I'm beginning to think not," Mrs. McGruder said.

"Mr. Fortis Alonzo Gridley died at his own hand. Trying to make people think he was rich enough to have an air-conditioned car. He didn't have it though and that's what killed him. The heat and no air at all. I was the one who got to him first the night he collapsed. Gridley's house was next door to ours and when I saw Mr. Gridley drive up weaving and wobbling I ran over and jerked the door of his car open and he fell out. He didn't have time to say one word. Just blew a bubble and died."

"What do you mean he blew a bubble?"

"He blew a bubble while he was dying. It looked like glass. Mrs. McGruder?"

"Yes, Ellen Grae?"

"Was that telegram that came a few minutes ago from Rosemary?"

"It was from her father. She'll be in on the ten o'clock train. Are you ready for more breakfast now?"

"No thanks. I still hate breakfast; I haven't changed that much. Will I have to room with her again?"

"That's my plan. Why?"

"Oh, nothing. It's just that I was thinking it might be better if I could have a room to myself this year. I forgot to tell you and I'll bet Grace did too that lately I have these strange seizures."

"Seizures? What kind of seizures?"

"Seizures. You know. They always come at night. I get up and crash around and cry out. I know when I'm doing it but I can't stop myself. Jeff says it's a very frightening thing to watch. He says it's almost as if I was disembodied. I was just thinking it might be better if Rosemary could be spared the sight. You know how frail she is."

"No, I hadn't noticed," Mrs. McGruder said, setting two scrambled eggs and a glass of milk in front of me. "I'll be on the lookout for one of your attacks but in the meantime could you just oblige me and eat so that we can get on to more important things?"

Mrs. McGruder is a MORE person. Everything, no matter what it is, always should be MORE.

Together we went down the hall to the room that I was again to share with Rosemary and

Mrs. McGruder looked at my bed and said that the sheets and spread could stand a little MORE smoothing and the pillow a little MORE plumping. Then she watched while I finished unpacking my suitcases which contained MORE books than clothes and said that I should have brought MORE dresses and that those I did bring needed MORE starch.

She looked at my white shoes and made a noise with her tongue against the roof of her mouth. "Who polished these shoes, Ellen Grae?"

"I did. Don't they look nice?"

"Yes. Except they've got MORE white on the soles than on the tops."

About ten o'clock we drove down to the village of Thicket to meet Rosemary's train but as usual it was late. Mrs. McGruder parked the car off to one side and tried to settle down to reading a magazine which she had had the foresight to bring along but couldn't because I was there.

"Goodness, Ellen Grae. Stop fidgeting."

"I'm not fidgeting. I'm itching myself. It's all those baths I've been taking. Wouldn't some boiled peanuts taste good right about now? Just to take our minds off things?"

Mrs. McGruder frowned but when she turned her head to look at me there was a gentleness in her eyes. "Oh, honey, you don't really want any boiled peanuts now, do you?"

"Some nice, salty, juicy ones. The way Ira fixes them. While we're just sitting here waiting for Rosemary I could just hop over to his stand and get us a couple of bags. I'd hurry."

Mrs. McGruder sighed but reached into her handbag and found her change purse and extracted a quarter. "All right but don't make me come after you. And watch when you cross the street."

She meant for cars, of course, but there were only three parked ones. First Street lay hot and quiet under the September sun. The only humans in sight were the clerk from Sangster's Grocery Store who was busy letting down the green window awnings, a man in white coveralls who had his head stuck in the door of the barber shop, and Ira who was setting up his stand in its customary oak-shaded spot.

A lot of people in Thicket think that Ira is crazy but he's not. He's just different. He never wears shoes even when the cold winds come sweeping down from the north, he can't read or write and he lives in a two-room tin shack down near the river bend all by himself. Mrs. McGruder told me that once upon a time Ira had a mother and father, at least a stepfather, but that one day they just picked up and left and never came back. Nobody knows how old Ira is. Mrs. McGruder says maybe thirty but I think maybe he's older because he's got white in his black hair and sometimes his dark eyes have a very old man's sadness in them. Ira lives on what money he can make selling boiled and parched peanuts and sometimes somebody patient will pay him to mow a yard. He could make a lot of money mowing yards because he's neat and careful but he won't talk to people. He just nods and points which makes everybody nervous. Even when he goes into a store to buy something that's all he does. Mrs. McGruder told me that in all the years she's been seeing Ira around town she's never heard him speak. I reckon nobody has except me. He talks to me all the time.

I skipped up to his stand and whacked the board that was his counter and said, "Hey, Ira."

He turned around and gave me his slow, quiet look. "Hey, Ellen Grae. I wuz hopin' you'd come

by to see me this mornin'. I saw you yistiddy when you come on the train."

"You did? I didn't see you. Why didn't you holler?"

"They wuz people around. Ellen Grae, I got me a goat now."

"Oh, Ira, that's wonderful!"

"When can you come and see her?"

"I don't know. Maybe Sunday after church. I'll get Grover to come with me. I brought back a whole pile of books with me. If you want me to I'll bring one when I come and read you a story. What's your goat's name?"

"Missouri."

"Missouri? That's a funny name for a goat."

"My mother's name wuz Missouri," Ira explained softly, setting two waxed paper bags of boiled peanuts up on the counter. "My goat reminds me of my mother. Did I ever tell you what happened to my mother, Ellen Grae?"

I laid my quarter on the counter and waited for Ira to lay back a nickel change but he didn't. Which wasn't unusual. Ira didn't know how to make change. If you handed him a dollar for one bag of peanuts he'd keep the whole thing. But, by the same token, if you only handed him a penny for a half dozen bags that was all right too. So, if you traded with him for any length of time, things kind of evened themselves out.

"Yes, you told me what happened to your mother, Ira. Listen, I have to go now. Mrs. McGruder and I just came down to the train station to meet Rosemary. When Grover and I come over Sunday afternoon I'll read to you."

"She died in the swamp, she and her husband. While they wuz tryin' to run away from me. They had 'em this ol' rattler in a box and they wuz draggin' me alongside an' pokin' at him with a stick but instead of bitin' me like he wuz suppose' to, he stuck his ol' head out 'n bit 'em. They swoll up and threshed around some afterward but they wa'n't nothin' I could do for 'em. We wuz too far back in the swamp. So I buried 'em 'longside of that ol' snake. I killed the snake first so he wouldn't bite 'em no more. I didn't tell you 'bout this before, did I, Ellen Grae?"

"No, I reckon this is the first time, Ira. Listen, I'll see you Sunday." I picked up the two bags of peanuts and started to turn away and leave but something in the way Ira looked caused me to

turn back. "Listen, Ira, you feel all right, don't you? You aren't sick or anything, are you?"

For a second I thought there were tears on Ira's black lashes but it was only the sun glinting on them. He said, "No, I'm not sick, Ellen Grae. Just tuckered out from talkin' so much."

Poor Ira. He has these hallucinations.

from HOMER PRICE

Robert McCloskey

The doughnut episode in Homer Price *has long been a favorite of readers of Robert McCloskey's amusing boy stories. He won the Caldecott Medal in 1942 for* Make Way for Ducklings, *and in 1958 for* Time of Wonder. *Any one of his other picture-stories might also have won it—* Lentil, Blueberries for Sal, *or* One Morning in Maine. *His illustrations for* Trigger John's Son *by Tom Robinson are equally delightful.*

The Doughnuts

One Friday night in November Homer overheard his mother talking on the telephone to Aunt Agnes over in Centerburg. "I'll stop by with the car in about half an hour and we can go to the meeting together," she said, because tonight was the night the Ladies' Club was meeting to discuss plans for a box social and to knit and sew for the Red Cross.

"I think I'll come along and keep Uncle Ulysses company while you and Aunt Agnes are at the meeting," said Homer.

So after Homer had combed his hair and his mother had looked to see if she had her knitting instructions and the right size needles, they started for town.

Homer's Uncle Ulysses and Aunt Agnes have a very up and coming lunch room over in Centerburg, just across from the court house on the town square. Uncle Ulysses is a man with advanced ideas and a weakness for labor saving devices. He equipped the lunch room with automatic toasters, automatic coffee maker, automatic dish washer, and an automatic doughnut maker. All just the latest thing in labor saving devices. Aunt Agnes would throw up her hands and sigh every time Uncle Ulysses bought a new labor saving device. Sometimes she became unkindly disposed toward him for days and days. She was of the opinion that Uncle Ulysses just frittered away his spare time over at the barber shop with the sheriff and the boys, so, what was the good of a labor saving device that gave you more time to fritter?

When Homer and his mother got to Centerburg they stopped at the lunch room, and after Aunt Agnes had come out and said, "My, how that boy does grow!" which was what she always said, she went off with Homer's mother in the car. Homer went into the lunch room and said, "Howdy, Uncle Ulysses!"

"Oh, hello, Homer. You're just in time," said Uncle Ulysses. "I've been going over this automatic doughnut machine, oiling the machinery and cleaning the works . . . wonderful things, these labor saving devices."

"Yep," agreed Homer, and he picked up a cloth and started polishing the metal trimmings while Uncle Ulysses tinkered with the inside workings.

"Opfwo-oof!!" sighed Uncle Ulysses and, "Look here, Homer, you've got a mechanical mind. See if you can find where these two pieces fit in. I'm going across to the barbershop for a spell, 'cause there's somethin' I've got to talk to the sheriff about. There won't be much business here until the double feature is over and I'll be back before then."

Then as Uncle Ulysses went out the door he said, "Uh, Homer, after you get the pieces in place, would you mind mixing up a batch of doughnut batter and put it in the machine? You could turn the switch and make a few doughnuts to have on hand for the crowd after the movie . . . if you don't mind."

"O.K." said Homer, "I'll take care of everything."

A few minutes later a customer came in and said, "Good evening, Bud."

Homer looked up from putting the last piece in the doughnut machine and said, "Good evening, Sir, what can I do for you?"

"Well, young feller, I'd like a cup o' coffee and some doughnuts," said the customer.

"I'm sorry, Mister, but we won't have any doughnuts for about half an hour, until I can mix some dough and start this machine. I could give you some very fine sugar rolls instead."

"Well, Bud, I'm in no real hurry so I'll just have a cup o' coffee and wait around a bit for the doughnuts. Fresh doughnuts are always worth waiting for is what I always say."

"O.K." said Homer, and he drew a cup of coffee from Uncle Ulysses' super automatic coffee maker.

"Nice place you've got here," said the customer.

"Oh, yes," replied Homer, "this is a very up and coming lunch room with all the latest improvements."

"Yes," said the stranger, "must be a good business. I'm in business too. A traveling man in outdoor advertising. I'm a sandwich man, Mr. Gabby's my name."

"My name is Homer. I'm glad to meet you, Mr. Gabby. It must be a fine profession, traveling and advertising sandwiches."

"Oh no," said Mr. Gabby, "I don't advertise sandwiches, I just wear any kind of an ad, one sign on front and one sign on behind, this way. . . . Like a sandwich. Ya know what I mean?"

"Oh, I see. That must be fun, and you travel too?" asked Homer as he got out the flour and the baking powder.

"Yeah, I ride the rods between jobs, on freight trains, ya know what I mean?"

"Yes, but isn't that dangerous?" asked Homer.

"Of course there's a certain amount a risk, but you take any method a travel these days, it's all dangerous. Ya know what I mean? Now take airplanes for instance . . ."

Just then a large shiny black car stopped in front of the lunch room and a chauffeur helped a lady out of the rear door. They both came inside and the lady smiled at Homer and said, "We've stopped for a light snack. Some doughnuts and coffee would be simply marvelous."

Then Homer said, "I'm sorry, Ma'm, but the doughnuts won't be ready until I make this batter and start Uncle Ulysses' doughnut machine."

"Well now aren't you a clever young man to know how to make *doughnuts!*"

"Well," blushed Homer, "I've really never done it before but I've got a receipt to follow."

"Now, young man, you simply must allow me to help. You know, I haven't made doughnuts for years, but I know the best receipt for doughnuts. It's marvelous, and we really must use it."

"But Ma'm . . ." said Homer.

"Now just *wait* till you taste these doughnuts," said the lady. "Do you have an apron?" she asked, as she took off her fur coat and her rings and her jewelry and rolled up her sleeves. "Charles," she said to the chauffeur, "hand me that baking powder, that's right, and, young man, we'll need some nutmeg."

So Homer and the chauffeur stood by and handed things and cracked the eggs while the lady mixed and stirred. Mr. Gabby sat on his stool, sipped his coffee, and looked on with great interest.

"There!" said the lady when all of the ingredients were mixed. "Just *wait* till you taste these doughnuts!"

"It looks like an awful lot of batter," said Homer as he stood on a chair and poured it into the doughnut machine with the help of the chauffeur. "It's about *ten* times as much as Uncle Ulysses ever makes."

"But wait till you taste them!" said the lady with an eager look and a smile.

Homer got down from the chair and pushed a button on the machine marked, "Start." Rings of batter started dropping into the hot fat. After a ring of batter was cooked on one side an automatic gadget turned it over and the other side would cook. Then another automatic gadget gave the doughnut a little push and it rolled neatly down a little chute, all ready to eat.

"That's a simply *fascinating* machine," said the lady as she waited for the first doughnut to roll out.

"Here, young man, *you* must have the first one. Now isn't that just *too* delicious!? Isn't it simply marvelous?"

"Yes, Ma'm, it's very good," replied Homer as the lady handed doughnuts to Charles and to Mr. Gabby and asked if they didn't think they were simply divine doughnuts.

"It's an old family receipt!" said the lady with pride.

Homer poured some coffee for the lady and her chauffeur and for Mr. Gabby, and a glass of milk for himself. Then they all sat down at the lunch counter to enjoy another few doughnuts apiece.

"I'm so glad you enjoy my doughnuts," said the lady. "But now, Charles, we really must be going. If you will just take this apron, Homer, and put two dozen doughnuts in a bag to take along, we'll be on our way. And, Charles, don't forget to pay the young man." She rolled down her sleeves and put on her jewelry, then Charles managed to get her into her big fur coat.

"Good night, young man, I haven't had so much fun in years. I *really* haven't!" said the lady, as she went out the door and into the big shiny car.

"Those are sure good doughnuts," said Mr. Gabby as the car moved off.

"You bet!" said Homer. Then he and Mr. Gabby stood and watched the automatic doughnut machine make doughnuts.

After a few dozen more doughnuts had rolled down the little chute, Homer said, "I guess that's about enough doughnuts to sell to the after theater customers. I'd better turn the machine off for a while."

Homer pushed the button marked *Stop* and there was a little click, but nothing happened. The rings of batter kept right on dropping into the hot fat, and an automatic gadget kept right on turning them over, and another automatic gadget kept right on giving them a little push and the doughnuts kept right on rolling down the little chute, all ready to eat.

"That's funny," said Homer, "I'm sure that's the right button!" He pushed it again but the automatic doughnut maker kept right on making doughnuts.

"Well I guess I must have put one of those pieces in backwards," said Homer.

"Then it might stop if you pushed the button marked *Start*," said Mr. Gabby.

Homer did, and the doughnuts still kept rolling down the little chute, just as regular as a clock can tick.

"I guess we could sell a few more doughnuts," said Homer, "but I'd better telephone Uncle Ulysses over at the barber shop." Homer gave the number and while he waited for someone to answer he counted thirty-seven doughnuts roll down the little chute.

Finally someone answered, "Hello! This is the sarber bhop, I mean the barber shop."

"Oh, hello, sheriff. This is Homer. Could I speak to Uncle Ulysses?"

"Well, he's playing pinochle right now," said the sheriff. "Anythin' I can tell 'im?"

"Yes," said Homer. "I pushed the button marked *Stop* on the doughnut machine but the rings of batter keep right on dropping into the hot fat, and an automatic gadget keeps right on turning them over, and another automatic gadget keeps giving them a little push, and the doughnuts keep right on rolling down the little chute! It won't stop!"

"O.K. Wold the hire, I mean, hold the wire and I'll tell 'im." Then Homer looked over his shoulder and counted another twenty-one doughnuts roll down the little chute, all ready to eat. Then the sheriff said, "He'll be right over. . . . Just gotta finish this hand."

"That's good," said Homer. "G'by, sheriff."

The window was full of doughnuts by now so Homer and Mr. Gabby had to hustle around and start stacking them on plates and trays and lining them up on the counter.

"Sure are a lot of doughnuts!" said Homer.

"You bet!" said Mr. Gabby. "I lost count at twelve hundred and two and that was quite a while back."

People had begun to gather outside the lunch room window, and someone was saying, "There are almost as many doughnuts as there are people in Centerburg, and I wonder how in tarnation Ulysses thinks he can sell all of 'em!"

Every once in a while somebody would come inside and buy some, but while somebody bought two to eat and a dozen to take home, the machine made three dozen more.

By the time Uncle Ulysses and the sheriff arrived and pushed through the crowd, the lunch room was a calamity of doughnuts! Doughnuts in the window, doughnuts piled high on the shelves, doughnuts stacked on plates, doughnuts lined up twelve deep all along the counter, and doughnuts still rolling down the little chute, just as regular as a clock can tick.

"Hello, sheriff, hello, Uncle Ulysses, we're having a little trouble here," said Homer.

"Well, I'll be dunked!" said Uncle Ulysses.

"Dernd ef you won't be when Aggy gits home," said the sheriff.

"Mighty fine doughnuts though. What'll you do with 'em all, Ulysses?"

Uncle Ulysses groaned and said, "What will Aggy say? We'll never sell 'em all."

Then Mr. Gabby, who hadn't said anything for a long time, stopped piling doughnuts and said, "What you need is an advertising man. Ya know what I mean? You got the doughnuts, ya gotta create a market . . . Understand? . . . It's balancing the demand with the supply . . . That sort of thing."

"Yep!" said Homer. "Mr. Gabby's right. We have to enlarge our market. He's an advertising sandwich man, so if we hire him, he can walk up and down in front of the theater and get the customers."

"You're hired, Mr. Gabby!" said Uncle Ulysses.

Then everybody pitched in to paint the signs and to get Mr. Gabby sandwiched between. They painted "SALE ON DOUGHNUTS" in big letters on the window too.

Meanwhile the rings of batter kept right on dropping into the hot fat, and an automatic gadget kept right on turning them over, and another automatic gadget kept right on giving them a little push, and the doughnuts kept right on rolling down the little chute, just as regular as a clock can tick.

"I certainly hope this advertising works," said Uncle Ulysses, wagging his head. "Aggy'll certainly throw a fit if it don't."

The sheriff went outside to keep order, because there was quite a crowd by now—all looking at the doughnuts and guessing how many thousand there were, and watching new ones roll down the little chute, just as regular as a clock can tick. Homer and Uncle Ulysses kept stacking doughnuts. Once in a while somebody bought a few, but not very often.

Then Mr. Gabby came back and said, "Say, you know there's not much use o' me advertisin' at the theater. The show's all over, and besides almost everybody in town is out front watching that machine make doughnuts!"

"Zeus!" said Uncle Ulysses. "We must get rid of these doughnuts before Aggy gets here!"

"Looks like you will have ta hire a truck ta waul 'em ahay, I mean haul 'em away!!" said the sheriff who had just come in. Just then there was a noise and a shoving out front and the lady from the shiny black car and her chauffeur came pushing through the crowd and into the lunch room.

"Oh, gracious!" she gasped, ignoring the doughnuts, "I've lost my diamond bracelet, and I know I left it here on the counter," she said, pointing to a place where the doughnuts were piled in stacks of two dozen.

"Yes, Ma'm, I guess you forgot it when you helped make the batter," said Homer.

Then they moved all the doughnuts around and looked for the diamond bracelet, but they couldn't find it anywhere. Meanwhile the doughnuts kept rolling down the little chute, just as regular as a clock can tick.

After they had looked all around the sheriff cast a suspicious eye on Mr. Gabby, but Homer said, "He's all right, sheriff, he didn't take it. He's a friend of mine."

Then the lady said, "I'll offer a reward of one hundred dollars for that bracelet! It really *must* be found! . . . it *really* must!"

"Now don't you worry, lady," said the sheriff. "I'll get your bracelet back!"

"Zeus! This is terrible!" said Uncle Ulysses. "First all of these doughnuts and then on top of all that, a lost diamond bracelet . . ."

Mr. Gabby tried to comfort him, and he said, "There's always a bright side. That machine'll probably run outta batter in an hour or two."

If Mr. Gabby hadn't been quick on his feet Uncle Ulysses would have knocked him down, sure as fate.

Then while the lady wrung her hands and said, "We must find it, we *must!*" and Uncle Ulysses was moaning about what Aunt Agnes would say, and the sheriff was eyeing Mr. Gabby, Homer sat down and thought hard.

Before twenty more doughnuts could roll down the little chute he shouted, "SAY! I know where the bracelet is! It was lying here on the counter and got mixed up in the batter by mistake! The bracelet is cooked inside one of these doughnuts!"

"Why . . . I really believe you're right," said the lady through her tears. "Isn't that *amazing?* Simply *amazing!*"

"I'll be durn'd!" said the sheriff.

"OhH-h!" moaned Uncle Ulysses. "Now we have to break up all of these doughnuts to find it. Think of the *pieces!* Think of the *crumbs!*

Think of what *Aggy* will say!"

"Nope," said Homer. "We won't have to break them up. I've got a plan."

So Homer and the advertising man took some cardboard and some paint and printed another sign. They put this sign

FRESH DOUGHNUTS
2 for 5¢
WHILE THEY LAST
$100.00 PRIZE
FOR FINDING
A BRACELET
INSIDE A DOUGHNUT
P.S. You have to give the
bracelet back

in the window, and the sandwich man wore two more signs that said the same thing and walked around in the crowd out front.

THEN . . . The doughnuts began to sell! *Everybody* wanted to buy doughnuts, *dozens* of doughnuts!

And that's not all. Everybody bought coffee to dunk the doughnuts in too. Those that didn't buy coffee bought milk or soda. It kept Homer and the lady and the chauffeur and Uncle Ulysses and the sheriff busy waiting on the people who wanted to buy doughnuts.

When all but the last couple of hundred doughnuts had been sold, Rupert Black shouted, "I GAWT IT!!" and sure enough . . . there was the diamond bracelet inside of his doughnut!

Then Rupert went home with a hundred dollars, the citizens of Centerburg went home full of doughnuts, the lady and her chauffeur drove off with the diamond bracelet, and Homer went home with his mother when she stopped by with Aunt Aggy.

As Homer went out of the door he heard Mr. Gabby say, "Neatest trick of merchandising I ever seen," and Aunt Aggy was looking sceptical while Uncle Ulysses was saying, "The rings of batter kept right on dropping into the hot fat, and the automatic gadget kept right on turning them over, and the other automatic gadget kept right on giving them a little push, and the doughnuts kept right on rolling down the little chute just as regular as a clock can tick—they just kept right on a comin', an' a comin', an' a comin', an' a comin'."

from **THE EGYPT GAME**

Zilpha K. Snyder

While never definitely labeled, the setting of this story is Berkeley, California, a college community where children of all races and nationalities play together with only the ordinary conflicts of childhood present. Once launched into "the Egypt game," Melanie and April plunge themselves into ancient times with all the enthusiasm of youth. In this selection, Melanie and April meet, and April is introduced to "the imagining games." The Egypt Game *was a runner-up for the 1968 Newbery Medal.*

Enter Melanie—and Marshall

On that same day in August, just a few minutes before twelve, Melanie Ross arrived at the door of Mrs. Hall's apartment on the third floor. Melanie was eleven years old and she had lived in the Casa Rosada since she was only seven. During that time she'd welcomed a lot of new people to the apartment house. Apartment dwellers, particularly near a university, are apt to come and go. Melanie always looked forward to meeting new tenants, and today was going to be especially interesting. Today, Melanie had been sent up to get Mrs. Hall's granddaughter to come down and have lunch with the Rosses. Melanie didn't know much about the new girl except that her name was April and that she had come from Hollywood to live with Mrs. Hall who was her grandmother.

It would be neat if she turned out to be a real friend. There hadn't been any girls the right age in the Casa Rosada lately. To have a handy friend again, for spur-of-the-moment visiting, would be great. However, she had overheard something that didn't sound too promising. Just the other day she'd heard Mrs. Hall telling Mom that April was a strange little thing because she'd been brought up all over everywhere and never had much of a chance to associate with other children. You wouldn't know what to expect of someone like that. But then, you never knew what to expect of any new kid, not really. So Melanie knocked hopefully at the door of apartment 312.

Meeting people had always been easy for Melanie. Most people she liked right away, and they usually seemed to feel the same way about her. But when the door to 312 opened that morning, for just a moment she was almost speechless. Surprise can do that to a person, and at first glance April really was a surprise. Her hair was stacked up in a pile that seemed to be more pins than hair, and the whole thing teetered forward over her thin pale face. She was wearing a big, yellowish-white fur thing around her shoulders, and carrying a plastic purse almost as big as a suitcase. But most of all it was the eyelashes. They were black and bushy looking, and the ones on her left eye were higher up and sloped in a different direction. Melanie's mouth opened and closed a few times before anything came out.

April adjusted Dorothea's old fur stole, patted up some sliding strands of hair and waited—warily. She didn't expect this Melanie to like her—kids hardly ever did—but she *did* intend to make a very definite impression; and she could see that she'd done that all right.

"Hi," Melanie managed after that first speechless moment. "I'm Melanie Ross. You're supposed to have lunch with us, I think. Aren't you April Hall?"

"April Dawn," April corrected with an offhand sort of smile. "I was expecting you. My grandmother informed me that—uh, she said you'd be up."

It occurred to Melanie that maybe kids dressed differently in Hollywood. As they started down the hall she asked, "Are you going to stay with your grandmother for very long?"

"Oh no," April said. "Just till my mother finishes this tour she's on. Then she'll send for me to come home."

"Tour?"

"Yes, you see my mother is Dorothea Dawn—" she paused and Melanie racked her brain. She could tell she was supposed to know who Dorothea Dawn was. "Well, I guess you haven't happened to hear of her way up here, but she's a singer and in the movies, and stuff like that. But right now she's singing with this band that travels around to different places."

"Neat!" Melanie said. "You mean your mother's in the movies?"

But just then they arrived at the Ross's apartment. Marshall met them at the door, dragging Security by one of his eight legs.

"That's my brother, Marshall," Melanie said.

"Hi, Marshall," April said. "What in the heck is that?"

Melanie grinned. "That's Security. Marshall takes him everywhere. So my dad named him Security. You know. Like some little kids have a blanket."

"Security's an octopus," Marshall said very clearly. He didn't talk very much, but when he did he always said exactly what he wanted to without any trouble. He never had fooled around with baby talk.

Melanie's mother was in the kitchen putting hot dog sandwiches and fruit salad on the table. When Melanie introduced April she could tell that her mother was surprised by the eyelashes and hairdo and everything. She probably didn't realize that kids dressed a little differently in Hollywood.

"April's mother is a movie star," Melanie explained.

Melanie's mother smiled. "Is that right, April?" she asked.

April looked at Melanie's mother carefully through narrowed eyes. Mrs. Ross looked sharp and neat, with a smart-looking very short hairdo like a soft black cap, and high winging eyebrows, like Melanie's. But her smile was a little different. April was good at figuring out what adults meant by the things they didn't quite say—and Mrs. Ross's smile meant that she wasn't going to be easy to snow.

"Well," April admitted, "not a star, really. She's mostly a vocalist. So far she's only been an extra in the movies. But she almost had a supporting role once, and Nick, that's her agent, says he has a big part almost all lined up."

"Gee, that's neat!" Melanie said. "We've never known anyone before whose mother was an extra in the movies, have we Mom?"

"Not a soul," Mrs. Ross said, still smiling.

During lunch, April talked a lot about Hollywood, and the movie stars she'd met and the big parties her mother gave and things like that. She knew she was overdoing it a bit but something made her keep on. Mrs. Ross went right on smiling in that knowing way, and Melanie went right on being so eager and encouraging that April thought she must be kidding. She wasn't sure though. You never could tell with kids— they didn't do things in a pattern, the way grown-ups did.

Actually Melanie knew that April was being pretty braggy, but it occurred to her that it was probably because of homesickness. It was easy to see how much she'd like to be back in Hollywood with her mother.

While they were having dessert of ice cream and cookies, Mrs. Ross suggested that April might like to look over Melanie's books to see if there was anything she'd like to borrow.

"Do you like to read?" Melanie asked. "Reading is my favorite occupation."

"That's for sure." Mrs. Ross laughed. "A fulltime occupation with overtime. Your grandmother tells me that you do a lot of reading, too."

"Well, of course, I'm usually pretty busy, with all the parties and everything. I do read some though, when I have a chance."

But after lunch when Melanie showed April her library, a whole bookcase full in her bedroom, she could tell that April liked books more than just a little. She could tell just by the way April picked a book up and handled it, and by the way she forgot about acting so grown-up and Hollywoodish. She plopped herself down on the floor in front of the bookcase and started looking at books like crazy. For a while she seemed to forget all about Melanie. As she read she kept propping up her eyelashes with one finger.

All of a sudden she said, "Could you help me get these darn things off? I must not have put them on the right place or something. When I look down to read I can't even see the words."

So Melanie scratched the ends of the eyelashes loose with her longest fingernail, and then April pulled them the rest of the way off. They were on pretty tight, and she said, "Ouch!" several times and a couple of other words that Melanie wasn't allowed to say.

"— —!" said April, looking in the mirror. "I think I pulled out most of my real ones. Does it look like it to you?"

"I don't think so," Melanie said. "I still see some. Is this the first time you've worn them? The false ones, I mean?"

April put back on her haughty face. "Of course not. Nearly everybody wears them in Hollywood. My mother wears them all the time. It's just that these are new ones, and they must be a different kind."

April put her eyelashes away carefully in her big bag and they went back to looking at books. Melanie showed her some of her favorites, and April picked out a couple to borrow. It was then that April took a very special book off the shelf.

It was a very dull-looking old geography book that no one would be interested in. That was why Melanie used it to hide something very special and secret. As April opened the book some cutout paper people fell out on the floor.

"What are those?" April asked.

"Just some old things of mine," Melanie said, holding out her hand for the book, but April kept on turning the pages and finding more bunches of paper people.

"Do you really still play with paper dolls?" April asked in just the tone of voice that Melanie had feared she would use. Not just because she was April, either. It was the tone of voice that nearly anyone would use about a sixth grade girl who still played with ordinary paper dolls.

"But they're not really paper dolls," Melanie said, "and I don't really play with them. Not like moving them around and dressing them up and everything. They're just sort of a record for a game I play. I make up a family and then I find people who look like them in magazines and catalogues. Just so I'll remember them better. I have fourteen families now. See they all have their names and ages written on the back. I make up stuff about their personalities and what they do. Sometimes I write it down like a story, but usually I just make it up."

April's scornful look was dissolving. "Like what?"

"Well," Melanie said, "this is the Brewster family. Mr. Brewster is a detective. I had to cut him out of the newspaper because he was the only man I could find who looked like a detective. Don't you think he does?"

"Yeah, pretty much."

"Well anyway, he just—that is, I just made up

about how he solved this very hard mystery and caught some dangerous criminals. And then the criminals escaped and were going to get revenge on Mr. Brewster. So the whole family had to go into hiding and wear disguises and everything."

April spread the Brewsters out on the floor. Her eyes were shining and without the eyelashes they were pretty, wide and blue. "Have they caught the criminals yet?" she asked. Melanie shook her head. "Well, how about if the kids catch them. They could just happen to find out where the criminals were hiding?"

"Neat!" Melanie said. "Maybe Ted," she pointed to the smallest paper Brewster, "could come home and tell the other kids how he thinks he saw one of the criminals, going into a certain house."

"And then," April interrupted, "the girls could go to the house pretending to sell Girl Scout cookies, to see if it really was the crooks."

From the Girl-Scout-cookies caper, the game moved into even more exciting escapades, and when Mrs. Ross came in to say that Marshall was down for his nap and that she was leaving for the university where she was taking a summer course for schoolteachers, the criminals were just escaping, taking one of the Brewster children with them as a hostage. An hour later, when Marshall came in sleepy-eyed and dragging Security, several of the other paper families had been brought into the plot. Marshall seemed content to sit and listen, so the game went on with daring adventures, narrow escapes, tragic illnesses and even a romance or two. At last, right in the middle of a shipwreck on a desert island, April noticed the time and said she'd have to go home so she'd be there when Caroline got back from work.

As they walked to the door Melanie said, "Do you want to play some more tomorrow?"

April was adjusting her fur stole around her shoulders for the trip upstairs. "Oh, I guess so," she said with a sudden return to haughtiness.

But Melanie was beginning to understand about April's frozen spells, and how to thaw her out. You just had to let her know she couldn't make you stop liking her that easily. "None of my friends know how to play imagining games the way you do," Melanie said. "Some of them can do it a little bit but they mostly don't have

any very good ideas. And a lot of them only like ball games or other things that are already made up. But I like imagining games better than anything."

April was being very busy trying to get her stole to stay on because the clasp was a little bit broken. All at once she pulled it off, wadded it all up and tucked it under her arm. She looked right straight at Melanie and said, "You know what? I never did call them that before, but imagining games are just about all I ever play because most of the time I never have anybody to play with."

She started off up the hall. Then she turned around and walked backward waving her fur stole around her head like a lasso. "You've got lots of good ideas, too," she yelled.

from A DOG ON BARKHAM STREET

Mary Stolz

Edward Frost wants two things from life: a dog, and Martin Hastings, the bully next door, to disappear from his world. Mary Stolz, long recognized as an outstanding writer of stories for teenage girls, here turns her attention to a real boy with real problems.

[Edward Cleans His Room]

Edward stood at the window and watched the rain tossing in sudden gusts along the street when the wind caught it, then falling straight again. Once in a while a car went by, its tires hissing, and once a wet, ruffled robin bounded across the grass and then took to its wings and flew, apparently, over the roof.

Now a dog came running along, its nose to the ground, its back quite sleek with water. Edward watched it hopefully. There were no end of stories in which the boy wanted a dog but didn't get one until a wonderful dog came along and selected *him*. In the stories these dogs were either stray ones, or the people who owned them saw how the boy and the dog loved each other and gave the dog up.

In the stories the parents agreed to keep the dog, even if they'd been very much against the idea before.

Edward was always looking around for some dog that would follow him home from school and refuse to leave. In a case like that, he didn't see how his mother could refuse. He had even, a couple of times, tried to lure a dog to follow him. Whistling at it, snapping his fingers, running in a tempting way. But he must have picked dogs that already had homes and liked them. Now if this dog, this wet dog running along by itself in the rain, should suddenly stop at his house, and come up to the door and cry to be let in . . . wouldn't his mother be *sure* to let Edward have him? You couldn't leave a dog out in the rain, could you? The dog ran across the street, ran back, dashed halfway over the lawn, stopped to shove its nose in a puddling flowerpot, backed off sneezing, sat down and scratched its chin.

Edward held his breath, waiting. After a moment he tapped lightly on the windowpane. The dog cocked its head in an asking gesture, got to its feet, then wheeled around and continued down the street. Edward sighed. He was not at all surprised—the dog had a collar with at least four license tags dangling from it—but still he sighed. He was pretty sure he'd forgotten to make his bed and suspected that a hammer he'd been using yesterday was now lying in the back yard getting pretty wet. Mr. Frost was particular about his tools, and Edward felt that dogs, if they weren't getting further away from him, certainly weren't coming any nearer. He decided to go up and make his bed. He didn't see what there was to do about the hammer just now, since his mother would notice if he went out in the rain to get it.

The mailman turned the corner, and Edward lingered to watch him. Mr. Dudley had his mail sack and a tremendous black umbrella to juggle. He wore a black slicker that glistened in the rain and shining mud-splashed rubbers and a plastic cover on his hat. He was late already but he moved slowly, as if he were tired.

"Mr. Dudley's coming," Edward said, as his mother came in the room.

Mrs. Frost came over to the window. "Poor man," she said. "Stay and ask him if he'd like to come in for a cup of coffee."

Edward waited, and when Mr. Dudley turned up their walk, he ran to the front door and opened it. "Mother says do you want some coffee, Mr. Dudley," he asked, as he took the mail.

"Well now, that's a handsome offer," Mr. Dudley said, frowning down at his rubbers, "but does your mother know I'm just this side of drowned?"

"Oh, that's all right," Edward said cheerfully. "You take off your rubbers and raincoat here on the porch."

Mr. Dudley laid down the mail sack and his huge black umbrella. "Can't say a cup of coffee won't be welcome," he observed, as he and Edward made for the kitchen.

Mrs. Frost gave the mailman a sweet bun with his coffee, and Edward a cup of cocoa. They sat in the breakfast nook and the rain beat against the window, making things quite snug. Edward glanced out in the back yard. There was the hammer, all right. In perfectly plain view. He guessed his mother hadn't noticed it yet, and decided that rain or no rain he was going to leave there until his father got home and to have to go after it. It was too good a hammer saw it.

"Notice you have a letter there from Arizona, Mrs. Frost," said Mr. Dudley. He licked the sugar daintily from his fingers and Edward watched with admiring envy. He wondered if Mr. Dudley's mother had told him, when he was a little boy, "Don't lick your fingers, dear, use the napkin." He decided she probably had and now Mr. Dudley, all grown up, was doing as he pleased. It was satisfying to watch and look forward to. Edward was really looking forward to growing up. And the first thing I'll do, he said to himself now, is move to some city that Martin Hastings never heard of.

Mrs. Frost had picked up the letter from Arizona. Her forehead wrinkled the way it did when a pie came out of the oven not looking as she'd planned it to. Edward and Mr. Dudley waited for her to say who it was from. Or, perhaps, "How strange—who can it be from?" Or, "So it is—a letter from Arizona." But she said none of these things. She frowned at the letter, and then, in a funny gesture, put the other letters on top of it, and asked Mr. Dudley if he wanted another cup of coffee.

After the mailman had gone, Edward began to say, "Who is that letter from—" but his mother interrupted him. This was something she practically never did, since she was always telling Edward how he shouldn't, and it made him begin to be very curious about the letter. His mother asked if he'd made his bed and he said maybe he ought to go up and see, so he climbed the stairs to his room, wondering all the way (about the letter, not the bed), and found that sure enough everything was rumpled and tossed around just as he had left it.

Suddenly, because that possible dog was on his mind, and because there was nothing else to do, Edward decided to make a tremendous gesture. He would clean his entire room. He would stack the books that lay around so carelessly. He would straighten his toys and his clothes. He'd get out the vacuum and do the rug. Maybe he'd even clean the closet. Yes, that was a great idea. He'd never cleaned the closet in his life. His mother would be so bowled over she'd probably offer him a St. Bernard on the spot.

He plunged in at once, dragging out clothes, books, fishing equipment, old forgotten trucks and games. He put the clothes on the still-unmade bed, shoved everything else out on the floor. It seemed to take an awfully long time to get the closet emptied, and then when he thought he was done he looked up, saw the shelves, and wished he'd never started.

They were absolutely jammed with junk. Well, maybe it wasn't all junk, but it looked it. And now his room was filled to brimming with things that would have to be put away again. He sat on his heels and stared around, thinking that the whole idea of cleaning up was pretty silly. Everything was just going to have to be put back in the closet, so what was the point of taking it out in the first place?

"My word, Edward," said his mother at the door, "what are you doing?"

"Cleaning my room," he said glumly.

"That's a good idea," she said, coming in. "Did all that come out of the closet?"

Edward nodded. "And it all has to go back," he said. "And I was just thinking, what's the point? I mean, where do you get *ahead*? I don't think I'll clean it after all."

"You can't leave it this way," said Mrs. Frost.

She picked up a battered green dump truck. "Do you ever use this?" When Edward said he didn't suppose so, at least he hadn't in a long time, she said, "Why don't you get a box from the cellar and put the things you don't really want in it, and we'll give it to the Salvation Army? They're marvelous at fixing things up for Christmas. It seems to me there must be a lot of things you've outgrown. When you get all that sorted out, you won't have so much to put back, and you'll be neater, *and* ahead. Sweep the closet out before you put your things away, of course, and put them away tidily. I see you hadn't made your bed after all."

There was no reasonable answer to this, so Edward stumped down to the basement for a box, wondering if dogs appreciated what people had to go through to get them. He paused at the cellar door, looking out. The rain hadn't slackened any. Or had it? He leaned forward, pressing his nose to the glass. He wasn't fifteen feet from that hammer, and his mother was busy upstairs, so if he just dashed out . . .

Pulling his sweater up so that it partly covered his head, he opened the door and dashed. The grass was sopping, the earth beneath it marshy, and, though he got the hammer all right, his shoulders and feet were drenched even in so short a run. Back in the cellar, he dried the hammer thoughtfully and stared at his shoes. Finally he removed them. The socks were dry enough. He took a towel from the hamper and rubbed his head and the sweater. Picking up the box, he went upstairs in his stocking feet, hoping his mother wouldn't notice anything.

"Here's the box," he said in a loud cheerful voice. "Think it's big enough?"

His mother had her back to him. She was on a chair, getting things down from the shelves. "I thought," she said, not turning around yet, "that I'd help you out a little. This is really quite a big job. Here, you take these things, and I'll hand you down some more—" She glanced around and stopped talking. Her eyes went from his head to his feet.

"I suppose," she said, "you had some reason for going out in the pouring rain? Aside from its nuisance value, that is?"

Edward wiggled his shoulders. He disliked that kind of remark, and would have preferred to have her come right out and ask what the heck he thought he was doing. But just saying something right out was a thing grownups rarely did. In this, as in so many matters concerning adults, Edward failed to see the reason but accepted the fact.

"Somebody had left the hammer out in the rain," he mumbled. "It might've got rusty."

"Somebody?" said Mrs. Frost, lifting one eyebrow.

Edward debated, and then said with inspiration, "Well, *I'm* somebody, aren't I?"

Mrs. Frost began to scowl, looked at the ceiling, half-smiled, turned back to the closet, and said, "How about all these jigsaw puzzles?"

"They're a bit on the simple side," said Edward. He almost added that they could get him some harder ones, but decided this wasn't the best time for requests of any sort. His mother was being very nice about the rain and the hammer, so there was no point in annoying her.

It was a funny thing, he mused, piling things in the box for the Salvation Army, that lots of times he asked for things not really much wanting them at all. For instance, jigsaw puzzles. He didn't actually want any, he didn't even like doing them very much when he got them, but the habit of *asking* was just one he sort of had. He asked for Good Humors if the Good Humor man happened to be around, clothes if he happened to be in a store where they sold them, toys if he happened to see them in an advertisement or a shop window. He guessed that one way and another he asked for something or other every single day whether he wanted it or not. Sometimes he got the thing and sometimes he didn't but anyone could see that the asking annoyed parents. Rod said he'd found that, too. Once Mr. Frost had said, "Edward, don't you ever bore yourself with these constant requests?" and Edward had said he didn't think so.

Still, thinking it over now, he wondered if it wouldn't be wiser to limit all the asking to a dog. If he concentrated on that, one of several things might happen. Either he'd wear them down so that at last they'd give in, or he'd impress them so much with how he wanted a dog and nothing else that they'd give in, or they'd get to be so sorry for him that they'd give in. Or—he had to admit—they'd get so irritated that he'd never see a dog until he was grown-up himself. He piled a fleet of little trucks in the box, and sat back on his heels to think.

"Problems?" said his mother, coming away from the closet to inspect the box. Edward nodded. "Could I help?" Mrs. Frost asked.

"Probably not," he said sadly. Then he looked up and met his mother's blue, friendly eyes. *"How* responsible do I have to be before I can have a dog?"

"Quite a bit, I'm afraid. Now, Edward . . . look at today. Bed unmade again, hammer out in the rain, *you* out in the rain—"

"But I'm cleaning my whole room," he protested.

"You started to," his mother reminded him. "If you recall, you got everything out and then changed your mind."

"When I grow up," Edward said, "my boy will have a dog as soon as he asks for it. In fact, I bet having the dog will *teach* him to be responsible," he added hopefully.

"But suppose it doesn't? Suppose you get the dog, and he doesn't take care of it at all?"

"I wouldn't mind taking care of it myself."

"Well, that's where you and I differ," said Mrs. Frost. "I would mind."

Edward, realizing that he hadn't handled his end of the argument well at all, gave up for the time being.

So now he could either get on with the room because he'd started and ought to finish, or he could get on with it because his mother was perfectly sure to make him. He decided on the former, and, in as responsible a voice as he could manage, he said, "Guess I might as well finish up here, eh?"

"I guess you might as well," said Mrs. Frost with a smile. "I'll have to leave you. I'm making a lemon meringue pie."

"You are?" said Edward with pleasure. There were few things he preferred to lemon meringue pie. "Gee, that's great." He went and fetched the vacuum cleaner and set to work in a good humor, the matter of dogs dwindling to the back of his mind.

Even people who wanted something badly couldn't think about it every single minute.

from **THE ADVENTURES OF**

TOM SAWYER

Mark Twain

This is one of the most famous scenes in American literature, and it should lead children to the book.

The Glorious Whitewasher

Saturday morning was come, and all the summer world was bright and fresh, and brimming with life. There was a song in every heart; and if the heart was young the music issued at the lips. There was cheer in every face and a spring in every step. The locust trees were in bloom and the fragrance of the blossoms filled the air. Cardiff Hill, beyond the village and above it, was green with vegetation, and it lay just far enough away to seem a Delectable Land, dreamy, reposeful, and inviting.

Tom appeared on the sidewalk with a bucket of whitewash and a long-handled brush. He surveyed the fence, and all gladness left him and a deep melancholy settled down upon his spirit. Thirty yards of board fence nine feet high. Life to him seemed hollow, and existence but a burden. Sighing he dipped his brush and passed it along the topmost plank; repeated the operation, did it again; compared the insignificant whitewashed streak with the far-reaching continent of unwhitewashed fence, and sat down on a tree-box discouraged. Jim came skipping out at the gate with a tin pail, and singing "Buffalo Gals." Bringing water from the town pump had always been hateful work in Tom's eyes, before, but now it did not strike him so. He remembered that there was company at the pump. White, mulatto, and Negro boys and girls were always there waiting their turns, resting, trading playthings, quarreling, fighting, skylarking. And he remembered that although the pump was only a hundred and fifty yards off, Jim never got back with a bucket of water under an hour—and even then somebody generally had to go after him. Tom said:

"Say, Jim, I'll fetch the water if you'll whitewash some."

From *The Adventures of Tom Sawyer* by **Mark Twain** (pseud. for Samuel L. Clemens), 1876

Jim shook his head and said:

"Can't, Mars Tom. Ole missis, she tole me I got to go an' git dis water an' not stop foolin' roun' wid anybody. She say she spec' Mars Tom gwine to ax me to whitewash, an' so she tole me go 'long an' 'tend to my own business—she 'lowed *she'd* 'tend to de whitewashin'."

"Oh, never you mind what she said, Jim. That's the way she always talks. Gimme the bucket—I won't be gone only a minute. *She* won't ever know."

"Oh, I dasn't, Mars Tom. Ole missis she'd take an' tar de head off'n me. 'Deed she would."

"*She!* She never licks anybody—whacks 'em over the head with her thimble—and who cares for that, I'd like to know. She talks awful, but talk don't hurt—anyways it don't if she don't cry. Jim, I'll give you a marvel. I'll give you a white alley!"

Jim began to waver.

"White alley, Jim! And it's a bully taw."

"My! Dat's a mighty gay marvel, *I* tell you! But Mars Tom, I's powerful 'fraid ole missis —"

"And besides, if you will I'll show you my sore toe."

Jim was only human—this attraction was too much for him. He put down his pail, took the white alley, and bent over the toe with absorbing interest while the bandage was being unwound. In another moment he was flying down the street with his pail and a tingling rear, Tom was whitewashing with vigor, and Aunt Polly was retiring from the field with a slipper in her hand and triumph in her eye.

But Tom's energy did not last. He began to think of the fun he had planned for this day, and his sorrows multiplied. Soon the free boys would come tripping along on all sorts of delicious expeditions, and they would make a world of fun of him for having to work—the very thought of it burnt him like fire. He got out his worldly wealth and examined it—bits of toys, marbles, and trash; enough to buy an exchange of *work*, maybe, but not half enough to buy so much as half an hour of pure freedom. So he returned his straitened means to his pocket, and gave up the idea of trying to buy the boys. At this dark and hopeless moment an inspiration burst upon him! Nothing less than a great, magnificent inspiration.

He took up his brush and went tranquilly to work. Ben Rogers hove in sight presently—the very boy, of all boys, whose ridicule he had been dreading. Ben's gait was the hop-skip-and-jump —proof enough that his heart was light and his anticipations high. He was eating an apple, and giving a long, melodious whoop, at intervals, followed by a deep-toned ding-dong-dong, ding-dong-dong, for he was personating a steamboat. As he drew near, he slackened speed, took the middle of the street, leaned far over to starboard and rounded to ponderously and with laborious pomp and circumstance—for he was personating the *Big Missouri,* and considered himself to be drawing nine feet of water. He was boat and captain and engine-bells combined, so he had to imagine himself standing on his own hurricane-deck giving the orders and executing them:

"Stop her, sir! Ting-a-ling-ling!" The headway ran almost out and he drew up slowly toward the sidewalk.

"Ship up to back! Ting-a-ling-ling!" His arms straightened and stiffened down his sides.

"Set her back on the stabboard! Ting-a-ling-ling! Chow! ch-chow-wow! Chow!" His right hand, meantime, describing stately circles—for it was representing a forty-foot wheel.

"Let her go back on the labboard! Ting-a-ling-ling! Chow-ch-chow-chow!" The left hand began to describe circles.

"Stop the stabboard! Ting-a-ling-ling! Stop the labboard! Come ahead on the stabboard! Stop her! Let your outside turn over slow! Ting-a-ling-ling! Chow-ow-ow! Get out that head-line! *Lively* now! Come—out with your spring-line—what're you about there! Take a turn round that stump with the bight of it! Stand by that stage, now— let her go! Done with the engines, sir! Ting-a-ling-ling! *Sh't! s'h't! sh't!*" (trying the gaugecocks).

Tom went on whitewashing—paid no attention to the steamboat. Ben stared a moment and then said:

"Hi-*yi! You're* up a stump, ain't you!"

No answer. Tom surveyed his last touch with the eye of an artist, then he gave his brush another gentle sweep and surveyed the result, as before. Ben ranged up alongside of him. Tom's mouth watered for the apple, but he stuck to his work. Ben said:

"Hello, old chap, you got to work, hey?"

Tom wheeled suddenly and said:

"Why, it's you, Ben! I warn't noticing."

"Say—*I'm* going in a-swimming, *I* am. Don't you wish you could? But of course you'd druther *work*—wouldn't you? Course you would!"

Tom contemplated the boy a bit, and said:

"What do you call work?"

"Why, ain't *that* work?"

Tom resumed his whitewashing, and answered carelessly:

"Well, maybe it is, and maybe it ain't. All I know is, it suits Tom Sawyer."

"Oh come, now, you don't mean to let on that you *like* it?"

The brush continued to move.

"Like it? Well, I don't see why I oughtn't to like it. Does a boy get a chance to whitewash a fence every day?"

That put the thing in a new light. Ben stopped nibbling his apple. Tom swept his brush daintily back and forth—stepped back to note the effect—added a touch here and there— criticized the effect again—Ben watching every move and getting more and more interested, more and more absorbed. Presently he said:

"Say, Tom, let *me* whitewash a little."

Tom considered, was about to consent; but he altered his mind:

"No—no—I reckon it wouldn't hardly do, Ben. You see, Aunt Polly's awful particular about this fence—right here on the street, you know—but if it was the back fence I wouldn't mind and *she* wouldn't. Yes, she's awful particular about this fence; it's got to be done very careful; I reckon there ain't one boy in a thousand, maybe two thousand, that can do it the way it's got to be done."

"No—is that so? Oh come, now—lemme just try. Only just a little—I'd let *you*, if you was me, Tom."

"Ben, I'd like to, honest injun; but Aunt Polly—well, Jim wanted to do it, but she wouldn't let him; Sid wanted to do it, and she wouldn't let Sid. Now don't you see how I'm fixed? If you was to tackle this fence and anything was to happen to it——"

"Oh, shucks, I'll be just as careful. Now lemme try. Say—I'll give you the core of my apple."

"Well, here— No, Ben, now don't. I'm afeared——"

"I'll give you *all* of it!"

Tom gave up the brush with reluctance in his face, but alacrity in his heart. And while the late steamer *Big Missouri* worked and sweated in the sun, the retired artist sat on a barrel in the shade close by, dangled his legs, munched his apple, and planned the slaughter of more innocents. There was no lack of material; boys happened along every little while; they came to jeer, but remained to whitewash. By the time Ben was fagged out, Tom had traded the next chance to Billy Fisher for a kite, in good repair; and when *he* played out, Johnny Miller bought in for a dead rat and a string to swing it with—and so on, and so on, hour after hour. And when the middle of the afternoon came, from being a poor poverty-stricken boy in the morning, Tom was literally rolling in wealth. He had beside the things before mentioned, twelve marbles, part of a jews'-harp, a piece of blue bottle-glass to look through, a spool cannon, a key that wouldn't unlock anything, a fragment of chalk, a glass stopper of a decanter, a tin soldier, a couple of tad-

poles, six firecrackers, a kitten with only one eye, a brass door-knob, a dog-collar—but no dog—the handle of a knife, four pieces of orange-peel, and a dilapidated old window-sash.

He had had a nice, good, idle time all the while—plenty of company—and the fence had three coats of whitewash on it! If he hadn't run out of whitewash, he would have bankrupted every boy in the village.

Tom said to himself that it was not such a hollow world, after all. He had discovered a great law of human action, without knowing it—namely, that in order to make a man or a boy covet a thing, it is only necessary to make the thing difficult to attain. If he had been a great and wise philosopher, like the writer of this book, he would now have comprehended that Work consists of whatever a body is *obliged* to do, and that Play consists of whatever a body is not obliged to do. And this would help him to understand why constructing artificial flowers or performing on a treadmill is work, while rolling tenpins or climbing Mont Blanc is only amusement. There are wealthy gentlemen in England who drive four-horse passenger-coaches twenty or thirty miles on a daily line, in the summer, because the privilege costs them considerable money; but if they were offered wages for the service, that would turn it into work and then they would resign.

The boy mused awhile over the substantial change which had taken place in his worldly circumstances, and then wended toward headquarters to report.

from JENNIFER, HECATE, MACBETH, WILLIAM McKINLEY, AND ME, ELIZABETH

E. L. Konigsburg

When Elizabeth, who is desperately lonely, meets Jennifer, it is Halloween—and what better time to meet a witch who promises to train her in the ways of witchcraft! From that moment on, Elizabeth's life is not the same; and neither is Jennifer's, for in the end, the two friendless girls have found the greatest magic of all—friendship. This book was a runner-up for the 1968 Newbery Medal.

[The School Halloween Parade]

I first met Jennifer on my way to school. It was Halloween, and she was sitting in a tree. I was going back to school from lunch. This particular lunch hour was only a little different from usual because of Halloween. We were told to dress in costume for the school Halloween parade. I was dressed as a Pilgrim.

I always walked the back road to school, and I always walked alone. We had moved to the apartment house in town in September just before school started, and I walked alone because I didn't have anyone to walk with. I walked the back way because it passed through a little woods that I liked. Jennifer was sitting in one of the trees in this woods.

Our apartment house had grown on a farm about ten years before. There was still a small farm across the street; it included a big white house, a greenhouse, a caretaker's house, and a pump painted green without a handle. The greenhouse had clean windows; they shone in the sun. I could see only the roof windows from our second floor apartment. The rest were hidden by trees and shrubs. My mother never called the place a farm; she always called it THE ESTATE. It was old; the lady who owned it was old. She had given part of her land to the town for a

park, and the town named the park after her: Samellson Park. THE ESTATE gave us a beautiful view from our apartment. My mother liked trees.

Our new town was not full of apartments. Almost everyone else lived in houses. There were only three apartment buildings as big as ours. All three sat on the top of the hill from the train station. Hundreds of men rode the train to New York City every morning and rode it home every night. My father did. In the mornings the elevators would be full of kids going to school and fathers going to the train. The kids left the building by the back door and ran down one side of the hill to the school. The fathers left the building by the front door and ran down the other side of the hill to the station.

Other kids from the apartment chose to walk to school through the little woods. The footsteps of all of them for ten years had worn away the soil so that the roots of the trees were bare and made steps for walking up and down the steep slope. The little woods made better company than the sidewalks. I liked the smells of the trees and the colors of the trees. I liked to walk with my head way up, practically hanging over my back. Then I could see the patterns the leaves formed against the blue sky.

I had my head way back and was watching the leaves when I first saw Jennifer up in the tree. She was dressed as a Pilgrim, too. I saw her feet first. She was sitting on one of the lower branches of the tree swinging her feet. That's how I happened to see her feet first. They were just about the boniest feet I had ever seen. Swinging right in front of my eyes as if I were sitting in the first row at Cinerama. They wore real Pilgrim shoes made of buckles and cracked old leather. The heel part flapped up and down because the shoes were so big that only the toe part could stay attached. Those shoes looked as if they were going to fall off any minute.

I grabbed the heel of the shoe and shoved it back onto the heel of that bony foot. Then I wiped my hands on my Pilgrim apron and looked up at Jennifer. I didn't know yet that she was Jennifer. She was not smiling, and I was embarrassed.

I said in a loud voice, which I hoped would sound stout red but which came out sounding thin blue, "You're going to lose that shoe."

Jennifer neither laughed nor answered. But I was sure she'd got it. She looked at me hard and said, "Give me those three chocolate chip cookies, and I'll come down and tell you my name, and I'll walk the rest of the way to school with you."

I wasn't particularly hungry for the cookies, but I was hungry for company, so I said, "Okay," and reached out my hand holding the cookies. I wondered how she could tell that they were chocolate chips. They were in a bag.

As she began to swing down from the branches, I caught a glimpse of her underwear. I expected that it would look dusty, and it did. But that was not why it was not like any underwear I had ever seen. It was old fashioned. There were buttons and no elastic. She also had on yards and yards of petticoats. Her Pilgrim dress looked older than mine. Much older. Much, much older. Hers looked ancient. Of course, my Pilgrim costume was not new either. I had worn it the year before, but then I had been in a different grade in a different school. My cousin had worn the costume before that. I hadn't grown much during the year. My dress was only a little short, and only a little tight, and only a little scratchy where it was pinned, and it was only absolutely uncomfortable. In other words, my costume was a hand-me-down, but Jennifer's was a genuine antique.

After Jennifer touched the ground, I saw that she was taller than I. Everybody was. I was the shortest kid in my class. I was always the shortest kid in my class. She was thin. Skinny is what she really was. She came toward my hand and looked hard at the bag of cookies.

"Are you sure you didn't bite any of them?" she demanded.

"Sure I'm sure," I said. I was getting mad, but a bargain's a bargain.

"Well," she said, taking one cookie out of the bag, "My name is Jennifer. Now let's get going." As she said "going," she grabbed the bag with the other two cookies and started to walk.

"Wait up," I yelled. "A bargain's a bargain. Don't you want to know my name?"

"I told you witches are never late, but I can't be responsible for you yet . . . Elizabeth."

She knew my name already! She walked so fast that I was almost convinced that she was a witch; she was practically flying. We got to school just as

The first thing Jennifer ever said to me was, "Witches never lose anything."

"But you're not a witch," I said. "You're a Pilgrim, and look, so am I."

"I won't argue with you," she said. "Witches convince; they never argue. But I'll tell you this much. Real witches are Pilgrims, and just because I don't have on a silly black costume and carry a silly broom and wear a silly black hat, doesn't mean that I'm not a witch. I'm a witch all the time and not just on Halloween."

I didn't know what to say, so I said what my mother always says when she can't answer one of my questions. I said, "You better hurry up now, or you'll be late for school."

"Witches are never late," she said.

"But witches have to go to school." I wished I had said something clever.

"I just go to school because I'm putting the teacher under a spell," she said.

"Which teacher?" I asked. "Get it? *Witch* teacher?" I laughed. I was pleased that now I had said something clever.

the tardy bell began to ring. Jennifer's room was a fifth grade just off the corridor near the entrance, and she slipped into her classroom while the bell was still buzzing. My room was four doors further down the hall, and I got to my room *after* the bell had stopped.

She had said that witches are never late. Being late felt as uncomfortable as my tight Pilgrim dress. No Pilgrim had ever suffered as much as I did. Walking to my seat while everyone stared at me was awful. My desk was in the back of the room; it was a long, long walk. The whole class had time to see that I was a blushing Pilgrim. I knew that I was ready to cry. The whole class didn't have to know that too, so I didn't raise my eyes until I was seated and felt sure that they wouldn't leak. When I looked up, I saw that there were six Pilgrims: three other Pilgrim girls and two Pilgrim boys. That's a lot of Pilgrims for a class of twenty. But none of them could be witches, I thought. After checking over their costumes and shoes, I decided that at least three of them had cousins who had been Pilgrims the year before.

Miss Hazen announced that she would postpone my detention until the next day because of the Halloween parade. Detention was a school rule; if you were late coming to school, you stayed after school that day. The kids called it "staying after." I didn't feel grateful for the postponement. She could have skipped my "staying after" altogether.

Our lesson that afternoon was short, and I didn't perform too well. I had to tug on my dress a lot and scratch under my Pilgrim hat a lot. I would have scratched other places where the costume itched, but they weren't polite.

At last we were all lined up in the hall. Each class was to march to the auditorium and be seated. Then one class at a time would walk across the stage before the judges. The rest of the classes would be the audience. The classes at the end of the hall marched to the auditorium first.

There were classes on both sides of the hall near my room, and the space for the marchers was narrow. Some of the children had large cardboard cartons over them and were supposed to be packages of cigarettes or sports cars. These costumes had trouble getting through. Then there

was Jennifer. She was last in line. She looked neither to the right nor to the left but slightly up toward the ceiling. I kept my eye on her hoping she'd say "Hi" so that I wouldn't feel so alone standing there. She didn't. Instead, well, I almost didn't believe what I actually saw her do.

But before I tell what I saw her do, I have to tell about Cynthia. Every grown-up in the whole U.S. of A. thinks that Cynthia is perfect. She is pretty and neat and smart. I guess that makes perfect to almost any grown-up. Since she lives in the same apartment house as we do, and since my mother is a grown-up, and since my mother thinks that she is perfect, my mother had tried hard to have us become friends since we first moved to town. My mother would drop hints. HINT: Why don't you call Cynthia and ask her if she would like to show you where the library is? Then you can both eat lunch here. Or HINT: Why don't you run over and play with Cynthia while I unpack the groceries?

It didn't take me long to discover that what Cynthia was, was not perfect. The word for what Cynthia was, was *mean*.

Here's an example of mean. There was a little boy in our building who had moved in about a month before we did. His name was Johann; that's German for John. He moved from Germany and didn't speak English yet. He loved Cynthia. Because she was so pretty, I guess. He followed her around and said, "Cynsssia, Cynsssia." Cynthia always made fun of him. She would stick her tongue between her teeth and say, "Th, th, th, th, th. My name is Cyn-*th*-ia not Cyn-*sss*-ia." Johann would smile and say, "Cyn-*sss*-ia." Cynthia would stick out her tongue and say, "Th, th, th, th, th." And then she'd walk away from him. I liked Johann. I wished he would follow me around. I would have taught him English, and I would never even have minded if he called me Elizabessss. Another word for what Cynthia was, was *two-faced*. Because every time some grown-up was around, she was sweet to Johann. She'd smile at him and pat his head . . . only until the grown-up left.

And another thing: Cynthia certainly didn't need me for a friend. She had a very good friend called Dolores who also lived in the apartment house. They told secrets and giggled together whenever I got into the elevator with them. So I

got into the habit of leaving for school before they did. Sometimes, on weekends, they'd be in the elevator when I got on; I'd act as if they weren't there. I had to get off the elevator before they did because I lived on the second floor, and they lived on the sixth. Before I'd get off the elevator, I'd take my fists, and fast and furious, I'd push every floor button just the second before I got out. I'd step out of the elevator and watch the dial stopping at every floor on the way up. Then I'd skip home to our apartment.

For Halloween Cynthia wore everything real ballerinas wear: leotards and tights and ballet slippers and a tutu. A tutu is a little short skirt that ballerinas wear somewhere around their waists. Hers looked like a nylon net doughnut floating around her middle. Besides all the equipment I listed above, Cynthia wore rouge and eye make-up and lipstick and a tiara. She looked glamorous, but I could tell that she felt plenty chilly in that costume. Her teeth were chattering. She wouldn't put on a sweater.

As we were standing in the hall waiting for our turn to go to the auditorium, and as Jennifer's class passed, Cynthia was turned around talking to Dolores. Dolores was dressed as a Pilgrim. They were both whispering and giggling. Probably about Jennifer.

Here's what Jennifer did. As she passed Cynthia, she reached out and quicker than a blink

unsnapped the tutu. I happened to be watching her closely, but even I didn't believe that she had really done it. Jennifer clop-clopped along in the line with her eyes still up toward the ceiling and passed me a note almost without my knowing. She did it so fast that I wasn't even sure she did it until I felt the note in my hand and crunched it beneath my apron to hide it. Jennifer never took her eyes off the ceiling or broke out of line for even half a step.

I wanted to make sure that everyone saw Cynthia with her tutu down, so I pointed my finger at her and said, "O-o-o-o-oh!" I said it loud. Of course, that made everyone on both sides of the aisle notice her and start to giggle.

Cynthia didn't have sense enough to be embarrassed. She loved attention so much that she didn't care if her tutu had fallen. She stepped out of it, picked it up, shook it out, floated it over her head, and anchored it back around her waist. She touched her hands to her hair, giving it little pushes the way women do who have just come out of the beauty parlor. I hoped she was itchy.

Finally, our class got to the auditorium. After I sat down, I opened the note, holding both my hands under my Pilgrim apron. I slowly slipped my hands out and glanced at the note. I was amazed at what I saw. Jennifer's note looked like this:

Meet for Trick or Treat
at
Half after six P.M. o'clock
of this evening.
By the same tree.
Bring two (2) bags.
I hope were good cookies

I studied the note a long time. I thought about the note as I watched the Halloween parade; I wondered if Jennifer used a quill pen. You can guess that I didn't win any prizes for my costume. Neither did Cynthia. Neither did Jennifer (even though I thought she should have). We all marched across the stage wearing our masks and stopped for a curtsy or bow (depending on whether you were a girl or a boy) in front of the judges who were sitting at a table in the middle of the stage. Some of the girls who were disguised as boys forgot themselves and curtsied. Then we marched off. Our class was still seated when Jennifer clop-clopped across the stage in those crazy Pilgrim slippers. She didn't wear a mask at all. She wore a big brown paper bag over her head and *there were no holes cut out for her eyes.* Yet, she walked up the stairs, across the stage, stopped and curtsied, and walked off without tripping or falling or walking out of those gigantic shoes.

from HARRIET THE SPY

Louise Fitzhugh

Having learned from her friend Janie that they are destined to go to dancing school, Harriet Welsch, girl spy and author-in-training, decides to take the initiative in getting her parents to change their minds about dancing school.

Harriet the Spy by Louise Fitzhugh. Copyright © 1964 by Louise Fitzhugh. Reprinted with permission of Harper & Row, Publishers, and McIntosh & Otis, Inc.

The response of her parents, the way Ole Golly copes, and the relationships among the children are seen in this excerpt. Harriet's arrival in the book world was like an atomic explosion; some adults strongly object to the book. Other adults and most children find Harriet believable and unforgettable.

[Harriet Changes Her Mind]

That night at dinner everything was going along as usual, that is, Mr. and Mrs. Welsch were having an interminable, rambling conversation about nothing in particular while Harriet watched it all like a tennis match, when suddenly Harriet leaped to her feet as though she had just then remembered, and screamed, "I'll be *damned* if I'll go to dancing school."

"Harriet!" Mrs. Welsch was appalled. "How dare you use words like that at the table."

"Or any other place, dear," interjected Mr. Welsch calmly.

"All right, I'll be FINKED if I'll go to dancing school." Harriet stood and screamed this solidly. She was throwing a fit. She only threw fits as a last resort, so that even as she did it she had a tiny feeling in the back of her brain that she had already lost. She wouldn't, however, have it said that she went down without a try.

"Where in the world did you learn a word like that?" Mrs. Welsch's eyebrows were raised almost to her hairline.

"It's not a verb, anyway," said Mr. Welsch. They both sat looking at Harriet as though she were a curiosity put on television to entertain them.

"I *will not, I will not, I will not,*" shouted Harriet at the top of her lungs. She wasn't getting the right reaction. Something was wrong.

"Oh, but you will," said Mrs. Welsch calmly. "It really isn't so bad. You don't even know what it's like."

"I hated it," said Mr. Welsch and went back to his dinner.

"I *do so* know what it's like." Harriet was getting tired of standing up and screaming. She wished she could sit down but it wouldn't have done. It would have looked like giving up. "I went there once on a visit with Beth Ellen because she had to go and I was spending the night, and you have to wear party dresses and all the boys are too short and you feel like a *hippopotamus.*" She said this all in one breath and screamed "hippopotamus."

Mr. Welsch laughed. "An accurate description, you must admit."

"Darling, the boys get taller as you go along."

"I just *won't.*" Somehow, indefinably, Harriet felt she was losing ground all the time.

"It isn't so bad." Mrs. Welsch went back to her dinner.

This was too much. The point wasn't coming across at all. They had to be roused out of their complacency. Harriet took a deep breath, and in as loud a voice as she could, repeated, "I'll be *damned* if I'll go!"

"All right, that does it." Mrs. Welsch stood up. She was furious. "You're getting your mouth washed out with soap, young lady. Miss Golly, Miss Golly, step in here a minute." When there was no response, Mrs. Welsch rang the little silver dinner bell and in a moment Cook appeared.

Harriet stood petrified. *Soap!*

"Cook, will you tell Miss Golly to step in here a minute." Mrs. Welsch stood looking at Harriet as though she were a worm, as Cook departed. "Now Harriet, to your room. Miss Golly will be up shortly."

"But . . ."

"Your *room,*" said Mrs. Welsch firmly, pointing to the door.

Feeling rather like an idiot, Harriet left the dining room. She thought for half a second about waiting around and listening outside but decided it was too risky.

She went up to her room and waited. Ole Golly came in a few minutes later.

"Well, now, what is this about dancing school?" she asked amiably.

"I'm not going," Harriet said meekly. There was something that made her feel ridiculous when she shouted at Ole Golly. Maybe because she never got the feeling with Ole Golly that she did with her parents that they never heard anything.

"Why not?" Ole Golly asked sensibly.

Harriet thought a minute. The other reasons weren't really it. It was that the thought of being in dancing school somehow made her feel undignified. Finally she had it. "*Spies* don't go to dancing school," she said triumphantly.

"Oh, but they do," said Ole Golly.

"They do *not,*" said Harriet rudely.

"Harriet"—Ole Golly took a deep breath and sat down—"have you ever thought about how spies are trained?"

"Yes. They learn languages and guerrilla fighting and everything about a country so if they're captured they'll know all the old football scores and things like that."

"That's *boy* spies, Harriet. You're not thinking."

Harriet hated more than anything else to be told by Ole Golly that she wasn't thinking. It was worse than any soap. "What do you mean?" she asked quietly.

"What about *girl* spies? What are they taught?"

"The same things."

"The same things and a few more. Remember that movie we saw about Mata Hari one night on television?"

"Yes . . ."

"Well, think about that. Where did she operate? Not in the woods guerrilla fighting, right? She went to parties, right? And remember that scene with the general or whatever he was—she was dancing, right? Now how are you going to be a spy if you don't know how to dance?"

There must be some answer to this, thought Harriet as she sat there silently. She couldn't think of a thing. She went "Hmmmph" rather loudly. Then she thought of something. "Well, do I have to wear those silly dresses? Couldn't I wear my spy clothes? They're better to learn to dance in anyway. In school we wear our gym suits to learn to dance."

"Of course not. Can you see Mata Hari in a gym suit? First of all, if you wear your spy clothes everyone knows you're a spy, so what have you gained? No, you have to look like everyone else, then you'll get by and no one will suspect you."

"That's true," said Harriet miserably. She couldn't see Mata Hari in a gym suit either.

"Now"—Ole Golly stood up—"you better march downstairs and tell them you changed your mind."

"What'll I say?" Harriet felt embarrassed.

"Just say you've changed your mind."

Harriet stood up resolutely and marched down the steps to the dining room. Her parents were having coffee. She stood in the doorway and said in a loud voice, "I've changed my mind!" They looked at her in a startled way. She turned and left the doorway abruptly. There was nothing further to be said. As she went back up the steps she heard them burst out laughing and then her father said, "Boy, that Miss Golly is magic, sheer magic. I wonder where we'd be without her?"

Harriet didn't know how to approach Janie about her defection, but she decided she must. At lunch Sport and Janie sat laughing over the new edition of *The Gregory News* which had just come out. *The Gregory News* was the school paper. There was a page reserved for every grade

in the Middle School and every grade in the Upper School. The Lower School were such idiots they didn't need a page.

"Look at that. It's ridiculous." Janie was talking about Marion Hawthorne's editorial about candy wrappers everywhere.

"She just did that because Miss Whitehead talked about them on opening day," Harriet sneered.

"Well, what else? She hasn't got the sense to think of anything original." Sport bit into a hard-boiled egg. Sport made his own lunch and it was usually hard-boiled eggs.

"But it's so dumb and boring," Harriet said. "Listen to this: 'We must not drop our candy wrappers on the ground. They must be put into the wastebaskets provided for this purpose.' It's not even news; we hear it practically every day."

"I'll put *her* in a wastebasket," said Janie with satisfaction.

"My father says you have to catch the reader's attention right at first and then hold it," said Sport.

"Well, she just lost it," said Harriet.

"You oughta write it, Harriet, you're a writer," said Sport.

"I wouldn't do it now if they paid me. They can have their dumb paper." Harriet finished her sandwich with a frown.

"They should be blown up," said Janie.

They ate in silence for a moment.

"Janie . . ." Harriet hesitated so long that they both looked up at her. "I think they've got me," she said sadly.

"What? Was that sandwich poisoned?" Janie stood up. The egg fell right out of Sport's mouth.

"No," Harriet said quickly. Now it was anticlimactic. "I mean dancing school," Harriet said grimly.

Janie sat down and looked away as though Harriet had been impolite.

"Dancing school?" Sport squeaked, picking the egg out of his lap.

"Yes," said Janie grimly.

"Oh, boy, am I glad. My father never even *heard* of that." Sport grinned around his egg.

"Well," said Harriet sadly, "It looks like I'm gonna have to if I'm gonna be a spy."

"Who ever heard of a dancing spy?" Janie

was so furious she wouldn't even look at Harriet.

"Mata Hari," Harriet said quietly; then when Janie didn't turn around she added very loudly, "I can't *help* it, Janie."

Janie turned and looked at her. "I know," she said sadly, "I'm going too."

It was all right then, and Harriet ate her other tomato sandwich happily.

After school, when Harriet went home for her cake and milk, she remembered that it was Thursday and that Thursday was Ole Golly's night out. As she was running down the steps to the kitchen she was struck by a thought so interesting that it made her stop still on the steps. If Ole Golly had a boy friend and she went out on her night out—wouldn't she meet the boy friend? And . . . if she were to meet the boy friend—couldn't Harriet follow her and see what he looked like? Extraordinary thought. She decided that she would have to be extra careful and terribly crafty to find out when, where, and with whom Ole Golly was spending her free evening. If Ole Golly went to places like the Welsches did, like night clubs, Harriet wouldn't be able to follow. Out of the question. She would have to wait until she was Mata Hari for that.

But *IF*, for instance, this boy friend were to come to the house and pick up Ole Golly. *THEN* Harriet could at least see what he looked like. She decided to pursue this as she clattered down the rest of the way into the kitchen. Ole Golly was having her tea. The cook put out the cake and milk as Harriet slipped into place at the table.

"Well," said Ole Golly in a friendly manner.

"Well?" said Harriet. She was looking at Ole Golly in a new way. What was it like for Ole Golly to have a boy friend? Did she like him the way Harriet liked Sport?

"Well, iffen it don't rain, it'll be a long dry spell," Ole Golly said softly, then smiled into her tea.

Harriet looked at her curiously. That was one thing about Ole Golly, thought Harriet, she never, never said dull things like, 'How was school today?' or 'How did you do in arithmetic?' or 'Going out to play?' All of these were unanswerable questions, and she supposed that Ole Golly was the only grown-up that knew that.

from

FROM THE MIXED-UP FILES OF
MRS. BASIL E. FRANKWEILER

E. L. Konigsburg

This winner of the 1968 Newbery Medal is the story of Claudia Kincaid and her brother Jamie, told by Mrs. Basil E. Frankweiler. Claudia was not running away from home permanently; she planned to return home "after everyone had learned a lesson in Claudia appreciation." But long after "everyone" had learned his lesson, Claudia and her brother were still hiding out in the Metropolitan Museum of Art, taking baths in the fountain, sleeping in a sixteenth-century bed, and being intrigued with the identification of the sculptor whose beautiful statue was on display. Mrs. Frankweiler, donor of the statue, holds the answer to Claudia's questions, and from her mixed-up files emerges the answer that finally allows Claudia and Jamie to return home. The following selection is Chapter 3 in the book; notice how Mrs. Frankweiler alternately "narrates" the story from the children's point of view and "tells" their story from her own point of view. The Saxonberg mentioned in this selection is Mrs. Frankweiler's lawyer, to whom she has sent these "files."

["Checking-In" at the Museum]

As soon as they reached the sidewalk, Jamie made his first decision as treasurer. "We'll walk from here to the museum."

"Walk?" Claudia asked. "Do you realize that it is over forty blocks from here?"

"Well, how much does the bus cost?"

"The bus!" Claudia exclaimed. "Who said anything about taking a bus? I want to take a taxi."

"Claudia," Jamie said, "you are quietly out of your mind. How can you even think of a taxi? We have no more allowance. No more income. You can't be extravagant any longer. It's not my money we're spending. It's *our* money. We're in this together, remember?"

"You're right," Claudia answered. "A taxi is

expensive. The bus is cheaper. It's only twenty cents each. We'll take the bus."

"*Only* twenty cents each. That's forty cents total. No bus. We'll walk."

"We'll wear out forty cents worth of shoe leather," Claudia mumbled. "You're sure we have to walk?"

"Positive," Jamie answered. "Which way do we *go?*"

"Sure you won't change your mind?" The look on Jamie's face gave her the answer. She sighed. No wonder Jamie had more than twenty-four dollars; he was a gambler and a cheapskate. If that's the way he wants to be, she thought, I'll never again ask him for bus fare; I'll suffer and never, never let him know about it. But he'll regret it when I simply collapse from exhaustion. I'll collapse quietly.

"We'd better walk up Madison Avenue," she told her brother. "I'll see too many ways to spend *our* precious money if we walk on Fifth Avenue. All those gorgeous stores."

She and Jamie did not walk exactly side by side. Her violin case kept bumping him, and he began to walk a few steps ahead of her. As Claudia's pace slowed down from what she was sure was an accumulation of carbon dioxide in her system (she had not yet learned about muscle fatigue in science class even though she was in the sixth grade honors class), Jamie's pace quickened. Soon he was walking a block and a half ahead of her. They would meet when a red light held him up. At one of these mutual stops Claudia instructed Jamie to wait for her on the corner of Madison Avenue and 80th Street, for there they would turn left to Fifth Avenue.

She found Jamie standing on that corner, probably one of the most civilized street corners in the whole world, consulting a compass and announcing that when they turned left, they would be heading "due northwest." Claudia was tired and cold at the tips; her fingers, her toes, her nose were all cold while the rest of her was perspiring under the weight of her winter clothes. She never liked feeling either very hot or very cold, and she hated feeling both at the same time. "Head due northwest. Head due northwest," she mimicked. "Can't you simply say turn right or turn left as everyone else does? Who do you think you are? Daniel Boone? I'll bet no one's

used a compass in Manhattan since Henry Hudson."

Jamie didn't answer. He briskly rounded the corner of 80th Street and made his hand into a sun visor as he peered down the street. Claudia needed an argument. Her internal heat, the heat of anger, was cooking that accumulated carbon dioxide. It would soon explode out of her if she didn't give it some vent. "Don't you realize that we must try to be inconspicuous?" she demanded of her brother.

"What's inconspicuous?"

"Un-noticeable."

Jamie look all around. "I think you're brilliant, Claude. New York is a great place to hide out. No one notices no one."

"Anyone," Claudia corrected. She looked at Jamie and found him smiling. She softened. She had to agree with her brother. She was brilliant. New York was a great place, and being called brilliant had cooled her down. The bubbles dissolved. By the time they reached the museum, she no longer needed an argument.

As they entered the main door on Fifth Avenue, the guard clicked off two numbers on his people counter. Guards always count the people going into the museum, but they don't count them going out. (My chauffeur, Sheldon, has a friend named Morris who is a guard at the Metropolitan. I've kept Sheldon busy getting information from Morris. It's not hard to do since Morris loves to talk about his work. He'll tell about anything except security. Ask him a question he won't or can't answer, and he says, "I'm not at liberty to tell. Security.")

By the time Claudia and Jamie reached their destination, it was one o'clock, and the museum was busy. On any ordinary Wednesday over 26,000 people come. They spread out over the twenty acres of floor space; they roam from room to room to room to room to room. On Wednesday come the gentle old ladies who are using the time before the Broadway matinee begins. They walk around in pairs. You can tell they are a set because they wear matching pairs of orthopedic shoes, the kind that lace on the side. Tourists visit the museum on Wednesdays. You can tell them because the men carry cameras, and the women look as if their feet hurt; they wear high heeled shoes. (I always say that those who wear 'em deserve 'em.) And there are art students. Any day of the week. They also walk around in pairs. You can tell that they are a set because they carry matching black sketchbooks.

(You've missed all this, Saxonberg. Shame on you! You've never set your well-polished shoe inside that museum. More than a quarter of a million people come to that museum every week. They come from Mankato, Kansas, where they have no museums and from Paris, France, where they have lots. And they all enter free of charge because that's what the museum is: great and large and wonderful and free to all. And complicated. Complicated enough even for Jamie Kincaid.)

No one thought it strange that a boy and a girl, each carrying a book bag and an instrument case and who would normally be in school, were visiting a museum. After all, about a thousand school children visit the museum each day. The guard at the entrance merely stopped them and told them to check their cases and book bags. A museum rule: no bags, food, or umbrellas. None that the guards can see. Rule or no rule, Claudia decided it was a good idea. A big sign in the checking room said NO TIPPING, so she knew that Jamie couldn't object. Jamie did object, however; he pulled his sister aside and asked her how she expected him to change into his pajamas. His pajamas, he explained, were rolled into a tiny ball in his trumpet case.

Claudia told him that she fully expected to check out at 4:30. They would then leave the museum by the front door and within five minutes would re-enter from the back, through the door that leads from the parking lot to the Children's Museum. After all, didn't that solve all their problems? (1) They would be seen leaving the museum. (2) They would be free of their baggage while they scouted around for a place to spend the night. And (3) it was free.

Claudia checked her coat as well as her packages. Jamie was condemned to walking around in his ski jacket. When the jacket was on and zipped, it covered up that exposed strip of skin. Besides, the orlon plush lining did a great deal to muffle his twenty-four-dollar rattle. Claudia would never have permitted herself to become so overheated, but Jamie liked perspiration, a little bit of dirt, and complications.

Right now, however, he wanted lunch. Claudia wished to eat in the restaurant on the main floor, but Jamie wished to eat in the snack bar downstairs; he thought it would be less glamorous, but cheaper, and as chancellor of the exchequer, as holder of the veto power, and as tightwad of the year, he got his wish. Claudia didn't really mind too much when she saw the snack bar. It was plain but clean.

Jamie was dismayed at the prices. They had $28.61 when they went into the cafeteria, and only $27.11 when they came out still feeling hungry. "Claudia," he demanded, "did you know food would cost so much? Now, aren't you glad that we didn't take a bus?"

Claudia was no such thing. She was not glad that they hadn't taken a bus. She was merely furious that her parents, and Jamie's too, had been so stingy that she had been away from home for less than one whole day and was already worried about survival money. She chose not to answer Jamie. Jamie didn't notice; he was completely wrapped up in problems of finance.

"Do you think I could get one of the guards to play me a game of war?" he asked.

"That's ridiculous," Claudia said.

"Why? I brought my cards along. A whole deck."

Claudia said, "*Inconspicuous* is exactly the opposite of that. Even a guard at the Metropolitan who sees thousands of people every day would remember a boy who played him a game of cards."

Jamie's pride was involved. "I cheated Bruce through all second grade and through all third grade so far, and he still isn't wise."

"Jamie! Is that how you knew you'd win?"

Jamie bowed his head and answered, "Well, yeah. Besides, Brucie has trouble keeping straight the jacks, queens, and kings. He gets mixed up."

"Why do you cheat your best friend?"

"I sure don't know. I guess I like complications."

"Well, quit worrying about money now. Worry about where we're going to hide while they're locking up this place."

They took a map from the information stand; for free. Claudia selected where they would hide during that dangerous time immediately after the museum was closed to the public and before all the guards and helpers left. She decided that she would go to the ladies' room, and Jamie would go to the men's room just before the museum closed. "Go to the one near the restaurant on the main floor," she told Jamie.

"I'm not spending a night in a men's room. All that tile. It's cold. And, besides, men's rooms make noises sound louder. And I rattle enough now."

Claudia explained to Jamie that he was to enter a booth in the men's room. "And then stand on it," she continued.

"Stand on it? Stand on what?" Jamie demanded.

"You know," Claudia insisted. "Stand on it!"

"You mean stand on the toilet?" Jamie needed everything spelled out.

"Well, what else would I mean? What else is there in a booth in the men's room? And keep your head down. And keep the door to the booth very slightly open," Claudia finished.

"Feet up. Head down. Door open. Why?"

"Because I'm certain that when they check the ladies' room and the men's room, they peek under the door and check only to see if there are feet. We must stay there until we're sure all the people and guards have gone home."

"How about the night watchman?" Jamie asked.

Claudia displayed a lot more confidence than she really felt. "Oh! there'll be a night watchman, I'm sure. But he mostly walks around the roof trying to keep people from breaking in. We'll already be in. They call what he walks, a cat walk. We'll learn his habits soon enough. They must mostly use burglar alarms in the inside. We'll just never touch a window, a door, or a valuable painting. Now, let's find a place to spend the night."

They wandered back to the rooms of fine French and English furniture. It was here Claudia knew for sure that she had chosen the most elegant place in the world to hide. She wanted to sit on the lounge chair that had been made for Marie Antoinette or at least sit at her writing table. But signs everywhere said not to step on the platform. And some of the chairs had silken ropes strung across the arms to keep you from even trying to sit down. She would have to wait until after lights out to be Marie Antoinette.

At last she found a bed that she considered perfectly wonderful, and she told Jamie that they would spend the night there. The bed had a tall canopy, supported by an ornately carved headboard at one end and by two gigantic posts at the other. (I'm familiar with that bed, Saxonberg. It is as enormous and fussy as mine. And it dates from the sixteenth century like mine. I once considered donating my bed to the museum, but Mr. Untermyer gave them this one first. I was somewhat relieved when he did. Now I can enjoy my bed without feeling guilty because the museum doesn't have one. Besides, I'm not that fond of donating things.)

Claudia had always known that she was meant for such fine things. Jamie, on the other hand, thought that running away from home to sleep in just another bed was really no challenge at all.

He, James, would rather sleep on the bathroom floor, after all. Claudia then pulled him around to the foot of the bed and told him to read what the card said.

Jamie read, "Please do not step on the platform."

Claudia knew that he was being difficult on purpose; therefore, she read for him, "State bed—scene of the alleged murder of Amy Robsart, first wife of Lord Robert Dudley, later Earl of . . ."

Jamie couldn't control his smile. He said, "You know, Claude, for a sister and a fussbudget, you're not too bad."

Claudia replied, "You know, Jamie, for a brother and a cheapskate, you're not too bad."

Something happened at precisely that moment. Both Claudia and Jamie tried to explain to me about it, but they couldn't quite. I know what happened, though I never told them. Having words and explanations for everything is too modern. I especially wouldn't tell Claudia. She has too many explanations already.

What happened was: they became a team, a family of two. There had been times before they ran away when they had acted like a team, but those were very different from *feeling* like a team. Becoming a team didn't mean the end of their arguments. But it did mean that the arguments became a part of the adventure, became discussions not threats. To an outsider the arguments would appear to be the same because feeling like part of a team is something that happens invisibly. You might call it *caring*. You could even call it *love*. And it is very rarely, indeed, that it happens to two people at the same time—especially a brother and a sister who had always spent more time with activities than they had with each other.

They followed their plan: checked out of the museum and re-entered through a back door. When the guard at that entrance told them to check their instrument cases, Claudia told him that they were just passing through on their way to meet their mother. The guard let them go,

knowing that if they went very far, some other guard would stop them again. However, they managed to avoid other guards for the remaining minutes until the bell rang. The bell meant that the museum was closing in five minutes. They then entered the booths of the rest rooms.

They waited in the booths until five-thirty, when they felt certain that everyone had gone. Then they came out and met. Five-thirty in winter is dark, but nowhere seems as dark as the Metropolitan Museum of Art. The ceilings are so high that they fill up with a lot of darkness. It seemed to Jamie and Claudia that they walked through miles of corridors. Fortunately, the corridors were wide, and they were spared bumping into things.

At last they came to the hall of the English Renaissance. Jamie quickly threw himself upon the bed forgetting that it was only about six o'clock and thinking that he would be so exhausted that he would immediately fall asleep. He didn't. He was hungry. That was one reason he didn't fall asleep immediately. He was uncomfortable, too. So he got up from bed, changed into his pajamas and got back into bed. He felt a little better. Claudia had already changed into her pajamas. She, too, was hungry, and she, too, was uncomfortable. How could so elegant and romantic a bed smell so musty? She would have liked to wash everything in a good, strong, sweet-smelling detergent.

As Jamie got into bed, he still felt uneasy, and it wasn't because he was worried about being caught. Claudia had planned everything so well that he didn't concern himself about that. The strange way he felt had little to do with the strange place in which they were sleeping. Claudia felt it, too. Jamie lay there thinking. Finally, realization came.

"You know, Claude," he whispered, "I didn't brush my teeth."

Claudia answered, "Well, Jamie, you can't always brush after every meal." They both laughed very quietly. "Tomorrow," Claudia reassured him, "we'll be even better organized."

It was much earlier than her bedtime at home, but still Claudia felt tired. She thought she might have an iron deficiency anemia: tired blood. Perhaps, the pressures of everyday stress and strain had gotten her down. Maybe she was light-headed from hunger; her brain cells were being robbed of vitally needed oxygen for good growth and, and . . . yawn.

She shouldn't have worried. It had been an unusually busy day. A busy and unusual day. So she lay there in the great quiet of the museum next to the warm quiet of her brother and allowed the soft stillness to settle around them: a comforter of quiet. The silence seeped from their heads to their soles and into their souls. They stretched out and relaxed. Instead of oxygen and stress, Claudia thought now of hushed and quiet words: glide, fur, banana, peace. Even the footsteps of the night watchman added only an accented quarter-note to the silence that had become a hum, a lullaby.

They lay perfectly still even long after he passed. Then they whispered good night to each other and fell asleep. They were quiet sleepers and hidden by the heaviness of the dark, they were easily not discovered.

(Of course, Saxonberg, the draperies of that bed helped, too.)

from MY SIDE OF THE MOUNTAIN

Jean George

Almost every human being, boy or girl, man or woman, occasionally wishes to escape the complexities of modern life and return to nature, but few follow through on their desires. Readers, young and old, can vicariously share such an experience in reading about Sam Gribley's adventures on his side of the mountain during the year he lived alone and off the land.

This Is about the Old, Old Tree

I knew enough about the Catskill Mountains to know that when the summer came, they were covered with people. Although Great-grandfather's farm was somewhat remote, still hikers and campers and hunters and fishermen were sure to wander across it.

Therefore I wanted a house that could not be

seen. People would want to take me back where I belonged if they found me.

I looked at that tree. Somehow I knew it was home, but I was not quite sure how it was home. The limbs were high and not right for a tree house. I could build a back extension around it, but that would look silly. Slowly I circled the great trunk. Halfway around, the whole plan became perfectly obvious. To the west, between two of the flanges of the tree that spread out to be roots, was a cavity. The heart of the tree was rotting away. I scraped at it with my hands; old, rotten insect-ridden dust came tumbling out. I dug on and on, using my ax from time to time as my excitement grew.

With much of the old rot out, I could crawl in the tree and sit cross-legged. Inside I felt as cozy as a turtle in its shell. I chopped and chopped until I was hungry and exhausted. I was now in the hard good wood, and chopping it out was work. I was afraid December would come before I got a hole big enough to lie in. So I sat down to think.

You know, those first days, I just never planned right. I had the beginnings of a home, but not a bite to eat, and I had worked so hard that I could hardly move forward to find that bite. Furthermore it was discouraging to feed that body of mine. It was never satisfied, and gathering food for it took time and got it hungrier. Trying to get a place to rest it took time and got it more tired, and I really felt I was going in circles and wondered how primitive man ever had enough time and energy to stop hunting food and start thinking about fire and tools.

I left the tree and went across the meadow looking for food. I plunged into the woods beyond, and there I discovered the gorge and the white cascade splashing down the black rocks into the pool below.

I was hot and dirty. I scrambled down the rocks and slipped into the pool. It was so cold I yelled. But when I came out on the bank and put on my two pairs of trousers and three sweaters, which I thought was a better way to carry clothes than in a pack, I tingled and burned and felt coltish. I leapt up the bank, slipped, and my face went down in a patch of dogtooth violets.

You would know them anywhere after a few looks at them at the Botanical Gardens and in colored flower books. They are little yellow lilies on long slender stems with oval leaves dappled with gray. But that's not all. They have wonderfully tasty bulbs. I was filling my pockets before I got up from my fall.

"I'll have a salad type lunch," I said as I moved up the steep sides of the ravine. I discovered that as late as it was in the season, the spring beauties were still blooming in the cool pockets of the woods. They are all right raw, that is if you are as hungry as I was. They taste a little like lima beans. I ate these as I went on hunting food, feeling better and better, until I worked my way back to the meadow where the dandelions were blooming. Funny I hadn't noticed them earlier. Their greens are good, and so are their roots—a little strong and milky, but you get used to that.

A crow flew into the aspen grove without saying a word. The little I knew of crows from following them in Central Park, they always have something to say. But this bird was sneaking, obviously trying to be quiet. Birds are good food. Crow is certainly not the best, but I did not know that then, and I launched out to see where it was going. I had a vague plan to try to noose it. This is the kind of thing I wasted time on in those days when time was so important. However, this venture turned out all right, because I did not have to noose that bird.

I stepped into the woods, looked around, could not see the crow, but noticed a big stick nest in a scrabbly pine. I started to climb the tree. Off flew the crow. What made me keep on climbing in face of such discouragement, I don't know, but I did, and that noon I had crow eggs and wild salad for lunch.

At lunch I also solved the problem of carving out my tree. After a struggle I made a fire. Then I sewed a big skunk cabbage leaf into a cup with grass strands. I had read that you can boil water in a leaf, and ever since then I had been very anxious to see if this were true. It seems impossible, but it works. I boiled the eggs in a leaf. The water keeps the leaf wet, and although the top dries up and burns down to the water level, that's as far as the burning goes. I was pleased to see it work.

Then here's what happened. Naturally, all this took a lot of time, and I hadn't gotten very far on my tree, so I was fretting and stamping out the fire when I stopped with my foot in the air.

The fire! Indians made dugout canoes with fire. They burned them out, an easier and much faster way of getting results. I would try fire in the tree. If I was very careful, perhaps it would work. I ran into the hemlock forest with a burning stick and got a fire going inside the tree.

Thinking that I ought to have a bucket of water in case things got out of hand, I looked desperately around me. The water was far across the meadow and down the ravine. This would never do. I began to think the whole inspiration of a home in the tree was no good. I really did have to live near water for cooking and drinking and comfort. I looked sadly at the magnificent hemlock and was about to put the fire out and desert it when I said something to myself. It must have come out of some book: "Hemlocks usually grow around mountain streams and springs."

I swirled on my heel. Nothing but boulders around me. But the air was damp, somewhere—I said—and darted around the rocks, peering and looking and sniffing and going down into pockets and dales. No water. I was coming back, circling wide, when I almost fell in it. Two sentinel boulders, dripping wet, decorated with flowers, ferns, moss, weeds—everything that loved water—guarded a bathtub-sized spring.

"You pretty thing," I said, flopped on my stomach, and pushed my face into it to drink. I opened my eyes. The water was like glass, and in it were little insects with oars. They rowed away from me. Beetles skittered like bullets on the surface, or carried a silver bubble of air with them to the bottom. Ha, then I saw a crayfish.

I jumped up, overturned rocks, and found many crayfish. At first I hesitated to grab them because they can pinch. I gritted my teeth, thought about how much more it hurts to be hungry, and came down upon them. I did get pinched, but I had my dinner. And that was the first time I had planned ahead! Any planning that I did in those early days was such a surprise to me and so successful that I was delighted with even a small plan. I wrapped the crayfish in leaves, stuffed them in my pockets, and went back to the burning tree.

Bucket of water, I thought. Bucket of water? Where was I going to get a bucket? How did I think, even if I found water, I could get it back to the tree? That's how citified I was in those days. I had never lived without a bucket before—scrub buckets, water buckets—and so when a water problem came up, I just thought I could run to the kitchen and get a bucket.

"Well, dirt is as good as water," I said and ran back to my tree. "I can smother the fire with dirt."

Days passed working, burning, cutting, gathering food, and each day I cut another notch on an aspen pole that I had stuck in the ground for a calendar.

In Which I Meet One of My Own Kind and Have a Terrible Time Getting Away

Five notches into June, my house was done. I could stand in it, lie down in it, and there was room left over for a stump to sit on. On warm evenings I would lie on my stomach and look out the door, listen to the cicadas and crickets, and hope it would storm so that I could crawl into my tree and be dry. I had gotten soaked during a couple of May downpours, and now that my house was done, I wanted the chance to sit in my hemlock and watch a cloudburst wet everything but me. This opportunity didn't come for a long time. It was dry.

One morning I was at the edge of the meadow. I had cut down a small ash tree and was chopping it into lengths of about eighteen inches each. This was the beginning of my bed that I was planning to work on after supper every night.

With the golden summer upon me, food was much easier to get, and I actually had several hours of free time after supper in which to do other things. I had been eating frogs' legs, turtles, and best of all, an occasional rabbit. My snares and traps were set now. Furthermore, I had a good supply of cattail roots I had dug in the marsh.

If you ever eat cattails, be sure to cook them well, otherwise the fibers are tough and they take more chewing to get the starchy food from them than they are worth. However, they taste just like potatoes after you've been eating them a couple of weeks, and to my way of thinking are extremely good.

Well, anyway, that summer morning when I was gathering material for a bed, I was singing and chopping and playing a game with a raccoon I had come to know. He had just crawled in a hollow tree and had gone to bed for the day when I came to the meadow. From time to time I would tap on his tree with my ax. He would hang his sleepy head out, snarl at me, close his eyes, and slide out of sight.

The third time I did this, I knew something was happening in the forest. Instead of closing his eyes, he pricked up his ears and his face became drawn and tense. His eyes were focused on something down the mountain. I stood up and looked. I could see nothing. I squatted down and went back to work. The raccoon dove out of sight.

"Now what's got you all excited?" I said, and tried once more to see what he had seen.

I finished the posts for the bed and was looking around for a bigger ash to fell and make slats for the springs when I nearly jumped out of my shoes.

"Now what are you doing up here all alone?" It was a human voice. I swung around and stood face to face with a little old lady in a pale blue sunbonnet and a loose brown dress.

"Oh! gosh!" I said. "Don't scare me like that. Say one word at a time until I get used to a human voice." I must have looked frightened because she chuckled, smoothed down the front of her dress, and whispered, "Are you lost?"

"Oh, no, Ma'am," I stuttered.

"Then a little fellow like you should not be all alone way up here on this haunted mountain."

"Haunted?" said I.

"Yes, indeed. There's an old story says there are little men up here who play ninepins right down in that gorge in the twilight." She peered at me. "Are you one of them?"

"Oh, no, no, no, no," I said. "I read that story. It's just make-believe." I laughed, and she puckered her forehead.

"Well, come on," she said, "make some use of yourself and help me fill this basket with strawberries."

I hesitated—she meant *my* strawberry supply.

"Now, get on with you. A boy your age should be doing something worth while, 'stead of play-ing mumbly peg with sticks. Come on, young man." She jogged me out into the meadow.

We worked quite a while before we said any more. Frankly, I was wondering how to save my precious, precious strawberries, and I may say I picked slowly. Every time I dropped one in her basket, I thought how good it would taste.

"Where do ye live?" I jumped. It is terribly odd to hear a voice after weeks of listening only to birds and crickets and raccoons, and what is more, to hear the voice ask a question like that.

"I live here," I said.

"Ye mean Delhi. Fine. You can walk me home."

Nothing I added did any good. She would not be shaken from her belief that I lived in Delhi. So I let it go.

We must have reaped every last strawberry before she stood up, put her arm in mine and escorted me down the mountain. I certainly was not escorting her. Her wiry little arms were like crayfish pinchers. I couldn't have gotten away if I had tried. So I walked and listened.

She told me all the local and world news, and it was rather pleasant to hear about the national league, an atom bomb test, and a Mr. Riley's three-legged dog that chased her chickens. In the middle of all this chatter she said, "That's the best strawberry patch in the entire Catskill

range. I come up here every spring. For forty years I've come to that meadow for my strawberries. It gits harder every year, but there's no jam can beat the jam from that mountain. I know. I've been around here all my life." Then she went right into the New York Yanks without putting in a period.

As I helped her across the stream on big boulders, I heard a cry in the sky. I looked up. Swinging down the valley on long pointed wings was a large bird. I was struck by the ease and swiftness of its flight.

"Duck hawk," she said. "Nest around here ever year. My man used to shoot 'em. He said they killed chickens, but I don't believe it. The only thing that kills chickens is Mr. Riley's three-legged dog."

She tipped and teetered as she crossed the rocks, but kept right on talking and stepping as if she knew that no matter what, she would get across.

We finally reached the road. I wasn't listening to her very much. I was thinking about the duck hawk. This bird, I was sure, was the peregrine falcon, the king's hunting bird.

"I will get one. I will train it to hunt for me," I said to myself.

Finally I got the little lady to her brown house at the edge of town.

She turned fiercely upon me. I started back.

"Where are you going, young man?"

I stopped. Now, I thought, she is going to march me into town. Into town? Well, that's where I'll go then, I said to myself. And I turned on my heel, smiled at her, and replied, "To the library."

The King's Provider

Miss Turner was glad to see me. I told her I wanted some books on hawks and falcons, and she located a few, although there was not much to be had on the subject. We worked all afternoon, and I learned enough. I departed when the library closed. Miss Turner whispered to me as I left, "Sam, you need a haircut."

I hadn't seen myself in so long that this had not occurred to me. "Gee, I don't have any scissors."

She thought a minute, got out her library scissors, and sat me down on the back steps. She did a fine job, and I looked like any other boy who had played hard all day, and who, with a little soap and water after supper, would be going off to bed in a regular house.

I didn't get back to my tree that night. The May apples were ripe, and I stuffed on those as I went through the woods. They taste like a very sweet banana, are earthy and a little slippery. But I liked them.

At the stream I caught a trout. Everybody thinks a trout is hard to catch because of all the fancy gear and flies and lines sold for trout fishing, but, honestly, they are easier to catch than any other fish. They have big mouths and snatch and swallow whole anything they see when they are hungry. With my wooden hook in its mouth, the trout was mine. The trouble is that trout are not hungry when most people have time to fish. I knew they were hungry that evening because the creek was swirling, and minnows and everything else were jumping out of the water. When you see that, go fish. You'll get them.

I made a fire on a flat boulder in the stream, and cooked the trout. I did this so I could watch the sky. I wanted to see the falcon again. I also put the trout head on the hook and dropped it in the pool. A snapping turtle would view a trout head with relish.

I waited for the falcon patiently. I didn't have to go anywhere. After an hour or so, I was rewarded. A slender speck came from the valley and glided up the stream. It was still far away when it folded its wings and bombed the earth. I watched. It arose, clumsy and big—carrying food—and winged back to the valley.

I sprinted down the stream and made myself a lean-to near some cliffs where I thought the bird had disappeared. Having learned that day that duck hawks prefer to nest on cliffs, I settled for this site.

Early the next morning, I got up and dug the tubers of the arrow-leaf that grew along the stream bank. I baked these and boiled mussels for breakfast, then I curled up behind a willow and watched the cliff.

The hawks came in from behind me and circled the stream. They had apparently been out hunting before I had gotten up, as they were returning with food. This was exciting news. They were feeding young, and I was somewhere near the nest.

I watched one of them swing in to the cliff and disappear. A few minutes later it winged out empty-footed. I marked the spot mentally and said, "Ha!"

After splashing across the stream in the shallows, I stood at the bottom of the cliff and wondered how on earth I was going to climb the sheer wall.

I wanted a falcon so badly, however, that I dug in with my toes and hands and started up. The first part was easy; it was not too steep. When I thought I was stuck, I found a little ledge and shinnied up to it.

I was high, and when I looked down, the stream spun. I decided not to look down any more. I edged up to another ledge, and lay down on it to catch my breath. I was shaking from exertion and I was tired.

I looked up to see how much higher I had to go when my hand touched something moist. I pulled it back and saw that it was white—bird droppings. Then I saw them. Almost where my hand had been sat three fuzzy whitish-gray birds. Their wide-open mouths gave them a startled look.

"Oh, hello, hello," I said. "You are cute."

When I spoke, all three blinked at once. All three heads turned and followed my hand as I swung it up and toward them. All three watched my hand with opened mouths. They were marvelous. I chuckled. But I couldn't reach them.

I wormed forward, and *wham!*—something hit my shoulder. It pained. I turned my head to see the big female. She had bit me. She winged out, banked, and started back for another strike.

Now I was scared, for I was sure she would cut me wide open. With sudden nerve, I stood up, stepped forward, and picked up the biggest of the nestlings. The females are bigger than the males. They are the "falcons." They are the pride of kings. I tucked her in my sweater and leaned against the cliff, facing the bulletlike dive of the falcon. I threw out my foot as she struck, and the sole of my tennis shoe took the blow.

The female was now gathering speed for another attack, and when I say speed, I mean 50 to 60 miles an hour. I could see myself battered and torn, lying in the valley below, and I said to myself, "Sam Gribley, you had better get down from here like a rabbit."

I jumped to the ledge below, found it was really quite wide, slid on the seat of my pants to the next ledge, and stopped. The hawk apparently couldn't count. She did not know I had a

youngster, for she checked her nest, saw the open mouths, and then she forgot me.

I scrambled to the river bed somehow, being very careful not to hurt the hot fuzzy body that was against my own. However, Frightful, as I called her right then and there because of the difficulties we had had in getting together, did not think so gently of me. She dug her talons into my skin to brace herself during the bumpy ride to the ground.

I stumbled to the stream, placed her in a nest of buttercups, and dropped beside her. I fell asleep.

When I awoke my eyes opened on two gray eyes in a white stroobly head. Small pinfeathers were sticking out of the stroobly down, like feathers in an Indian quiver. The big blue beak curled down in a snarl and up in a smile.

"Oh, Frightful," I said, "you are a raving beauty."

Frightful fluffed her nubby feathers and shook. I picked her up in the cup of my hands and held her under my chin. I stuck my nose in the deep warm fuzz. It smelled dusty and sweet.

I liked that bird. Oh, how I liked that bird from that smelly minute. It was so pleasant to feel the beating life and see the funny little awkward movements of a young thing.

The legs pushed out between my fingers, I gathered them up, together with the thrashing wings, and tucked the bird in one piece under my chin. I rocked.

"Frightful," I said. "You will enjoy what we are going to do."

It is well for American children to discover early that their country is made up of many kinds of people, races, religions, and ethnic groups with varying customs. After they have learned this, the transition to thinking about people of other countries is an easy and a natural one, founded on familiarity with and liking for the many kinds of people in their own land.

Like the varied peoples of the United States, the heroes and heroines of books set in other lands are a diverse group. No matter where people live, they have the same basic needs—to love

LIFE IN OTHER LANDS

and to be loved, to belong, to feel secure—and they have similar emotional responses—they feel fear when threatened, they enjoy being approved of, and they resent being looked down upon. How they dress and the customs they practice may differ, but the fundamental needs are the same throughout the world.

Both Kate in *The Good Master* (see p. 149) and Caddie in *Caddie Woodlawn* (see p. 212) are high-spirited, sometimes mean, girls who need to learn to accept their roles as members of the "weaker sex." The two books have many similarities, but it is interesting to contrast the Hungarian countryside with the American setting and discover how land itself can be a character in books. The role natural environment plays in our lives is further emphasized in *Avalanche!* (see p. 168) and *Boy Alone* (see p. 176), two books in which nature is cast in a destructive role. The land on which people live dictates the kind of life they will lead, what their problems will be, what joys they will experience. But nature is no more consistent than man, and the mountain that provides the climber with a magnificent view can also bury him under tons of snow.

Fear is a universal emotion. Almost every child has a fear: of dogs, of the dark, of deep water, or of moving to a new neighborhood and making new friends in a new school. These are among the everyday fears of children, and they are experienced whether the child lives in a small American town or in a Swiss village.

While fear is an unpleasant emotion, one of the points made by good children's books is that it can be conquered. Most often, it is conquered by the individual through his devotion to someone or something important to him. In *Call It Courage* (see Bibliography, p. 254) Mafatu eventually overcomes his fear of the ocean because his love for his father and his dog is stronger than his fear of the ocean.

Almost all problems can be coped with, if not overcome, through affection and the need to belong. This is shown clearly in *North to Freedom* (see Bibliography, p. 254), in which David, the central character, cannot enjoy fully the happy moments he finds in being free because he cannot trust people. David's fear of being pursued and captured by the concentration camp police dominates his life, and it is only when he finds himself beginning to count on people that his fear lessens.

When books portray characters having similar fears, they ease the child reader's mind by helping him see that he is not alone in being afraid. When books move beyond the ordinary and present fears which threaten to destroy the character's entire life, as in *Call It Courage* or *North to Freedom*, the child begins to realize that his own fears are minute in relationship to those of Mafatu and David. When he realizes how small his own fears are, there begins a sense of perspective, a sign of maturing in the child.

Criteria for books about other lands

While books set in other lands should provide the reader with a sense of common humanity, they should also show clearly the differences among cultures. The authenticity of details is essential if the author is to provide a true picture of everyday life in another land. When writing about India, for example, the author must not leave the reader with the impression that it is an exotic, romantic land. He must concern himself with the overwhelming poverty, with the huge population that produces thousands of city beggars and threatens to starve millions, with the illiteracy that keeps India from using modern tools, and with the multiplicity of languages which makes communication among provinces difficult. Life in India need not be morbidly described, but it should be clear enough so the reader is not left with the idea that India is only a land of maharajahs riding on elephants and being pampered by an army of servants.

Townsend's *Good-Bye to the Jungle* (see Bibliography, p. 251) is an important view of modern England in that, for once, the characters come from the lower class. Too many English books leave the impression that all Englishmen live in mansions and have nannies, gardeners, and butlers. The French children in Berna's *The Horse Without a Head* (see Bibliography, p. 252) are street waifs, children of the lower class who must make do with what comes along.

These books, and many others like them, represent major progress in books about other lands. For too many years most of the books we had were written by Americans who had never been to the country they wrote about, or by those who had seen only a distorted view—that of the pampered tourist. Few looked beyond the comforts provided for the tourist; few wandered from the main streets and the tourist attractions to see the lives of the ordinary citizens. When such authors wrote, they produced glowing accounts reminiscent of travel brochures.

While we still get some books of this type, most of the new books about other lands are vastly improved. An American who writes of another country is expected to have traveled in that country, or, at the very least, to have done extensive research on it before he sits down to write. In recent years we have received large numbers of imported books, written by Frenchmen about France, by Germans about Germany, etc. American children can now read the books written for and about children in other countries, and thus can receive a more balanced picture of life as it is really lived, not as it is imagined by authors who are unfamiliar with the countries.

The stories chosen for this section and those listed in the Bibliography present everyday people faced with everyday problems, sometimes worried or frightened, sometimes gay or triumphant, but normally doing the best they can at work and at play. They are themselves, not Americans in disguise, with their own peculiarities, influenced by their own history and geography.

Stories about people of other lands must, first and foremost, be good stories. Then, they must help the youthful reader see that all men are brothers regardless of where they live; and finally, they must help the young reader understand that each nation has its own heritage, its own national and familial traditions, its own way of life.

While identifying with *Heidi* (see p. 156), *Young Fu of the Upper Yangtze* (see Bibliography, p. 253), or Kate in *The Good Master* (see p. 149), the reader must also see how different his own life would be if he had been born in Switzerland, China, or Hungary, instead of in the United States. By seeing both the similarities and the differences, children are laying the groundwork for a better understanding of world problems when they become adults. They will not be so quick to assume that the American way of life is best for everyone; they will not be arrogant in their assumptions that other people are worse off for not being Americans. They will, hopefully, recognize that the diversity of life is one of its miracles. They will see that diversity is not something to be stamped out, but rather that it is to be cherished.

from KOBI, A BOY OF SWITZERLAND

Mary and Conrad Buff

Conrad Buff, who made the beautiful pictures for Kobi, *is a Swiss and in this story he has recalled his childhood experiences in that beautiful country. His wife, Mary Buff, wrote them down, and together they made this book. So also they made* The Apple and the Arrow, *a thrilling story of the Swiss people's fight for freedom.* Dash and Dart *is about twin fawns and reflects the Buffs' California life, part of which is spent high in the mountains where deer, squirrel, and other small animals share the forest with them.*

A Lonely Night

When Kobi had finished milking the cows, he carried the milk into the hut and poured it out into flat wooden bowls, which he put away in the cool milk room. Then he ate his usual supper of goats' milk and great hunks of heavy bread. Supper over, the boy sat on an old bench just outside the cabin, watching the evening shadows.

It was a warm summer evening, and so clear that Kobi could see the cows grazing on Schwarz Alp across the valley. He could even hear Sepp's dog bark.

Shadows slowly drowned each bright green Alp in gray, as night crept up and up along both sides of the valley. In a short time, only the tops of the mountains shone with the last rays of the sun. Soon the gray shadows covered them too, and the world faded into darkness.

Slowly stars came out. By the faint glow in the eastern sky, Kobi knew the moon would rise. As it grew still darker, a bird called sadly in the forest beyond the hut. It sang as if it had lost something it would never find again.

Kobi saw a light flicker in Sepp's hut. On Hoch Alp the cows grazed restlessly. Every few minutes they stopped in their feeding and looked around as if they heard someone coming. Blass the dog lay panting at Kobi's feet, his red tongue hanging from his mouth, for it was warm. Usually when the sun went down the night was cold, but this night Kobi thought the air very sultry.

The world outside was so unfriendly that Kobi went into the cabin and lit the lamp. Blass always slept in the barn, but on this strange night Kobi called him into the hut for company.

But even with the light shining in the old lamp on the rough table and Blass panting beside him, Kobi still felt the world was unfriendly. Earlier than usual he put out the light, and crawled into bed. But it too was lonely, without Uncle Jacob.

Kobi lay thinking about the day that had just gone: the edelweiss he had picked high on the top of the mountain; the chamois that crept along the cliffs; Grittli, Mother, Aunt Marie.

It was so hot, Kobi threw off the goose-feather pad. The wind rose. A shutter banged. Kobi heard a stick of wood slip from the woodpile outside. An ax leaning against the hut fell to the ground with a soft thud.

Kobi would never have heard these little noises if Uncle Jacob had been there. But tonight they made him afraid.

He thought of Franzli in the story Grandfather had told so often, the old story of "The Boy Who Wanted to Yodel." That boy had slept all alone in an Alpine hut too. What if a giant should come to this cabin tonight and give to him, Kobi, the gift of yodeling like Uli the cheesemaker? Everything seemed possible tonight.

The wind whined louder as it rose. Kobi heard the goats bleating outside. Even Blass was restless. He could not find a comfortable place to sleep. He walked around the cabin from spot to spot, never quiet.

Suddenly the door blew open. Blass growled. Kobi was so startled he jumped out of bed to bolt the door. But before he did this, he peered out of doors. The sky was overcast with clouds. The stars were gone. Was a storm coming?

Hurriedly he climbed back into bed. But he did not stay long, for drops of rain began to fall gently upon the roof. Through the window Kobi saw a bright fork of lightning flare and disappear.

Grandfather had told him many a story from his own boyhood of storms that came and disappeared in an hour, leaving behind them ruined bridges, dead cattle, broken barns.

He knew how suddenly the weather changed in the mountains. Animals felt it before people did. Kobi thought of the panting dog, the restless cows, the sad bird in the forest. He must drive the cows into the barn at once.

He jumped out of bed and lit the lamp. He pulled on his heavy woolen trousers, his hob-nailed shoes, and a warm coat. By the time his black leather cap was on his head, the rain was pouring down.

He unbolted the door and ran into the storm; it was so dark he could see only when the lightning flashed. When he reached the barn he pulled open the door, and the cows and goats piled in pell-mell, happy for a roof. Kobi lit a lantern. Each cow stood in her own stall. But thirteen stalls were still empty. Thirteen cows were missing. He must find them.

When Kobi, followed by Blass, raced once again into the night, the rain was coming down so hard he was soon wet to the skin. His feet sloshed about in his soggy shoes as he ran here and there over Hoch Alp, looking everywhere for the lost cows. The thunder was deafening. Each peal bounded back from the sides of the mountains, echoing time and time again. Before one died away another peal of thunder had taken its place. The noise was earsplitting. Lightning flashed every second. Kobi could see everything clearly, but he did not see any cows.

Then he remembered Uncle Jacob had told him never to let cows stand under trees during a storm. He said lightning often hit the trees.

There was but one tree on Hoch Alp. That was the crooked old pine tree on the north side, near the steep cliffs. It's a long way to the old tree, thought Kobi as he slipped through the wet grass. Once he fell headlong on his face. But he struggled up and on. He was so worried about the lost cows that he had no time to fear the wind, the thunder, the lightning.

When at last he reached the tree, Kobi saw a dark mass of animals huddled together under it. Cows! He yelled and called; Blass barked; each tried to make himself heard above the storm. Boy and dog ran this way and that, chasing the frightened animals toward the distant barn. It took a long time, but when at last each cow stood in her stall, Kobi saw by the light of the flickering lantern that one stall was still empty. It was Roslie's stall—Roslie, the fine prize heifer he had promised Mrs. Bach to guard so carefully and bring back to Wolfram's Castle in September. Where could Roslie be?

Once more the boy and his dog went into the storm. It was even worse than before. Peals of thunder boomed against the rocks like giant cannon. Kobi and Blass raced from one end of the Alp to the other, looking everywhere.

Perhaps I have missed her near the tree, thought Kobi, and he ran on and on until he could hardly breathe and his heart beat wildly.

He was near the old tree when suddenly a sheet of living white fire dropped out of the sky and struck the ground before him. Kobi fell on his knees. He covered his eyes with his hands. He smelled burning wood.

He was helpless, afraid, trembling all over. His ears hurt and he could not see—he could not get to his feet.

Strangely enough this last fierce blinding stroke of lightning was the last to flash that night on Hoch Alp. Kobi heard the thunder die slowly away, growing fainter and fainter, as the sound of the great bells died in the church tower on feast days. The wind drove the sullen clouds before it like an army beaten in battle. The rain stopped. The moon looked through a clear bit of sky.

Kobi could hardly believe the world had not ended. As he looked around, his trembling stopped. He saw where the lightning had struck. It had split the tree in two. One great gnarled limb lay across the fence, breaking it down. The old pine had lost its last battle with the storm.

In the strange calm that followed, Kobi heard a faint sound. It seemed to come up from between the canyon walls. He ran to the tree and leaned over the broken fence, peering down into the dark canyon. He heard a soft sad "moo." As he looked into the darkness, he thought he saw something move. He called:

"Roslie, Roslie!" and another "moo" came out of the canyon.

Kobi knew the cliff wall as well in the darkness as he knew it in the daylight. Many an afternoon he had sat there and studied its rocky forms from the edge, the cliff sloped gently down and ended in a narrow shelf of rock in the side of the canyon wall. Then it plunged straight down for over a hundred feet to meet the noisy stream far below.

Roslie must have been knocked over by the broken limb. Or she might have jumped over in fright. "Be still, Roslie." He slid down the incline and landed beside the heifer. She licked his hands.

"Don't move, Roslie," Kobi whispered to her. "Don't move." And with these words the boy clambered up the cliff and raced with all his strength toward the distant barn, to get a rope. Fear lent him wings.

When Kobi returned to the edge of the canyon, and once more slid down to the rocky shelf, Roslie was still there. He tied the rope around her neck and fastened it to a stout root that stuck out of the rocks. Then he said to her: "Roslie, I'm going away. But I'll be back soon and pull you up. Stay here, Roslie, I'll be back."

As Kobi had raced to the barn for the rope, he had thought of a plan. He would go down into the valley, cross the river, climb up to Schwarz Alp, and get Sepp. Sepp was strong. He and Sepp together could pull the heifer out of the canyon.

The moon shone so brightly as Kobi hurried down the muddy trail into the valley that he could hardly believe death had walked on the Alp only a few minutes before. The creek in the

bottom of the valley roared, swollen into a river. The foot bridge seemed to hang by a thread. Kobi crossed it carefully. As he climbed up toward Schwarz Alp Sepp saw him coming.

"Come and help me!" cried Kobi to his friend, and then he hurriedly told him the story of Roslie. "Hurry up," he cried, plucking at Sepp's sleeve. "Of course I'll come," Sepp said. He ran to the barn, and came back with a thick heavy rope curled over his shoulder.

When the boys arrived on Hoch Alp a half-hour later, Roslie was still there. They could hear her chewing her cud on her little haven of rock.

"Imagine that," laughed Sepp, out of breath with the steep climb, "chewing her cud! She's not hurt at all."

Kobi grabbed one end of the rope, and slid down the embankment. He put the rope around the heifer's neck, and threw the other end to his friend on the bank, who wound it around the old tree-trunk, which was still standing. Then Sepp called: "Steady, Kobi. Push!"

Kobi pushed, Sepp pulled on the rope. Roslie did her best. She knew the boys were trying to help her, but the rocks were slippery and she always slid back. The boys tried time and time again until they were both out of breath.

"We may have to wait until Uncle Jacob comes," cried Kobi.

"Let's try once more," argued Sepp. "If she doesn't come up then, I'll go and get Father."

So once more they pushed and pulled Roslie. The bank was full of holes, washed out by the storms that had fallen on the Alp in many years. By accident Roslie put a hind foot in a hole just as Kobi pushed her from behind. Suddenly, almost without knowing how it happened, Roslie walked up the cliff and stood safely on the Alp.

The faint gray of dawn was pouring over the mountains as the tired, sleepy boys drove the heifer into the barn. "Come and have something to eat," said Kobi to Sepp, putting his arm over his shoulder in affection.

"No, sorry, Kobi. I've got to get home and help Father milk. But tonight I'll come over." Sepp hurried down the trail.

Kobi could hardly drag himself into the cabin, he was so tired and hungry.

He took off his muddy shoes and his wet coat; he poured himself a bowl of milk and cut a thick piece of bread. Then he sat down on a bench, his back to the door.

Kobi did not hear the quick footstep, until he felt a pair of strong arms around him, holding him tight. And Uncle Jacob's voice was saying: "Kobi, Kobi, my brave herder."

Uncle Jacob had met Sepp as he crossed the broken bridge in the valley, and Sepp had told him about the long fight to save Roslie. But Kobi was so tired he could not say a single word. He burst into tears as Uncle Jacob patted him on the shoulder and said: "Never mind, Kobi. You are a brave boy! I woke up when I heard the thunder and saw lightning flash on the mountain. I came as fast as I could, my boy, but the roads were rivers of mud. Many of the bridges were washed away. In all of my life in the mountains I've never seen a storm like this. Many a cow was lost, I know. I prayed for you, Kobi, all alone with those cows in such a storm. Your mother will be proud of you. You are a real cowherd now, Kobi, as good as any man!" But the real cowherd was fast asleep, worn out with the work and the excitement.

Early in September, a snow storm fell over the Alps. In the morning when Kobi woke, everything was white. When the sun came out, the snow melted. But it was a warning to the herders that autumn had come.

Uncle Jacob told Kobi: "If we have another snow storm like this, we must go home. The grass is short now. When snow covers it for a few hours, the cows don't get enough to eat."

The grass was very short. Only a few fall flowers still bloomed in the pastures. On a clear day Kobi could see the beech trees, in the valley below, turned red.

Then another snow storm came, covering the roofs of the barn and hut. The snow did not melt quickly.

"Kobi," said Uncle Jacob as they were milking that morning, "I think we must go home, and go today. Bring down the big bells. We will start as soon as the hut and barn are in order."

So without any more talk, Kobi and Uncle Jacob drove the cows down the trail toward home. When they reached the lowlands, everything seemed new to Kobi. The villages were so crowded. There were so many people everywhere. He had lived for three months in a world of only Uncle Jacob, Sepp, Uli, the cows, Blass, the goats; he had forgotten how crowded the villages were, how close to each other the farmhouses were, and how tiny the fenced pastures of the lowlands.

As he and Uncle Jacob went through the villages they saw many other processions of cattle. The snow storm had driven the wise herders from the mountains that September day.

When they reached Uncle Jacob's house, Kobi did not stay long enough to eat. He wanted to get home. He wanted to see Mother, Grandfather, Father. He wanted to play with Grittli, and he wanted to eat fried potatoes covered with caraway seeds, and hot sausage.

It was late afternoon when he saw his old brown house far in the distance. The red geraniums were not in the windows. The fields were shaved close by the mowers. The leaves were falling from the pear trees. There were late apples still clinging to the apple trees.

Kobi ran the last half mile, he was so anxious to get home. He pulled open the heavy kitchen door, and rushed through the house, calling: "Grittli, Mother, where are you? I'm home! It's me—Kobi!"

Then he saw his mother. She was very beautiful, for she wore her fine dress that she wore only on Sundays and feast days. But this is not Sunday, thought Kobi.

As the boy hugged her, he cried: "Mother, you have on your Sunday dress; this is not Sunday. And how beautiful you are, Mother!"

Mother smiled down at him, tears in her eyes, as she said: "Brave Kobi, I heard all about that night in the storm. Do you remember that Aunt Marie told you we had a surprise at home for you? It is upstairs in my room. Come, Grittli, we'll show him."

Up the rickety stairs Kobi followed his Mother. Grittli danced on ahead of them both. The three entered Mother's bedroom. Beside her bed was the old wooden cradle. Kobi's grandfather had slept in it when he was a baby; so had Kobi's father, and Kobi himself. There were roses painted on the headboard, and between the roses it read: "1842."

Kobi's mother lifted a white cloth. Kobi peered inside as she said:

"This is the surprise for you, Kobi. This is why I have on my best dress. We have just come from the christening. This is your baby brother —Conrad Tobler."

from PEDRO'S COCONUT SKATES
Esther Wood

Esther Wood has the knack of re-creating the work and play, longings and achievements, the sadness and fun of children of other lands. Pedro's Coconut Skates is the tender story of a little Filipino boy's desire to have a house for his grandmother.

Singing Souls

Hundreds of little candles twinkled in the darkness of All Saints' Eve. They looked as if the stars might have fallen, and, just for one night, snuggled down against the earth.

Aunt Valentina dressed herself in her best clothes. She put on a long skirt, tucking the train up neatly to show her embroidered petticoat and her green velvet chinelas. Her blouse was thin and crisp with big, bell-like sleeves. When she had tied on her best black apron, she called to Uncle Manuel that she was ready.

He finished the song he was singing and tucked his guitar under his arm. "Time for bed," he called to the children, who were playing tubigan in the moonlight.

Pedro stamped out the water marks they had made in the road for their game and followed the three little girls into the house. Great Aunt Trinidad had spread their mats on the floor, and hung up the mosquito nets around each bed. In no time at all the four of them were in bed; even Magellan was tucked in, much against his will.

"Well," said Great Aunt Trinidad, "you never know about children. It's always trouble, trouble, trouble, putting them to bed; and now on All Saints' Eve they're asleep almost before I get the mats on the floor." She held the lamp high that Aunt Valentina might see her way down the ladder and out the gate.

"They're too good to be true," she said, holding the lamp to look at the children, who already seemed to be sound asleep. With that she blew out the light, and leaned back against the wall where her eyes were shaded from the moonlight coming through the door. In a few minutes she was asleep and snoring softly.

Pedro raised his head. "Are you ready?" he whispered.

Three black heads popped out from under three mosquito nets, and nodded. Three little girls slipped on their dresses and quietly stole down the ladder to the gate where Pedro waited for them.

"Where is Magellan?" asked Pedro. "I thought you had him."

Magellan scampered out from under the house. He was carrying Pedro's coconut skates.

"Oh, Magellan," cried Pedro, "I don't want them now." He put the skates back of the fence and picked up the monkey. "But—" he said, "you're a smart monkey. You gave me a good idea."

Juana stopped. "I forgot the coconut shell," she said. "Singing souls always carry a coconut shell."

"And the candle," said Marciana.

"And the bell," said Nene.

Juana climbed back into the house and presently came out with a bell, a candle, and half a coconut shell. She gave the bell to Nene and the candle to Marciana, keeping the coconut shell for herself.

Pedro led the way down the dark street, staying well in the shadows that no one might see them. Instead of crossing the moonlit plaza, they slipped around its edge where the houses cast deep, black shadows. Past the old stone church they crept and across the market place, until they came to the big house of the landlord.

"Do you think they'll hear us?" whispered Nene.

"Perhaps they aren't at home," said Juana.

The shell windows had been closed and the house looked quite dark.

"Well, sing as loudly as you can," said Marciana. She started the song, for she was the only one who knew all the verses of the long ballad that told of the travels of the Singing Souls from heaven to earth. Nene rang her bell, and they all sang very loudly when Marciana came to the parts they knew.

The door was opened a crack, and someone looked out at them. Then it was opened wider. A servant in a long, white apron shuffled out and put five centavos in Juana's coconut shell.

Juana excitedly poked Marciana. "Look!" she whispered. "Five centavos!"

The man shuffled back into the house, but just as he was about to close the door, he popped his head out again. "Is that Magellan?" he asked, peering at the monkey in Pedro's arms.

"Yes," said Pedro. "I found him, and I am bringing him back to the Señor."

Magellan jumped to the ground, bounded through the man's outstretched arms, and ran into the hall.

"Oh, Magellan!" cried a woman's voice from inside. "Where have you been?"

"The Señora was very sad to lose that little monkey," said the servant to the children. Then he whispered behind his hand, "As for myself—" He shrugged.

"Bring the children inside," said the Señora, coming to the door, with Magellan sitting on her shoulder. "And, Vicente, bring my purse to me."

The servant ran down the hall, the wooden soles of his shoes clattering on the floor.

"Come in." The Señora smiled at them.

The four children followed her down the hall and out into the patio. The moonlight made everything look white in the little garden, surrounded by the four walls of the house. They climbed the stairs and crossed the balcony to a sitting room where the Señor sat reading.

"Look! Here is Magellan home again!" cried the Señora.

Magellan bounded across the room and jumped on the Señor's shoulder, where he snuggled his head against the man's collar.

"Where did you find him?" the Señor asked, as he stroked the monkey's back. His stern face softened, and he smiled.

The three girls said nothing. They were afraid of the landlord.

"In—the haunted house," stammered Pedro.

"That old house by the river?" asked the Señor.

"Yes," said Pedro.

"What were you doing there?" asked the man sharply.

"I—I just wanted to see what it was like," explained Pedro. "I didn't touch anything."

The Señora interrupted, "Oh, I know you didn't," she said. "It's such a tumble-down house, anyway." She took the purse the servant had brought her.

"Weren't you afraid to go there?" asked the landlord.

"No. It's just like any other house," said Pedro, "only old."

"What's your name?" asked the Señor.

"Pedro."

"Well, Pedro, I like you," said the Señor. "You're one boy who doesn't believe the old women's stories."

The Señora slipped five centavos apiece into the coconut shell. "For the Singing Souls," she said. "And now," she said to her husband, "what about a reward for bringing back Magellan?"

"Good," said the man, turning to Pedro. "What do you want?"

"Well—" said Pedro, "I don't want a reward. But, you know, that little, old house by the river is just the kind of house my grandmother has always wanted."

"Yes?" said the Señor.

"It's very old," said Pedro, "but she wouldn't mind. We could mend it."

"Yes?" said the Señor.

"Well—it's like this," said Pedro. "I haven't any money, but I could work for you. I'm a good houseboy; I could bring my coconut skates and polish your floors every day."

The old servant poked the Señora and vigorously nodded his head. She smiled and nodded to her husband.

"I could come every day on my way to school," said Pedro.

"It seems to me," said the Señor, "that would be enough rent for the little old house."

"Do you mean it?" cried Pedro. "Could we really have it?"

"Yes, of course," said the landlord, "but don't let it fall down on you."

"Oh, thank you, Señor," said Pedro.

The man laughed and patted his head. "I like you, Pedro," he said. "Do whatever you want with the little old house."

The children went down the stairs and across the moonlit patio to the hall, where the servant held the door open for them. Pedro saw nothing. He was too excited. Christmas was coming, and maybe—! Perhaps it was too much for a little boy to do, but it wasn't too much for a little boy to think about.

Mending the Nipa House

Early the next morning the Cruz family went down to the bamboo grove to see Pedro's house. Even Great Aunt Trinidad left her sunny doorway and stomped along with her cane. She took a special interest in the house, for wasn't it she who had told Pedro to find out about things? And if it had not been for Pedro's curiosity, he would not have had the little house.

Pedro was proud to show them his house, old and wornout though it was. To be sure, it was very small, but Grandmother Paz had always wanted a wee nipa house. There were four windows, one on each side, and a door. In the open space beneath the house, Grandmother Paz could keep her chickens.

"It's a bit dilapidated, to be sure," said Uncle Manuel, shaking the old ladder by the front door.

"And there are holes in the roof," said Aunt Valentina, peering up at the ceiling.

"And the floor sags a little," said Great Aunt Trinidad, poking through the cracks in the bamboo floor with her cane.

"Oh, but we can fix it!" cried Pedro. "We can mend the holes and make a new ladder."

"Well, you children go to work," said Uncle Manuel. "There's plenty of bamboo and nipa palm around."

"There's a nice mango tree out there," said Aunt Valentina.

Pedro looked out the door. "Grandmother Paz likes mangoes," he said.

"And Pedro can have his bananas," said Great Aunt Trinidad, poking her cane into the banana tree by the window.

Uncle Manuel took down the shutters, the worn and sagging shutters that all but fell apart when they were touched. The house looked bare, but much neater without them. They made a great bonfire and burned up all the rubbish they could find.

With great enthusiasm Pedro and the three girls started mending the house for Grandmother Paz. Before they knew it, the bamboo grove had become the most popular place in the village. It was like a new game; after school everyone raced down to the river to see who would be allowed to help the Cruz children that day.

Even the older boys and girls came to help, for building a house by themselves was fun. The boys borrowed their fathers' bolo-knives and cut down the bamboo shoots in the yard. The girls brought mangrove leaves and mended the holes in the walls. With the help of Uncle Manuel they made four new shutters, weaving strips of bamboo into mats and tying them tightly with rattan. Each one they hung by rings on a bamboo pole, so that it could be slipped back along the wall, or propped out to make a window shade.

Finally, the parents had heard so much about Pedro's house, that they, too, came to the bamboo grove by the river. They came to watch, but they stayed to help. Some said it should be done this way, and others that, and before they knew it, they were putting in new beams of nibong to make the house stronger and weaving new laths of bamboo to make the floor firmer.

There was little need for furniture inside the house. Few people had tables and chairs. Grandmother Paz would have her own mats and mosquito nets and a woven tampipi basket for her clothes.

The only thing that bothered Pedro was the roof. To be sure it could be mended with nipa palm that would do very well in good weather. But perhaps, when the rainy season came, it would leak like a fish net. Pedro decided not to think about the roof for a while. The dry season was ahead.

One day Ignacio, the rope maker, and his wife came to see what was happening in the bamboo grove. "Oy," cried Ignacio, "I see you have a fine house here."

"But what about a kitchen?" said Maria. "Now to my mind, every house needs a kitchen. You can't live on mangoes and bananas day in and day out."

"I forgot about a kitchen," said Pedro. "Maybe we could build a bonfire at mealtime."

"No, you must have a stove," said Maria.

"And a stove you shall have," said Ignacio, "if you don't mind a stove that's a bit used."

"Oh, no!" cried Pedro.

Then the two of them brought out their gift for Grandmother Paz's nipa house. Ignacio carried an earthen pot which he put down on the ground by the door. "That's for the fire," he said,

Maria brought a round earthen pot that fitted on top and put it in place. "And that's for the rice and the fish and the stew," she said. "Now you have a kitchen."

For plates Grandmother Paz could use banana leaves, and for cups and bowls she could use coconut shells. It was very simple, for they grew right in the yard.

Then Great Aunt Trinidad came hobbling over with a treat for all the children. She had a basketful of coconut cakes and suman, which was sweetened rice sticks. She made a fire in the lower part of the stove, and in the pot on top she put cacao beans, ground up and mixed with sugar and water. In no time at all there was a pot full of hot chocolate. Each child found a coconut shell for his cup.

With most of the children of the village there, the little nipa house had its first housewarming.

Christmas

Pedro and the three girls could hardly wait for Christmas. The little nipa house, with its new roof, was to be a Christmas surprise for Grandmother Paz.

Pedro built a chicken coop, and Aunt Valentina said she would give him two of her chickens to put in it. Uncle Manuel hollowed out the trunk of a bamboo tree for a water bucket. Marciana and Juana scrubbed the little stove until it looked almost new.

When everything was ready, they wrote a letter to Grandmother Paz and asked her to come to visit them for Christmas. They didn't say a word about the little house. They only asked her to bring her sleeping mat and her mosquito net. Pedro asked her to bring something for him, but he wouldn't tell anyone what it was. He wanted it very much, he said.

At last the day came when Uncle Manuel was to bring her from Manila in the carabao cart. He would get back in time for Christmas Eve, he said, as he left.

Pedro put a banana tree by the gate and tied it to the fence post. Then he helped the three girls trim it with lanterns and chains of colored paper. It was a gay little Christmas tree. In the window they hung a star lantern with a long swishing tail and a candle to light at night.

All through the village banana trees and arches were trimmed with lanterns and colored papers. A warm breeze, blowing through the palms, stopped to touch the Christmas trees and make them dance.

"And now it's time for a siesta," said Aunt Valentina, spreading their mats on the floor. "If you're going to stay up until midnight, you'll have to have your siesta."

The children slowly climbed up the ladder and lay down on the floor. That night they would go to church, at the nativity hour, and after that there would be a midnight feast. Small wonder they couldn't sleep, thinking about it all.

Pedro lay on his back, watching the lizards scamper up the walls in search of mosquitoes. Outside Aunt Valentina was swishing rice back and forth in her flat bamboo basket to let the wind blow the chaff away. She sang happily to herself:

My nipa house is very small
But in gathering seeds, it houses
    them all;
Sincamas and talong,
Seguidillas and mani,
Sitao, batao, patani.

Great Aunt Trinidad sat in the doorway, grinding cacao beans with a stone. The smell of chocolate made Pedro hungry. He could smell, too, the chicken adobo in the pot on the stove.

Just as he was about to ask for something to eat, he heard the squeaking of cart wheels down the street. He rolled over, and looked out the door. There was Domingo, and behind him sat Uncle Manuel and Grandmother Paz with the tampipi basket between them.

"Oy!" shouted Pedro, jumping out of the door with one bound. Behind him came Marciana and Juana and Nene. The four of them raced down the street to meet their grandmother.

"Well," said Grandmother Paz, gathering them all in her arms, "if my children can't come 'to

kiss the hand of Grandmother' at Christmas, then Grandmother will come to them."

Joyfully they led her back to the house where Aunt Valentina and Great Aunt Trinidad came to the gate to meet her.

"Did you bring my Christmas present?" whispered Pedro when Uncle Manuel had carried the tampipi basket indoors.

"Do you want it now?" asked Grandmother Paz.

"Yes," said Pedro. "I am going to give it to Uncle Manuel."

Grandmother Paz opened the tampipi basket and took out a package tied up in red tissue paper.

"Uncle Manuel," called Pedro, "here is a Christmas present for you."

Everyone crowded around to watch Uncle Manuel open the package from Manila. Out of the red tissue paper came a round black record. "For your victrola," said Pedro.

"For my victrola!" exclaimed Uncle Manuel, beaming. "Where is my victrola?"

The three little girls dragged it from the corner and lifted the lid. They all listened in delight while the music came from somewhere in the box:

Jingle bells, jingle bells,
    jingle all the way
Oh, what fun it is to ride
    in a one-horse open sleigh!

They loved it. None of them had ever seen snow or even heard of a sleigh, but it was such a jolly tune that they all began to sing with the victrola. The three little girls and Pedro danced round and round the room, until their mother said they'd fall through the floor if they didn't watch out.

"When are we going to give Grandmother Paz her surprise?" asked Nene, in a whisper so loud that it could be heard all through the house. Everyone laughed, while Grandmother Paz pretended she hadn't heard.

Pedro, who was almost bursting with the secret, jumped up. "Right now," he cried, taking Grandmother Paz's hand and leading her down the ladder.

The whole family went with them. Even Great Aunt Trinidad left her sunny doorway and stomped along with her cane. Grandmother Paz was quite breathless by the time she reached the river bank. "Wherever are we going, Pedro?" she asked, as she followed them through the bamboo grove.

"Here it is!" cried Pedro, who had run on ahead.

Then she saw the wee nipa house sitting in the middle of a tidy yard. In every window hung a star lantern with a long swishing tail.

"It's for you," said Pedro.

"Oh-h-h," breathed Grandmother Paz. "What a dear little house." Then she turned to her grandson. "What did you say, Pedro?"

"It's for you," said Pedro.

Everyone began talking at once, telling Grandmother Paz how Pedro had found the little house and the whole village had helped mend it for her.

Grandmother Paz couldn't say a word. But her shining eyes told everyone she was too happy to speak.

"There is a mango tree near the door," said Nene, remembering that her grandmother liked mangoes.

"So there is," said Grandmother Paz.

"And look!" cried Pedro. "Here is the chicken coop; there are two chickens in it."

"It is just as I have dreamed a little house should be," said Grandmother Paz.

They went inside and lighted the candles in the star lanterns that hung in the windows. Then the neighbors began to come to welcome Grandmother Paz home. Each one brought a gift—a few eggs or a basket of rice or even a live chicken to put in her chicken coop.

Uncle Manuel played his guitar. What with the laughing, and the talking, and the singing, and the noise of firecrackers, it was a very gay housewarming.

Darkness came quickly, and outside the Christmas stars twinkled through the palm trees. The candles in the windows lighted the laughing faces of friends and neighbors. Pedro stood in the doorway watching them. He said, "Grandmother, do you think this little old house was ever so happy before?"

"Oh, Pedro," Grandmother Paz laughed, "are you still asking funny questions?"

"You're all right, Pedro," said Great Aunt Trinidad, playfully tapping him on the head with her knuckles, "if you don't ask questions, you'll never know anything."

from THE GOOD MASTER

Kate Seredy

Life is not the same for Jancsi after his hotheaded cousin Kate arrives from Budapest to spend time on the farm. Kate is a willful child, given to tantrums and unfunny pranks. As the book progresses, the peacefulness of the Hungarian countryside, the serenity of the peasants, and the strength of the "Good Master" combine to make Kate a more reasonable girl.

Cousin Kate from Budapest

Jancsi was up bright and early that morning and at work milking the cows. He was so excited he couldn't stay in bed. For today Cousin Kate was coming. She was the only cousin he had, and she was a city girl. A real city girl from Budapest. Ever since the letter came from his uncle, Jancsi had been the proudest boy on the big Hungarian plain. He was the only boy in the neighborhood who had a cousin in the city. And she was coming today, to stay for a long time. Father had told Jancsi what was in the letter. It said that Kate had had the measles last winter. Jancsi had never had the measles—he thought it must be something wonderful to have. And she was delicate, the letter said, too, so she was coming to the country. A *delicate* city cousin, who had had the *measles*—that was something.

If it were only Sunday, they would go to church and he could tell everybody about her. Sunday was the only time when Jancsi saw anyone outside his own family. Father had a ranch, with thousands of sheep, horses, cows, and pigs. He had chickens and ducks and geese; he even had donkeys, but he didn't have enough children to suit Jancsi. It got so lonesome for poor Jancsi, he would have given ten horses for a brother. He had it all figured out—he would give a donkey for even a sister. Not horses, just a donkey.

The ranch was miles and miles from the village. It was too far to walk, and they were too

From *The Good Master* by Kate Seredy. Copyright 1935, © 1963 by Kate Seredy. Reprinted by permission of The Viking Press, Inc.

busy to drive on weekdays. So, although Jancsi was ten years old and quite a man if you asked his opinion, he had never been to school, and he did not know how to read or write. The ranch was the only reality to him—the world outside was just a fairy story. Mother knew lots of fairy stories about dragons and golden-haired princesses who lived in glittering castles. Jancsi thought that houses in Budapest were made of gold and had diamond windows. All the city people rode around on pure white horses and wore silk gowns. Cousin Kate would have golden curls, rosy cheeks, big blue eyes; she would wear a white silk flowing gown, and her voice would be like honey. Now—Jancsi is off in dreamland—some day a dragon will capture her, and it will be up to Jancsi to go to the rescue. He is clad in green velvet, red boots, riding a coal-black steed. Here comes the dragon! Jancsi pulls out his golden sword, and one-two-three heads are at his feet! All good dragons have twelve perfectly hideous heads. Four—slash, five—swish goes his sword——

"Mo-o-o-o!" bellowed something close to him. And crash-bang went Jancsi together with the milking-stool. He sat and blinked. Máli, the mottled cow, looked at him with reproachful eyes. Reality closed around the hero—oh yes, here he was in the barn, milking the cow.

"Jancsi! Ja-a-ncsi-i! Hurry up with the milk or you'll be late for the train!" It was his mother's voice calling from the house. He scrambled to his feet, scowled at Mali, and picking up the full pails made his way back to the kitchen. Mother took the milk from him. "I'll strain it today, Jancsi. You eat your breakfast and get dressed. And get a good scrub—why, you're all full of mud!"

Jancsi kept his back out of Mother's sight—the seat of his white pants would need explaining. He gulped down his bread and milk. Then, backing out of the kitchen, he ran to the well. He filled a wooden bucket with the icy water and, stripping off his clothes, stepped into it. With great splutters and groans he scrubbed himself, using sand on the most disgraceful spots. Then he took a bit of salt from a mug and scrubbed his teeth with his fingers. Squirting out the salty water, he set a new long-distance record; he even paused long enough to gaze at it admiringly and mark the spot with a stone. "Can spit almost as far as Father," he muttered with pride.

He ran back to the house. His very best Sunday clothes were all laid out on the bench, near the big white stove—his embroidered shirt, the wide pleated pants, his shiny black boots, his round hat with the bunch of flowers. He put them on. Mother wasn't in the kitchen. He went to the bedroom. No Mother in the bedroom. But on the windowsill, glittering in the sunshine, was a green bottle. He gazed at it for a while, torn between desire and discipline. It was too much for him. Tiptoeing to the window, he took the bottle and the little red comb next to it. It was perfumed hair oil—and only *men* used perfumed hair oil! He put a little on his hair. Then a little more, and still more, until his hair looked as if it were made of black enamel. Then with a sigh of satisfaction he put on his hat and strutted out. He heard the wagon—time to go!

When he saw the wagon drive up to the door, he gave a whoop of joy. Father had harnessed his four black horses with the very best brass-studded harness. Each horse had a big bunch of geraniums fastened to the headband, and long streamers of gayly colored ribbons floated in the breeze. He jumped up next to Father, and off they went down the long poplar-lined lane leading to the main road.

It was early April, and fields and pastures were a fresh pale green. The poplars stood like solemn sentinels, whispering to the wind. Father was a man of few words; men never spoke, he believed, unless they had something important to say. Gossip was only for the womenfolks. Jancsi was quiet, too, busy with his own thoughts. He was going to the town for the first time in his life—he would see a train. Trains were a mystery to him. One of the shepherds had told him trains were fire-eating dragons; they roared, and snorted black smoke. "They pull little houses; people go from one place to another in the little houses. And trains kill everybody who gets in their way." Jancsi wondered if he could hitch their own house to one of these dragons. Then he could go and see the world. But he would take his dog Peti, he'd take his favorite horse, he'd take Máli, the cow . . . No, he scowled and rubbed his side, remembering this morning. No, he wouldn't take Máli. Deeply absorbed in deciding whom he would take with him, he hardly noticed how fast they were traveling. Soon they left the open country and entered the long village street. The village was always interesting to him, so he began to look around. Father turned to him. "I'll stop at the store to buy some tobacco. You hold the reins, Jancsi." Jancsi slid over to Father's seat and grabbed the reins. He sat there, head up, shoulders erect, looking straight ahead. Just then a village boy walked by. He stopped and looked at Jancsi with open admiration.

"Hey! You driving *alone?*"

Jancsi gulped and replied evasively: "Going to fetch my cousin from the train. She comes from Budapest." Then, unable to keep from gossiping like womenfolks, he blurted out his news: "She had the measles and is delicate and her name is Kate! She'll live with us!"

Father came down the store steps, stuffing his pipe. Jancsi prayed for a miracle. If the boy would only go away or if Father would only let him drive . . . !

The miracle came. Father walked around the wagon and, getting up next to Jancsi, said: "Let's see how you handle wagon and four!"

So they left the boy staring after them open-mouthed. Jancsi drove through the village like a king in a golden coach. The clouds of white dust around the horses' hoofs were like stardust to him. The glittering hoofs were made of diamonds. Everything looked new and beautiful to him today. The endless rows of snow-white houses with their gayly painted doors and shutters were like pearls in a row. The geraniums in the windows were a brighter red than ever. The church seemed taller, the grass greener. He flipped his whip impatiently at the barking dogs and almost rode over a flock of honking geese slowly plodding across the street. Then they were in the open country again. It was almost noon; the spring sun beat down on the shimmering fields. They passed a long fence. Horses were grazing placidly in the pasture.

"Good horseflesh," remarked Father. "See how meek they look now, but it's a man's job to stay on one of those beasts."

"I can get on one and stay on it, Father. Those aren't worse than your own horses."

"Think you can, Son?"

"I *know* I can!" asserted Jancsi hastily, forgetting that this would call for explanations.

He was not yet allowed to ride unbroken horses.

"You *know* you can?" said Father, reaching for his pocket knife. Jancsi watched him in shocked silence. He knew he was in for it, but somehow he didn't mind. After the pocket knife came a little round stick of wood with many cross-marks cut into it. It was the score pad. One notch was cut for each sin Jancsi committed, and after a while it was crossed out. But the "after a while" usually included moments Jancsi didn't like to remember. Holding knife and stick in his hands, Father looked at Jancsi. Jancsi looked far, far ahead. Suddenly Father laughed and, putting away the "score," slapped Jancsi on the back.

"You're no worse than I was at your age, Son. You'll make a good rancher."

Jancsi heaved a sigh of relief. This was a man's world, and he was accepted!

Father pointed ahead. "See those houses and chimneys? That's the town and the station." Jancsi was all eyes and ears now. Soon the wagon was rattling on the cobbled street. They passed lots of buildings, and there were a great many people walking around. Father told him where to stop and, after the horses were hitched to a post, said: "Well done, boy!" This made Jancsi feel still better. Praises from Father were few and far between, but they were all the more satisfying.

Walking through the station building, they came to the platform. "Those long shiny snakes are rails, Son; the train travels on them. It'll be here soon now."

Jancsi heard a great rumbling, snorting, and pounding in the distance. He felt the platform shake under his feet. Casting a frightened look at his father, he saw that Father wasn't afraid, so it must be all right. Then he saw a black monster rushing around the curve. It must be the dragon. It had an immense eye glittering in the sunshine. Vicious-looking black teeth, close to the ground. And black smoke poured out of its head. Then it gave a shrill scream, blew white smoke out of its ears, and came to a groaning halt. Men jumped down, opened the doors of the funny little black houses. Jancsi waited with eyes round and shiny like big black cherries. He expected to see people in silks and velvets, glorious people. But not one of them had good clothes on; they were just everyday people dressed in drab grays and browns. Then he heard someone shouting: "Már-ton Nagy! Is Márton Nagy here?"

Father yelled back: "Here! Márton Nagy!" A man hurried toward them, dragging a little girl with him. Just any kind of little girl, with plain black hair, a smudgy face, and skinny legs.

"Well, thank goodness you're here," said the man, wiping his forehead. "Here, take this—this imp, this unspeakable little devil—take her and welcome." He pushed the girl to Father. "Never again in my life will I take care of girls. I'm a self-respecting railroad guard. I handle anything from baggage to canaries, but I'd rather travel with a bag of screaming monkeys than her, any time." He gave her a final push. "Here's your uncle, he'll take care of you now. G'bye and—good luck to you, Mister Nagy!"

All this tirade left Jancsi and Father speechless. Here was Kate, looking as meek as Moses, but evidently something was wrong with her. Father bent down and said: "Well, Kate, I am your Uncle Márton and this is Jancsi, your cousin. We'll take you home now."

Cousin Kate looked up. Her dirty little face broke into a grin. "Oh, but you look funny!" she cried. "And I thought my cousin was a boy, and she's nothing but a girl!"

"But, Kate," said Father, "can't you see he's a boy?"

"I only see that she has skirts on and an embroidered blouse. Nobody's wearing embroidered blouses this season, they're out of style!"

Jancsi just began to realize that this dirty, skinny little girl in the plain blue dress was his cousin. He felt cheated—that was bad enough—but she called Father "funny" and said he was a *girl*—that was really too much! With fists clenched, chin stuck out, he advanced toward Kate. "I am a girl, am I? . . . I'm funny, am I? . . . I'll show you!"

Kate was ready. She dropped her bag, took a threatening step toward Jancsi. They were face to face now, tense, poised like two little bantam roosters, ready to settle the argument on the spot. Suddenly Father's hearty laugh broke the tension. "You two little monkeys," he cried, "now I'll tell you that you are both funny! Stop this nonsense, both of you. Jancsi! Gentlemen don't fight girls. Come on, we'll go home."

He grabbed their hands and, still laughing, walked to the baggage-room. Jancsi and Kate had no choice, they had to go, but at least they could make faces at each other behind his back. The fight was not over, it was just put off for the moment.

When they reached the wagon, there was more trouble. Kate declared that since the wagon had no top, she'd get a sunstroke. It didn't have cushions on the seat, so she'd break to pieces. She told Father to "phone" for a "taxicab."

"I'll wash your mouth out with soap, if you swear at *my* father!" cried Jancsi. "Phone" and "taxicab" sounded like swearing to him.

"She wasn't swearing, Jancsi," said Father; "she is just talking city language. 'Phone' is a little black box, you can talk into it, and people many miles away hear you. 'Taxicab' is a horseless wagon city people travel in." He turned to Kate. "We haven't any taxicabs here, Kate, so come on, hop on the seat."

Kate shook her head. "I will not. Ride in this old wagon indeed! Why, everybody will laugh at me."

Father's patience was wearing out. He just grabbed Kate under the arms and lifted her into the seat before she knew what had happened. "Come on, Son, we can't waste the whole day. You sit on the outside so she won't fall off." They both got on the wagon. Kate almost disappeared between them. Father was a very big man, and Jancsi a big husky boy for his age. But what Kate lacked in size, she made up in temper. When she realized what had happened, she turned into a miniature whirlwind. She kicked and screamed, she pinched Jancsi, she squirmed like a "bag of screaming monkeys."

"Father, the man was right, she's a bag of screaming monkeys!" said Jancsi, half angry, half amused, holding on to Kate.

Father was busy holding the horses in check. They were respectable farm horses, not used to the unpleasant sounds Kate managed to make. Soon they left the town and were traveling at a fast clip on the country road. Little by little Kate subsided. The long trip in the train and all the excitement were beginning to wear her out. She looked around. She saw the great Hungarian plain unfold before her eyes. Something in her was touched by the solemn beauty of it. Its immense grassy expanses unbroken by mountains or trees, shimmering under the spring sun. The dark blue sky, cloudless, like an inverted blue bowl. Herds of grazing sheep, like patches of snow. No sound, save the soft thud of the horses' hoofs on the white dusty road, and now and then the distant tinkle of sheep's bells, or the eerie sound of a shepherd's flute, the tilinkó. At times these plains, called the "puszta," are the very essence of timeless calm. At times the puszta wakes up and resembles an ocean in a storm. Clouds, so low it seems you can reach up and touch them, gather above. Hot winds roar over the waving grass. Frightened herds stampede, bellowing and crying. But calm or stormy, it is magnificent. Its people are truly children of the soil, they are like the puszta itself. Good-natured, calm, smiling, they, like the plain, can be aroused to violent emotions.

Kate did not know all this, but she was touched by the greatness and calm of it. She was very quiet now. Jancsi looked at her and touched Father's shoulder. They smiled at each other—she seemed asleep. Jancsi felt almost sorry for her now, she was so little and thin, so funny with her dirty little face. "Like a kitten," he thought, "the poor little kitten I found after the storm." He moved, to give her more room. She leaned heavily against him, her head nodding. He didn't see her face now, didn't see the slow impish grin, the awakening mischief in her eyes. He moved a little more, balancing on the edge of the seat. "Poor little kitten," he thought again—and "poor little kitten" suddenly gave him a hearty push which sent him off the wagon like a bag of flour. He landed in the dusty road, resembling a bag of flour indeed. He hurt something awful where he landed; it was the same spot Máli the cow had kicked that morning. Through the dust he saw the wagon come to a stop.

Father jumped down and, reaching Jancsi, began to feel his arms and legs for broken bones. "You great big baby," he scolded, "you want to ride wild horses? Can't even stay on a wagon!"

"Hey! Hey! Father! Stop Kate! Look, Father!" Jancsi yelled, struggling away from Father.

There was Kate, standing bolt upright on the seat, reins and whip in hand. She was grinning from ear to ear.

"Pushed you off, didn't I, little girl? Catch me if you can!" She whipped the horses, screaming at them: "Gee, git up, git up!" This was too much for one day even for the horses. They lunged forward, and broke into a wild gallop.

Father, shocked speechless for a moment, grabbed Jancsi by the arm.

"Come on, Son, we've got to catch this screaming monkey before the horses break their legs, or she breaks her neck!"

They ran, panting and choking in the hot dust. The wagon was almost out of sight now.

"Got-to-get-horses!" panted Father.

"We-could-catch-two from the herd here!" choked Jancsi, pointing to the herd they had passed that morning.

They jumped the fence and were among the surprised horses before the animals became alarmed.

"Run with the horse, Son," cried Father. "Run with it, grab its mane, and *swing!*"

Exciting moments followed. They were used to horses, but this was hard business, without rope or halter. Jancsi singled out a young chestnut horse. The animal reared, shied, baring his teeth, and started to run. But Jancsi's hands were already clutching his mane. The horse broke into a wild run, Jancsi clinging to him for dear life. He was carried like a piece of cloth, almost flying beside the horse. With a supreme effort he pulled himself up. Clutching his legs around the animal's neck, he reached forward to pull its nose down. Horse and rider were a mass of plunging, snorting animation. Jancsi was dizzy, but he gritted his teeth and hung on. Then he heard Father's voice through the tumult. "Let him run and guide with your knees. Come on, 'csikós,' you're a real son of mine!"

Slowly the horse quieted down. Jancsi pulled him around and headed for the fence. Father was riding a big mare, waving to him to follow. Soon they were traveling side by side—hot, dirty, exhausted, and, judging by Father's face, madder than hornets.

They rode through the village without stopping to ask questions. The poplars on the ranch road whizzed past them. There was the house now! There was Mother, at the gate, waving madly with one hand. With her other hand she was clutching the blue skirts of a dancing, struggling little imp—a dirty, disheveled, but grinning little girl—Cousin Kate from Budapest!

Motherless Lamb

While Kate told her story, Jancsi cast half-amused, half-admiring glances at her. She might be just a plain little girl, but she certainly wasn't a sissy.

She was sitting in Mother's ample and protective lap, looking once more like a sleepy kitten. Father was very angry at first, but he was so relieved to see her alive, he just couldn't stay angry.

"We were going almost as fast as Ben Hur in the movies," Kate said. "Only I lost those long strings tied to the horses and then I had to sit down, I had nothing to hang on to. And the chariot was swaying so I got dizzy!" She kept on calling the wagon a "chariot." Jancsi didn't like it, it sounded almost as bad as "taxicab." "Then we came to a long street with houses. Men in petticoats, like yours, Jancsi, came running out of the houses. They were all yelling, but couldn't stop the horses. But after a while the horses got tired running, an' I was sick to my stomach anyway, so I crawled back and lay down on the straw, and went to sleep."

"The poor mite was still sleeping when I found her," said Mother. "I saw the wagon turn in at the gate without a living soul on it. The horses were heading for the stable. I ran out. There was a girl curled up in the straw! When I woke her up, she started to jabber a lot of nonsense about 'chariots' and 'Ben Hurs' and Uncle Márton and Jancsi. 'Glory be,' I said, 'are you Cousin Kate from Budapest?' I picked her up and brought her in! The very idea, leaving a delicate child alone in the wagon with four wild horses!"

"Leaving—what's this?" cried Father, but Kate broke in hurriedly: "And then we saw you and Jancsi riding like the devil was after you!"

"Only it was the other way round—*we* were riding after the devil!" said Father. "Luckily the horses had sense enough to bring you home. But listen, my girl, you are rather a wolf in sheep's clothing!"

"M-m-m," said Kate with satisfaction. "I know. That's what Father always said. Oh! He sent you a letter!" She reached down into her blouse and produced an envelope.

Father read the letter aloud:

"My dear Brother:

"I feel guilty for misleading you, so forgive me. My dear daughter Kate had the measles, and she is delicate and in need of fresh country air—all this is true. But she is more than delicate. She is the most impossible, incredible, disobedient, headstrong little imp. And she needs more than fresh air—she needs a strong hand! Pray don't let her innocent face take you in; when she looks like an angel, she's contemplating something disastrous. She is beyond me. I confess I have spoiled her since her blessed mother died. You always had a good hand with wild young things, your people always called you the Good Master, so I send Kate to you. I'll miss her terribly, but this is the best thing I can do for her.

"So forgive me, Márton, and try to put a halter on my wild colt.

"Your loving brother,
"Sándor."

There was a long silence. Everybody looked at Kate. She, with her eyes cast down demurely, was the very picture of innocence.

"My poor little motherless lamb," cried Mother, gathering Kate in her arms. "I don't believe a word of it. Why, look at her, Father, isn't she like an angel?"

Jancsi felt gooseflesh creeping up his spine. He had seen this angelic expression before—his uncle was right, it was a danger signal. He looked at Father and caught his eye. Father was actually winking at him. Then he stood up, and said:

"Jancsi and I are going to look after those 'wild horses,' Mother; you watch our new angel. See that she doesn't fly away."

The horses were a sorry sight indeed, caked with dust. Father and Jancsi worked hard for a long time. Under the currycomb and brush the black coats of the animals were glossy once more. After the cleaning Father gave them their rations. The stable was spick and span, the wagon put in the shed. "Time for our supper, Jancsi. Let's see what Mother is doing with the 'angel.'"

"There's Mother calling now," cried Jancsi, "but she's calling Kate."

Mother was running toward them, flushed, with all her numerous petticoats swaying around her.

"Kate! Where is Kate? Have you seen Kate? She was in the kitchen one minute, making the most awful faces at the bowl of milk I gave her for supper. Then she disappeared in thin air while I went out for water!"

They looked high and low. No Kate. No sign, no sound, of Kate. In the sheep house, the chicken coop, pigsty, cowbarn—no Kate. They looked up the roof and down the well. Back to the house, maybe she was just hiding. She wasn't in the house.

Utterly exhausted, Father sank into a kitchen chair. "If she's still alive, she's going back to the city tomorrow, so help me! I wasn't made for this sort of thing, it gives me a pain in my side," he said.

"Send the poor little motherless lamb away, Father? You couldn't," cried Mother. "Her very own father calling her names. I just know her poor little heart is broken. And you two looking at her as if she were a bug. It's enough to kill the child!"

"Tee-hee!" a sound came from the rafters. "Tee-hee!"

"Mice or rats after the sausages again. Light a candle, Jancsi," said Father. He was very fond of sausages. Mother made quantities of them in the winter. Thin long ones with lots of paprika, short fat ones with liver; she made head cheese, smoked hams. When they were ready, Father hung them on the rafters in the kitchen. He hung long rows of peppers and strings of corn on the cob. He kept bacon on one rafter, his carving tools on another. Even Jancsi wasn't allowed to touch anything stored up there.

When the candle flared up, Father was ready with a broom. Rats were his personal enemies.

"Tee-hee!" came the sound again. There sat Kate, straddling the smoky beam, skinny legs dangling, munching one end of a long sausage. Gulping down a huge mouthful, she volunteered an explanation to her thunderstruck relatives. "She gave me milk for supper. Hate milk! I like sausages!"

As long as Jancsi lived, he never forgot the uproar that followed the discovery of Kate. He wanted to laugh, but didn't dare, Father was too mad! Grasping the broom, Father roared: "Come down!" Kate shook her head. "COME DOWN!" Kate moved like lightning, out of the path of the swinging broom. Mother was wringing her hands, trying to calm Father, and imploring Kate to come down, all at once. There was a cascade of assorted sausages, pepper, and corn. Father got red and redder in the face. Kate was scurrying like a monkey from one beam to the other, screaming like a tin whistle. It went on and on. It was Father who gave in first. He sank into his chair, wiping his forehead. "Angel . . . motherless lamb," he panted. "Look at her now. Her little heart is broken." And with utter contempt: "Delicate! Devouring yards of sausages!"

"Come down, my lamb, he won't hurt you." Mother held out her arms to Kate.

"Can't," was the laconic answer.

"How did you get up there anyway? If you went up, you can come down," growled Father.

"I climbed on that big white beehive in the corner, but it's hot now, she made a fire in it," said Kate. She meant the stove. It did look like a beehive, squatting in the corner. There was a bench around it. Jancsi loved to cuddle on the bench, propping his back against the warm side of the "kemence."

"Well, now you'll stay there until the 'beehive' cools down. Jancsi! Mother! I forbid you to take her down. She can stay there all night!" said Father. And no amount of Mother's begging and crying softened him. There she was, and there she stayed.

Mother began to serve supper. They ate in silence. Jancsi was grinning secretly. Once he looked up. Kate was peering down, her face black, her dress smoky, her stockings torn, but she grinned back.

Suddenly Father began to laugh. "Screaming monkey! Poor kitten! Colt! Motherless lamb! Why, she's a whole menagerie! You always wanted to go to a circus, Jancsi; now the circus has come to you!"

"I'm thirsty," announced Kate unexpectedly.

"Anybody would be after eating two yards of sausages. If you want a drink, come down and get it!" was Father's answer.

She tried "I'm sleepy," "I'm tired," without any satisfactory results. In fact, they were going to bed, actually leaving her perched on the rafters, and the "beehive" still too hot. She began to whimper. Jancsi felt sorry for her, but orders were orders.

Mother prepared the beds. The guest bed for Kate. This was seldom in use, all the fancy embroidered pillows were piled up to the ceiling on it. Mother carried them to a chest, put down

two huge featherbeds for mattresses, and a lighter featherbed for a cover. She was shaking her head, looking at Kate, looking at Father, but he wouldn't soften. Finally they put out the candles and silence settled upon the house.

Jancsi fell asleep. The sound of soft footsteps woke him up. Then he heard whispers and a giggle. He tiptoed to the kitchen door. There was Father, holding Kate in his arms, stroking her hair.

Something made Jancsi feel all shaky inside— he felt like crying, but he was happy.

He crawled back to his bed. A little later he heard Father's voice whisper: "Good night, little screaming monkey."

Dozing off to a contented sleep, Jancsi's last thought was: "I'm glad she isn't a golden-haired princess—she's almost as good as a real boy!"

from HEIDI

Johanna Spyri

Heidi is a homeless, forlorn child trying to make a place for herself. In this selection, Heidi arrives at her grandfather's and gets acquainted with him and his surroundings. This is a reassuring book, and the gallant spirit of the little girl is unforgettable.

At the Grandfather's

After Dete had disappeared, the uncle sat down again on the bench and blew great clouds of smoke from his pipe, while he kept his eyes fixed on the ground without saying a word. Meanwhile Heidi was content to look about her. She discovered the goats' shed built near the hut and peeped into it. It was empty.

The child continued hunting about and came to the fir trees behind the hut. The wind was blowing hard, and it whistled and roared through the branches, high up in the tops. Heidi stood still and listened. When it stopped somewhat she went round to the other side of the hut and came back to her grandfather. When she found him in the same place where she had left him, she

From *Heidi* by Johanna Spyri, translated by Helen B. Dole. Used by permission of the publishers, Ginn and Company placed herself in front of him, put her hands behind her, and gazed at him. Her grandfather looked up.

"What do you want to do?" he asked, as the child continued standing in front of him without moving.

"I want to see what you have in the hut," said Heidi.

"Come along, then!" and the grandfather rose and started to go into the hut.

"Bring your bundle of clothes," he said as he entered.

"I shan't want them any more," replied Heidi.

The old man turned round and looked sharply at the child, whose black eyes shone in expectation of what might be inside the hut.

"She's not lacking in brains," he said half to himself. "Why won't you need them any more?" he asked aloud.

"I'd rather go like the goats, with their swift little legs."

"So you shall, but bring the things along," commanded the grandfather; "they can be put into the cupboard."

Heidi obeyed. The old man opened the door, and Heidi followed him into a good-sized room, which occupied the whole hut. In it were a table and a chair; in one corner was the grandfather's bed, in another the fireplace where hung the large kettle; on the other side, in the wall, was a large door, which the grandfather opened; it was the cupboard. There hung his clothes, and on one shelf lay his shirts, stockings, and linen; on another were plates, cups, and glasses, and on the topmost a loaf of bread, smoked meat, and cheese. Everything the Alm-Uncle owned and needed for his living was kept in this closet. As soon as he had opened the door, Heidi came running with her bundle and pushed it in, as far back of her grandfather's clothes as possible, that it might not be easy to find it again. Then she looked carefully round the room and said:

"Where shall I sleep, grandfather?"

"Wherever you like," he replied.

This was quite to Heidi's mind. She looked into every nook and corner to see where would be the best place for her to sleep. In the corner by her grandfather's bed stood a little ladder, which led to the hayloft. Heidi climbed this.

There lay a fresh, fragrant heap of hay, and through a round window one could look far down into the valley below.

"This is where I will sleep," Heidi called down; "it is lovely! Just come and see how lovely it is up here, grandfather!"

"I know all about it," sounded from below.

"I am going to make a bed," called out the child again as she ran busily to and fro in the loft; "but you must come up here and bring a sheet, for the bed must have a sheet for me to sleep on."

"Well, well," said the grandfather below; and after a few moments he went to the cupboard and rummaged about; then he drew out from under his shirts a long, coarse piece of cloth, which might serve for a sheet. He came up the ladder and found that a very neat little bed had been made in the hayloft; the hay was piled up higher at one end to form the pillow, and the bed was placed in such a way that one could look from it straight out through the round open window.

"That is made very nicely," said the grandfather; "next comes the sheet; but wait a moment,"—and he took up a good armful of hay and made the bed as thick again, in order that the hard floor might not be felt through it; "there, now put it on."

Heidi quickly took hold of the sheet, but was unable to lift it, it was so heavy; however, this made it all the better because the sharp wisps of hay could not push through the firm cloth. Then the two together spread the sheet over the hay, and where it was too broad or too long Heidi quickly tucked it under. Now it appeared quite trim and neat, and Heidi stood looking at it thoughtfully.

"We have forgotten one thing, grandfather," she said.

"What is that?" he asked.

"The coverlet; when we go to bed we creep in between the sheet and the coverlet."

"Is that so? But supposing I haven't any?" asked the old man.

"Oh, then it's no matter," said Heidi soothingly; "we can take more hay for a coverlet"; and she was about to run to the haymow again, but her grandfather prevented her.

"Wait a moment," he said, and went down

the ladder to his own bed. Then he came back and laid a large, heavy linen bag on the floor.

"Isn't that better than hay?" he asked. Heidi pulled at the bag with all her might and main, trying to unfold it, but her little hands could not manage the heavy thing. Her grandfather helped, and when it was finally spread out on the bed, it all looked very neat and comfortable, and Heidi, looking at her new resting-place admiringly, said:

"That is a splendid coverlet, and the whole bed is lovely! How I wish it were night so that I could lie down in it!"

"I think we might have something to eat first," said the grandfather. "What do you say?"

In her eagerness over the bed, Heidi had forgotten everything else; but now that eating was suggested to her, a great feeling of hunger rose within her, for she had taken nothing all day, except a piece of bread and a cup of weak coffee early in the morning, and afterward she had made the long journey. So Heidi heartily agreed, saying:

"Yes, I think so too."

"Well, let us go down, since we are agreed," said the old man and followed close upon the child's steps. He went to the fireplace, pushed the large kettle aside and drew forward the little one that hung on the chain, sat down on the three-legged wooden stool with the round seat and kindled a bright fire. Almost immediately the kettle began to boil, and the old man held over the fire a large piece of cheese on the end of a long iron fork. He moved it this way and that, until it was golden yellow on all sides. Heidi looked on with eager attention. Suddenly a new idea came to her mind; she jumped up and ran to the cupboard, and kept going back and forth. When the grandfather brought the toasted cheese to the table, it was already nicely laid with the round loaf of bread, two plates, and two knives, for Heidi had noticed everything in the cupboard, and knew that all would be needed for the meal.

"That is right, to think of doing something yourself," said the grandfather, laying the cheese on the bread and putting the teapot on the table; "but there is something still lacking."

Heidi saw how invitingly the steam came out of the pot, and ran quickly back to the cupboard. But there was only one little bowl there. Heidi was not long puzzled; behind it stood two glasses;

the child immediately came back with the bowl and glasses and placed them on the table.

"Very good. You know how to help yourself; but where are you going to sit?"

The grandfather himself was sitting in the only chair. Heidi shot like an arrow to the fireplace, brought back the little three-legged stool and sat down on it.

"Well, you have a seat, sure enough, only it is rather low," said the grandfather; "but in my chair also you would be too short to reach the table; still you must have something anyway, so come!"

Saying which he rose, filled the little bowl with milk, placed it on the chair, and pushed it close to the three-legged stool, so that Heidi had a table in front of her. The grandfather laid a large slice of bread and a piece of the golden cheese on the chair and said:

"Now eat!"

He seated himself on the corner of the table and began his dinner. Heidi grasped her bowl and drank and drank without stopping, for all the thirst of her long journey came back to her. Then she drew a long breath and set down the bowl.

"Do you like the milk?" asked her grandfather.

"I never tasted such good milk before," answered Heidi.

"Then you must have some more"; and the grandfather filled the bowl again to the brim and placed it before the child, who looked quite content as she began to eat her bread, after it had been spread with the toasted cheese soft as butter. The combination tasted very good, with frequent drinks of milk.

When the meal was over, the grandfather went out to the goat-shed to put it in order, and Heidi watched him closely as he first swept it clean with a broom and then laid down fresh straw for the animals to sleep on. Then he went to his little shop, cut some round sticks, shaped a board, made some holes in it, put the round sticks into them, and suddenly it was a stool like his own, only much higher. Heidi was speechless with amazement as she saw his work.

"What is this, Heidi?" asked the grandfather.

"It is a stool for me, because it is so high; you made it all at once," said the child, still deeply astonished.

"She knows what she sees; her eyes are in the right place," remarked the grandfather to himself as he went round the hut driving a nail here and there; then he repaired something about the door, and went from place to place with hammer, nails, and pieces of wood, mending and clearing away wherever it was needed. Heidi followed him step by step and watched him with the closest attention, and everything he did interested her very much.

Evening was coming on. It was beginning to blow harder in the old fir trees, for a mighty wind had sprung up and was whistling and moaning through their thick tops. It sounded so beautiful in Heidi's ears and heart that she was quite delighted, and skipped and jumped under the firs as if she were feeling the greatest pleasure of her life. The grandfather stood in the doorway and watched the child.

A shrill whistle sounded. Heidi stopped her jumping, and the grandfather stepped outside. Down from above came goat after goat, leaping like a hunting train, and Peter in the midst of them. With a shout of joy Heidi rushed in among the flock and greeted her old friends of the morning one after the other.

When they reached the hut, they all stood still, and two lovely slender goats—one white, the other brown—came out from the others to the grandfather and licked his hands, in which he held some salt to welcome them. This he did each evening. Peter disappeared with his flock. Heidi gently stroked first one goat and then the other and ran round them to stroke them on the other side; she was perfectly delighted with the little creatures.

"Are they ours, grandfather? Are they both ours? Will they go into the shed? Will they stay with us always?" asked Heidi, one question following the other in her delight. When the goats had finished licking their salt, the old man said:

"Go and bring out your little bowl and the bread."

Heidi obeyed, and came back at once. The grandfather milked the goat and filled the bowl and cut off a piece of bread, saying:

"Now eat your supper and then go up to bed! Your Aunt Dete left a bundle for you; your nightgowns and other things are in it. You will find it downstairs in the closet if you need it.

time. In the night the wind blew with such force that its blasts made the whole hut tremble, and every rafter creaked. It howled and groaned down the chimney like voices in distress, and outside in the fir trees it raged with such fury that now and then a bough was broken off.

In the middle of the night the grandfather rose and said half aloud to himself:

"She may be afraid."

He climbed the ladder and went to Heidi's bedside. The moon outside shone brightly in the sky for a moment and then disappeared behind the driving clouds, and everything grew dark. Then the moonlight came again brightly through the round opening and fell directly on Heidi's couch. Her cheeks were fiery red as she slept under the heavy coverlet, and she lay perfectly calm and peaceful on her little round arm. She must have been dreaming happy dreams, for a look of happiness was on her face. The grandfather gazed long at the sweetly sleeping child until the moon went behind a cloud again and it was dark. Then he went back to his own bed.

from DOBRY

Monica Shannon

Dobry won the Newbery Medal in 1935, and it still remains one of the finest in the list of Newbery winners. Beautifully written and rich in unique characters, this slow-moving story does not make an immediate appeal to children. Reading it aloud and discussing it will help. Should Dobry do as his mother wishes, stay on the farm, or go away to study art as he yearns to do?

[Everything Is Different]

Dobry ran to a window, slid back its window-panel carved with buffalo heads. "Snow! Why, it's snowing, Grandfather! The courtyard is white already." Snow was never rare in a mountain village of Bulgaria, but nobody, not even Dobry's grandfather, had seen snow coming down to hide red apples on the tree, late corn on the stalk, ripe peppers in the field, grapes on the vine. The golden-leaved poplar tree in the

I must attend to the goats now; so sleep well!"

"Good night, grandfather! Good night—what are their names, grandfather? what are their names?" cried the child, running after the old man and the goats as they disappeared into the shed.

"The white one is named Schwänli[1] and the brown one Bärli,"[2] answered the grandfather.

"Good night, Schwänli! good night, Bärli!" called Heidi at the top of her voice. Then Heidi sat down on the bench and ate her bread and drank her milk; but the strong wind almost blew her off the seat; so she finished hastily, then went in and climbed up to her bed, in which she immediately fell asleep and slept as soundly and well as if she had been in the loveliest bed of some royal princess.

Not long after, even before it was entirely dark, the grandfather also went to bed; for he was always up with the sun, and it came climbing over the mountain very early in the summer

[1] Schwänli = little swan
[2] Bärli = little bear

courtyard of Dobry's peasant home was completely hushed with snow. Wool, too, from the autumn shearing was hanging out to dry. The wool grew thicker, the thickest wool imaginable as more and more snow came down. Without making a sound, the sky itself seemed to be coming down bit by bit.

"Nobody has ever seen a happening like this one," Dobry's grandfather said, and followed the little boy to the window. "Snow already, even before the gypsy bear gets here! My back, my legs complain of getting in the grass and the early corn. They wanted a good rubbing before snow set in. Snow? To the devil with gypsies! They should be here with the massaging bear!"

Dobry hung out of the window as far as he could. The rickety outside stairway going down to the ground floor where their two oxen lived had a carpet of snow, immaculate, and the oxen looked up from their stalls each wearing a furry hat of new snow.

Dobry shouted, "Look! Sari and Pernik are surprised too. Look, Grandfather, they wear white fur hats like royalty!"

The grandfather leaned out. "It's true." He shook his head instead of nodding because in Bulgaria you shake your head for "yes" and nod your head for "no." "They do look like royalty," the grandfather said. He drew in his head, shivered, muttered, "You feel the first cold. Anyway, you feel it when one day is like summer and the next day like winter. Come in out of that."

Dobry pulled his head in, turned around. His hair and eyelashes had gone completely white.

"St. Nicholai, the Miracle Maker, bless us all!" The grandfather stared at Dobry. "You look just like me with all that white on you. Snow is blowing in! Close that window tight."

"Wait, wait," Dobry begged and cupping his hands he put them out for snowflakes. "Look, they are beauties," he told the grandfather. "Look at the shapes! Flowers from the sky."

The grandfather shook his head vigorously instead of saying, "Yes, yes." "Each flake is a different one. Perfect! All white flowers—little, new, and no two alike."

Dobry asked him, "And why aren't the snowflakes alike, Grandfather? Different, each one different?"

The grandfather said, "Everything is different,

each leaf if you really look. There is no leaf exactly like that one in the whole world. Every stone is different. No other stone exactly like it. That is it, Dobry. God loves variety." Grandfather found it hard to say exactly what he meant. "God makes better icons than those in the church. He makes a beautiful thing and nothing else in the whole world is exactly like it. That is it, Dobry. Something for you to remember."

"Why?" Dobry asked him.

"Well, it's as good a thing to remember as anything. I never went like you do to the school but I know it. No two things are exactly alike. In odd days like these—snow comes too early, the gypsy bear too late—people study how to be all alike instead of how to be as different as they really are."

Grandfather slid back the window-panel, threw a log on the open fire, pushed it in farther with his foot, and sat himself down on the three-legged stool under the fireplace hood reaching far out into the room.

Dobry, his mother Roda, his grandfather, all of them called their fireplace a "jamal" and a jamal it really was. It stood out from the wall, tiles green, yellow, blue, glimmering in the firelight, and its big yellow chimney was stuccoed to make a picture of quail hiding in ripe grass.

Dobry squatted on the hearth. Above his head under the jamal's hood dangled copper pots, copper kettles, and copper pans, tarnished now because the gypsy cleaner had not yet come to brighten them up for the winter. He looked at the flames, content to watch their colors, their motions, and listen to their chat, but his grandfather interrupted.

"Ours is the most beautiful jamal in the whole village," he said. "No other like it. It knows its work, too. Never smokes. Heats up the whole house instead of trying to change the weather outside. Only Maestro Kolu could have made a jamal like this one."

"Couldn't you make a jamal like this one? You could, couldn't you, Grandfather? And the blacksmith could make one too, couldn't he?"

Grandfather said very loud, "Pff, Pff! Not Pinu, the blacksmith. That fellow! Maestro Kolu is a Macedonian and almost a magician besides. He puts little pipes into a chimney the way God puts blood vessels into our bodies. Perfect! The heat goes around but stays in the house. Maestro Kolu knows the secret and that secret has been growing up for centuries. He knows how to make a jamal as no other man knows it—tiles colored up like our stony earth, the chimney a picture like one of our fields. I tell you, if Maestro Kolu lives to be five hundred years old he'll never have time enough to make the jamals people ask him to make. And——"

Realizing all of a sudden that he was roaring instead of talking, the grandfather stopped to laugh at himself. "Some day you will see Maestro Kolu, maybe, and then you will know for yourself what he is."

The old man got a pipe out from the sash winding seven times around his middle and, his pipe filled, going, he felt around in his sash for a red pepper and gave it to Dobry to nibble. Dobry never could guess at all the things his grandfather tucked away in that broad red sash making a middle for his blue homespun suit. Pipes, coins, red peppers, cheese, bread, garlic, wooden boxes of spices to brighten up his bread in the fields, a painted flute—Dobry often saw these things come out and always asked himself, "What else may be in there?"

Dobry's mother hurried in from the kitchen fetching a bucket of water to heat in the cauldron hanging from big iron chains over the open fire. She added to the brightness the firelight made in this room of plain wooden walls and carved wooden panels—there was so much color to Roda that in the summer field bees often sought her out. Her cheeks and black eyes glowed, her white lace petticoat swirled below a sunflower-colored dress and an apron woven over with roosters just about to crow. A white kerchief topped her head and her hair danced behind her in two long braids.

"What is this?" she asked them. "A boy thinks of everything except going to bed. A big, sleepy boy and long after his supper time! A boy grows big enough to down four bowls of buttermilk at a sitting and he can't tell bedtime yet! We must be up and out before the sun is up and out tomorrow. Peppers to come in and be dried, corn to come in and be husked! When are the roads going to be cleaned up for hauling? There is too much to do now that it snows when

it shouldn't. Pop yourself into bed, Dobry!"

Dobry said, "Everybody expects me to go to bed the way bread goes into the oven. Pop! Am I bread? Mother, you should see the way Sari and Pernik go to bed. You should see it! Close one eye, eat a little more, open that eye, close the other, and eat a little more. Very slow. And Grandfather said they were good beasts fit to wear tall fur hats like royalty. Didn't you, Grandfather? You should see their hats, Mother. Snow, very new. Perfect!"

His mother said, "There it is! A boy can think of everything except going to bed. Bread, ovens, fur hats, royalty even. Go to bed!" She stooped and kissed Dobry. "The whole world taken by surprise! All these snowflakes dancing the horo outside—and this boy! Well, I must go and look after the bread. The bread is growing up now."

Dobry said, "Good night, Grandfather," and kissed him.

The grandfather told him, "Don't forget to pray to St. Triffon about the gypsy bear, will you now? How late those gypsies are and the snow early! Ask St. Triffon to bring the gypsies soon with the massaging bear."

"Do your back and legs complain much tonight?" Dobry asked him.

"Yes, always a little. Ever since I weeded tomatoes when the fields were wet."

"Do we eat the tomatoes now, Grandfather? We always eat tomatoes after the first snow comes."

The grandfather nodded his head emphatically to say, "No, no. It's not winter yet. Tomatoes are for winter. Later snows will cover them just right. Then we'll have tomatoes, a few at a time, and a whole vineful of tomatoes for Christmas Day—the way we always do."

Dobry's grandfather alone of all the villagers knew how to make snow take care of his tomatoes for him. He picked the tomato vines with their ripe fruits, wove them together in a weaving dense enough so that not the smallest chink was left for frost to get through. Snow covered his pyramid of tomatoes on their vines and all winter long he had only to dig down into the snow to bring up tomatoes as fresh but crisper than the morning they first ripened.

"But can't I eat some tomatoes right away?" Dobry begged. "This snow will make them crisp. You said all summer, when I helped you weed the tomatoes, you said to me, 'When snow comes you will be very happy, Dobry, for all this work. When snow comes we will both be warmed to red inside with tomatoes.' Don't you remember, Grandfather? And snowflakes are dancing a horo dance outside right now."

"Oh, yes, the snowflakes dance but without the music." The Grandfather hummed and made gestures with his hands—he imitated a peasant beating a drum, playing a fiddle, blowing a pair of bagpipes. "I love the music," he cried.

Dobry jumped up, whirled about, dancing the rachanitza. Like every other Bulgarian child, he had learned the national dance when he first learned walking. The grandfather took a flute from his sash, closed his eyes, swayed his body and played the rachanitza music. Dobry danced faster and faster and Grandfather began stamping his feet.

The room was lighted up again with Dobry's mother. She called out, grabbed at them both. The flute stopped, the dance stopped. "Now, good night!" she said crossly and turned back to the kitchen.

Happy from the music, the grandfather said, "Yes, yes, I think we had better have tomatoes

now that the snow is here. Bring me in some, Dobry, when there is time. I'll be so busy getting our peppers in out of the snow. Tomatoes—we will both eat a big plateful! Nice and crisp after the snow. The first snow of the year—it is true we should celebrate. The snow comes too early, the gypsy bear too late—we need them, tomatoes to warm us to red inside. Lots of tomatoes!"

Dobry said, "Perfect!" and kissed his grandfather good night.

Dobry lay in his bed, but excitement had him awake. The snow was all down, the moon up. A full-grown harvest moon, it stared at Dobry through the window.

"Why do you always follow me around?" Dobry asked the moon. "Everywhere I go there you come looking, looking, looking. Everything happens at once—snow comes when it shouldn't, the gypsy bear doesn't come when it should and you—you say nothing. Just follow me about, staring! How do you expect me to sleep? Nobody could sleep while you stare the way you do and say nothing. I should go for the tomatoes, anyway. Grandfather needs them to warm him to red inside and there will be little time tomorrow. Everything to do."

While he talked, Dobry got out of bed, picked up the homespun breeches he had just taken off and knotted the legs at the bottom, making twin sacks. "One to hold tomatoes enough for my grandfather, the other to hold tomatoes enough for me," he told the moon. He put on goatskin sandals and a long, belted sheepskin coat, slung the breeches like sacks over his shoulder and, calling to the moon, "Well, come on!"—ran out on and down the snow-piled stairway.

Dobry stopped at the floor below to look in on Sari and Pernik. He said to them, "What! No hats? You look just like yourselves. One eye open, one eye closed, eating away. You think of everything, don't you? Everything except going to bed!" He opened the heavy stall door, went in, patted them both and said firmly, "Good night, Sari. Good night, Pernik."

It took Dobry and the moon only a few minutes to go to the small forest of pine and fir trees separating Dobry's home from his mother's fields beyond. He could hear the happy whistle of his own breathing and his feet sounded nice in his ears as he broke through fresh snow. But in a little while the going seemed hard. Dobry stopped to pant freely on a hilltop while the moon rested too, but very far up on a cloud.

Below them the forest was deep in new snow, immaculate with the heavy snowfall. Trees had gathered to themselves all the snow they could hold; only the points of black fir trees and pines were still uncovered. They branched out like horns and made blue shadows on the freshly covered earth. Dobry could not speak to the moon now. Silence was alive here, he knew, and the moon gave it light. A radiant silence took possession of Dobry as well.

But on a sudden two owls began calling to each other, "Hoot—oo! Hoot—oo!" One of them flew low over the boy's head and he picked up an owl's feather. Then he slid down the hill, loose snow giving way behind him. ("Chasing me," he told himself.) His heart stopped thumping when he saw his mother's fields just ahead. They looked homely, familiar even in the moonlight. Walnut trees and corn-stalks Dobry knew well stood up in the snow. A very fat rabbit out to get carrots instead of tomatoes bounded across the fields, off for his hole, and Dobry noticed how dimly yellow a rabbit can look by moonlight, becoming almost a piece of it.

"Rabbits are always out when you are," Dobry told the moon. "Whenever you are following me around I have only to go outside to see rabbits going places in a big hurry. If you tried to follow a rabbit, first you would have to go very fast—hippetty hop, and besides that you would have to squeeze down a hole. With me you have only to look in through a window."

He stooped over the pyramid of tomatoes, dug down through the snow, filled up both legs of his breeches with tomatoes, slung the pack over his shoulder, called out to the moon, "Come on, moon," and ran for home. The tomatoes felt heavy enough at the start and got heavier as he ran on. But he kept going, running slower and slower down the trail his coming had broken through the new snow. Perspiration squeezed out all over him and he ate handfuls of snow to quench his thirst.

Tired out and hardly able to keep his eyes open, Dobry sat up in bed eating his share of the tomatoes, skin and all just as if they were apples,

while the moon stared in at him through the window.

"There is sense to your staring now," Dobry told the moon. "Me—I should hate to just look on while somebody else ate the first tomatoes of the year. Crisp, too, juicy and really cold. Perfect!"

from THE FAMILY UNDER THE BRIDGE

Natalie Savage Carlson

After World War II, there was a time in Paris when there were not enough houses and apartments for people to live in. The poor lived in tents, slept in doorways, or made homes for themselves under bridges. In this selection old Armand, the hobo, first encounters the children. Before the story is finished they have had some funny, some sad, and some exciting adventures together. Get the book and enjoy the wonderful illustrations by Garth Williams along with the heart-warming story.

[A Hobo Adventure]

Once there was an old hobo named Armand who wouldn't have lived anywhere but in Paris. So that is where he lived.

Everything that he owned could be pushed around in an old baby buggy without any hood, so he had no worries about rents or burglars. All the ragged clothing he owned was on his back, so he didn't need to bother with trunks or dry-cleaners.

It was easy for him to move from one hideyhole to another so that is what he was doing one late morning in December. It was a cold day with the gray sky hanging on the very chimney pots of Paris. But Armand did not mind because he had a tickly feeling that something new and exciting was going to happen to him today.

He hummed a gay tune to himself as he pushed his buggy through the flower market at the side of Notre Dame cathedral. The flowers reminded him that someday it would be spring even though it wasn't bad winter yet.

There were pots of fragile hyacinths and tulips crowded together on planks in front of the stalls. There were pink carnations and oleanders in great tin pails. Most of all there were bouquets of red-beaded holly, clumps of white-pearled mistletoe and little green fir trees because it would soon be Christmas.

Armand's keen eye caught sight of a pile of broken branches and wilted flowers swept away from one stall. "Anabel" was the name written over the stall, and Armand touched his black beret to the stocky woman whose blue work apron hung below her wooly coat.

"By your leave and in gratitude for your generosity, madame," he said to the woman who was surely Anabel. He piled the broken branches on top of his belongings in the baby buggy. Then he fastidiously picked a sprig of dried holly from the litter and pulled it through his torn buttonhole. He wanted to look his best for whatever gay adventure was waiting for him this day.

The woman who must have been Anabel only frowned at Armand as he trundled his buggy toward the Rue de Corse. Past the ancient buildings he shuffled, his buggy headed for the far branch of the Seine River.

But as he entered the square in front of Notre Dame, a hand grasped his arm from behind.

"Your fortune, monsieur," wheedled a musical voice. "You will meet with adventure today."

Armand let go of the handle of the buggy and whirled around to face a gypsy woman in a short fur coat and full, flowered skirt.

He gave her a gap-toothed smile. "You, Mireli," he greeted her. "Your people are back in Paris for the winter?"

The gypsy woman's dark face beamed under the blue scarf. "Doesn't one always spend the winters in Paris?" she asked, as if she were a woman of fashion. "But have you taken to the streets so early?"

Armand shrugged his shoulders under the long overcoat that almost reached to his ankles. "It's back under the bridge for me," he answered. "I've had enough of the crowded corners and tight alleys in the Place Maubert. And I'm tired of sorting rags for that junk dealer. I'm ready for that adventure you're promising me."

Mireli could understand. "That courtyard we rent seems like a cage after the freedom of the long, winding roads," she said, "but the men have found plenty of work for the winter. A city with as many restaurants as Paris has more than enough pots and pans to be mended. Of course the children can talk of nothing but the fields and woods of spring."

"I can't abide children," grumped Armand. "Starlings they are. Witless, twittering, little pests."

Mireli shook her finger at him. "You think you don't like children," she said, "but it is only that you are afraid of them. You're afraid the sly little things will steal your heart if they find out you have one."

Armand grunted and took the handle of the buggy again. Mireli waved him away, swaying on bare feet squeezed into tarnished silver sandals. "If you change your mind about the bridge, you can come to live with us," she invited. "We're beyond the Halles—where they're tearing down the buildings near the old Court of Miracles."

Armand tramped under the black, leafless trees and around the cathedral by the river side without even giving it a glance.

In the green park behind the flying buttresses, some street urchins were loitering. Two of them played at dueling while a third smaller one watched, munching a red apple. The swordsmen, holding out imaginary swords, circled each other. Closer and closer came the clenched fists, then the boys forgot their imaginary swords and began punching each other.

They stopped their play as Armand went by. "Look at the funny old tramp!" one cried to his playmates.

Armand looked around because he wanted to see the funny old tramp too. It must be that droll Louis with his tall black hat and baggy pants. Then he realized that he was the funny old tramp.

"Keep a civil tongue in your head, starling," he ordered. He fingered the holly in his lapel. "If you don't, I'll tell my friend Father Christmas about your rude manners. Then you'll get nothing but a bunch of sticks like these on my buggy."

The boys looked at him with awe. Father

Christmas is the Santa Claus of France. He rides down from the north on his little gray donkey and leaves presents for good children.

The small boy held out his half-eaten apple. "Are you hungry, monsieur?" he asked. "Would you like the rest of this apple?"

But the biggest boy mockingly punched the air with his fist. "Pouf!" he scoffed. "There's no Father Christmas. He's just make-believe."

"If you doubt my word," said Armand with dignity, "just take a look in the Louvre store. You'll find him on the mezzanine floor."

He grinned like one of the roguish gargoyles on the cathedral. There really was a Father Christmas and it was his friend Camille, who felt the urge to work when the weather turned cold.

"I believe you, monsieur," said the boy with the apple. "I saw Father Christmas outside the store yesterday. He was eating hot chestnuts on the street."

Armand hunched his shoulders and quickly walked toward the bridge. Mireli was right. These starlings would steal your heart if you didn't keep it well hidden. And he wanted nothing to do with children. They meant homes and responsibility and regular work—all the things he had turned his back on so long ago. And he was looking for adventure.

Down a few blocks was the bridge under which he lived when the weather wasn't too raw. And plenty of company he had during the summer with all the homeless of Paris staking their claims to this space or that.

"But first I must have dinner," he told himself, looking up at the restaurant across the street. He licked his thumb and held it up. "The wind is just right," he decided.

So he parked his buggy beside the low wall and settled himself in the breeze that came from the restaurant. He pulled all the kitchen smells deep into his lungs. "Ah, steak broiled over charcoal," he gloated. "And the sauce is just right. But they scorched the potatoes."

For two hours Armand sat on the curb enjoying the food smells because that is the length of time a Frenchman allows himself for lunch in the middle of the day.

Then he daintily wiped his whiskered lips with his cuff and rose to his knobby shoes. "And just keep the change, waiter," he said generously, although there wasn't a white-uniformed waiter in sight. "You'll need it for Christmas."

He started down the steps that dropped from the street to the quay beside the Seine. He bounced the back wheels of the buggy down each step. "I am really quite stuffed," he told himself, "but I wish I had taken that apple. It would have been the right dessert after such a rich sauce."

Down the quay he pushed the buggy toward the bridge tunnel that ran along the shore. On the cobbled quay a man was washing his car with the free Seine water. A woman in a fur coat was airing her French poodle. A long barge, sleek as a black seal, slid through the river. It was like coming home after a long absence, thought Armand. And anything exciting could happen under a Paris bridge.

As he neared the tunnel, his eyes widened with surprise and anger. A gray canvas was propped over the niche that had always been his own. And a market pushcart was parked by the pillar.

He raced his buggy across the cobblestones toward the arch. When he arrived there, he reached up and angrily tore down the canvas with one swoop of his arm. Then he jumped back in surprise and horror.

"Oh, là, là!" he cried. "Starlings! A nest full of them!"

Because three startled children snuggled into a worn quilt looked up at him with eyes as surprised as his own. The little girl and the boy cowered deeper into the quilt. But the older girl quickly jumped to her feet. She had direct blue eyes and they matched her determined chin and snubbed nose and bright red hair.

"You can't take us away," she cried, clenching her fists. "We're going to stay together because we're a family, and families have to stick together. That's what mama says."

As Armand glared at the children, a shaggy dog that should have been white came bounding across the quay. It protectively jumped between the tramp and the children, barking fiercely at Armand. The hobo quickly maneuvered his buggy between himself and the dog.

"If that beast bites me," he cried, "I'll sue you for ten thousand francs."

The girl called the dog to her. "Here, Jojo!

Come, Jojo! He won't take us away. He's only an old tramp."

The dog stopped barking and sniffed at the wheels of Armand's baby buggy.

The man was insulted. "I'll have you know that I'm not just any old tramp," he said. And he wasn't. "I'm not friendless, and I could be a workingman right now if I wanted. But where are your parents and who are you hiding from? The police?"

He studied the children closely. Redheads they were, all of them, and their clothes had the mismatched, ill-fitting look of poverty.

The older girl's eyes burned a deep blue. "Our landlady put us out because we don't have enough money to pay for the room since papa died," she explained. "So mama brought us here because we haven't any home now. And she told us to hide behind the canvas so nobody could see us, or they'd take us away from her and put us in a home for poor children. But we're a family, so we want to stay together. I'm Suzy and they're Paul and Evelyne."

The boy swaggered a little. "If I was bigger, I'd find a new place for us to live," he boasted.

"It looks to me like you've already found a new place," said Armand, "and it's my old place. You've put me out of my home just like that landlady did to you."

Suzy was apologetic. She moved the pushcart over and measured Armand with one eye closed. Then she carefully drew a long rectangle on the concrete with a piece of soft coal.

"That's your room," she said. "You can live with us." On second thought, she scrawled a small checkered square at the foot of the rectangle. "There's a window," she said gravely, "so you can look out and see the river."

Armand grumbled to himself and pulled his coat tighter across his chest as if to hide his heart. Oh, this starling was a dangerous one. He'd better move on. Paris was full of bridges, the way the Seine meandered through it. No trouble finding another one. But as he started away, the girl ran over and clutched him by his torn sleeve.

"Please stay," she begged. "We'll pretend you're our grandfather."

Armand snorted. "Little one," he said, "next to a millionaire, a grandfather is the last thing I hope to be." But even as he grumbled, he began unpacking his belongings.

He stacked the branches and twigs, and made a pile of the dead leaves he had gathered. He pulled out a dirty canvas and a rusty iron hook. He set a blackened can with a handle near the leaves. He sorted some bent spoons and knives. Last of all, he pulled out an old shoe with a hole in the sole.

"Might come across its mate one of these days," he explained to the children. "And it fits me just right."

The children wanted to help him. Oh, these starlings were clever. They knew how to get around an old man. Lucky he wasn't their grandfather. But he laid his canvas over the rectangle Suzy had made for him.

He started a fire with the branches and dead leaves. Then he hung a big can over the fire. Into it he dropped scraps of food he unwrapped from pieces of newspaper.

"In the good old days of Paris," he told the children, "they used to ring bells in the market places at the close of day so the tramps would know they were welcome to gather up the leftovers. But no more. Nowadays we have to look after ourselves."

They watched him eating his food. Even the dog that should have been white watched each morsel that went into his mouth and drooled on the concrete. Armand wriggled uneasily. "What's the matter?" he asked gruffly. "Haven't you ever seen anybody eat before?" They said nothing in reply, but four pairs of eyes followed each move of his tin spoon. "I suppose you're hungry," he growled. "Starlings always have to be eating. Get your tinware."

Suzy pulled some stained, cracked bowls and twisted spoons from the pushcart. Armand carefully divided the food, even counting in the dog.

It was dark by the time the children's mother joined them. The lights of Paris were floating in the river, but the only light in the tunnel flickered from a tiny fire Armand had made. He could not see the woman's face well, but he felt the edge of her tongue.

"What are you doing here?" she demanded of the hobo.

Armand was angered. "And I might ask you the same, madame," he retorted. "You have taken my piece of the bridge."

"The bridges don't belong to anybody," said the woman. "They're the only free shelter in Paris."

Suzy tried to make peace. "He's a nice, friendly old tramp, mama," she explained, "and he's going to live with us."

"I'm not a friendly old tramp," said Armand indignantly. "I'm a mean, cranky old tramp, and I hate children and dogs and women."

"Then if you hate us," said Paul, "why did you give us some of your food?"

"Because I'm a stupid old tramp," replied Armand. "Because I'm a stupid, soft-hearted old tramp." Oh, là, là! There it was. He had let slip that he really had a heart. Now this homeless family would surely be after that too.

The mother was displeased to hear that the children had accepted the hobo's food. "We are not beggars," she reminded them. "I have a steady job at the laundry, and that is more than he can say."

She went to work warming a pan of soup and breaking a long loaf of bread that she had brought with her. Armand sat in the rectangle marked by Suzy and thought that this woman's trouble was pride, and that pride and life under the bridge weren't going to work out well together.

By the dying light of the fire, the woman went back and forth to her pushcart, pulling out moth-eaten blankets and making bed-places on the concrete. Just overhead the automobiles roared, lights garlanded the bridge and people walking along the higher quay laughed lightly. But it could have been a million miles away from the little group under the bridge.

"You ought to put the starlings in some charity home until you find a place of your own, madame," suggested Armand, after the children had dropped off to sleep. "This life is not for them. Now, you wouldn't want them to end up like me, would you?"

"Families should stick together through the lean times as well as the fat," replied the woman. "And I have hopes. I'm going to see my sister-in-law soon. She may know of a place for us out in Clichy."

Armand stretched out on his canvas without bothering about any covering. He was used to the cold. He never felt it any more. But he was sure these children would feel it. As he lay on the hard concrete an uneasy thought worried him, like a mouse gnawing at his shoestring. Now that he had befriended these starlings, his life would never again be completely his own.

from AVALANCHE!

A. Rutgers van der Loeff

Natural disaster is man's sternest teacher. When nature intrudes upon our organized lives, whether it is a flood, a hurricane, or an avalanche in a Swiss village, we are tested seemingly beyond human endurance. In this excerpt, Werner, the hero, has returned from helping rescue people buried beneath tons of snow. Physically weakened by his efforts and mentally worn out from worrying about his own family, Werner asks the question we all ask, "Why do all these things happen?" The answer he receives provides one of the most important messages in juvenile literature within the framework of a thoroughly spellbinding book.

Where Do We Go from Here?

When he came to, he was lying on his camp bed in the station restaurant at Brachen. It was broad daylight and only one or two people here and there were sitting or lying on their beds. The place seemed less full than before. He looked at the corner over by the coffee machines to see if Klaus were lying there, but the bed had been taken away.

He looked round slowly. He had a queer, light-headed feeling and wondered how long he had been asleep.

Paolo was in the next bed. He was asleep, but his hands moved restlessly on the coverlet, and now and then he muttered something. Farther along, Nikolai and Giuseppe lay fast asleep.

The camp beds of the others had been tidily made. They were empty. The boys must have gone off to the village. Werner raised himself on one elbow and gave a little grunt of pain. All his muscles hurt. He looked round a bit farther. Then he saw Hans Peter sitting behind him a little distance away. He was sitting on a pile of knapsacks between two beds with his back against the wall, staring gloomily before him. Werner beckoned, but Hans Peter did not see. He was sunk in thought.

Was he angry at their having gone off without him? He would have been a great help, but he could never have given Mr. Hutamäki the slip like the rest of them. Would he know how Klaus and Marie were? And whether their parents had been found?

Werner heaved himself up a bit farther and all his muscles seemed to protest. He was aching everywhere—back, shoulders, arms.

"Hans Peter!" he said in an urgent whisper.

Hans Peter jumped. He stood up rather reluctantly and came over to Werner's bed. "How do you feel?" he asked gruffly.

"I'm fine. How are the others?"

"I've been left here as watchdog," said Hans Peter. "You're none of you to get up till the doctor says you may. He's coming back this afternoon. There was no room for you in the hospital."

"But there's nothing wrong with us!" exclaimed Werner in surprise.

Hans Peter did not answer.

"How long have we been asleep?" asked Werner.

"Two nights and a day and a half."

Werner's jaw dropped.

"They gave you injections to make you sleep. You were suffering from exhaustion or something. They made quite a song and dance about you."

"But I feel fine," protested Werner. "My muscles ache a bit, that's all."

Hans Peter shrugged his shoulders. "Well, you looked pretty moldy, all the lot of you, when they brought you in here the day before yesterday. You all had jabs at the hospital. You looked more dead than alive, I can tell you, and Hutamäki had the scare of his life. It was a mean trick you played us, creeping out while we were asleep, instead of taking us with you."

"We couldn't help that," said Werner. "Mr. Hutamäki would never have approved of your coming and you might have let on to him about us."

"Honestly, I don't know what I should have done," Hans Peter admitted. He was not so gruff now. "But I've never been so angry in all my life."

Werner glanced over to the corner where he had expected to see Klaus. He hesitated and then asked, "How are Klaus and his sister?"

Hans Peter looked uncomfortable. He began to say something and then stopped, looking away so as not to meet Werner's eyes.

"D'you mean it was all for nothing?" Werner asked suddenly, with his heart in his mouth.

Hans Peter shook his head. "Marie's alive, but they don't know if she'll pull through." He paused. "They found the parents; they were both dead." He paused again and it was a minute before he added, "And Klaus is very ill. He's delirious."

Werner felt the blood beating in his temples. His heart was thumping. He felt dizzy and lay down again on his back.

"Everyone here is getting on fine," Hans Peter went on presently, in a flat, expressionless voice. "Most of them are out now. It's visiting time at the hospital. And the trains are running again. A lot of the evacuees have left."

But Werner was not listening any more. He could see Klaus, and Marie's pinched white face. Should not he and the other boys have done what they did? Had they just been crazy fools?

Then he remembered Klaus when he was brought in that evening, sobbing and kicking because he had had to leave the place where his parents were buried. He had kept on shouting, but no one had listened to him. He had known they had been searching in the wrong place. In his helplessness there was nothing Klaus could do but howl. But later he had dug frantically for hours.

And had it all been wrong? Had they just caused more misery? Klaus was delirious, his parents were dead after all, and Marie . . . .

"What exactly is wrong with Marie?" he asked. Hans Peter hesitated, but after a bit he answered. "She bled an awful lot inside," he said. "She's got to have an operation. They wanted to do it yesterday afternoon, but they couldn't because they hadn't any blood for her."

"No blood?" asked Werner, puzzled.

"She's got to have a blood transfusion before the operation, and after it's over. But they couldn't find anyone that had exactly the same kind of blood. As a rule it isn't so tricky, but with Marie it was very difficult. A lot of us went over to let them test our blood. They tried me and Mr. Hutamäki and Bartel. But our blood wasn't right either. There were two doctors and three nurses working on us, and word kept on coming up from the lab that it wasn't the right kind of blood. And you'll never guess who had the right kind in the end."

"Who?" demanded Werner excitedly.

"Your Aunt Augusta. First they wouldn't try her. They said she was too old and her blood pressure wasn't high enough, or something. She was so cross with the doctors when they wouldn't try her that they gave in. And then they found she had exactly the right kind."

"Well, what happened?" Werner asked. "Were they in time?"

"I'm not quite sure about what happened after that. They took Aunt Augusta away with them and we were all sent back here."

"Have they operated on Marie?"

"Yesterday evening, but they don't know yet if it was successful or not. It should have been done much sooner. Your aunt had to stay in the hospital."

Werner lay quite still on his back. It was all too much for him to take in at once. Aunt Augusta and Marie . . . it was all so wonderful. He knew just what his father would have said about it—"It was meant."

He tried to think. If he and his father had not brought the boys down from the hut above Urteli, they would not have been evacuated together. If they had not come here to Brachen, Klaus would not have been able to take them up to his home. In that case Marie would be dead by now, for she could have lasted only a couple of hours longer. And if Aunt Augusta had not been evacuated with them she would not have been able to give her blood. It was meant!

But what about the avalanches? Were they meant too? That could not be right. There must be something wrong somewhere. All those people killed and injured, all that grief and suffering! His whole heart revolted against the idea of so much pain. It was senseless for the snow to come hurtling down from the mountains. Why did it happen? Why? Why? Why did Klaus and Marie have to lose their father and mother?

"*I* don't know," he muttered suddenly half aloud.

"What is it?" asked Hans Peter. "What don't you know?"

"Why do all these things happen? Why can't people just live happy and ordinary lives?"

"Happy and ordinary aren't the same," said Hans Peter slowly. "I believe you're only happy if you *know* you're happy. And you only know that after you've been miserable. A lot of us in the Children's Village have learned that."

Werner said nothing. Hans Peter went on rather uncertainly, "The head of our Village told us something once. He said misfortune shakes you awake, and it's only when you're awake that life becomes quite real, because then you've learned what it's worth."

from THE BUSHBABIES

William Stevenson

This is much more than the story of a foolish young girl's attempt to return her beloved bushbaby to its natural habitat. As the journey to return the bushbaby progresses across Africa, Jackie is faced with a growing awareness of the danger in which she has placed Tembo—everyone thinks he has kidnaped her—since the orders are to shoot him on sight. But she also comes to appreciate his tremendous knowledge of the country and to understand that numerous skills are required for survival in different environments. The Bushbabies is one of the few juvenile books which lay the groundwork for the young adult to read with compassion Alan Paton's Cry the Beloved Country.

[Kamau Goes Home]

"Are you the little girl with the bushbaby?" asked the second engineer of the United States motor vessel *Thoreau*.

Jackie, picking her way between coils of tarred rope, said: "Yes. Want to see him?"

She lifted the lid to the basket which was his second home, displaying Kamau asleep in his nest of old sweaters.

"That's a rare 'un," said the engineer. "Worth his weight in gold, I bet."

He stood in front of her, face red against the brilliant white of his starched shirt and shorts. "You've got a game permit, of course."

"Of course," Jackie replied quickly, and flushed.

"Good kid." The engineer let her pass. "It'd be a bad thing if all the rare animals of Africa were taken away, eh?" he called after her.

But Jackie was already running, gripped by the sudden fear that she had forgotten the vital permit with the impressive words: *"Granting permission hereby for the export of one bushbaby— to wit: galagos senegalensis zanzibaricus."* She could remember even the Latin name. Where had she put the permit?

She flew to her cabin and hooked the door shut. Then she threw open her suitcase and whirled through its contents.

The permit was nowhere to be found.

She searched Sally's bag on the adjacent bunk. She went carefully through all her own pockets. She combed her memory.

She had no recollection of packing the permit. With growing certainty and alarm, she knew she had left it behind.

Her heart flipped.

She tried to remember the restriction on animals leaving Africa. Of one thing she was sure. It would be illegal to keep Kamau.

There was a knock at the door. Trembling, she unhooked it.

"I come to make bunks ready." It was the Swahili steward. He moved to the two-tiered bunks and saw the basket.

"Little missie has *galago*, bushbaby?"

"You know?"

"All the ship knows."

She thought in that case it would be impossible to keep Kamau as a stowaway.

"Does the captain know?"

"The captain." He paused, crouching over the coverlet, eyes dark and expressionless. "The captain will find out, missie. He is not liking animals on board. One time he makes the ship's carpenter leave a pet monkey behind, in Madagascar."

This was worse news still.

"Please don't tell him."

"Why for should I tell the captain?" The steward gave her an indignant look. "I do my work. Captain does his." He turned and busied himself with the blankets.

Jackie picked up the basket and took it into the small shower room. She closed the door and lifted Kamau gently out. He disliked being disturbed and drew back his ears, blowing between sharp little teeth with a sound like a muted roar.

From outside came the whine and screech of cranes. Soon the ship must sail. She had to think fast. If she tried to keep Kamau hidden, the captain was bound to find out. If she somehow deceived the captain, there would be customs men to face later. Either way she would certainly lose her bushbaby.

She let him leap to the rail of the shower curtain, where he clung upside down, head twisted so that he could watch her.

She remembered how her father had gone to some trouble to get Kamau's export license from the Kenya Game Department.

And now she had forgotten the permit.

She remembered, too, going to the public library and reading: "These are among the strangest animals in existence. Their relatives of the *tarsier* family are found only in equatorial forests of Asia. The animal commonly called the bushbaby, however, has been known to survive in cold climates."

Jackie winced. Here she was, planning to expose Kamau to the wintry blasts of a northern climate. Yet she could not even preserve the piece of paper that protected his life.

She heard the outer door clunk open again.

"Daddy!" She rushed to meet him.

"What is it?" He caught the urgency in her voice and looked at her with such frank and honest eyes that she faltered.

"Nothing." She was suddenly afraid to mention the permit. Her father was a square sort of man; square of shoulders and with a face that seemed to be chiseled from stone. He had an old-fashioned square-dealing approach to life. She could see no way of enlisting his help in breaking regulations.

"Come on deck and join the others." Trapper Rhodes took her arm in the belief that her evident distress was due to the tension of recent days.

She let him lead her to the main deck, her mind working furiously. There was only one solution that she could see. Kamau must be released here, in Mombasa dockyard.

Shrinking from the thought, she took her place at the rail. The dock was almost deserted. The last of the cargo had swung aboard. Big arc lights swayed in the humid night breeze, casting an eerie glow on the greasy concrete below. Chains rattled. Davits creaked.

A voice behind her said: "We'll be another coupla hours before sailing."

It was the second engineer talking quietly to Rhodes.

"In that case," said Penny firmly, "we'd better get some sleep." She herded the children together. "It's been a long day. And truth to tell, I'd sooner not be here when we cast off. We'll say goodbye to Africa tomorrow, at a good long distance."

Later when they were all bunked down, Penny said to her husband: "Did you see how upset Jackie was?"

His answer was lost in the metallic whir of the fan.

"You know," Penny continued, "that girl has changed a great deal since we gave her the bush-baby. She's still awfully clumsy. And forgetful. She breaks cups and trips over her own legs,

which are certainly too long for her age. She's awkward and dreamy and moves like a young colt. But she's a gentle child," said Penny, closing her eyes. "And a kind heart is worth a ton of cleverness."

In the next cabin Jackie waited until she heard Sally's breathing deepen into slumber.

Then she crept into the shower room. Kamau squatted beside the dish of milk and corn flakes she had smuggled from the cook's galley. He was clasping a mint candy, licking it with rapture in his eyes. She knew from long experience that mints had an almost hypnotic power over him, glueing his attention just as firmly as his twig-fingers were glued to the candy itself.

With a movement so swift it was scarcely perceptible, she scooped him up.

"Kek-kek-kek!" His screech was somewhat muffled by the mint. She bundled him into the basket, crammed down the lid, and pegged it into place.

She checked again that Sally was asleep, and slipped into the clothes she had worn in the train; riding breeches, a yellow shirt, and a brown whipcord jacket. Into a pocket of the jacket she stuffed a paper bag full of Kamau's remaining mints.

She tied her long golden hair at the back

hastily, using an old piece of blue ribbon. She donned her favorite chukka boots made from the ear of an elephant. Finally, on impulse, she bent and kissed Sally. "Back soon," she whispered, and slipped away.

The gangway was down and still unattended. Men scurried about the decks, absorbed in their own pursuits. Jackie was grateful that nobody· had come to see them off. All farewells, except for Tembo's, had been made upcountry. And Tembo, once he saw the baggage safely stowed away, had not lingered to drag out the agony.

Jackie scampered down the gangway and stood for a moment in the shadows. A stumpy locomotive of the port railway fussed along the gleaming metal of the line. A group of stevedores, bared backs glistening in the artificial light, stood arguing in a group.

She waited, and when the way seemed clear, she ran to the shelter of a nearby godown. There, in the thick smell of diesel oil and coffee, Jackie took stock.

She could let Kamau out of his basket now, and pray that somehow he would find his way safely back to the highland forests that were his natural home.

But then she thought of all his enemies. The hooting owls. The giggling hyena. The fish eagle whose harsh cry sounded across the marshes. The baboons who worked in teams, so clever and ruthless they could tear a leopard to pieces, never mind a bushbaby.

She shuddered.

Her mind went back to the very first time she had seen the basket she now clutched in her arms.

It had been their last Christmas Day in Africa.

The African workers and their children were gathered under the tall pine tree growing outside the bungalow. The tree was decorated with lights, and gifts were scattered on the grass below.

She had seen nothing at first but the straw basket tied with red ribbon.

"How do I open it?"

Jackie remembered how her father had bent down and freed the ribbon. "It will open itself."

The lid of the basket had lifted a fraction, making her jump.

And then, for the first time in her life, she had seen a bushbaby.

A tiny hand had groped along the basket's edge, followed by a face like a furry walnut.

"What is it?"

"Galago." Tembo's deep voice boomed in her ear.

She clapped her hands. "What a super, super surprise."

At the sound of her voice the bushbaby had jumped clean out of the basket and into her lap, tail thrashing like a propeller.

"His name is Kamau." Again it was Tembo who spoke. "The sprite who lives in the jungle. Kamau."

Now, as Jackie peered out of the darkness of the godown, she smiled sadly at the recollection of those happy months that followed. Kamau had been comforted by the warmth of her body, and made a permanent haven inside her shirt. She had to teach him to give up his nocturnal habits, for he was by nature a night animal.

"He's got the face of a fox, the ears of a bat, the eyes of an owl," Jackie had written to a distant uncle. "He's the color of a squirrel and he grins like a monkey and he's got the fingers of an old man. And he jumps like a kangaroo!"

She listened to him now, astir in the basket.

She stood alone on the dockside, in an agony of doubt, and heard the locomotive come clattering and clanging down the line again. It stopped and there was a moment of silence.

Away in the distance she caught faint notes of a toy harmonica. At first she thought the sound came from the ship. She heard Kamau scratching to be let out of the basket, and she lifted the lid. The bushbaby scrambled onto her arm and stiffened, his big paper thin ears pricked forward, his head twisting in every direction to pick up the sound.

Tembo!

She knew it must be Tembo, for the bushbaby had responded to the same harmonica notes.

Long ago, her father had said: "The most constructive thing the army ever taught Tembo was to play the mouth organ." And he had given the African headman a big old-fashioned German harmonica made of engraved metal and carved walnut. In camp, at night, Tembo would play this impressive instrument while the women husked coconuts or pounded the evening meal of posho made from corn meal.

Now, straining her ears like Kamau, the girl

was sure she recognized the notes. They were lost again in the deep and sudden thunder of the *Thoreau*'s siren.

It reminded her of the foghorn near the family cottage, a few miles along the coast from Mombasa. Its desolating thunder made her think of shipwrecks and storm-tossed seas. When it stopped, and the echoes dwindled away, she listened again for the notes of a mouth organ, but heard nothing.

Kamau slipped under her shirt and, hugging the basket, she ran the length of the godown. Part of her mind insisted that she had imagined the mouth organ. Deep down inside herself, she was not so sure.

Again the ship's siren blew, and still she felt this strange compulsion to run away from it. She slipped her hand inside the basket and felt the comforting furry warmth of the bushbaby. She stopped running, and looked back.

There was a great deal of activity now around the *Thoreau*. She saw figures moving about the stern and on the fantail. A rope snaked astern and fell with a clear splash into the murky water.

She stood, breathing fast.

A loud clatter drew her attention to the gangway. It was moving away from the ship's hull. Mesmerized, she saw more ropes curl through the air. Her legs were rooted to the ground. Common sense told her to shout, to run to the trundling gangway some fifty yards away.

But nothing on earth would have made her drop Kamau.

The ship's propellers began to churn. She heard small waves slap against the wharfside.

As if in a bad dream she saw the ship detach itself from the black density of the docks. Lights twinkled along the hull. The gap between the *Thoreau* and the quay began to widen with surprising speed. The ship had moved so slowly at first. Now it surged forward in a great hurry to be free from Africa. In the wake came a stench of fuel and tar, of stale cooking pots and sacks of coffee. A stream of garbage shot through a chute in the stern, and again the siren blew.

The girl stared unbelievingly at the black and deepening gulf between herself and her family. The basket in her arms, however, was like an anchor. While her head spun with the enormity of her situation, her legs refused to move. And

then, quite slowly at first, came a wave of relief. Kamau was safe. He was still with her.

When she heard the notes of the harmonica again, she was certain it must be Tembo.

She followed the sound, half-sobbing, until she came to the end of the main wharf. There she saw him, seated on a bollard, silhouetted against the city's glow.

"Tembo!" She was still too far away to be heard. He was playing a mournful African song. Jackie had heard it many times when he crouched over the charcoal brazier at night. It was a song of his own people, made long ago when Arab slavers laid waste this part of the continent. The song was a lament for the lost freedom of the chained African slaves, and for the slaughtered children they left behind. It was a dirge that recalled the endless march of the slaves, and in it were echoes of the wide horizons and the great forests they would never see again.

Tembo stopped. Moving softly, anxious not to alarm him, Jackie whispered: "Hullo, old friend. It's me. Do not be disturbed. Tembo?"

She spoke in Swahili.

The man jumped to his feet. His eyes shone, whites gleaming. He was on the very edge of the shifting pool of light cast by the swinging flood lamps, and he peered dubiously into the surrounding dark.

"Baba?" His voice was a hiss. "What are you doing here. *Wafanyajee?*"

"Come quickly, Tembo, out of the light."

He took a firm grip on the short club hanging from his wrist and moved toward her.

"Is it really you?"

"It is me, Tembo. I want your help." She touched his arm.

When his eyes had adjusted to the dark, and he saw truly that the girl stood there, the man sucked his breath. "What have you done?" He dropped to one knee and pressed her face between his callused hands. Then he saw the basket.

"Kamau?"

"Yes." She began to explain.

The African groaned. "You have done this thing for the galago? You have left the ship?"

"There was nothing else I could do," Jackie said simply. She hesitated. "I must get him home, to the place where he was caught. To the Place of the Hippopotamus."

Until this moment she had given no thought to such a plan. It rose unbidden to her mind. At once, however, she saw what a sensible solution it would be. Among his own family, he would be safe.

"That is a long way," Tembo was saying. "It is beyond Ndi." He added slowly: "Your father will be angry."

"He will understand." She spoke with more confidence than she felt. "If I had stayed on the ship, Kamau would die."

Tembo nodded slowly. He had never pretended to share the Rhodes' curious love of animals. As a young Kamba warrior, one of the fleetest hunters in his village, he regarded animals as either a nuisance or as a source of food. He passed no judgments on white-skinned foreigners who took a different view. He thought of them quite simply as mad. There was no telling how far they might go in their craziness.

He fingered the bracelet on his scarred wrist. It was made from the hairs plucked from a lion's tail, and it was the most powerful of his charms. He turned it slowly between his thick fingers, standing there in the darkness while the girl waited patiently at his side.

"How will the bushbaby make such a long journey?" he asked.

"With your help."

His friendship with Trapper Rhodes went back a long way. He had not expected to have it tested so severely by the daughter.

"You will help?" she persisted.

She was interrupted by a long blast from the ship's siren and she waited, head cocked, watching Tembo's face.

He was wearing the old desert kepi, with a neck flap at the back, that he used on safari. Over his thin shoulders he had flung an army greatcoat, worn like a cloak. His feet were thrust into black boots that were several sizes too large. The leather was cracked and the boots lacked laces. In these clothes he had gladly suffered the most acute discomfort, considering them to be appropriate to the sad occasion of parting.

The siren echoed across the harbor, and faded. Again the girl remembered the foghorn, and her father's cottage.

"I know!" She seemed to explode with the idea. "We will go to the cottage at Vipingo. It's a short

bus journey from here. And tomorrow, when the post office is open, I will send a telegram—a letter by radio—to the ship."

She saw the doubt lingering in his face.

"You have not seen the cottage but it is beside the farm of Major Bob."

Tembo's face cleared slightly. He knew about Major Bob and felt less apprehensive.

"Is it not possible to take the northern train?"

"No." She spoke decisively, detecting from his voice that the battle was half won. "In the cottage at Vipingo we shall be safe tonight. Major Bob will tell us what to do in the morning. If we go to the train, there will be questions at the barrier. There will be white policemen."

She knew the beefy red-faced police. They seldom understood small girls as her African friends did. The red-faced whites were too busy blustering around. Her family's cottage, on the other hand, was far off the beaten track. There she could plan her next move.

Tembo wiped his harmonica across the knee of his torn pants. Perhaps if he humored the girl now, she would see sense in the morning. "You are sure this is what you wish?"

"I am sure, old friend." She slipped her free hand into his gnarled fist. "Remember when we all went climbing on Kilimanjaro?"

Tembo chuckled softly.

"And we got lost in the mist, you and I?" She grinned up at him. Behind her, the *Thoreau's* lights twinkled in the harbor mouth. "We had such fun, just the two of us, singing and shouting down the mountain. It will be like that, Tembo, like climbing a mountain together."

The African smiled and hunched his shoulders under the greatcoat. It was a coat far too big, and much too warm, but he wore it with pride. He wore it as he had once worn the skin of the colobus monkey, in days when he carried a spear and shield, before he went to war in the service of a foreign king. The coat was a link with those distant days when he shouldered a rifle to fight the white king's enemies.

He looked down at the towheaded child. His days as an askari in the King's African Rifles had taught him many things. His days as a tribal warrior had also taught him much. He had learned to accept the passing of these days—the great days of hunting the lion; and other, more bewildering days, marching against an unknown army. Time had taught him never to grieve over his lost youth; never to look back in sadness at what had gone beyond recall. Despite this he had been sitting on the dockside in great despair as the ship sailed away with those he had served with loyalty and affection. A few minutes ago, the world had seemed a forlorn and lonely place. Age had come creeping into his bones.

He held the girl's hand and felt a warm surge of joy. Jackie's mother had once said he would follow the girl to the end of the earth; and he himself had believed this; and hidden his unhappiness when he saw that the girl had no further need of him. Foolishly, he had nursed a secret hope that Trapper Rhodes would take him away too. But the ship had sailed, with no word said. A little time ago he was blaming himself for being a failure. Now fate had provided him with an opportunity to show that, if need be, he would follow this girl anywhere.

He laughed, the deep booming laugh that Jackie knew so well. He was a religious man, respectful of tribal gods, and devoted to the biblical figures he had learned about at the mission school. He released the girl's hand and cupped the harmonica between his horny palms.

There was a marching song they both remembered, played on ceremonial parades by the King's African Rifles. It was called: "When the Saints Go Marching In."

He squared his shoulders. "Come, then, baba. You will be my captain-bwana and give me orders." He blew out his cheeks, the wooden club dangling by a thong from his wrist. "Let us go." He sucked in a lungful of air and began to play.

"Forward!" cried Jackie, falling into the spirit of the game. "To the bus for Vipingo."

On the hot sticky night of October the twenty-fourth a puzzled Sikh policeman patrolling the Kilindini dockyard in Mombasa heard the strains of a familiar military march float down the tarmac road by the ferry. He thought he saw an African in flowing robes, accompanied by a slender blond girl, flit in the shadows between the street lamps. He was sure he had heard "When the Saints Go Marching In" when the record was played several days later. By that time the unusual spectacle had assumed an importance that even the most efficient Sikh officer could never have foreseen.

from BOY ALONE

Reginald Ottley

The opening chapter of this powerful book reflects all of its qualities. There are the harshness of life on the Australian desert, the lack of sentimentality characteristic of such a rugged life, and the gentleness of those who love things smaller and weaker than themselves—the boy's love for the pup, and the small touches of friendship for the boy shown by those around him. Although it is set in the Australia of the 1930's, the mixture of harshness and tenderness needed to survive in such an environment is universal. Ottley's Roan Colt *is a worthy sequel.*

Kanga's Choice

The boy crouched, to peer under the huge feed-bin. In a scooped-out hole, he could see a bitch being nuzzled by newborn pups. The little mites were wiggling, crawling blindly on top of each other.

Gentle-handed, the boy reached under the bin. When the bitch's tongue licked wetly on his fingers, he rubbed her ears. "It's all right, Brolga," he whispered. "It's on'y me. I'm jus' feelin' in, t' count 'em." As he said it, he slid his fingers along her sleek body. Lightly, he touched each squirming pup. Their eagerness choked him in the throat. He wanted to stay there. Just him, the bitch, and the pups. But he couldn't. He could sense the tall old man staring down.

Slowly, the boy straightened. Worry lines creased his freckles. "There's seven of 'em, Kanga," he said. "Seven little beauts. An' they're all snuggin' up." He hoped to sound confident, but his voice broke.

Kanga's lean height stooped. His hard, wide shoulders brushed down past the boy. Stiffly, the old man groped, to pull out the seven pups. One after the other, he set them on the strawed floor. When the seven squirmed in a line, he rolled each one with a finger. The finger was calloused, yet its touch on the pups was light. The mites wriggled, then scratched fatly at their bellies.

The boy watched every movement. His heart seemed swollen inside his shirt. "Cor," he thought, "I wish I could grab 'em all an' run, run, run. But there ain't nowhere to go. Just sand an' waste an' desert. You couldn't get far before old Kanga'd have you." He waited while the pups wheezed faintly.

Finally, Kanga towered to his height. The boy saw a pup in the old man's hand. "This 'un 'll do," Kanga said. "He's got the most bone. You'd best git rid of the others." He slid the pup onto the boy's cupped palms. Dejectedly, the boy held it close to his chest. "Come on, little feller," he said with a sigh, "I'll put you back with your mum." He knelt to slip the pup under the bitch. She whimpered, calling to the rest of her litter.

The boy swiveled around. The six remaining pups squirmed at his feet. He tucked them together, pushing each little ball against the other. "Couldn't she keep 'em, Kanga?" he whispered. "Couldn't she keep 'em all, jus' for a while?"

Kanga rubbed tobacco in his hand. The battered felt hat masked his gaunt, seamed face. He had the tobacco tamped in his pipe when he said, "There's enough strife about for a good dawg,

son; never mind for them that ain't wanted. An' if you want a 'king' dawg, you have t' rear 'im right. On 'is own, so he'll grow big an' strong."

The boy stroked the pups. They wriggled when he bunched them. Their tiny heads reached in search of their mother's teats. He wished they were his, to give back to the bitch. Kanga struck a match. Through encircling hands, he puffed and drew on the pipe. The bowl glowed as he added, "You'd better get a shovel an' bucket. I'll have 'em set when you git back."

The boy choked. He tried to speak, but words blurred in his throat. With a final pat, he rebunched the pups and walked toward the door. Kanga watched the boy go.

When he returned, the shed had darkened. Kanga knelt with his back to the feedbin. In front of him lay the now still pups. Blindly, the boy gave the bucket to Kanga and kept the spade.

Kanga took the bucket with one hand and lifted the pups with the other. They settled limply, piled in a soft-skinned heap. Rising, he gave the bucket to the boy. "Here you are," he said. "They're better orf out of it. Take 'em out t' the sandhills an' dig a hole. They'll be right when you tip 'em into it."

For a long, long moment the boy stared up at Kanga, then down at the bucket. Slowly, he turned and went out through the doorway again. Kanga heard him stumble on the rough timber step.

Outside, the sun had set. Under the peppercorn trees surrounding the homestead, it was already dark. The boy saw a light glitter brightly in the kitchen. Up in the trees, galah cockatoos scrambled for their roosts. "They're all alive," he thought. "Warm, an' waitin' for t'morrow. Yet the pups—they're all dead. All except one. You can't understand a man like Kanga. He's like an old tree that doesn't think or feel." Clear of the peppercorns, the boy trudged westward.

Where the red-earthed plains merged into drifting sand, he set down the bucket, then leaned on the spade. The handle felt cool and smooth to his grasp. Overhead, an odd star or two began to show through the haze. Slowly, the boy dug a hole. He finished it with his hands, making the sides clean and straight. Then he lined the hole with dry, withered tussock grass. "You'll be right, there," he said, and gently placed the pups, side by side, in the hole. "An' when I cover you, I won't press hard. That way"—he wiped a hand under his eyes—"you won't feel bad. You'll know that the light ain't too far away." He covered the pups by letting sand trickle down. When he leveled the top, the hole was lost in a vast sea of desert.

Trudging back, he thought of many things: the mystery of death when it comes; the quick way life has of going. One minute the pups were warm and wriggling; the next they were limp and still. And where had it gone? Life, as it's called. The boy didn't know. But he *did* know the pups were dead. They were nice little fellers. Every one a beaut. He set down the bucket to rub a hand under his eyes.

At the bunkhouse, he left the spade and bucket outside. In his room, the air felt hot and heavy. Through the window came the whisper of leaves rustling on the peppercorns. Sprawled flat on his bunk, the boy let tears flow freely. He didn't mind when nobody was there to see.

But on the other side of a timber partition, old Kanga heard. He puffed his pipe, then shook the ash. The bowl glowed redly in his hand. Hard-knuckled, he rapped the partition. "You there, boy?" he said. "You ain't ate yet. Your tucker's in the kitchen. Mrs. Jones was askin' for you."

The boy wiped his face. His boots clumped when he sat up. "Yeah," old Kanga went on, "there's pie an' cream. I saw it on your table." He lay back and closed his teeth on the pipe.

The boy wavered. "I'd just as soon stay," he thought. "But if I do, she'll be over for me. Then I'll have to go, or she'll think I'm crook an' send for the boss." His feet shuffled as he edged toward the door. It was dark in the room, and he couldn't see too well. "Thanks, Kanga," he said. "I nearly forgot. The trouble was that job I had t' do." He went out through the doorway and clumped down the steps. On his bunk, old Kanga puffed. Smoke drifted up in the darkness.

In the kitchen, Mrs. Jones rolled dough to fit the bread tins. She smiled when the boy came in. "Set down," she told him. "Your tea's cold. I'll make a fresh pot." She wiped her hands on her apron.

The boy pulled out a chair. He had a knife and fork in his hands when he said, "It don't matter, Mrs. Jones. A feller c'n drink it cold, the same

as if it's hot. I'm sorry I'm late in for tea." He paused and looked up. Mrs. Jones saw the smudge where he'd rubbed his eyes. She had heard from Kanga about the pups. She wished there was more she could do. "Never mind," she said. "You couldn't help it. Now pass me that pot. I can't have you drink cold tea."

Later, the boy stood up. The pie crust and cream tasted sweet in his mouth; he'd scraped the last crumb from the plate. "Do you want me," he asked, "to give you a hand? Help with the washin' up?" He reached for the door as he spoke; one leg held it partly open.

Mrs. Jones smiled. She liked the ways he had. Always willing to help, yet always half away somewhere else. "No," she told him, "there's not much to do. You go along, an' don't get worrying. Good night. An' make sure you wash. There's dust still on your face."

The boy nodded. "It ain't dust," he thought. "It's sand from them sandhills. I had it on me hands."

"Good night, Mrs. Jones," he said. "I'll be around early t' get wood t' cook breakfast." He let the door rub, sliding across his back, as he went out.

In the morning, Kanga rode away before dawn. Behind him trotted his rabbit-hunting pack of thirty-four dogs. At his side, loose-muscled and scarred, loped Skipper, his "king" dog. Kanga couldn't see him but knew he was there. He always had been, since his training as a pup; he always would be, until he died, unless Kanga chained him to a peg or whistled him to control the dogs. Then Skipper would hurtle to rip and slash, to bring the pack to order. The dog was Kanga's life. If he knew love, it was for the dog. If the dog knew love, it was for Kanga. The two were inseparable, except by chain or command.

An hour after Kanga had gone, Yamboorah homestead stirred. Stockmen came from the buildings to yard their saddle horses. Wild galahs, squawking in the peppercorn trees, woke the boy. As a rule, he liked to hear them. They flocked in great numbers on Yamboorah, and the big old trees were a favorite roosting place. But this morning their angry chattering seemed more raucous. "Get out," he shouted, as he pulled on his boots, "an' start the day right. You've all got rotten tempers." Then he thought about Brolga and the pup. Under a tap, he splashed his face with water, then went out through the gateway.

Near the stables, he waited while horses galloped by. An aboriginal stockman riding behind them waved and smiled; his white teeth flashed over the bobbing rumps. The boy saw the whip in his hand swing up, then down. As it cracked, the big mob of horses surged. Squint-eyed in the dust, the boy entered the shed. Its door hung open, propped by a stone.

On the floor, he settled on hands and knees. Brolga was still there, under the bin. The pup was asleep, curled in a ball. A tiny snuffle sniffled through its jaws.

The bitch nuzzled the boy's hands for scent of her pups. "I'm sorry," he whispered, "but I couldn't do a thing. You know how it is with Kanga. He's hard, Brolga. Hard as a Mulga log." Unknowing of words but keen to the boy's tone, Brolga licked his hand. She pushed her muzzle deep into the cupped palm. The scent of her pups stayed strong on the boy's skin.

He let her push. His fingers touched her warm jaws. "So there it is," he thought. "She loved her pups, but I buried 'em. Lay 'em deep in that round sandy hole. An' all because Kanga wants to breed a 'king' dog—a dog that'll fight an' kill if the old man wants him to." The boy stroked the bitch, then scrambled up. "I'll get you a feed," he said, "an' something to drink. It's me best, Brolga. I tried t' save 'em, but I didn't have a chance."

At the door, he bumped into a man. Ross, the overseer, stood craglike on the step. "Good day, son," he said with a nod. "You're about bright an' fresh. How's the bitch an' her brood?" He held a bridle hooked on his arm, a stockwhip coiled on his shoulder.

The boy sighed. "She's right," he said, "but there's only one pup. Kanga killed the rest, an' I had t' bury 'em." He said it the way he felt— as if he'd helped to kill them.

Ross nodded. He rolled a cigarette and stared over the boy's shoulder at the horse yards. A stockman was saddling a young horse; the horse bucked and threw the saddle from its back. Ross held the cigarette. "Git hold of 'is ear," he shouted, then looked down at the boy. "Yeah," he said, in a softer voice, "that's how it is with Kanga. He's got t' rear a pup t' take the place of Skipper. He's gittin' old an' mightn't last much longer. Believe me, old Kanga knows his dawgs. Now git on over t' see the cook. She might want some wood or something." His face creased as the boy left. A smile blurred the set, weathered lines. "An' keep that chin up," he added. "Then you won't knock into a man. You ain't safe, with your head down." He heel-rocked toward the stables, chuckling. He stood six foot and weighed fifteen stone.

At the woodheap, the boy split a log into short, neat lengths, then trundled them to the kitchen. As he set down the barrow, he sniffed the warm, still air. The smell of bread, fresh-baked from the oven, drifted out through the door. When he opened it, the smell grew richer. Frying chops added to the odor. Arm-loaded, he carried in the wood. Mrs. Jones bustled near the fire. Pans of bread glowed brownly on their racks. The wood rattled as the boy dumped it down. He noticed the box was empty. Mrs. Jones must have used the last stick to bake her bread. "I'm late," he said, "an' I promised you. But I had t' look at Brolga. She's doin' fine with her pup." He stared at the chops sizzling in the pan.

Mrs. Jones fussed with a turning fork. "Don't worry," she told him. "I had enough. There's a mug of tea there, waiting on the table." Fat hissed when she turned a chop.

The boy nodded. Near the mug stood another pan of chops, salted but uncooked. Reaching for the mug, he inched a chop into his hand, along with the mug. Carefully he carried both outside. Mrs. Jones glanced over when the door had closed. The smile grew broader across her face. "That's one less," she thought. "But God bless his soul. He'll put it to good use. It'll help make milk for Brolga's puppy." She turned the rest of the chops, then lifted the other pan from the table.

Outside, the boy gulped his tea. It washed down hot and tasty. Mrs. Jones always sugared it just right.

With the chop rammed into his pocket, he headed for the stables. A group of stockmen, coming in for their breakfasts, said the usual "Good day, son." But the boy just nodded. The chop felt greasy and cold in his pocket; he could feel it sticky against his leg. "They might see the bulge," he thought. "These trousers are pretty tight."

The men walked on, bowlegged, on their heels. One of them rubbed his chin. "He looked kind of scary-like," he said. "An' not too good in the gait. Seemed t' have a limp." He spat as he went through the gateway.

In the shed, the boy hunkered down against the wall. He eased the chop until the bone end showed. The raw red tip poked out invitingly. "Come on, Brol'," he said. "Come an' see what's here." He pulled the chop to show another inch. Excitement made him jerky. The chop almost fell, and he had to push it back.

Brolga crawled slowly, mindful of her pup. Her head showed first, then her sleek, slender body. Tail held low, she feathered straw on the floor. Close to the boy, she crouched, nuzzling his hands. The scent of meat overpowered all other—even that of her pups. And hunger made her drool.

The boy chuckled. He twisted over, till his pocket was fully showing. The chop protruded on his lean, boyish rump. "You ain't lookin'," he told her. "You're in the wrong place. Jus' sniff along till you find it."

Brolga sniffed. Then she lifted her head to sniff again. Inquiringly, she snuffled along his trousers, into every crease and wrinkle. Near the pocket she questioned the boy. Her soft eyes begged for permission. The boy nodded. His hand slid over her ears. "Sure," he whispered, "I brought it for you. You an' your little bloke, asleep under there." He nodded again, this time toward the bin.

Sight of the bin reminded him. He had two horses to feed, as well as Brolga. Patches and Powder were gray Arabs, kept especially for the boss. He could hear them stamping in their stalls. Scuffle-footed, he scrambled up from the wall. "You see how it is," he said to Brolga. "I look after you an' forget them. They'll kick down their stalls if I don't feed 'em."

The bitch wagged her tail. Jaws clamped on the chop, she crept under the bin. The boy heard her crunch as he threw up the lid. With stomach flattened, he hung over, groping for two buckets. He buried them in chaff, then pulled them out. The short golden stems overflowed when he lifted. Carefully, he plodded toward the door. The buckets swung as he turned, before going out. "I'll be back," he called. "Jes' you stay there.

Next time I'll bring some water." The crunch of bone was Brolga's answer.

In the stalls he worked fast. Patches nipped him on the trousers, right where the chop had been. Powder tried to bump him. The boy dodged neatly. "I'm awake to you," he told them. "An' don't think I ain't. If you'll give me time, I'll tip it in." While they ate, he cleaned their stalls. The floors were raked and the straw bedding stacked when he slapped each snowy rump. "So long," he said. "You're right for another day. The boss'll feed you lunchtime." He ducked and scurried away when each took a flying kick.

After breakfast, Mrs. Jones wanted eggs. "It's cake day today," she said, while the boy wiped his plate. "And I'll need some eggs. A billyful will do." The boy was halfway through the doorway when she added, "You could look along the hedge. But be careful of the nests. I want fresh eggs, not stale." The boy let the door close. He flipped up the billycan, then caught it as he walked along the path. "She talks a lot," he thought, "but means her best. A feller knows not to touch the broodies. You c'n tell 'em by their feathers an' the shine they put on their eggs."

Under the hedge, he scraped and crawled. The rough limbs clawed his back. He kept one eye searching for eggs, the other for slithering snakes. Goannas he didn't mind; they hissed and spat, but you could hunt them away. Snakes reared up to strike; you had to be quick to get away in time.

The billy was full when he saw a snake in the dust. A long, thin tongue flickered questing from its jaws. Startled, the boy pushed backwards. The gaping head seemed almost under his chin. He heard it hiss as he crawled on backwards. "Phew!" he gasped as, clear of the hedge, he scrambled upright. "You made me puff. Another yard and I'd 've touched you." The thought made him shiver. He was glad of the sun flaring down on his shoulders. Glad, too, that he'd balanced the billy. Not an egg was cracked or broken.

In the kitchen, Mrs. Jones lifted out the eggs, then set them in a bowl. "They're lovely," she said. "Lovely and fresh. Did you have any trouble finding them?"

The boy shook his head. A leaf or two still clung to his hair. "No," he told her. "They were jus' lyin' about. I didn't go near the broodies.

There's a few of 'em, too. On their nests."

Mrs. Jones nodded. Broody hens meant more chickens. More chickens meant more fowls for the table. "That's good," she said with a smile. "We must look out for them. There's a pen in the garden to put them in." She rinsed the billy under a tap.

The boy watched her hands. They were large and white, with smooth round fingers. He'd seen them often lift great steaming pots. "She's strong," he thought: "though her arms look soft. You can't see any muscle." The billy was back in his grasp when he said, "Yeah, I like the little 'uns. They're all fluff an' wool." He remembered the snake, beady-eyed and waiting. "But they get a rough trot if a snake gets at 'em."

Mrs. Jones came from Sydney, far away on the New South Wales coast. She had read about snakes but seldom seen one—only in Taronga Zoo. The thought of them made her cold. "Yes," she agreed. "I believe they *are* bad. We'll have to be careful." She looked directly at the boy. "And you be careful, too."

The boy chuckled. "I will," he said, and left her wondering if he really would. Later, she talked about it to Ross, the overseer. He was sitting straddle-legged in the men's dining room. The back of the chair poked up through his arms; his chin hung over the top. He liked to sit that way after a day in the saddle; it rested his legs, he said.

He rocked up straight when she entered. The chair legs squeaked on the hard, bare floor. Crag-faced, he listened while she talked. "Don't worry, ma'am," he told her. "He'll live t' grow. But I'll talk to him just the same—if it'll help to ease your mind." He added the last in the hope she would smile. It lighted her face when she did.

"Thank you," she said, "I thought you would," and left him holding the chair.

When children are very young, last week is long ago and the next town is very far away. Developing perspective about time and space is one of the signs of increasing maturity within the individual. Many adults have had the experience of seeing a child show wide-eyed amazement upon learning that television has not always existed and that there have been people who have gone through childhood without it. Or, they have encountered children who associate Franklin D. Roosevelt, say, with the Civil War. We laugh about such incidents and repeat them to others, but behind these seemingly amusing episodes lies an important point: children need

HISTORICAL FICTION

guidance in developing a sense of time and place in history.

Children need to come to understand that the world did not begin with their birth and will not end with their death. They need to learn that their lives are a part of the continuity of existence, and that what is the present for them will be history for future generations.

In the 1961 edition of *Time for True Tales*, it was noted that the reading tastes of children often parallel adult tastes. We have seen this point dramatically illustrated in the intervening years when the publication of adult historical fiction has declined. Despite the celebration of the centennial of the Civil War in 1965, we find few new books of fiction written on that period for children. The new emphasis is on nonfiction—as it is in the world of adult books.

Of course good historical fiction continues to be written and published. It will always be possible to entrance children with accounts of times past; they are intrigued by a world without electricity or jet planes, and there is a romantic fascination in reliving through books the times when Indians rode the plains of our country and when primitive tribes occupied England.

Good fiction makes bare facts in the history textbook come alive, and good teachers have always supplemented the dates of battles and treaties with stories in order to help children see that history *is* people.

Three types of historical fiction

There are three distinct levels or types of books within the category called historical fiction. Authenticity is the only criterion they have in common. They should be true to place, period, and the people who lived during the time in which the book is set. It is impossible to overemphasize the importance of authenticity, since without it the book is valueless; with it, a less than perfect style or inadequate characterization can be, and often is, forgiven.

The purest type of historical fiction is that in which history itself is the center of interest, no matter how thrilling the plot or how well developed the characters. Such books can be written only about pivotal points in man's history; they are set in periods when the old way was giving way to the new. It is fairly easy to recognize such books. One has only to ask the question: could this plot and these characters have been superimposed upon any other period of history? When the answer is a resounding No, as it is in *Eagle of the Ninth* (see Bibliography, p. 257) by Rosemary Sutcliff and in *Johnny Tremain* (see p. 196) by Esther Forbes, we know that these books represent historical fiction at its very finest.

The majority of such books come from England. This is not to denigrate the efforts of American writers; it is merely to observe that Britain has had more pivotal points about which to write; and, being a much older nation, it can look at its history with a degree of objectivity few Americans can match. Aside from the American Revolution, only the Civil War has actually been pivotal, and it is still too close to us; the scars are still too raw for it to be written about in the grand manner.

The second type of historical fiction can best be analyzed in relationship to the books we produce about the Civil War. Factual history here takes a back seat to the reporting of human values. The real point of books like William O. Steele's *Perilous Road* (see Bibliography, p. 257) or Harold Keith's *Rifles for Watie* (see Bibliography, p. 256) is not the war itself, or even the issues which led to it, but rather the fact that men of good will and intelligence fought on both sides of the conflict. This point is important and must be made repeatedly, not only for children but for adults as well, since the human tendency is to divide the world into good guys and bad guys; good guys being those who agree with us and bad guys being those who don't. The same point needs to be made in books about the American Indian; for all too many years, juvenile fiction failed to depict the Indian as a human being with his own sense of values and his own civilization. He was a savage who was worthy of being exterminated if he resisted acceptance of the white man's culture. Now, all good books about Indians strive to show that, while they did not have the white man's values, they had their own, and the best of the books suggest that certain aspects of Indian culture were superior to those of the white man.

In short, this second type of historical fiction is more concerned with human aspects of history than with events themselves—a concern which does not make the category less important than the first, just different.

The third category is often classified in libraries as "Frontier and Pioneer Life Stories," which means that the books are set in the past but that no historical event is involved. An excellent example of such a book is *Caddie Woodlawn* (see p. 212), which takes place during the Civil War, but the impact of the war plays no part in the lives of the characters. (One knows only incidentally the time period involved.)

All three types of books are important. They are differentiated here only because they serve different purposes and have greater appeal to varied age levels. Young children should begin with books in the third category, like Alice Dalgliesh's *The Courage of Sarah Noble* (see Bibliography, p. 255), or hear read aloud *Caddie Woodlawn*—books which will introduce them gradually to a way of life far different from that in which they live. As children reach the fifth and sixth grades and United States history begins to take on form and meaning for them, they are ready for books in the second category; they are then ready to begin trying to understand that "right" is never the exclusive property of one side in a conflict. Finally, they should progress to books in the first category, to an understanding that there are certain landmark periods in history when the entire course of events is altered; the invasion of Britain by the Romans and the American Revolution are examples of two such momentous events.

Some criteria for historical fiction

The major defect to watch for in evaluating books with historical settings is the tendency on the part of authors who have done inadequate research to attribute modern attitudes to historical characters. One of the true joys in reading history stems from the fact that it shows how much progress mankind has made through the centuries; that people are no longer burned at the stake for deviate opinions, and that strides have been made toward recognizing the dignity of all men. We do a disservice to children to let them think that such progress comes as a matter of course.

Betty Baker's *Walk the World's Rim* (see Bibliography, p. 255) is a fine book to demonstrate this progress of mankind through the years. The Spaniards in the book see nothing wrong in Esteban's being a slave; for them, slavery is an accepted way of life. But the young Indian, Chakoh, has been taught that slaves are only slaves because they are cowardly and unworthy of freedom. Miss Baker makes it obvious that Chakoh would have immediately rejected Esteban as a friend if he had known Esteban as a slave from their first meeting. It takes the entire book for Chakoh to learn that Esteban was never a slave within his own heart, the place where real slavery begins. The point is made, and made well, but within the framework of authentic attitudes of the time. There is no distortion of history, no sentimentality.

This emphasis on avoiding historical distortion and sentimentality brings us back to authenticity. An author who knows history well writes books which convey to the youthful reader both the joys and hardships of life in times past. There is the joy of little Laura's listening to Papa tell the story of the time he met the bear; there is the pain of picking up and moving on because the present homestead will not support the family (see *Little House in the Big Woods,* Laura Ingalls Wilder, Bibliography, p. 257).

Before the technological revolution, all men, from primitive times on, worked from dawn to sunset clearing land, planting crops, hunting animals for food and clothing, and fighting off enemies. But there were always the good times: the harvest festival of primitive man which we celebrate as Thanksgiving; the neighbor with the fiddle who could make the pioneers forget for an evening that dawn would see them again bending their backs in endless toil; the house-raisings and corn husking bees which brought men together and even while they were working helped their spirits rise because the occasions renewed human bonds.

History has a lesson to tell, and historical fiction makes the lesson come alive; whatever the hardships, whatever the challenges, the human heart has always dared the impossible.

from AWAY GOES SALLY

Elizabeth Coatsworth

Elizabeth Coatsworth is a versatile author. Many of her lovely poems, some of which are reprinted in Time for Poetry, *are tucked away between the chapters of* Away Goes Sally *and other books. Her fanciful tale,* The Cat Who Went to Heaven, *won the Newbery Medal.*

Whether she writes prose or poetry, she writes with rare distinction. Away Goes Sally is the first of a series of historical stories about Sally. Sally's uncles, Joseph and Eben, wanted to move the whole family to Maine, but her Aunt Nannie vowed, "I will never leave my own fire nor sleep in any but my own bed." Sally and her young Aunt Esther were as disappointed as the uncles. They gave in, but Uncle Joseph did not.

Aunt Nannie's House

They drove home quickly. When Dorcas stopped at the back door it was still light, but there was no sign of the uncles, or of Jehoshaphat Mountain. Then, as Sally started to take the mare to the barn, she was stopped by several voices coming down the wood-road, men's voices gee-hawing oxen, and the screech of heavy runners on snow. The three aunts paused on the doorstep and Sally jumped from the sleigh to watch, as out of the darkness of the last pine thicket appeared the strangest thing she had ever seen. First came Peacock, Uncle Joseph's big horse, with Uncle Joseph on his back, and then six yoke of oxen, led by the red pair from their own farm, treading through the heavy snow in a slow procession of swaying heads and thick necks. Beside them walked Uncle Eben and Jehoshaphat Mountain with long poles, and behind them—wonder of wonders!—came a little house on runners, a house with windows whose small panes sparkled in the late light, with a doorstep, and a water-barrel under the drip of the roof, and a chimney pipe from which smoke was actually rising.

Sally jumped up and down, clapping her mittened hands, Aunt Esther uttered a cry of delight, and Uncle Joseph stood up in his stirrups and waved. But Aunt Nannie made no motion, and uttered no sound.

Slowly the line drew to the step and stopped.

"Nannie," said Uncle Joseph in a solemn voice, "here is a house I have built for you and which I give you with all my heart, so that you may travel to the district of Maine and yet never leave your own fire."

He paused and they all waited, Peacock pawing the snow.

But Aunt Nannie's face was still blank with surprise, and did not show her thoughts. She felt

behind her for the door to support herself, and once she tried to speak but could not. In the long silence Sally heard her own heart pounding like a colt galloping over a frozen meadow.

"Thank you, Brother Joseph," said Aunt Nannie at last in a small gentle voice, "thank you, my dear, I shall go willingly."

Sally let her breath out in a gasp of joy, and Uncle Joseph jumped from the saddle and kissed Aunt Nannie, who cried a little, mostly from relief because he had made it easy for her to give in and yet keep her word.

"Dorcas will take herself to the barn, Sally," Uncle Joseph called. "Come and see Aunt Nannie's house," and they all crowded in together. It was small, of course, but bright with windows, and warm with the Franklin stove which had a little fire burning in it. Two big beds stood in two corners of the room, covered with the blue eagle woven quilts. There was a smooth wooden sink and several chairs, and china in racks on the walls. Behind the larger room was a small room with two bunks in it for the uncles.

"There will be sleds for the rest of the furniture, Nannie," went on Uncle Joseph. "I have hired some men and their teams from down the road. You will, I imagine, wish to take our own cows, and Dorcas and the sleigh will bring up the rear, so that you may all take an airing when you grow tired of being in the house. And here, Deborah, are your seeds for a new garden, and we will carry some of your bulbs and roots on the sleds."

"And Aunt Esther will be a bride before the leaves turn yellow in Tuggie Noyes' woods!" cried Sally.

"Sally!" protested Aunt Esther laughing a little.

"I may come back and fetch someone to take your place, if it's not too much trouble," said Uncle Eben.

"Eliza is worth a good deal more trouble than that, Brother Sit-by-the-fire!" exclaimed Aunt Esther indignantly.

"How soon do we flit, Brother Joseph?" Aunt Nannie asked as she hung up her cloak on a peg and seated herself in her own chair, taking out her go-abroad sewing which she had brought back with her from Great-aunt Colman's.

"It's a picture to see you," said Uncle Joseph, smiling at her. They looked at each other and made their peace without a word being spoken. "I wanted this to be a surprise for you like the doll's house I made when you were a little girl. That's why I packed you all off to Quincy to have you out of the way while we furnished the house. But you asked when we would leave, Nannie. In a week, if you can be ready, my dear, so that we may have the advantage of the snow. The neighbors will help you."

"It doesn't matter what else you take," said Uncle Eben, "so long as you have plenty of meat-pies and apple-pies, baked beans, doughnuts, chocolate cake, pound cake, roasted chickens, hams——"

"Here, here," said Aunt Deborah, affectionately putting a hand across his lips, "you must not sound so greedy, Brother." She took her hand quickly away, for he had nipped it.

"Only a nibble," he joked her. "I've always said you had a sweet hand, Debby."

Meantime Jehoshaphat Mountain had been unyoking the oxen and taking them yoke by yoke to their quarters in the barn.

"I've been building the house for weeks in the wood lot," went on Uncle Joseph. "'Twill be a good way to carry our goods and ourselves without having to put up at the ordinaries, which they say are sometimes poor and dirty. And when we reach our land we shall have this to live in until we can build better. A new home, Nannie, on wider acres."

It was Sally who discovered the six little pots steaming in the rack that had been made for them on the stove. Uncle Eben, always ready to help in any matter of food, showed Sally where a pine table let down from the wall. She found the cloth and silver spoons and a jar of cookies, and soon six cups were filled, Uncle Joseph's with coffee, Uncle Eben's with chocolate, Aunt Nannie's with old Hyson, Aunt Deborah's with new Hyson, Aunt Esther's with Souchong, and Sally's with milk and chocolate. And so they shared their first meal in the house that was to carry them to a new land.

The Start

Uncle Joseph rode Peacock to the head of the procession, a dark figure in the early dawn. The men shouted, the oxen strained, and the little house shivered, then jerked forward with a screeching of runners, and the long journey was begun.

"They're off!" shouted Captain Dagget, waving his red muffler.

"They're off!" cried old Mrs. Captain Dagget, her white kerchief thrashing up and down in her mittened hand.

"Hip, hip, hurrah!" piped little John Hale from Sweet Brook Farm, running beside the oxen, waving his stocking cap.

"Good-bye, good-bye! Write me, my dearest Esther!" called Mrs. Caleb, beginning to cry.

All the neighbors were gathered at the door-step to see them go, although the sun had not yet fully risen, and the snow seemed dark and grave against the pale yellow sky.

Sally stood in the doorway of the little house in her red cloak, with her aunts behind her.

She could see the broad strong backs of the twelve oxen straining as they started on their road, and beyond them rose the farmhouse, the only home she had ever known. It looked so low and strong, with its wide chimney and a dark sparkle on the little panes of glass in the windows, and their friends standing on the doorstep! Her cheeks stung with cold and tears, and she felt suddenly a great hollow inside her. Then they came to the road and Uncle Joseph turned in his saddle and waved to her. Peacock was pulling at the bit, prancing, impatient to be off.

"To Maine!" called Uncle Joseph, making a gesture northward. "To Maine!"

The oxen quickened their pace on the beaten highway. Jehoshaphat Mountain shouted cheerfully at them. The sunlight caught the tops of the trees and the church weathervane in the distance. Sally heard a cow low behind her and knew it was old Brindle.

"We're off! We're off!" she thought, her mind turning to the future. "At last, we're off!"

"Come in, child, and shut the door," said Aunt Nannie, and Sally came in. Did ever a little girl go traveling like this before, in a doll's house on runners, seeing everything go by! She hung up her cloak and sat looking out of one of the little windows, watching how astonished people looked at seeing them. Whenever she waved, she did it stiffly, and she pretended she couldn't move her head at all.

"What is the matter, Sally?" asked Aunt Deborah, looking up from her sewing. "Have you caught rheumatism, child?"

"No, I'm being a doll," said Sally. "We're all dolls and this is our home."

Aunt Esther jumped up and did a doll's dance. Her eyes were shining, her curls bobbed up and down. Even Aunt Nannie smiled above the stocking she was knitting.

"Now, have we forgotten anything?" asked Aunt Deborah. "Where's Dinah's basket?"

Dinah was the black cat. She was shiny black all over, except for her paws and a star in the hollow of her throat, and a little white chin that always made her look as though she had just been drinking milk.

"Dinah, Dinah," called Sally.

"Mew," said Dinah, answering dismally from under one of the big beds.

Sally got down on her knees and pulled out the covered basket in which Dinah was imprisoned. When she took the cover off, Dinah jumped out, but she paid no attention to any of her mistresses. Round and round the room she went, with her nose extended, smelling everything, her tail stiff, her ears a little flattened. She smelled the pipe from the sink, she went into the corner, she disappeared under the beds, she sniffed at the furniture. She pushed open the door into the little room and investigated that. Then when she had thoroughly looked over every inch of this new home, she exclaimed, "Prrr!," stopped looking wary, and neatly jumped onto one of the beds, in the exact spot where the sunlight from the south window met the warmth of the stove. Kneading the place for a moment with her little white paws to make sure that it was soft, she turned round once, and went to sleep, as though traveling to Maine were something she had done all her life.

"Well, I declare, Dinah," said Aunt Nannie, "you do know how to make yourself comfortable! I suppose with all of us cooped up here together you'd best go where you've a mind to, but once in Maine I'll thank you to keep off the beds."

Getting dinner was great fun.

"We can't all be turning round in here like a lot of tops," said Aunt Nannie. "Deborah, you and Esther sit where you are and Sally and I will get things ready."

Sally gave her aunt a grateful look. And Aunt Nannie's ear-drops jingled back at her as Aunt Nannie nodded. They both had to learn to fit their walking to the movement of the house, especially when it jerked over a rut, but soon the potatoes were poked deep into the ashes, and the little table was laid with dishes taken down from the wall. Sally hung onto the doorstep while she dipped water from the barrel outside, breaking the thin skim of ice across it. It felt good outdoors in the cold, sunny air with the oxen pulling solemnly at their yokes and Peacock settled down to a slow walk, and the caw of a crow and the creak of snow for sound. Sally jumped down and ran along beside Jehoshaphat Mountain. An ox rolled his eyes at her, and she put her hand on his spotted white shoulder. It felt warm and muscular to her touch.

At noon they pulled the house to one side of

the road, and all the horses and cattle were given feed. The hired men built a fire and ate around it, but Uncle Joseph and Uncle Eben had their dinner in the little house.

"There's no room for me at the table," said Uncle Eben, "but I know where the warmest place in the room is. Scat, Dinah!" And he made himself comfortable where she had been. Dinah blinked her yellow eyes at him, stood up, stretched one leg after another, yawned so that her pink tongue showed stiff and curly, and then lay down again out of his way farther up on the bed.

"Dinah and I understand each other," said Uncle Eben, scratching her under the chin. "Don't we, Dinah?"

Dinah caught his finger between her two front paws and pretended to bite it, purring in gusts which, with her mouth open, sounded almost like growls.

"Careful, old girl," said Uncle Eben. "You must set an example of good behavior to all the cats in Maine."

That evening they stopped at a farm on the outskirts of Boston where they could find shelter for their animals in the big barn. The teamsters slept in the loft, but Sally and her family made themselves snug in the little house. It was drawn up in a barnyard, across which Sally could see the lighted kitchen windows of the farm, and the dim outlines of its roofs. A man came to see them, holding a lantern, but it was too late for visiting. By candlelight they had their supper of bread and cheese and warm milk just drawn from the cows.

"Twelve miles—a good journey for the first day," said Uncle Joseph, contentedly, after supper. "And now to bed, for we must be up early in the morning."

"Read us first the promise to Joseph, Brother Joseph," said Aunt Deborah, and Sally jumped up and brought the heavy Bible from its box and laid it on Uncle Joseph's knees. He drew the candle near and, after thumbing the pages until he found the place, read in his warm quiet voice:

"'Blessed of the Lord be his land, for the precious things of heaven, for the dew, and for the deep that coucheth beneath, and for the precious fruits brought forth by the sun, and for the precious things put forth by the moon, and

for the chief things of the ancient mountains, and for the precious things of the lasting hills, and for the precious things of the earth and the fulness thereof——' "

"That is God's blessing upon farmers," said Aunt Nannie.

"It makes me feel warm inside," whispered Sally to Aunt Esther. And then when the uncles had gone into the back room, they all raced one another to bed. Aunt Nannie and Aunt Deborah shared one bed, Aunt Esther and Sally the other. It was Sally who jumped in first, and she was asleep almost as soon as the blankets were under her chin. But once in the night she woke up to find the room growing cold and Dinah beside her—the cat had jumped up and now, rubbing against her cheek before she slipped in under the clothes, she curled up against Sally's chest, her black head on the pillow beside her mistress's.

from CALICO BUSH

Rachel Field

A number of Rachel Field's poems from Taxis and Toadstools *are to be found in* Time for Poetry. *They are always favorites, but* Calico Bush, *a historical novel, is one of the finest things she ever wrote. The heroine, Marguerite Ledoux, a French orphan, was "bound out" to Joel and Dolly Sargent. She traveled with them to a new settlement in Maine and, although she loved them and shared all of their hardships without complaint, they never made her feel that she was one of them. This Christmas excerpt from "Winter" has about it a poignant loneliness.*

Winter

It was a fairly warm day for December and she went out with Debby to watch him split the wood. It was pleasant to see his ax come down so swift and sure each time, and sometimes when he paused to rest he would talk to her for a minute or two. The baby was so well wrapped in a woolen shawl that she looked like a brownish caterpillar with a pink nose and tufts of light hair showing at one end.

"What time of year is it now?" Marguerite asked as Ira stopped to draw his sleeve across his streaming forehead.

"Let's see," he answered going over to the post where he still made his daily notches, dividing the months by means of long horizontal strokes. "Well, I declare, if it ain't got to be the middle o' December! Yes, tomorrow's the seventeenth, time I finished that beaver cap I promised Abby."

"Is it for Christmas?" asked Marguerite.

But he shook his head. "No," he said. "Our folks don't hold with such foolishness. We went to meetin' back in Marblehead on Christmas, I recollect, but there was a Dutch boy I knew told me how they had all kinds o' doin's where he come from."

"You mean, it will be no different from other days?" Marguerite's eyes grew wide with disappointment. "No carols, and no cakes, and no gifts from one to another?"

"I guess that's about right," he told her and went on with the chopping.

If Ira gave her no encouragement in Christmas festivities she knew it would be useless to expect more of Dolly and Joel Sargent. She tried to put the thought from her mind, but as each day came bringing it nearer she found herself remembering more and more the happy preparations for it she had helped to make at home. She dreamed of the Christmas cakes Grand'mère had always baked with such pride, of the seeded raisins and the picked nut-meats stirred ceremoniously in the rich batter. And then there were the carols, with the Sisters in the convent beating time and making sure that not a single "Noël" was left out when all their pupils' voices were lifted together. She tried to tell the children of the tiny carved statues of the Virgin and Joseph and the little Christ Child in the manger, with cattle and sheep and shepherds all painted as perfectly as life, that were brought out on Christmas Eve in the candle-lit chapel. Unfortunately Dolly had overheard part of this recital and had chided her roundly.

"I'll thank you to keep your Popishness to yourself," she had told her. "We may be in too God-forsaken a spot for a meetin' house, but that's no reason to put ideas in the children's heads."

And so it came to be Christmas Eve in the log cabin on Sargent's point with no smell of spice cakes, or incense, or candles, and none to feel the lack of them but Marguerite Ledoux.

She had been out to the post herself that noon, counting the month's notchings to be sure. There could be no doubt—tomorrow would make twenty-five. She would not have missed the holiday preparations so much, she thought, if she might have gone over to see Aunt Hepsa; but she knew there was no chance of this with such a high sea running and snow left in patches from last week's fall. It was rare, Joel had said, to have much fall near the sea. A bad winter ahead, Seth Jordan had predicted, and it looked as if he were right. Frost had covered the little square panes of glass with such feathery patternings, it required much breathing and scratching to make even a little hole to see out. Marguerite was tired of doing this. The room was almost dark, but she knew that outside there was still half an hour or so left of twilight. She went over to the pegs behind the door and took down the brown cloak and hood.

"What are you doin'?" Dolly asked her as she had her hand on the door.

"I'm—I want to bring more cones," she hazarded, grasping at the first idea that came into her head. "There are not so many left in the basket."

"Well, all right, then," Dolly told her, "only don't fetch in the wet ones that make the fire smoke. Pick 'em from underneath. No, Jacob," she added at a question from the child, "you can't go along—it's too cold."

Marguerite buckled on the shoes Aunt Hepsa had given her, tied on her cloak, and went out basket in hand. Once she shut the door behind her some of the depression which had weighed upon her spirit all day left her. It was impossible to feel so sad out in the snow with the pointed trees and all their shiny dark-green needles. They smelled of Christmas to her. There had been branches of evergreen in the chapel sometimes. Perhaps if she hunted at the edge of the tall woods behind the spring she might find some red partridge berries to bring back to the children. It was bad luck if you gave nothing on Christmas, and they need not know the reason for such a gift.

As she turned into the wood path behind the

house she looked across the water to Sunday Island. White places showed on the cleared field round the Jordan house where the snow remained, and the trees above it on the upper pasture where she and Aunt Hepsa had gathered bayberry looked more dark and bristling than ever in the winter twilight. She was glad that a curl of smoke rose from the chimney. Aunt Hepsa must be cooking supper, she told herself, and she paused to send her a Christmas wish across the water.

"I wonder if she's begun her new quilt yet?" she thought as she struck into the wood path. "She had the indigo dye Ethan brought her all ready to make a blue pot."

There were no red berries under the snow in the clearing by the spring where she had hoped to find them, so she went on farther along the blazed trail. It was very still there, with only a light wind stirring the spruce and fir boughs overhead. The light stayed longer there than she had expected, for the snow helped prolong the winter afternoon. Sometimes she stooped to gather cones, taking care to shake off the snow as Dolly Sargent had bidden her. The cold was intense, but her blood was quick and the old homespun cloak and hood enveloped her warmly. There was no sound except her footfalls in the snow. A sudden impulse came upon her to sing one of the carols which she knew the Sisters in the convent must even then be teaching other voices to raise.

She set down the half-filled basket of cones, folded her hands piously under the cloak, and began the first simple little chant that she had ever learned.

"*Noël—Noël—Noël!*"

Her own voice startled her in the stillness. Then at the sound of the familiar words she grew confident and began the one that had been Grand'mère's favorite because she also had sung it when she was a girl in the little village where she had lived.

"*J'entends le ciel retentir*
Des cantiques des Saints Anges,
Et la terre tressaillir
Des transports de leurs louanges.
C'est l'Oinct qui devoit venir,
Il est déjà dans ses langes.
Miracle! prodige nouveau,

Le fils de Dieu dans le berceau!
Mais plus grand prodige encore,
Ce grand Roi, que le ciel adore,
Doit expirer sur un poteau.
Noël! Noël! Noël!"[1]

As she sang there in the deepening twilight, she felt strangely comforted. The French words that had lain so long forgotten welled up out of her mind as easily as if she had been with the Sisters in the candle-lit chapel and not alone these thousands of miles away in a snowy wood.

"Noël! Noël!" she cried once more to the ranks of spruces, and then as she turned to retrace her steps something dark and swift moved towards her from behind a tree trunk.

There was not time enough to run away. The words were hardly cool on her lips before he stood beside her—a tall Indian in skins, with a musket that went oddly with his fringes and bright feathers. So silently did he come that not a twig snapped under his foot. He seemed not to dent the snow as he moved over it. His eyes showed bright in the copper of his skin, and a deep scar ran crookedly across one cheek. He came so close that she saw it plainly, and yet she could not move so much as an inch. Her feet seemed rooted in the snow, and if her heart continued to beat, she could not feel it. For what seemed like ages he continued to regard her fixedly with his black, unblinking eyes, while she waited for him to seize the tomahawk from his belt and make an end of her. But he did not move to do so. Instead, his lips parted in a queer smile.

"Noël!" he said, pronouncing the word carefully in a deep, guttural voice. "Noël!"

Marguerite felt her heart begin to beat again, though her knees were still numb and she continued to stare at him incredulously. Surely this must be a miracle, more extraordinary than any

[1] This old carol may be freely rendered as follows:—
I hear the heavens resound
To such angelic song
That trembling stirs the ground,
While rolls the news along—
The Heavenly Child is found,
To Whom all praise belong.
Oh! wondrous miracle,
A God in his cradle!
Yet must we wonder more,
This King the heavens adore
Must die upon a cross.

bestowed on Saint Catherine or Saint Elizabeth! A savage had come out of the woods to greet her in her own tongue on Christmas Eve! She forced herself to smile back and answer him.

His words were meager and hard to catch, but she made out from them and his signs that he had lived with the French in Quebec. He was bound there now, or so she guessed from his pointing finger. She could not tell how many of her words he understood, but whenever she said "Noël" his eyes would brighten with recognition and he would repeat it after her. "Les Pères Gris," he told her, had cured him. He touched the scar as he spoke and crossed his two lean forefingers to make a cross.

It was almost dark now; only a faint light lingered between the spruces. Pumpkin barked in the distance and Marguerite knew she must hurry back lest they grow alarmed. What would they think, Joel and Dolly Sargent and the rest, if they should come upon her there in the woods holding converse with an Indian? Prompted by an impulse she pulled the cord out from under her dress and jerked off Oncle Pierre's gilt but-

ton. It glittered in her hand as she held it out to the tall figure before her.

"Pour un souvenir de Noël," she said as she laid it in his hand before she turned and sped off towards the clearing.

Her heart was still pounding as she came out of the woods and in sight of the log house. Pumpkin bounded to meet her as she paused to put back the cord and its only remaining treasure. She had not thought to make such a Christmas gift, but surely she could not have done less. She could not but feel that somehow it was a fortunate sign, this strange meeting. Perhaps Le Bon Dieu had Himself arranged it that she might be less lonely on Christmas Eve. But she knew there must not be a word of it to the rest. She would never be able to make them understand what she scarcely understood herself. As for Caleb, she could well guess what he would say and that he would think ill of her ever after.

Dolly Sargent scolded her roundly for staying away so long.

"I declare you deserve a beatin'," she told her hotly, "strayin' so far at this time o' night. I vow Debby's got more sense 'n you show sometimes."

There was no mention made of Christmas next day save that Joel asked a lengthier blessing over their breakfast cornmeal than was usual with him. But Marguerite no longer minded. Had she not had her miracle the night before?

from FLAMING ARROWS

William O. Steele

There is no other writer today who can re-create pioneer life more vividly than William Steele. The particular story from which this chapter is taken is about an Indian raid and the terrifying experiences of the settlers living and fighting inside a stockade. It is also the story of two unusual boys you will not forget. For other exciting stories by this author be sure to read Wilderness Journey, Winter Danger, Tomahawks and Trouble, *and others listed in the Bibliography.*

From *Flaming Arrows*, copyright © 1957 by William O. Steele. Reprinted by permission of Harcourt, Brace & World, Inc. and Macmillan & Co. Ltd.

"I reckon it's suppertime," remarked Chad, letting his ax slip to the ground. He straightened up slowly. He was bone-tired, and his back was one fierce ache. But he was proud of himself. He figured he'd never worked so hard before in all his eleven years, for he'd spent this livelong day chopping trees and had done a man's work.

"I reckon it is," his father answered. "I heared Ambrose bringing the cows up a while ago."

Mr. Rabun turned back to stripping the limbs from a felled tree. His ax rose and fell in swift regular strokes, and the branches dropped neatly away from the trunk. Chad grinned. He admired to see his father work. Things never seemed to get all of a tangle for his pappy the way they did for other folks.

At last Mr. Rabun stood up and wiped his forehead on his sleeve. He looked around at the white-topped stumps and the sprawled logs. "We done a good day's work, Chad," he said slowly. "You was a big help. Two more days and we'll have us enough new ground for a cornfield."

Chad didn't say anything, but he was pleased. He'd worked hard and tried to do everything the right way, the way his pappy had taught him to.

Mr. Rabun slipped his shot pouch and powder horn straps over his shoulder. He shouldered his ax and then picked up his rifle.

Chad too reached for his musket. He hoped his pappy hadn't noticed that he'd almost forgot his gun. He hadn't had it long, and he wasn't yet used to fetching it along every place he went. Nobody in the Cumberland settlements went out in the fields without having his gun handy. At least not more than once.

They took the short cut home, through the woods. It was almost dark among the trees, and Chad wished they'd gone around by the edge of the field instead. The leaves hung dull and dusty, for it was the middle of September, dry and hot. "Injun weather," thought Chad, and he peered into the shadows.

Suddenly Mr. Rabun stopped dead still. Chad halted too, drawing in his breath quick and tightening his hand on his musket. His father stood with his head turned, listening, his rifle half-raised before him.

"I'll shoot the first one with my musket," Chad planned. "And Pappy can get one, and while he's reloading, I can use the ax. That'll take care of three or four of 'em. And if there's more than that, I reckon we'll have to run."

And then he heard what his father was hearing, the little clucking sounds, like water purling over stones, that a flock of turkeys makes calling to each other. It wasn't Injuns after all. Chad let out his breath silently, and his eyes went here and there, trying to make out the birds.

Pretty soon he saw them, walking slowly, stretching their long skinny necks and small heads out of their big bodies to look around suspiciously, and then leaning over to peck at acorns on the ground.

Slowly, carefully, Mr. Rabun raised his rifle to his shoulder. Chad could see his father's finger tighten on the trigger and the flash in the pan when he fired. There was a great noise of gobbling and flapping wings as the flock scattered in every direction. But one turkey lay on the ground, and its wings beat wildly for a minute before it lay still.

Chad ran to pick up the dead bird. It was a gobbler, not a big one, but a young one, tender and delicious.

"Mammy'll like this," he cried as he lifted the turkey by its feet. "I heared her say just this morning she hankered for a turkey."

"Well, it was luck to find 'em," Mr. Rabun answered. "When we first come here, there was turkeys under every bush. Now here it is not but three years later, and a body don't hardly see one 'lessen he goes way off hunting for 'em."

He reloaded his rifle as he talked. "There's just one thing about shooting a turkey," he went on. "When you've shot it, don't forget to put another ball in your gun. I've knowed a heap of men got scalped because they got to looking at the game they'd killed and never gave a thought to reloading, and the Injuns heard the shot and sneaked up on 'em."

"You don't reckon there's Injuns around now, do you?" asked Chad.

His father looked at him soberly. "It's the Injuns you don't reckon are around that kill you, most generally," he answered. "But you remember what I say and reload every time you fire."

"Yes, sir," Chad answered solemnly. "I'll carry the turkey," he offered as they set out again. Mr.

Rabun took both axes, and Chad slung the bird over his shoulder.

"You know what Amos Thompson said last summer?" Chad went on, keeping his eyes on the shadows ahead. "He said he'd seen a flock of turkeys kill a big old rattlesnake. Said they got around the rattler and took turns running and pecking at it till it was dead. Said the snake would strike at the turkeys, but it never fazed them. Do you reckon all that's really so, Pappy?"

Mr. Rabun pondered. "I've heard that tale," he answered. "I never saw any such thing, but I reckon it must be so. Amos Thompson ain't one to tell he'd seen something when he hadn't. There's some folks I wouldn't believe if'n I heared them tell a thing, for they'd be the kind of folks that might think they'd seen what they hadn't. But Amos ain't like that. If he says he seed it hisself, then he did."

Chad nodded. His pappy was always telling him not to believe everything he heard but to think things through and sift out the truth.

"You wouldn't reckon feathers would do much good when the rattler struck," Chad remarked, rubbing his cheek against the bird's soft feathers.

"You wouldn't, for a fact now," Mr. Rabun agreed. "I've seen a rattler's fangs go through stiff leather. But you study on it and you can see how it works out. Let a turkey ruffle up his feathers, and he's got a power of nothing and feathers between him and the snake. A snake's fangs ain't hardly long enough to get through, no matter how hard he strikes."

They walked on in silence, leaving the woods and stepping out into the red glow of the setting sun. The tall grass at the edge of the field brushed Chad's buckskins with a soft whisper. A bobwhite called three times as they struck out through the cornfield. It was a big field, Chad thought proudly, and there was another one this size near the creek.

Oh, his pappy was a fine farmer. In spite of the many Indian raids and having to rebuild their cabin and make new beds and tables, his father had managed to get the fields cleared and to raise a good crop. Not many in the Cumberland settlements could say as much, Chad reckoned.

They walked on between the rows of dry stalks.

Chad's dog Tumbler came running to meet them, and in a few minutes they reached the cabin clearing. Ambrose was standing in the open door. "Here they come, Mammy," he called.

Chad got a whiff of the good smell of stew. He began to run, the turkey flopping on his shoulder. He hadn't known he was so hungry. And wouldn't Mammy be glad to see what he was bringing her?

Sarah met him at the door. She took the turkey and held it up. "Mammy!" she cried. "Look what Pappy shot!"

Chad frowned. She might at least have wondered if Chad hadn't shot it. After all, he'd fetched it in. The trouble with Sarah was she was *too* good at sifting out the truth, even if she was only nine. He couldn't ever fool her the way he could Mammy.

"Oh, Chad, ain't he a fine one?" exclaimed Mammy. "After supper I'll clean him and pluck him."

"Now go wash," ordered Sarah. "Milking's done with and supper's most nigh ready."

Chad yanked her pigtail. A body would think Sarah was a grown-up married lady, the way she acted. She was always bustling about, so busy and important.

After the bowls and spoons were washed, the Rabuns went outside. Chad cleaned the turkey and his mother plucked it, working quickly before the sunlight faded. Mr. Rabun stood in the clearing watching the sky for a change in the weather.

"I reckon he's keeping an eye out for Injuns, too," thought Chad, but he didn't say anything. His mammy didn't like to have them always worrying and fretting about Indians.

She had said, "It's bad enough to have the savages in mind all the time without dinging away at 'em every time you open your mouth. A body can keep a lookout for Injuns and still talk about something else."

When the others had gone in, Chad stayed a few minutes longer enjoying the cool evening air. An owl flew over his head with a soft whish. Stars were coming out, and the night was clear.

"Injun weather, for sure," thought Chad, and went in.

He swung the door shut and barred it with the heavy boards. He hated doing it. It was hot and close in the cabin with the door shut and no window and the fire going. But who would be fool enough to leave a cabin door open at night and the woods full of redskins?

Mammy reached up on the fireboard for the Bible. Every night she made Chad and Sarah read a chapter out of the Book of Kings or Chronicles, for Mr. Rabun wanted all his children to be able to read and cipher well. He himself had gone to school in Pennsylvania and learned Latin and history.

Folks in the Cumberland settlements often traveled a good way to have Henry Rabun read or write a letter. He could survey too and knew some law. Oh, Chad was proud of his pappy. He wanted to be like him, so he struggled with Jehoshaphat and Moab and Elijah the Tishbite. Folks had a mighty hard time in Bible days, it seemed to him.

"I don't reckon I'll let Chad read tonight after all," said Mammy suddenly, laying down the Bible. "I want him to card. I aim to get started spinning tomorrow. Sarah's got to have a new short gown. And I had it in mind to make Pappy a new shirt."

Ambrose frowned darkly. Every year he hoped to have some new clothes, but he'd never yet had them. He got Chad's clothes, cut down from Pappy's.

Chad grinned. He never had any new clothes either, but it never bothered him the way it did Ambrose. It was a funny thing for a five-year-old to worry over.

Mr. Rabun looked up from the ax handle he was carving. "I talked to John Hart the other day about buying a ram from him," he said. "He's leaving here and going back to Virginny. Then in the spring I can get a ewe, and we'll have wool a-plenty—if'n the Injuns don't get 'em," he added in a low voice.

Mammy sighed. They'd had four sheep when they came here in 1781, but the wolves got one and the Indians killed two, and the last one died right after it was sheared. So this wool was the last the Rabuns would have till they got more sheep, unless they used buffalo wool. Chad writhed at the thought. Folks said buffalo wool itched worse than cloth made from nettles.

Chad took the wool carders his mother handed him. He hated to card. But Sarah was knitting

winter stockings, and Ambrose, who was stringing shucky beans on a long thong, wasn't handy enough.

He pulled his stool up on the hearth and laid the right-hand card close to the fire to warm. He took a handful of wool and drew it across the left card till it was caught in the teeth. When the right-hand card was hot, he began to stroke the wool with it, tumming it until the wool fibers were all straight.

Mr. Rabun held his wooden handle up and inspected it by the firelight. He turned suddenly to the others and smiled.

"There was a song my pappy used to sing, about a ram from Darby or some such place," he declared. "He was so big a heap of eagles built their nests in his wool or some such foolishment as that."

Mrs. Rabun laughed. "I remember that song," she cried. "His feet was so big they covered an acre. I can recollect the tune a little."

"Sing it, Mammy," begged Chad. He edged his stool back on the hearth. He was about to melt plumb away from the heat.

Mrs. Rabun hummed a little to herself, and then shook her head. "I can call the tune to mind, but I disremember the words. They were so foolish, they wouldn't stick in anybody's head."

"I reckon it would be fine to have a sheep like that," said Sarah. "We could all have new clothes then, even Ambrose."

Ambrose yawned. "I don't reckon we could card that much wool," he spoke up sleepily.

"And it would eat a heap," went on Mr. Rabun. "Clean up a whole savanna of grass in a day, I reckon. Then you'd have to kill it, else all the pasture between here and Kentuck would be used up in a week."

"Think of the mutton pie a ram like that could make," cried Chad. "Wheee, a whole cabin full! Mammy could cook one as big as a flatboat, and we could float it down to New Orleans and sell it for a heap of hard money."

"I can't abide mutton pie," said Sarah, wrinkling her nose. "I'm sick to death of deer meat, but I'd a heap rather eat it than greasy mutton."

"And I don't aim to cook one that big either," laughed Mrs. Rabun. "Ain't no need to talk of eating mutton when we ain't got any. Well, that turkey'll make a nice change from deer," she added. "You was lucky to get it so close to the cabin."

"Change! Why, we had squirrels only last week," Chad pointed out. He had shot the squirrels his very own self.

"Oh, and they was good," Mrs. Rabun cried. "You and Pappy always keep us in meat, and we get more change than most folks. But it's been a long spell since we had turkey."

Ambrose yawned again. He had long since ceased to work. His hands lay still in his lap, and the long string of beans dangled to the floor.

Mrs. Rabun took the beans from him. "Go to bed, Brose," she said gently. "You can finish them tomorrow night."

Ambrose stumbled to his feet and climbed the ladder to the loft. They could hear him moving around for a few minutes, taking off his moccasins and breeches, feeling around in the dark for his quilt, and then he was quiet.

Mr. Rabun ran his hand along the handle to check its smoothness. "Casper Mansker says he aims to build a mill over on his creek," he told them. "Me and Brose won't have to ride clean over to Frederick Stump's for a turn of meal, if'n he does that."

"Remember when we first come here, how we had to grind our corn with a mortar?" Mrs. Rabun asked. "We was lucky to have meal at all, I reckon. But mortar-ground meal ain't nowhere's near as good as stone-ground."

She laid a piece of leather on the floor by Chad. "Put your foot on that, so I can measure," she told him. Then she cut off a portion and sat back down.

Suddenly she dropped the buckskin and half-rose from the stool. "Listen, somebody's outside," she gasped.

Sarah looked up in fear. Mr. Rabun moved quickly toward his rifle.

"Naw," answered Chad. "It's just Tumbler scratching. He hits the wall with his legs."

Mrs. Rabun settled back to her work with a relieved sigh. "I declare I wish I wasn't so nervous about noises," she remarked. She picked up the awl by its horn handle and began to punch holes in the cut leather.

Mr. Rabun checked the powder in his rifle pan, and he too sat back down.

A stillness settled over the cabin. Chad could hear the fire crackle and hiss and the soft sound of the awl in the leather. Sarah put down her knitting and climbed to the loft. Chad watched her with eyes misted with sleep. He reckoned he wasn't going to keep awake much longer. But he kept on working the steel teeth of the card again and again through the wool.

At last Mrs. Rabun folded the deerskin shoes and laid them on a shelf. "Well, you most nigh finished all the wool, Chad," she told him, looking with pleasure at the long slender rolls he had carded. "I'll start spinning in the morning."

She took the two cards and placed them beside the half-finished moccasins. "Ain't it been nice this evening?" she went on. "We ain't talked one single time about Injuns or raids or scalping."

"Maybe not," answered Mr. Rabun gravely. "But I hope you ain't forgot about 'em. They've not bothered us folks north of the Cumberland River very much this summer." He stood the ax helve in the corner. "They're due to give us serious trouble soon, though. And we got to keep our eyes and ears open."

Chad, stooping to put another log on the fire, reckoned that was all Cumberland folks had done since they arrived here, keep their eyes and ears open for Chickamauga Indians. The raids had got so bad a couple of years ago that many of the settlers had been ready to pack up and leave. James Robertson, the leader of the settlement, had talked them out of it, and most had stayed on.

But still the Indians hung around the settlements, and it wasn't a week passed but what somebody was killed and scalped going to the spring or working in the fields. That was bad enough, but the early fall was the time of year the settlers dreaded most. Each year since the white men had come, the savages had made a big attack in September or October. Everybody had gone to the forts; their cabins and cornfields had been burned and their animals killed.

Again this fall a heavy feeling of fear lay over the settlements. Chad could see how his mammy fretted. But he couldn't help thinking things would be better now that he had a gun of his own, a musket he could shoot pretty well. Now he could help his pappy fight the Chickamaugas.

He kicked the logs in place, and Mrs. Rabun

banked the fire with ashes. When she stood up, the room was almost dark.

"Maybe there won't be no raids," she said hopefully. "Maybe this fall the Injuns will leave us alone."

Nobody in the shadowy room answered. But when Chad woke later in the night, his mammy's words were the first thing that popped into his head when he heard Tumbler barking outside and the sound of a galloping horse.

from JOHNNY TREMAIN

Esther Forbes

The first episode given here reveals the patience of the British soldiers with the rebellious colonists and the deadly earnestness of the rebels during the American Revolution. The second provides a glimpse of the plotters, their ideals and activities.

["That a Man Can Stand Up"]

Along down Old Country Road, marching through the meager, half-light of the new day, came a company of Minute Men up and out early, drilling for coming battles before it was yet the hour to get to their chores. Left, right, left, right, left . . . they did not march too well. A boy no bigger than Dusty Miller had put a fife to his lips, was trying to blow it. He made awkward little tootles. The men marched on past the defaced gates of the Lytes' country seat, never turning to look at them or Doctor Warren's chaise with Cilla and Johnny under the hood.

Oh, God help them, thought Johnny. They haven't seen those British troops in Boston. I have. They haven't seen the gold lace on the generals, those muskets—all so alike, and everyone has a bayonet. They haven't seen . . .

The chaise overtook and passed the marching farmers.

That musket which Rab did not have bothered Johnny. However, the soldiers never carried them while loitering about alehouses and wharves, or the stables of the Afric Queen. They

From *Johnny Tremain* by Esther Forbes. Reprinted by permission of and arrangement with Houghton Mifflin Company, the authorized publishers

stood guard with them. They drilled with them. They practiced marksmanship (very badly, Rab said), and now and then over at the foot of the Common they executed a deserter with them, but never, not once, as far as Johnny could make out, did they leave them about. Drilling, shooting, marching over, they stacked them at their barracks and there was always at least a sergeant guarding these stacked guns.

Johnny and Rab dropped their voices, even in the privacy of their attic, when they discussed these muskets. The Yankee gunsmiths were working from dawn to dusk preparing guns, making new ones, but as long as Rab had a weapon and was, after all, little more than a boy, he believed he had no chance for a modern gun unless he got it for himself from the British.

"How soon," Johnny whispered, "before they march out . . . and the war begins?"

"God knows," Rab murmured. "God and General Gage. Maybe not until next spring. Armies always move in the spring. But before then I must have a good gun in my hands. A man can stand up to anything with a good weapon in his hands. Without it, he's but a dumb beast."

Johnny had never seen Rab so blocked by anything. Apparently he went through every situation without friction, like a knife going through cheese. Now he was blocked and it made him restless, possibly less canny. One day he told Johnny that he had a contract with a farmer from Medway who was making a business of buying muskets from the British privates and selling them to Minute Men. Rab did not like to ask his aunt for so large a sum. She had little enough to buy food. But she had said, "Weapons before food."

One morning Johnny knew Rab was meeting the farmer at market. He knew that the soldier, returning from guard duty, was going, absentmindedly, to leave his musket on a pile of straw. It had all been worked out. But when he heard yells and shouts from the market-place and the rattle of British drums calling up reserves, he tore over to Dock Square. He had a feeling that the turmoil was over Rab's gun. He was right.

A solid block of redcoats faced out, presenting their muskets at the market people and inhabitants. The Captain was yelling to the churning hundreds. "Get back, stand back, good people of Boston. This is our own private affair."

"What's happened?" Johnny asked an old henwife.

"They've caught one of their own men selling a musket to a farmer."

"Happens he comes from Medway?"

"So 'tis said."

"Happens they caught more than the farmer and the soldier?"

"They caught three in all. They are taking them over to the Province House—for General Gage."

"Gage is in Salem."

"For some colonel, then."

No mob gathered to rescue the two Yankees. All, by now, felt a certain confidence in the British way of doing things. A general, or even a colonel, had the right to punish a soldier caught selling his arms, and also anyone who tempted him.

Johnny tagged the marching soldiers, but it was not until they turned into the Province House that he saw the three prisoners. The British soldier was grinning, and Johnny guessed that he had been put up to this game merely to snare "the yokels."

The farmer was in his market smock. He had long, straight gray hair and a thin, mean mouth. You could tell by looking at him he had gone into this little business for the love of money, not for the love of freedom. Rab had been shaken out of his usual nice balance between quick action and caution by his passionate desire for a good gun. Otherwise he would not have mixed himself up with such a man. Rab himself was looking a little sullen. He was not used to defeat. What would they do to him? They might imprison him. They might flog him. Worst of all, they might turn him over to some tough top sergeant to be taught "a lesson." This informal punishment would doubtless be the worst.

The Province House was a beautiful building and as Johnny hung about the front of it he had a chance to admire it for over an hour. It stood well back from the rattle and bustle of Marlborough Street, with its glassy-eyed copper Indian on top of the cupola and its carved and colored lion and unicorn of Britain over the door. Behind the house he heard orders called and soldiers were hallooing—but worst of all they were laughing. And that was Colonel Nesbit's boy bringing around the Colonel's charger. There was a large group of people still standing in the street. The hilarity of the British soldiers did not ease their fears as to the fate of the prisoners. Johnny could hear the rattle of the men's muskets as they came to attention, and then, all together, four drummers let their sticks fall as one.

Out onto Marlborough Street, with the drummers in black bearskin caps first, and then Colonel Nesbit on horseback, came almost the entire Forty-Seventh Regiment, surrounding a cart. In the cart sat a hideous blackbird, big as a man, shaped like a man, with head hung forward like a moulting crow. It was a naked man, painted with tar and rolled in feathers. Three times already the Whigs had tarred and feathered enemies and carted them through the streets of Boston. Now it was the British turn. The redcoats marched. The Colonel's horse pranced. The cart with its shameful burden bumped over the cobbles. One glance had convinced Johnny this was not Rab. The hideous blackbird had a paunch. Rab had none.

Before the Town House, Colonel Nesbit ordered a halt, and an orderly came forward and read a proclamation. It merely explained what was being done and why, and threatened like treatment to the next buyer of stolen weapons.

Then (Colonel Nesbit was evidently a newspaper reader) the regiment went to Marshall Lane and stopped before the office of the *Spy*. The threat was made that the editor of that paper would soon be treated like the bird in the cart. Then they were heading for Edes and Gill's office. Johnny guessed the *Observer* would come next after the *Boston Gazette*, and ran to Salt Lane to warn Uncle Lorne. He jumped into the shop, slamming the door after him, looking wildly about for the printer. Rab, in his printer's apron, was standing at his bench, quietly setting type.

"Rab! How'd you do it? How'd you get away?"

Rab's eyes glittered. In spite of his great air of calm, he was angry.

"Colonel Nesbit said I was just a child. 'Go buy a popgun, boy,' he said. They flung me out the back door. Told me to go home."

Then Johnny laughed. He couldn't help it.

Rab had always, as far as Johnny knew, been treated as a grown man and always looked upon himself as such.

"So all he did was hurt your feelings."

Rab grinned suddenly, but a little thinly. Johnny told of the tar-and-feathering of the farmer and also that he expected in a short time the Forty-Seventh Regiment would come marching down Salt Lane and stop before the door to read that proclamation about tar-and-feathering seditious newspaper publishers.

"And here they come—those dressed-up red monkeys. But they don't dare do anything but stop, read a proclamation, and move on."

When this was over and the troops moved on down the lane to Union, Johnny and Rab stood in the street and watched them.

"Luckily," said Rab, "I didn't give my money in advance. I'll return it to Aunt Jenifer."

But he still stood in the street watching the stiff rhythm of the marching troops, the glitter of their guns and bayonets, the dazzle of the white and scarlet disappearing at the bottom of the lane.

"They'll make good targets, all right," he said absent-mindedly. "Out in Lexington they are telling us, 'Pick off the officers first, then the ser-

geants.' Those white crosses on their chests are easy to sight on . . ."

His words frightened Johnny a little. Lieutenant Stranger, Sergeant Gale, Major Pitcairn . . . Johnny could not yet think of them as targets. Rab could.

. . . .

It was fall, and for the last time Sam Adams bade Johnny summon the Observers for eight o'clock that night.

"After this we will not meet again, for I believe Gage knows all about us. He might be moved to arrest Mr. Lorne. He might send soldiers to arrest us all."

"I hardly think they would hang the whole club, sir. Only you and Mr. Hancock."

Johnny had meant this for a compliment, but Sam Adams looked more startled than pleased.

"It has been noticed that every so often many of us are seen going up and down Salt Lane, entering the printing shop. We must, in the future, meet in small groups. But once more, and for the last time . . . And make as good a punch for us as you can."

. . . .

It would be a small meeting, for of the twenty-two original members many had already left town to get away from the threat of arrest by the British. Josiah Quincy was in England. Of the three revolutionary doctors, only Church and Warren remained. Doctor Young had gone to a safer spot. James Otis was at the moment in Boston. Johnny had not notified him, although he had founded this club in the first place. Ever since he had grown so queer, the other members did not wish him about, even in his lucid periods. He talked and talked. Nobody could get a word in edgewise when James Otis talked.

This, the last meeting, started with the punch bowl on the table instead of ending with it. There was no chairman nor was there any time when the two boys were supposed to withdraw. They were talking about how Gage had at last dared send out a sortie beyond the gate of Boston and, before the Minute Men got word of their plans, they had seized cannon and gunpowder over in Charlestown, got into their boats and back to Boston. Not one shot had been fired and it was all too late when the alarm had been spread and thousands of armed farmers had arrived. By then the British were safe home again. Yet, Sam Adams protested, this rising up of an army of a thousand from the very soil of New England had badly frightened General Gage. Once the alarm spread that the British had left Boston, the system of calling up the Minute Men had worked well indeed. The trouble had been in Boston itself.

"In other words, gentlemen, it was our fault. If we could have known but an hour, two hours, in advance what the British were intending, our men would have been there before the British troops arrived instead of a half-hour after they left."

Johnny had been told off to carry letters for the British officers, to keep on good terms with their grooms and stable boys over at the Afric Queen. Somehow he had failed. He hadn't known. Nobody had known that two hundred and sixty redcoats were getting into boats, slipping off up the Mystic, seizing Yankee gunpowder, and rowing it back to Castle Island for themselves.

Paul Revere was saying, "We must organize a better system of watching their movements—but in such a way that they will not realize they are being watched."

. . . .

There was a heavy footstep across the floor of the shop below. Rab leaped to the ladder's head.

"James Otis," he reported to the men standing about Adams.

"Well," said Sam Adams, a little crossly, "no one needs stay and listen to *him*. He shot his bolt years ago. Still talking about the natural rights of man—and the glories of the British Empire! You and I, John, had as well go home and get a good night's sleep before leaving at dawn tomorrow."

Otis pulled his bulk up the ladder. If no one was glad to see him, at least no one was so discourteous as to leave. Mr. Otis was immediately shown every honor, given a comfortable armchair and a tankard of punch. Seemingly he was not in a talkative mood tonight. The broad, ruddy, good-natured face turned left and right, nodding casually to his friends, taking it for granted that he was still a great man among them, instead of a milestone they all believed they had passed years before.

He sniffed at his punch and sipped a little.

"Sammy," he said to Sam Adams, "my coming interrupted something you were saying . . . 'We will fight,' you had got that far."

"Why, yes. That's no secret."

"For what will we fight?"

"To free Boston from these infernal redcoats and . . ."

"No," said Otis. "Boy, give me more punch. That's not enough reason for going into a war. Did any occupied city ever have better treatment than we've had from the British? Has one rebellious newspaper been stopped—one treasonable speech? Where are the firing squads, the jails jammed with political prisoners? What about the gallows for you, Sam Adams, and you, John Hancock? It has never been set up. I hate those infernal British troops spread all over my town as much as you do. Can't move these days without stepping on a soldier. But we are not going off into a civil war merely to get them out of Boston. Why are we going to fight? Why, why?"

There was an embarrassed silence. Sam Adams was the acknowledged ringleader. It was for him to speak now.

"We will fight for the rights of Americans. England cannot take our money away by taxes."

"No, no. For something more important than the pocketbooks of our American citizens."

Rab said, "For the rights of Englishmen—everywhere."

"Why stop with Englishmen?" Otis was warming up. He had a wide mouth, crooked and generous. He settled back in his chair and then he began to talk. It was such talk as Johnny had never heard before. The words surged up through the big body, flowed out of the broad mouth. He never raised his voice, and he went on and on. Sometimes Johnny felt so intoxicated by the mere sound of the words that he hardly followed the sense. That soft, low voice flowed over him; submerged him.

". . . For men and women and children all over the world," he said. "You were right, you tall, dark boy, for even as we shoot down the British soldiers we are fighting for rights such as they will be enjoying a hundred years from now.

". . . There shall be no more tyranny. A handful of men cannot seize power over thousands. A man shall choose who it is shall rule over him.

". . . The peasants of France, the serfs of Russia. Hardly more than animals now. But because we fight, they shall see freedom like a new sun rising in the west. Those natural rights God has given to every man, no matter how humble . . ." He smiled suddenly, and said . . . "or crazy," and took a good pull at his tankard.

". . . The battle we win over the worst in England shall benefit the best in England. How well are they over there represented when it comes to taxes? Not very well. It will be better for them when we have won this war.

"Will French peasants go on forever pulling off their caps and saying 'Oui, Monsieur,' when the gold coaches run down their children? They will not. Italy. And all those German states. Are they nothing but soldiers? Will no one show them the rights of good citizens? So we hold up our torch—and do not forget it was lighted upon the fires of England—and we will set it as a new sun to lighten a world . . ."

Sam Adams, anxious to get that good night's sleep before starting next day for Philadelphia, was smiling slightly, nodding his gray head, seeming to agree. He was bored. It does not matter, he was thinking, what James Otis says these days—sane or crazy.

Joseph Warren's fair, responsive face was aflame. The torch Otis had been talking about seemed reflected in his eyes.

"We are lucky men," he murmured, "for we have a cause worth dying for. This honor is not given to every generation."

"Boy," said Otis to Johnny, "fill my tankard."

It was not until he had drained it and wiped his mouth on the back of his hand that he spoke

again. All sat silently waiting for him. He had, and not for the first time, cast a spell upon them.

"They say," he began again, "my wits left me after I got hit on the head by that customs official. That's what you think, eh, Mr. Sam Adams?"

"Oh, no, no, indeed, Mr. Otis."

"Some of us will give our wits," he said, "some of us all our property. Heh, John Hancock, did you hear that? *Property*—that hurts, eh? To give one's silver wine-coolers, one's coach and four, and the gold buttons off one's sprigged satin waistcoats?"

Hancock looked him straight in the face and Johnny had never before liked him so well.

"I am ready," he said. "I can get along without all that."

"You, Paul Revere, you'll give up that silver-craft you love. God made you to make silver, not war."

Revere smiled. "There's a time for the casting of silver and a time for the casting of cannon. If that's not in the Bible, it should be."

"Doctor Warren, you've a young family. You know quite well, if you get killed they may literally starve."

Warren said, "I've thought of all that long ago."

"And you, John Adams. You've built up a very nice little law practice, stealing away my clients, I notice. Ah, well, so it goes. Each shall give according to his own abilities, and some—" he turned directly to Rab—"some will give their lives. All the years of their maturity. All the children they never live to have. The serenity of old age. To die so young is more than merely dying; it is to lose so large a part of life."

Rab was looking straight at Otis. His arms were folded across his chest. His head flung back a little. His lips parted as though he would speak, but he did not.

"Even you, my old friend—my old enemy? How shall I call you, Sam Adams? Even you will give the best you have—a genius for politics. Oh, go to Philadelphia! Pull all the wool, pull all the strings and all the wires. Yes, go, go! And God go with you. We need you, Sam. We must fight this war. You'll play your part—but what it is really about . . . you'll never know."

James Otis was on his feet, his head close against the rafters that cut down into the attic, making it the shape of a tent. Otis put out his arms.

"It is all so much simpler than you think," he said. He lifted his hands and pushed against the rafters.

"We give all we have, lives, property, safety, skills . . . we fight, we die, for a simple thing. Only that a man can stand up."

With a curt nod, he was gone.

Johnny was standing close to Rab. It had frightened him when Mr. Otis had said, "Some will give their lives," and looked straight at Rab. Die so that "a man can stand up."

Once more Sam Adams had the center of attention. He was again buttoning up his coat, preparing to leave, but first he turned to Revere.

"Now *he* is gone, we can talk a moment about that spy system you think you can organize in Boston."

Paul Revere, like his friend, Joseph Warren, was still slightly under the spell of James Otis.

"I had not thought about it that way before," he said, not answering Sam Adams's words. "You know my father had to fly France because of the tyranny over there. He was only a child. But now, in a way, I'm fighting for that child . . . that no frightened lost child ever is sent out a refugee from his own country because of race or religion." Then he pulled himself together and answered Sam Adams's remarks about the spy system.

That night, when the boys were both in bed, Johnny heard Rab, usually a heavy sleeper, turning and turning.

"Johnny," he said at last, "are you awake?"

"Yes."

"What was it he said?"

"That a man can stand up."

Rab sighed and stopped turning. In a few moments he was asleep. As often had happened before, it was the younger boy who lay wide-eyed in the darkness.

"That a man can stand up."

He'd never forget Otis with his hands pushed up against the cramping rafters over his head.

"That a man can stand up"—as simple as that.

And the strange new sun rising in the west. A sun that was to illumine a world to come.

from CHILDREN OF THE HANDCRAFTS

Carolyn Sherwin Bailey

There are many stories, books, and poems about Johnny Appleseed, but this story gives a long-range picture of the man from the standpoint of one of his beneficiaries. Look up the poem, "Johnny Appleseed," in The Book of Americans *by Rosemary and Stephen Vincent Benét. Carolyn Bailey has written many books for children including her unusual fairy tale,* Miss Hickory, *which won the Newbery Medal in 1947.*

Lost in the Apple Cave

Swinging her worn shoes from the steps of the covered wagon whose great canvas top had been her only roof for months, Rose looked back along the wilderness road. At its beginning lay the mountains. Where the road ended was a wide river. Rose and her father and mother were on their way from New England to that great unknown place beyond the Ohio River called the West. Everything they owned was packed in the great clumsy wagon, camped now on the banks of the Ohio until a flatboat should come to ferry it across. Rose had loved everything about the trip: the slow movement along strange roads, the tinkle of bells on some peddler's mule, the glimpse of a passing wain full of barrels of maple syrup or of raw hides and raw wool, the evening's camp beside some brook with a supper of cornmeal mush and salt pork cooked over an open fire.

The big wagon was like home to the twelve-year-old girl. In a corner crowded with pewter plates, patchwork quilts, sacks of cornmeal, and gourds of milk, Rose had a family of dolls made of great pine cones she had gathered on the road. She had dressed them in bits of her own calico frock as it had become torn. The little heads of these dolls, made of small wild apples, wore sunbonnets like Rose's own, or hats made of plaited rushes gathered by the brooks. The pine-cone dolls had a set of dishes made of acorns.

From *Children of the Handcrafts* by Carolyn Sherwin Bailey, Copyright 1935 by Carolyn Sherwin Bailey, © 1963 by Rebecca Davies Ryan. Reprinted by permission of The Viking Press, Inc.

Kicking her heels against the wagon step, feeling the warm harvest sun on her bare legs, Rose wished that she knew what lay within those deep woods at the right of their camp. She was sometimes lonely, for they had not happened to meet any other girl of her age all summer. She watched her mother bending over the knitting she was trying to finish before the sun dipped down into the river in flaming crimson. Her father was trying to catch some fish for supper. Rose stood up at last, swinging a little hand-made basket over her arm.

"I am going for a walk, Mother," she said. "Perhaps I can find some berries in the wood to eat with our porridge tonight."

"Do not go too far, Rose," her mother warned. "Your father saw a big brown bear quite close this morning."

"I will be back by suppertime," Rose said.

In five minutes from the time she left the wagon camp, Rose was out of all sight and sound of it. The faint stir of a passing snake among the fallen leaves in the forest, the rustle of a chipmunk's little feet, the flapping of a crow's wings or an owl's, were the only sounds. Rose hurried, remembering the bear. She never thought that she could lose the trail, but soon it seemed as if she were going round and round, each moment straying deeper into the wilderness. Her arms and legs were scratched by the bushes, each step was less sure. Rose ran. She clung to the little rush basket for comfort. It broke the force of her fall as she stepped down, tumbled, and found herself imprisoned in a cave. The entrance had been carefully screened by leafy boughs and bushes. When she got up and looked about, Rose could not believe her eyes.

The cave smelled deliciously of apples. Eating apples were a new fruit in those days, and rather rare. But here, in a roomy cave that had a little bubbling spring at the back to keep the fruit moist, was shelf upon shelf of wonderful apples such as Rose had never seen, stored away for the winter. There were August apples, the delight of harvesters. There were great golden pippins which made Rose think of the big bell on the church at home that had rung for their courage when the covered wagons started out; hard little russet apples that would keep all winter and be sweeter in March than they were now; and great red spicy apples, grown by grafting a shoot from a wild-apple bough into a bough of a sweet orchard-apple tree. Rose selected one of these apples and sat down in content on the mossy floor to munch it. This might be a bear's cave, she thought, but it was the pleasantest place she had seen in a long time.

Bright skin, delicious juice, crunchy pulp, Rose ate her apple down to its nest of big black seeds. She was just cupping her hands to drink from the spring, when a shadow darkened the door of the cave. Could it be the bear of whom her mother had warned her? Rose was dumb with terror as she saw a dark form closing the cave entrance. But a voice reassured her.

"Don't be afraid, little girl. It's only Appleseed Johnny. Welcome to my orchard!"

The man, strange indeed with his long hair, ragged clothes, and feet bare save for Indian moccasins, held out his hand to Rose.

"Come and see my trees, little girl," he said. "Many of the people of the covered wagons make this orchard of mine their halfway house before they cross the Ohio River. Come and see my house, too, and then I will show you the way to the camp again."

As the man led Rose out of the cave and into a clearing where grew more apple, cherry, peach, and plum trees than she had ever seen before, he talked about himself. He was still a young man, but he said that he had traveled on foot to Pittsburgh all the long way—across mountains, fording streams, and breaking trails through the wilderness—from Springfield in Massachusetts. His name was John Chapman. He was called Appleseed Johnny because he was the only orchardman of the pioneers. He loved apples, and he knew how much the West needed fruit. The rich soil was fairly aching to nourish the seeds that he had begged from farmers in Pennsylvania and planted there on the banks of the Ohio River.

Appleseed Johnny showed Rose the shed where he sorted and washed apple seeds, started shoots for new trees, and kept his spade and pruning shears. Then they went into the big comfortable cabin he had built for himself of forest wood, lusty logs of oak, chestnut, and pine. An apple bough, gnarled and crooked into the shape of a forest gnome, was perched on the ridge of Appleseed Johnny's cabin for its roof-tree. The nails that held the cedar planks of the door were handmade. So was the star-shaped iron latch that Appleseed Johnny lifted as he opened the heavy door and led Rose inside.

In the light of the big stone fireplace the girl thought that Appleseed Johnny looked like an Indian, as brown, sharp-eyed, and slender. He gave a low call, and down from a shelf near the roof fluttered a fluffy sleepy little owl and nestled on his shoulder.

"I came too far away from our wagon," Rose explained. "Folks say there are bears in these woods."

Appleseed Johnny laughed. He went to the door and made an odd growling sound. Fascinated, Rose saw a shaggy brown animal lumber out of the gathering darkness, sniff at Appleseed Johnny, and then pass by.

"All the wild creatures love this appleman," Rose thought.

Appleseed Johnny came in and filled a big pewter mug with milk for Rose. He put a comb of golden honey and three red apples in her basket. Last, he gave her a little apple tree, no taller than her pine-cone doll, and a small deerskin bag of seeds.

"Now I will guide you to the edge of the woods," he said. "And when you come to your new home in the wilderness, set out this young apple tree in the sunshine, and water it and build a little fence of brush about it to keep off the deer.

"In this bag are precious seeds of other apples, of berries, pears, cherries, grapes, plums, and peaches. Plant them and tend them, for there is no fruit in the wilderness. Your mother will want berries and fruits for her autumn pies, and jellies and preserves for the winter. Your new home in the West will need grapevines growing over it, and a pink cloud of orchard blossoms in the spring."

As Appleseed Johnny talked, he led Rose safely through the darkening forest until she could see her own campfire and smell the fish her mother was cooking.

"Good-by, and thank you," she said.

"Good-by, Little Pioneer," he said. "Remember Appleseed Johnny and plant your trees."

"I will!" she called as she ran over to hide her little tree and the seeds. She ate supper in a dream and in her sleep smelled apples under the canvas top. A flatboat was waiting for them in the morning, and they drifted, wagon and all, over the Ohio River and into the wild lands beyond.

Season after season Appleseed Johnny tended his trees, harvested his fruit, and sorted his seeds. He kept cows and had a row of beehives. Season after season the covered wagons carrying hundreds of pioneers West stopped by his cabin. The travelers were fed apples, honey, and milk and given little bags of Appleseed Johnny's precious seeds.

Rose's covered wagon rolled on into the untilled, wild country of Ohio. Her father told her about Appleseed Johnny. "He was only a boy when he left his home in Massachusetts and tramped out to Pennsylvania," he said. "He took apple seeds in payment for work for the farmers, and he built his house and planted his orchards

with his own hands. Hundreds of covered wagons stop at his door, rest, and go on, carrying his bags of seeds."

On, on went the wagon until Rose's father found a farm site. The seasons passed quickly, with so much work to be done. The land was cleared and a cabin built in two years. That was the year that Rose picked berries from the bushes that grew from Appleseed Johnny's seeds. In four years roads were built, the cabin made larger, and Rose's dresses were longer. That was the year that she picked peaches, cherries, and plums from the trees planted from Appleseed Johnny's seeds. In six years Rose was a young lady. It was another October, and the apples from the little tree that Appleseed Johnny had given her were harvested and waiting in the kitchen to be made into apple butter for the winter. Rose would trust no one but herself to do this.

In the sunny kitchen she had set out empty pans, tubs, sharp knives, and a great basket of juicy red apples. On linen thread, hanging from the beams of the kitchen were strips of apples drying. The strong crane in the open fireplace held a brass kettle filled with pared apples, sweet and sour in proportion, the sweet ones at the bottom, with quinces and molasses added for flavor. She had put straw in the bottom of the kettle to keep the cooking apples from burning. Rose would spend days preserving the apples for the winter. Down cellar, tubs of apple sauce would freeze and keep through the winter as sweet as when it was made. The dried apples would be made into pies.

Rose stirred the apple butter, her back to the open door. Suddenly she heard a low call, like that of a little screech owl. She turned and saw a surprising figure.

The man was as tall and straight as an Indian, keen-eyed, and on his back he carried a great sack. He was as ragged as a beggar, his hair had grown to his shoulders and he wore Indian moccasins. He gave his bird call again, and smiled at Rose. "You have grown, my child," he said.

"Appleseed Johnny!" she cried.

"Yes, I am Appleseed Johnny, still planting orchards in the wilderness. I gave away my house, filled this sack with seeds, crossed the Ohio River in a dugout canoe, and have been wandering for many years, scattering seeds, and teaching the pioneers how to plant and tend orchards."

"Come in," Rose begged. "Spend the night with us, and let us feed you as you fed me when I was a covered-wagon girl. These are your apples that I am cooking. Your little tree lived, and every one of your seeds grew and gave us fruit."

An old letter tells us the rest of the story: how Appleseed Johnny, pioneer nurseryman of the early nineteenth century, spent the night in the Rice cabin, made welcome by Roselle Rice and her family who had passed his door many years before. Many covered-wagon children knew Appleseed Johnny, but Rose was the only one who wrote about him. In the morning he started on again. He carried a Bible in the sack with his seeds, and left one leaf of it with Rose. Then he tramped off into the woods farther West and she never saw him again.

But Appleseed Johnny walked for forty years, leaving his little buckskin bags of seeds and his Bible pages at lonely cabins, planting the orchards that now cover acres of the West, sleeping outdoors, making friends with bears, wolves, and foxes, looked upon by the Indians as the Great Spirit. Pioneers went on with his work. Today skilled orchardmen cultivate the vast tracts of fruitland of our West. Following the trail he started, great freight trains return now to the East carrying barrels of Jonathan, Winesap, Spitzenburgh, Northern Spy, Delicious, King, Greening, and Golden Pippin apples for hungry boys and girls. The wild hardy stock poured into the spiced sap of the cultivated growth still gives us new, larger, tastier apples. The sturdy covered-wagon people, going West, gave us our beautiful Western cities, our fertile farms, our fine schools. And every pink apple blossom of the spring is scented with Appleseed Johnny's kindness to little Rose, and every bite of a rosy October apple tastes as sweet as those he laid away in his cave.

from AMERICA TRAVELS
Alice Dalgliesh

The period of the old canal boats comes as vividly to life in this story from America Travels *as the three little girls do. Harriet of the quick decisions meets her match in firmness in the unknown child who gets the kitten by sheer force of will. The author, Alice Dalgliesh, has written a variety of good books for children. One of the best is* The Bears on Hemlock Mountain, *which is a thriller and a chiller! For many years, Miss Dalgliesh was also juvenile editor at Scribner's and in that role was responsible for publishing many of our finest juvenile books.*

The Kitten on the Canal Boat

Harriet lay in her narrow bunk watching pictures move slowly past, framed in the small, square window. Each morning the pictures were different: sometimes a patch of blue sky, white clouds, or green fields, sometimes sheep grazing or cows lying lazily under a tree. Harriet was quite accustomed to moving scenery, for all of her nine summers had been spent on a canal boat. In the winter months Harriet lived in a house, but she much preferred the time spent on the canal where something interesting and different was always happening.

Now the sun was coming in the small, square window and it was time to get up. Harriet jumped out of bed and climbed on a box to look out. The *Red Lion of the West* was nosing slowly along the canal and there was nothing to be seen but fields full of buttercups. Harriet was glad that it was a fine day, for it meant that as the *Red Lion* passed through the next town gay picnic parties might come on board.

Two kinds of people traveled on the sturdy slow-moving canal boats. There were serious people who were really going somewhere. These slept on the boat and either brought their food with them or had their meals cooked by Harriet's mother in the tiny kitchen. These travelers sometimes were moving from one town or village to another, so they brought with them many bundles and baskets, with a large part of their household belongings. Then there were the gay people who were not really going anywhere but who thought it fun to take a trip on the boat. Harriet loved these picnic parties with laughing ladies who held little parasols over their heads to keep the sun from spoiling their beautiful complexions. They always carried the most interesting lunches put up in dainty baskets.

When Harriet was dressed she went to the

kitchen. It was a neat little kitchen with red-checked curtains and a red geranium in the window. These matched the rest of the *Red Lion* which was a trim boat painted red and white with a black stripe. As Harriet entered the kitchen a good smell of crisp bacon came from the frying pan on the small stove. There were other important things to be done, however, so she did not waste much time over breakfast. From a basket in the corner she took two kittens, a gray one and a black one. With a kitten tucked under each arm she went out on the roof of the boat, which was quite flat, like a deck. There she stood and watched her brother, who was walking along the towpath beside Jerry and Jim, the mules that pulled the boat. At the stern stood Harriet's father with his hand on the tiller; it was his job to steer the boat.

Harriet put the kittens down on the deck and sat looking along the canal. This was an exciting day, for on this day the *Red Lion* passed the *Blossoming Bough,* the boat on which lived Harriet's friend, Alice. As the boats passed each other Harriet and Alice waved, and even had time to talk. Now, as Harriet watched, the *Blossoming Bough* turned the corner and came slowly down the canal. She was a pretty boat, as trim as the *Red Lion* but painted green and white with a touch of yellow. As the boats came near each other the *Blossoming Bough* drew off to one side to allow the *Red Lion* to pass. The tow lines were dropped so that the mules pulling the *Red Lion* could step over them.

Harriet stood as close to the edge of the deck as she dared. There was Alice close to the edge of *her* boat. It was well to be careful, for the deck had no railing and canal water was dark and cold.

"Harriet!" called Alice, "I have a new dress."

"What is it like?" asked Harriet.

"Oh, it's white, for Sundays. I'm not allowed to wear it on week days."

"I'm going to have a new dress soon," said Harriet.

"A Sunday dress?"

"Yes, I think it will be white like yours."

The *Red Lion* had slipped past the *Blossoming Bough.*

"Good-by, Harriet!"

"Good-by, Alice!"

There would be no more excitement now until the *Red Lion of the West* reached the next town. Harriet sat on the deck and played with the kittens. Suddenly her father put a horn to his lips and blew a long blast. Harriet ducked her head, for this meant that they were about to pass under a low bridge. It seemed no time at all until they reached the town—and there was a picnic party! It was a particularly interesting picnic party.

There were two pretty ladies with parasols, and two gentlemen, their hats tied to their buttonholes with string to keep them from blowing away. And there was a little girl. Harriet thought, as the little girl stepped daintily onto the deck, that she had never seen anything so beautiful or so exactly like a picture come to life. The little girl had blue eyes, yellow curls, and pink cheeks. Her dress was of the palest pink, and below it showed white lace-trimmed pantalettes. Harriet stood there feeling very dark and solid and different in her calico dress. She could not take her eyes off the little girl. There above the golden curls was a bonnet, a dainty straw bonnet trimmed with pink roses and tied under its owner's chin with a pink bow.

The ladies moved gracefully to a seat, arranged their skirts and sat chatting with the gentlemen. The little girl's mother called her to sit beside her. For five minutes the little girl sat there as prim and as quiet as a china ornament on a shelf. Then she saw the kittens.

"Oh, Mamma!" she said, "look at the darling kittens! A black one and a gray one. The gray one is just the kitten I want!"

"They belong to the little girl who lives on the boat," said her mother.

"Oh, but I *want* one," said the pink child, who had always had what she wanted. "I *want* one, Mamma, I want the gray one. It's my birthday, you know." Two large tears came into the blue eyes.

"Mercy, Florence," said her mother, looking worried, "don't cry! Let's ask the little girl if she will sell us the gray kitten."

"Little girl," said Florence, "will you sell us the gray kitten?"

"No!" said Harriet, her brown eyes very large, her feet planted firmly on the deck.

"But I *want* her," fretted the child.

"He's my favorite kitten," said Harriet.

"She's my favorite *kind* of kitten," said Florence even more fretfully. Then, as suddenly as the sun comes out from behind a cloud, she changed her tone and began to coax. "Won't you let me have her? Please?"

"Well," said Harriet, weakening, "perhaps I will. But *you* must give *me* something that I want very much."

"Oh, I *will!*" smiled Florence. "What is it?"

"Your lovely pink bonnet," answered Harriet. There was a moment of chatter and fluttering.

"My pink bonnet?"

"Your lovely pink bonnet!"

"Your *new* pink bonnet. Florence, you *can't*."

But Florence usually had her own way and this was her birthday. Once more two big tears came into her eyes. This time they fell and splashed on the pink dress. Slowly one hand began to untie the strings of the pink bonnet.

"No, Florence."

"Oh, please, Mamma."

"The sun is much too hot."

"Mamma, it's such a lovely day and I can share your parasol." By this time the bonnet was untied. Harriet picked up the gray kitten. With one hand she took the bonnet, with the other she gave up the gray kitten. Then she hurried into the kitchen to find her mother.

Mother shook her head over the queer ways of little girls, but at last she was persuaded that the exchange was a fair one. It was well that she thought so, for by this time wild horses could not have dragged the kitten from Florence's arms.

When the picnic was over a little girl without a bonnet stood on the shore and waved to another little girl on the deck of the canal boat.

"I'll be very kind to your nice gray kitten," called Florence. "And I'm going to call her Velvet."

"*His* name is Tom!" shouted Harriet, but the *Red Lion* was too far along the canal for the pink child to hear. This was just as well, for never in the world could she have owned a kitten with the plain name of Tom.

It was Sunday morning when next the *Red Lion of the West* passed the *Blossoming Bough*. The sound of church bells came faintly across the fields. It was very quiet on the canal. The boats slipped silently along, for on Sundays they were not allowed to blow their horns. Harriet stood as close to the edge of the deck as she dared. Alice stood close to the edge too. Each little girl was wearing a Sunday dress. Each dress was white, with white pantalettes. Alice's hair was blowing in the breeze, but on Harriet's head there was a bonnet, a dainty straw bonnet with pink roses and pink ribbons tied under the chin.

"Look at my Sunday dress!" screamed Alice.

"Look at mine!"

"Why, Harriet, you have a pink bonnet!"

"Yes, isn't it beautiful?"

There was quite a long silence while Alice took in all the glory of the pink bonnet.

"It's the most beautiful bonnet I ever saw."

Harriet turned around to show the back of the bonnet.

"Did your mother give it to you?"

"No, I got it from a little girl in exchange for a kitten."

"For *what?*" The boats had passed each other. "*For a kitten!*"

But the *Red Lion of the West* was now too far away from the *Blossoming Bough*. There was nothing to do but wait until they passed again, then Harriet and Alice could finish their conversation. It was often like that!

MARTIN AND ABRAHAM LINCOLN

Catherine Cate Coblentz

The year before her death, Catherine Coblentz wrote a wonderful fairy tale, The Blue Cat of Castle Town, *which should be read aloud. It embodies her own spirit of service to the "bright enchantment" of "beauty, content and peace." This touching story,* Martin and Abraham Lincoln, *is a true incident of the Civil War.*

"Flour and sugar and butter and eggs. Flour and sugar and butter and eggs." Martin Emery kept saying the words over to himself as he went slowly up the lane.

He had heard his mother whispering them again and again these past days. The words reminded him of the songs which his friend, Snowden, sang. Only Martin felt sure Mother's words were not a song but a prayer. For Mother needed so many things for Martin, for Maria, and Amanda, and Anna, the baby.

Martin gulped. When Father was at the Fort near by he had seen to it that Mother had these things. But he was gone. He would be gone for a long time. Somehow or other Martin felt he must take his place and help. After all he wore a new uniform now with shiny buttons. It was

Martin and Abraham Lincoln by Catherine Cate Coblentz, Childrens Press, Inc., 1947. Used by permission of the publisher

just like the one Father was wearing the last time Martin had seen him.

By this time Martin had come to the end of the lane. So he climbed up on the big rock by the roadside. Then he turned about and waved at the little gray house. Maria and Amanda and Anna, the baby, were standing in the doorway. They all waved back. Though Maria had to start Anna's hand going.

Then Martin looked up the road. It was Saturday and time for Snowden and Nellie to appear around the curve. Pretty soon he saw Nellie's long white ears. He heard the bell on Nellie's neck, and the jingle of her harness. He heard the creaking wheels on Nellie's cart. He saw the baskets of fresh vegetables in the back.

He saw Snowden, but Snowden didn't see Martin. Snowden was bent over on the front seat. In his hand was a stub of a pencil; on his knee a piece of paper. He kept frowning and looking at the paper. "I sure got to make a lot of money today," he said loud enough for Martin to hear him. "I sure got to. There's flour to get for Rosebell, and sugar and butter and eggs."

But if Snowden didn't see Martin, Nellie did. As soon as she came to the rock, Nellie stopped still. She looked at Martin. Then she turned her head and looked at Snowden. Then she flicked her ears.

When Nellie flicked her ears it was a sign. As soon as Martin saw it, he began scrambling over the wheel. He climbed up on the seat beside Snowden. Snowden blinked with surprise.

"May I go to Washington with you?" Martin asked.

Snowden started to nod. Then he stopped and asked, "Does your mother know?"

"She knows," said Martin. "That's why she let me wear my new suit." He stood up so Snowden could see the suit better. He stretched his shoulders as high as he could.

Snowden looked him up and down. He didn't miss a quirk of the soldier-like cap or a single shiny button. "Hmm," he said. "Nice, Martin. Just like your father's."

"Father's regiment brought Mother the cloth," said Martin, "and the buttons."

"Snowden," began Martin, as the cart moved on toward Washington, "how do you get flour and sugar and butter and eggs?"

Snowden sighed, "Sometimes I declare I don't know myself, Martin. Rosebell and the children need so many things." He took up the pencil once more. When he put it down again, Martin asked another question.

"When the war is over, will my father come home, Snowden?"

Snowden drew a deep breath. "All the war prisoners will come home then, Martin. All those that the northern army has taken will go back south to their homes. And all those that the southern army has taken will go back to their homes."

"I wish the war was over now," burst out Martin.

Snowden looked at him. "So do I," he said. "Abraham Lincoln does, too, I reckon."

Martin knew who Abraham Lincoln was. His picture was in the little gray house at the end of the lane. He never could decide which picture he liked better, that of his father or of Abraham Lincoln. His mother said they were both very important people. "Mr. Lincoln is the best President this country ever had, Martin," she said. "And your father is the best cobbler."

Best cobbler, best cobbler went Nellie's iron shoes, as they thumped, thumped across the bridge that led from Alexandria into Washington. Martin kicked his feet back to feel whether the empty basket was under the seat. It was. Martin knew why it was there. He knew, too, what would happen to that basket.

At the very first house, Snowden began his morning song. Martin waited to hear what the song was. It was a different one every week. This week it was a good song. Martin joined in after the first time. He sang as loud as he could:

> Squash and beans and 'taters,
> Garden fresh, garden fresh,
> Beans and squash and 'taters.

After every sale, Snowden would put a scoop of beans or 'taters, or maybe a big squash into the basket under the seat.

The faster Snowden sold what he had, the bigger the gifts to the basket. And when everything else was sold that basket would be quite full. When Snowden and Martin and Nellie went home, Snowden would stop at the little gray house at the end of the lane.

"Got some left overs, Mrs. Emery." Snowden would say. "Thought maybe you'd help me out by using them." Then he always added, "Martin was a big help to me today, Mrs. Emery."

Had it not been for Snowden's left overs, Martin knew that he and Maria and Amanda and Anna would be hungry oftener than they were. Now, if they only had flour and sugar and butter and eggs, Mother wouldn't need to worry.

So on this Saturday Martin tried harder than ever to help Snowden as much as he could. He called:

> Squash and beans and 'taters,

at the top of his lungs. Earlier in the season it had been:

> Rhubarb and radishes, ripe and red.

Later there would be cabbages and parsnips and turnips, and Snowden would make up new songs for them to call.

"You are good at making up songs," said Martin as the cart rattled along the wide streets.

"And you are good at singing them," replied Snowden. "Words said over and over make a good song."

Words said over and over! That made Martin think of his mother, and the words she made into a prayer. He drew a long, quivering sigh.

"Wars, which put fathers in prison when they are needed at home, are a bad thing," Snowden said. He had been watching Martin closely.

Martin nodded. He swallowed the lump in his throat and called:

> Squash and beans and 'taters,
> Garden fresh, garden fresh,
> Beans and squash and 'taters.

However, his voice didn't sound nearly as cheerful as it usually did. Toward the end of the morning it began trailing after Snowden's like a small echo.

> Squash and beans and 'taters,

Snowden would sing.

> Beans and 'taters,

would come Martin's echo.

Snowden glanced at Martin several times. It was very hot. Martin looked pale. Snowden made up his mind he would take him to a cool spot, while he went off to buy the groceries which Rosebell needed.

So a little before noon, Snowden turned Nellie about. And when they came to a big parklike place filled with shade trees, Snowden pulled the reins.

"Whoa, Nellie," he said.

"Now, Martin," he went on, "you just stay here in the shade and rest until Nellie and I come back. It's a good place for anyone in a uniform like yours. There's been lots of soldiers on this lawn, I can tell you. I've seen them sleeping here at night sometimes. And all over the place in the day. And I've seen them jump up and stand just as proud and straight when Abraham Lincoln came along."

"Came along here, Snowden? Abraham Lincoln?"

"Of course, Martin. See that building there? That's the Capitol, Martin—our Capitol."

Martin stood on the ground and stared. Snowden and Nellie started to leave. Then Nellie stopped and flicked her ears. That made Snowden remember something. He reached in his pocket.

"I most forgot," he said. "Rosebell gave me a sandwich for you, Martin. And an apple."

"I have a sandwich." Martin pointed to his pocket. He did not take it out, for he did not want Snowden to see how small and thin that sandwich was. There was no butter on the bread, only a smear of molasses.

"You'd better take this," urged Snowden. "Rosebell made it special."

"Thank you," said Martin, reaching for the thick sandwich and the apple. He would just take a bite or two out of the sandwich and save the rest for Maria and Amanda and Anna. He would save the apple, too, most of it.

When Snowden and Nellie were gone, and when the last sound of Nellie's bell, the jingle of her harness, and the creaking of the cart wheels faded in the distance, Martin wandered about for a little. Then he climbed on a bench. He ate his thin sandwich. He ate a little of Snowden's thick one. It was so good. Half of it was gone before he knew it. He re-wrapped it in the paper Rosebell had put about it, and laid it on the bench. When Martin wasn't looking a fat squir-rel slipped up on the bench and grabbed at it. Martin felt the squirrel touch his hand. He jumped. The squirrel jumped. The sandwich fell and landed in a puddle.

Martin could have cried when he saw that. But he didn't. He would save all the apple, he decided, for Maria and Amanda and Anna. He would not take even a bite.

The sun was hot. Martin went over and sat down on the stone steps of the Capitol. The steps were clean and cool. His eyes closed a little as he leaned back, his head resting against the stone at one side.

Then, as always when he was alone and it was still, Martin began thinking about his father. The lump in his throat began to grow.

He heard someone coming down the steps in back of him. But there was plenty of room so Martin didn't move. He just sat there and watched dreamily as a long shadow moved over the step he was on, and went slither-sliding down the step ahead. And the next. And the next. And the next.

Then the shadow stopped still and stayed in one place. A voice just in back of Martin said, "Well, well! How's my little soldier?"

Soldier! When his father's friends said that, Martin had always done as his father had taught him, jumped to his feet and saluted. So, forgetting how tired and sad he had been, he sprang to his feet, flinging his head back and his hand up at the same time.

As his fingers touched the visor of his little blue cap, Martin's heart began to thud like a drum. For Abraham Lincoln was standing there looking down at him, his sad face losing its look of worry, and breaking slowly into a smile. Abraham Lincoln, himself!

"What is your name, soldier?" the great man asked, gravely returning the salute.

Martin told him.

"Where were you born, Martin?"

"In Vermont. In a log cabin."

The man nodded. "I was born in a log cabin, too."

"I know, Mother told me. She said some day I might get to be President like you."

"All mothers say that, Martin. What does your father say?"

"I don't know." Martin's voice slowed. "You

see, he is away. He used to be a cobbler, but now he is your soldier."

"What regiment? And where is he now?"

The lump in Martin's throat was growing worse. It was difficult to make the words come. "The First Vermont—" he managed. And then the sobs had him. "He's in Andersonville Prison," he jerked.

But the great man was bending over. Strong arms were lifting Martin. In another moment the man had taken Martin's place on the steps. Martin was folded into his lap.

The boy's face was hidden now, in Abraham Lincoln's vest.

Abraham Lincoln just sat there, holding the little boy whose sobbing had been so long kept back. A great hand patted him gently and understandingly between the shoulders. When Martin grew quieter the man began to talk.

"So your father is a cobbler. Is he a good cobbler, Martin?"

Martin nodded his head so hard that his nose

went up and down against Abraham Lincoln's ribs.

"Good cobblers are mighty important," said the man. "Never made a pair of shoes myself. But I saw a boy once that needed some mighty bad." The President settled his back a little more comfortably into the corner of the step and the wall.

"It happened when I was postmaster back in Illinois," he went on. "People didn't write many letters in those days, so I carried them in my hat. One cold day as I was going along with the letters in my hat, I saw Ab Trout. He was barefoot as the day he was born and chopping a pile of logs from an old barn that had been torn down. The logs were gnarled and tough. And Ab's ax kept going slower and slower.

" 'What do you get for this job, Ab?' I asked him.

" 'A dollar.'

" 'What do you aim to do with it?'

" 'Buy a pair of shoes,' he said.

" 'You'll never get one shoe at this rate, Ab,' I told him. 'Better go in and warm yourself and you'll work faster.' So he did. Funniest thing, Martin. When Ab came out, that wood was all chopped! Now, what do you think of that?"

Martin sat up and looked straight at Abraham Lincoln. "I think you chopped that wood," he said.

"Maybe you're right," smiled Lincoln. "After all, folks must help each other."

Martin nodded. "I help my mother all I can," he said. "I fix the rough places when they come in the shoes of Maria and Amanda and Anna. I can do it most as well as Father did. Mother says it helps a lot."

"I am sure it does." The President nodded.

"Vermont is a long way off," he went on. "Tell me, how do you happen to be here, Martin?"

Martin wiped the last tear from his cheek with the handkerchief Mr. Lincoln handed him. He could talk now. He wanted to.

"Father went to war," he began. "He was stationed at a fort near Alexandria. So, after a time he found a house near the fort, and sent for Mother and me and Maria and Amanda and Anna. We came on the train. At first we saw Father often. Then one night when some of the soldiers were sent out to take a railroad bridge, Father was captured. He was sent to prison."

"How does your mother manage to take care of you?" asked Abraham Lincoln.

"Well, it's like you said. Folks help. The soldiers—Father's friends—bring their mending to her. They ask her to cook for them. And sometimes they bring their washing for her to do. They pay as much as they can. The soldiers give us cloth for our clothes, too.

"And Snowden helps. Snowden is my friend. He sells vegetables and I help him call. Snowden fills the basket under the seat with vegetables and calls them left overs. He gives the basket to Mother. But the vegetables aren't left overs. Not really."

Martin didn't tell about his mother's prayer for flour and sugar and butter and eggs. He didn't need to. For Abraham Lincoln seemed to know all about that prayer.

"Hmm!" he began. "It seems to me, Martin, that part of this job of helping belongs to the army—your father's army, and mine. I will speak to somebody, and I'm pretty sure there will be food from the army stores every week for your mother. Things that Snowden and the soldiers can't supply, like butter and bacon and other things."

There wasn't any lump in Martin's throat now. He felt wonderful. But for some reason the tears began to pour down his face.

The man pretended not to see. Instead, he raised himself to his feet, and a sudden frown grew deep between his eyes. "It's my shoe, Martin," he explained. "There's a nail sticking right into my foot. And I keep forgetting to have it fixed."

"Oh, wait," cried Martin. "I can help you." He darted off to a pile of stones by the steps. Luckily he found the kind he wanted right away. When he came back Abraham Lincoln sat on the steps with his shoe off, waiting to be helped.

Martin sat down beside him. He slipped one stone inside the great shoe. With the other he pounded hard on the sole.

"My father showed me how," be boasted between pounds. "He is a good cobbler."

Abraham Lincoln smiled. "I'd like to be a cobbler myself, Martin. A good cobbler."

"That's what I am going to be," nodded Martin.

Down the street he could hear the sound of Nellie's bell, the jingle of her harness and the creaking of the wheels on Nellie's cart. But he finished the shoe and gave it to Abraham Lincoln.

The man put on the shoe. He stood up and set the foot, where the nail had been, down carefully. He pressed harder, while Martin watched his face. There was no frown between Abraham Lincoln's eyes.

"It's a good job, Martin," he praised. "It feels just fine." He paused and looked over Martin's head far into the distance. The worry had gone now from the President's face. "You have helped me, Martin," he said, "more than you know!"

Martin said nothing. He only slipped his hand inside Abraham Lincoln's. They came down the steps together.

They were waiting when Snowden and Nellie arrived.

Snowden's mouth popped wide open. Nellie stopped. She flicked her ears and Snowden swept off his hat.

The man beside Martin lifted his gravely in return. Then he bent and raised Martin high in the air and put him on the seat beside Snowden.

"Good-by, soldier," he said.

Martin saluted. Snowden saluted. Abraham Lincoln saluted. Nellie started toward home.

from CADDIE WOODLAWN

Carol Ryrie Brink

Caddie Woodlawn, *for which "Three Adventurers" is the first chapter, won the Newbery Medal in 1936, and time has not lessened its popularity. Indian John called Caddie Woodlawn "Missee Red Hair," and their friendship was to stand the whole community in good stead when the two of them were able to avert a bloody war between the Indians and the white settlers.*

Three Adventurers

In 1864 Caddie Woodlawn was eleven, and as wild a little tomboy as ever ran the woods of western Wisconsin. She was the despair of her mother and of her elder sister Clara. But her father watched her with a little shine of pride in his eyes, and her brothers accepted her as one of themselves without a question. Indeed, Tom, who was two years older, and Warren, who was two years younger than Caddie, needed Caddie to link them together into an inseparable trio. Together they got in and out of more scrapes and adventures than any one of them could have imagined alone. And in those pioneer days Wisconsin offered plenty of opportunities for adventure to three wide-eyed, red-headed youngsters.

On a bright Saturday afternoon in the early fall Tom and Caddie and Warren Woodlawn sat on a bank of the Menomonie River, or Red Cedar as they call it now, taking off their clothes. Their red heads shone in the sunlight. Tom's hair was the darkest, Caddie's the nearest golden, and nine-year-old Warren's was plain carrot color. Not one of the three knew how to swim, but they were going across the river, nevertheless. A thin thread of smoke beyond the bend on the other side of the river told them that the Indians were at work on a birch-bark canoe.

"Do you think the Indians around here would ever get mad and massacre folks like they did up north?" wondered Warren, tying his shirt up in a little bundle.

"No, sir!" said Tom, "not these Indians!"

"Not Indian John, anyhow," said Caddie. She had just unfastened the many troublesome little buttons on the back of her tight-waisted dress, and, before taking it off, she paused a moment to see if she could balance a fresh-water clam shell on her big toe. She found that she could.

"*No, not Indian John!*" she repeated decidedly, having got the matter of the clam shell off her mind, "even if he does have a scalp belt," she added. The thought of the scalp belt always made her hair prickle delightfully up where her scalp lock grew.

"Naw," said Tom, "the fellows who spread those massacre stories are just big-mouthed scared-cats who don't know the Indians, I guess."

"Big-mouthed scared-cats," repeated Warren, admiring Tom's command of language.

"Big-mouthed scared-cats," echoed a piping voice from the bank above. Seven-year-old Hetty,

Reprinted with permission of The Macmillan Company from *Caddie Woodlawn* by Carol Ryrie Brink. Copyright 1935 by The Macmillan Company, renewed 1963 by Carol Ryrie Brink

who fluttered wistfully on the outer edge of their adventures, filed away Tom's remark in her active brain. It would be useful to tell to Mother, sometime when Mother was complaining about Tom's language. The three below her paid no attention to Hetty's intrusion. Their red heads, shining in the sunlight, did not even turn in her direction. Hetty's hair was red, too, like Father's, but somehow, in spite of her hair, she belonged on the dark-haired side of the family where Mother and Clara and all the safe and tidy virtues were. She poised irresolutely on the bank above the three adventurous ones. If they had only turned around and looked at her! But they were enough in themselves. She could not make up her mind what to do. She wanted to go with them, and yet she wanted just as much to run home and tell Mother and Clara what they were about to do. Hetty was the self-appointed newsbearer of the family. Wild horses could not prevent her from being the first to tell, whatever it was that happened.

Tom and Caddie and Warren finished undressing, tied their clothes into tight bundles, and stepped out into the river. The water was low after a long, hot summer, but still it looked cold and deep. Hetty shuddered. She had started to undo one shoe, but now she quickly tied it up again. She had made up her mind. She turned around and flew across the fields to tell Mother.

Tom knew from experience that he could just keep his chin above water and touch bottom with his toes across the deep part of the river. It would have been over Caddie's and Warren's heads, but, if they held onto Tom and kept their feet paddling, they could just keep their heads above water. They had done it before. Tom went first with his bundle of clothes balanced on his head. Caddie came next, clutching Tom's shoulder with one hand and holding her bundle of clothes on top of her head with the other. Warren clung to Caddie's shoulder in the same manner, balancing his own clothes with his free hand. They moved slowly and carefully. If Tom lost his footing or fell, they would all go down together and be swept away by the current toward the village below. But the other two had every confidence in Tom, and Tom had not the slightest reason to doubt himself. They looked like three beavers, moving silently across the cur-

rent—three heads with three bundles and a little wake of ripples trailing out behind them. Last of all came Nero, the farm dog, paddling faithfully behind them. But Hetty was already out of sight.

Presently there was solid river bed beneath their feet again. The three children scrambled out on the other side, shook themselves as Nero did, and pulled on their dry, wrinkled clothing.

"Hurry up, Caddie," called Tom. "You're always the last to dress."

"So would you be, too, Tom, if you had so many buttons!" protested Caddie. She came out of the bushes struggling with the back of her blue denim dress. Relenting, Tom turned his superior intelligence to the mean task of buttoning her up the back.

"I wish Mother'd let me wear boy's clothes," she complained.

"Huh!" said Warren, "she thinks you're tomboy enough already."

"But they're so much quicker," said Caddie regretfully.

Now that they were dressed, they sped along the river bank in the direction of the smoke. Several Indian canoes were drawn up on shore in the shelter of a little cove and beyond them in a clearing the Indians moved to and fro about a fire. Propped on two logs was the crude framework of a canoe which was already partly covered with birch bark. The smell of birch smoke and hot pitch filled the air. Caddie lifted her head and sniffed. It was perfume to her, as sweet as the perfume of the clover fields. Nero sniffed, too, and growled low in his throat.

The three children stopped at the edge of the clearing and watched. Even friendly Indians commanded fear and respect in those days. A lean dog, with a wolfish look, came forward barking.

He and Nero circled about each other, little ridges of bristling hair along their spines, their tails wagging suspiciously. Suddenly the Indian dog left Nero and came toward Caddie.

"Look!" said Caddie. "It's Indian John's dog." The dog's tail began to wag in a friendlier manner, and Caddie reached out and patted his head.

By this time the Indians had noticed the children. They spoke among themselves and pointed. Some of them left their work and came forward.

In all the seven years since the Woodlawns had come from Boston to live in the big house on the prairie, the Indians had never got used to seeing them. White men and their children they had seen often enough, but never such as these, who wore, above their pale faces, hair the color of flame and sunset. During the first year that the children spent in Wisconsin, the Indians had come from all the country around to look at them. They had come in groups, crowding into Mrs. Woodlawn's kitchen in their silent moccasins, touching the children's hair and staring. Poor Mrs. Woodlawn, frightened nearly out of her wits, had fed them bread or beans or whatever she had on hand, and they had gone away satisfied.

"Johnny, my dear," Mrs. Woodlawn had complained to her husband, "those frightful savages will eat us out of house and home."

"Patience, Harriet," said her husband, "we have enough and to spare."

"But, Johnny, the way they look at the children's hair frightens me. They might want a red scalp to hang to their belts."

Caddie remembered very vividly the day, three years before, when she had gone unsuspecting into the store in the village. As she went in the door, a big Indian had seized her and held her up in the air while he took a leisurely look at her hair. She had been so frightened that she had not even cried out, but hung there, wriggling in the Indian's firm grasp, and gazing desperately about the store for help.

The storekeeper had laughed at her, saying in a reassuring voice: "You needn't be afraid, Caddie. He's a good Indian. It's Indian John."

That was the strange beginning of a friendship, for a kind of friendship it was, that had grown up between Caddie and Indian John. The boys liked Indian John, too, but it was at Caddie and her red-gold curls that the big Indian looked when he came to the farm, and it was for Caddie that he left bits of oddly carved wood and once a doll—such a funny doll with a tiny head made of a pebble covered with calico, black horsehair braids, calico arms and legs, and a buckskin dress! John's dog knew his master's friends. Caddie had been kind to him and he accepted her as a friend.

He rubbed his head against her now as she patted his rough hair. Indian John left his work on the canoe and came forward.

"You like him dog?" he said, grinning. He was flattered when anyone patted his dog.

"Yes," said Caddie, "he's a good dog."

"Will you let us see how you put the canoe together?" asked Tom eagerly.

"You come look," said the Indian.

They followed him to the half-finished canoe. Grunting and grinning, the Indians took up their work. They fastened the pliable sheaths of birch bark into place on the light framework, first sewing them together with buckskin thongs, then cementing them with the hot pitch. The children were fascinated. Their own canoe on the lake was an Indian canoe. But it had been hollowed out of a single log. They had seen the birch-bark canoes on the river, but had never been so close to the making of one. They were so intent on every detail that time slipped by unheeded. Even the squaws, who came up behind them to examine their hair, did not take their attention from the building of the canoe. Caddie shook her head impatiently, flicking her curls out of their curious fingers, and went on watching.

But after awhile Warren said: "Golly! I'm hungry." Perhaps it was the odor of jerked veni-son, simmering over the fire, which had begun to mingle with the odors of birch and pitch, that made Warren remember he was hungry.

"You're always hungry," said Tom, the lofty one, in a tone of disgust.

"Well, I am, too," said Caddie positively, and that settled it. The sun was beginning to swing low in the sky, and, once they had made up their minds, they were off at once. As quickly as they had come, they returned along the river bank to their crossing place. The Indians stared after them. They did not understand these curious red and white children of the white man, nor how they went and came.

Soon three bundles, three dirty faces, and three fiery heads, shining in the red autumn sun, crossed the river with a little trail of ripples behind them. Safe on the other bank, the three hastily pulled on their clothes and started to take a short cut through the woods, Nero trotting at their heels.

from JED

Peter Burchard

This is a simple, but moving, story of a sixteen-year-old Yankee soldier who befriends a young member of a Southern family and proves that not all enemies are ruthless.

[A Yankee Meets a Young Confederate]

Right after reveille Sergeant Charlie came around. "Well, Jed," Charlie said, "did you break up any Rebel raids this morning?"

"Only a little one," Jed said. "How does it happen you didn't come around before this?"

"Now, I'm sorry, Jed," Charlie said. "If I'd a knowed it would worry you so I'd have come around earlier."

"I'll forgive you just this once," Jed said. "But don't let it happen again."

Charlie smiled and walked toward the next picket.

Jed heard Charlie whistling a little tune. Almost as soon as the sound of Charlie's whistling died away Jed heard something else. At first he thought it might be the dog working his way out of the thicket, but he soon realized that a little dog couldn't make that much noise.

Jed curled his finger around the trigger of his rifle and stood stock-still, trying to see into the waves of light, rolling mist that veiled the lowland. For a minute he heard nothing, and then he heard the crackle of dead branches and a crash as if someone had fallen down.

"Halt!" Jed called. "Who is that out there?"

There was no answer.

"Come forward and make yourself known," Jed called, "or I'll start shooting."

Then a voice spoke up. It was a child's voice. "Go ahead, Yankee," the voice said.

Jed lowered his rifle. "You come out here fast," he yelled.

There was no answer. Jed held his rifle loosely in one hand and moved forward. It came to him that maybe this was some kind of trap. He found his way to where the dog had been, but he wasn't there any more. He stood listening. Suddenly the dog began to yelp. Jed moved forward, following the sound. He went through the thicket to a little clearing on the other side. There he saw a young boy sitting on a log and looking mad enough to

chew nails. He was bareheaded, his hair was the color of corn silk and his eyes were blue. The little dog was sitting at his feet and didn't make a sound as Jed walked up.

"What are you doing here?" Jed asked him.

The boy tilted his tan face up to Jed and looked at him with pure hate in his eyes. "Nothin' that matters to you," he said. "I woke up early and went out with my dog."

"It matters plenty to me," Jed said. "You should stay clear of this camp. It's lucky you didn't get shot."

"I need no Yankee mercy, soldier," the boy said.

Jed could feel himself getting hot under the collar. "You mind your tongue, boy," he said. "There are pickets all around this camp and some of them have itching trigger fingers."

"I hate Yankees," the boy said, "and most of all I hate Yankee soldiers. My pa's a Confederate soldier."

"Then I don't blame you for hating Yankee soldiers," Jed said, "but there's no call to get yourself shot to prove it."

He looked down at the blond head and at the dog sitting trustingly by the boy's feet. "Now you get up and cut out of here as fast as your legs will carry you," he said. "I go off duty soon and you'd best not be here when the next man comes around."

The dog got up and limped toward Jed, wagging his tail and looking up. He leaned down and gave the dog a pat. "Now take your dog and git," he said. "Walk straight out that way. Don't circle around or you're liable to get shot by one of the other pickets."

The boy sat on the log, not saying a word or making a move. Finally he said, "I can't walk. I fell in a chuckhole and when I walk my leg near kills me."

Jed faced the boy, holding his rifle in one hand, his other hand in a fist on his hip. He gazed at him thoughtfully.

"How far do you live from here?" he asked.

"Two or three miles I guess," the boy said, "but I'm not likely to tell you which way. You'd bring those other Yankees around to steal our pigs and chickens and burn our buildings."

"Well, you can't crawl home," Jed said. "Maybe your leg is broken. I better take you to our surgeon and get him to fix you up."

"If you're a mind to shoot me," the boy said, "shoot me here. No use to drag me back to that Yankee camp."

Jed found it hard to keep a straight face. "Now don't be a fool," he said. "Even Yankees don't shoot children."

He moved forward and reached out his hand so the boy could hang on and hop to the willow tree. "Come on," he said, "there's no use fighting me."

The boy drew back his hand. "Not while there's a breath in me," he said.

Jed turned on his heel. "You can't go far on a broken leg," he said, "and I don't have the heart to leave a tad like you to starve. You think things over. I'll come back later to see if you've changed your mind."

He walked back to the willow tree and looked around and listened and settled back against the tree.

His relief came about half an hour later when the sun had burned the mist away and stood like a red ball in the east.

"Well, how you been, Davy?" Jed asked the boy.

"Fine, Jed boy," his relief said. "I thought maybe you died of the fever, I haven't seen you for so long."

Davy was no taller than Jed, but he was thicker, and he had a bullet-shaped head. Jed looked him up and down. "I have a fever that makes me ache to get out of here and fight this war to a finish," he said.

"You ain't just waggin' your tongue, Jed boy," Davy said. "Most anything is better than this."

Jed hesitated and looked into Davy's eyes. "Davy," he said.

"What is it, boy?" Davy asked.

"Well, it might be hard to believe," Jed said, suddenly talking very fast, "but there's a little boy out there past that thicket. He's hurt his leg and I got to take him to the surgeon to get him fixed up. Maybe the surgeon can figure out a way to get him home without kicking up a fuss with Captain Pike and all. I'd like it if you could keep this a secret."

"Why, all right," Davy said. "How old is the boy?"

" 'Bout eight or nine I guess," Jed said. "I hav-

en't heard him stir since I found him, so he must still be there."

"Maybe it's some trick," Davy said.

"I thought of that," Jed said, "but I can't figure out what kind of trick it would be. Anyway I don't think he's play-acting."

"Well, go ahead and get him," Davy said. "If it was me I'd let the little Rebel crawl back home."

"Now you don't mean that, surely," Jed said.

from FARMER BOY

Laura Ingalls Wilder

Farmer Boy is the one book in the Wilder series devoted to the Wilder family. The other seven, beginning with Little House in the Big Woods, *are concerned with the adventures of the Ingalls family as it pioneers westward into new country. In the last three books, beginning with* The Long Winter, *the Ingalls family and Almanzo Wilder meet and share the same vicissitudes and adventures. Laura marries Almanzo and later writes this wonderful series of books, a saga of pioneering in this country. The Fourth of July described in the following episode must have been about 1867. One of the important things Almanzo Wilder's father did for his son was to give him a sense of values. Children will be interested perhaps in a comparison of prices then and now.*

Independence Day

Almanzo was eating breakfast before he remembered that this was the Fourth of July. He felt more cheerful.

It was like Sunday morning. After breakfast he scrubbed his face with soft soap till it shone, and he parted his wet hair and combed it sleekly down. He put on his sheep's-gray trousers and his shirt of French calico, and his vest and his short round coat.

Mother had made his new suit in the new style. The coat fastened at the throat with a little flap of the cloth, then the two sides slanted back to show his vest, and they rounded off over his trousers' pockets.

He put on his round straw hat, which Mother

From *Farmer Boy* by Laura Ingalls Wilder. Copyright 1933 Harper & Brothers. Reprinted with permission of Rose Wilder Lane, Harper & Row, and Lutterworth Press had made of braided oat-straws, and he was all dressed up for Independence Day. He felt very fine.

Father's shining horses were hitched to the shining, red-wheeled buggy, and they all drove away in the cool sunshine. All the country had a holiday air. Nobody was working in the fields, and along the road the people in their Sunday clothes were driving to town.

Father's swift horses passed them all. They passed by wagons and carts and buggies. They passed gray horses and black horses and dappled-gray horses. Almanzo waved his hat whenever he sailed past anyone he knew, and he would have been perfectly happy if only he had been driving that swift, beautiful team.

At the church sheds in Malone he helped Father unhitch. Mother and the girls and Royal hurried away. But Almanzo would rather help with the horses than do anything else. He couldn't drive them, but he could tie their halters and buckle on their blankets, and stroke their soft noses and give them hay.

Then he went out with Father and they walked on the crowded sidewalks. All the stores were closed, but ladies and gentlemen were walking up and down and talking. Ruffled little girls carried parasols, and all the boys were dressed up, like Almanzo. Flags were everywhere, and in the Square the band was playing "Yankee Doodle." The fifes tooted and the flutes shrilled and the drums came in with rub-a-dub-dub.

> "Yankee Doodle went to town,
>   Riding on a pony,
> He stuck a feather in his hat,
>   And called it macaroni!"

Even grown-ups had to keep time to it. And there, in the corner of the Square, were the two brass cannons!

The Square was not really square. The railroad made it three-cornered. But everybody called it the Square, anyway. It was fenced, and grass grew there. Benches stood in rows on the grass, and people were filing between the benches and sitting down as they did in church.

Almanzo went with Father to one of the best front seats. All the important men stopped to shake hands with Father. The crowd kept coming till all the seats were full, and still there were people outside the fence.

The band stopped playing, and the minister prayed. Then the band tuned up again and everybody rose. Men and boys took off their hats. The band played, and everybody sang.

> "Oh, say, can you see by the dawn's early light,
>   What so proudly we hailed at the twilight's
>   last gleaming,
> Whose broad stripes and bright stars through
>   the perilous night,
>   O'er the ramparts we watched were so gal-
>   lantly streaming?"

From the top of the flagpole, up against the blue sky, the Stars and Stripes were fluttering. Everybody looked at the American flag, and Almanzo sang with all his might.

Then everyone sat down, and a Congressman stood up on the platform. Slowly and solemnly he read the Declaration of Independence.

"When in the course of human events it becomes necessary for one people . . . to assume among the powers of the earth the separate and equal station. . . . We hold these truths to be self-evident, that all men are created equal. . . ."

Almanzo felt solemn and very proud.

Then two men made long political speeches. One believed in high tariffs, and one believed in free trade. All the grown-ups listened hard, but Almanzo did not understand the speeches very well and he began to be hungry. He was glad when the band played again.

The music was so gay; the bandsmen in their blue and red and their brass buttons tootled merrily, and the fat drummer beat rat-a-tat-tat on the drum. All the flags were fluttering and everybody was happy, because they were free and independent and this was Independence Day. And it was time to eat dinner.

Almanzo helped Father feed the horses while Mother and the girls spread the picnic lunch on the grass in the churchyard. Many others were picnicking there, too, and after he had eaten all he could Almanzo went back to the Square.

There was a lemonade-stand by the hitching-posts. A man sold pink lemonade, a nickel a glass, and a crowd of the town boys were standing around him. Cousin Frank was there. Almanzo had a drink at the town pump, but Frank said he was going to buy lemonade. He had a nickel. He walked up to the stand and bought a glass of the pink lemonade and drank it slowly. He smacked his lips and rubbed his stomach and said:

"Mmmm! Why don't you buy some?"

"Where'd you get the nickel?" Almanzo asked. He had never had a nickel. Father gave him a penny every Sunday to put in the collection-box in church; he had never had any other money.

"My father gave it to me," Frank bragged. "My father gives me a nickel every time I ask him."

"Well, so would my father if I asked him," said Almanzo.

"Well, why don't you ask him?" Frank did not believe that Father would give Almanzo a nickel. Almanzo did not know whether Father would, or not.

"Because I don't want to," he said.

"He wouldn't give you a nickel," Frank said.

"He would, too."

"I dare you to ask him," Frank said. The other boys were listening. Almanzo put his hands in his pockets and said:

"I'd just as lief ask him if I wanted to."

"Yah, you're scared!" Frank jeered. "Double dare! Double dare!"

Father was a little way down the street, talking to Mr. Paddock, the wagon maker. Almanzo walked slowly toward them. He was faint-hearted, but he had to go. The nearer he got to Father, the more he dreaded asking for a nickel. He had never before thought of doing such a thing. He was sure Father would not give it to him.

He waited till Father stopped talking and looked at him.

"What is it, son?" Father asked.

Almanzo was scared. "Father," he said.

"Well, son?"

"Father," Almanzo said, "would you—would you give me—a nickel?"

He stood there while Father and Mr. Paddock looked at him, and he wished he could get away. Finally Father asked:

"What for?"

Almanzo looked down at his moccasins and muttered:

"Frank had a nickel. He bought pink lemonade."

"Well," Father said, slowly, "if Frank treated you, it's only right you should treat him." Father put his hand in his pocket. Then he stopped and asked:

"Did Frank treat you to lemonade?"

Almanzo wanted so badly to get the nickel that he nodded. Then he squirmed and said:

"No, Father."

Father looked at him a long time. Then he took out his wallet and opened it, and slowly he took out a round, big silver half-dollar. He asked:

"Almanzo, do you know what this is?"

"Half a dollar," Almanzo answered.

"Yes. But do you know what half a dollar is?"

Almanzo didn't know it was anything but half a dollar.

"It's work, son," Father said. "That's what money is; it's hard work."

Mr. Paddock chuckled. "The boy's too young, Wilder," he said. "You can't make a youngster understand that."

"Almanzo's smarter than you think," said Father.

Almanzo didn't understand at all. He wished he could get away. But Mr. Paddock was looking at Father just as Frank looked at Almanzo when he double-dared him, and Father had said Almanzo was smart, so Almanzo tried to look like a smart boy. Father asked:

"You know how to raise potatoes, Almanzo?"

"Yes," Almanzo said.

"Say you have a seed potato in the spring, what do you do with it?"

"You cut it up," Almanzo said.

"Go on, son."

"Then you harrow—first you manure the field, and plow it. Then you harrow, and mark the ground. And plant the potatoes, and plow them, and hoe them. You plow and hoe them twice."

"That's right, son. And then?"

"Then you dig them and put them down cellar."

"Yes. Then you pick them over all winter; you throw out all the little ones and the rotten ones. Come spring, you load them up and haul them here to Malone, and you sell them. And if you get a good price, son, how much do you get to show for all that work? How much do you get for half a bushel of potatoes?"

"Half a dollar," Almanzo said.

"Yes," said Father. "That's what's in this half-dollar, Almanzo. The work that raised half a bushel of potatoes is in it."

Almanzo looked at the round piece of money that Father held up. It looked small, compared with all that work.

"You can have it, Almanzo," Father said. Almanzo could hardly believe his ears. Father gave him the heavy half-dollar.

"It's yours," said Father. "You could buy a sucking pig with it, if you want to. You could raise it, and it would raise a litter of pigs, worth four, five dollars apiece. Or you can trade that half-dollar for lemonade, and drink it up. You do as you want, it's your money."

Almanzo forgot to say thank you. He held the half-dollar a minute, then he put his hand in his pocket and went back to the boys by the lemonade-stand. The man was calling out,

"Step this way, step this way! Ice-cold lemonade, pink lemonade, only five cents a glass! Only half a dime, ice-cold pink lemonade! The twentieth part of a dollar!"

Frank asked Almanzo:

"Where's the nickel?"

"He didn't give me a nickel," said Almanzo, and Frank yelled:

"Yah, yah! I told you he wouldn't! I told you so!"

"He gave me half a dollar," said Almanzo.

The boys wouldn't believe it till he showed them. Then they crowded around, waiting for him to spend it. He showed it to them all, and put it back in his pocket.

"I'm going to look around," he said, "and buy me a good little sucking pig."

The band came marching down the street, and they all ran along beside it. The flag was gloriously waving in front, then came the buglers blowing and the fifers tootling and the drummer rattling the drumsticks on the drum. Up the street and down the street went the band, with all the boys following it, and then it stopped in the Square by the brass cannons.

Hundreds of people were there, crowding to watch.

The cannons sat on their haunches, pointing their long barrels upward. The band kept on playing. Two men kept shouting, "Stand back! Stand back!" and other men were pouring black powder into the cannons' muzzles and pushing it down with wads of cloth on long rods.

The iron rods had two handles, and two men pushed and pulled on them, driving the black powder down the brass barrels. Then all the boys ran to pull grass and weeds along the railroad tracks. They carried them by armfuls to the cannons, and the men crowded the weeds into the cannons' muzzles and drove them down with the long rods.

A bonfire was burning by the railroad tracks, and long iron rods were heating in it.

When all the weeds and grass had been packed tight against the powder in the cannons, a man took a little more powder in his hand and carefully filled the two little touchholes in the barrels. Now everybody was shouting.

"Stand back! Stand back!"

Mother took hold of Almanzo's arm and made him come away with her. He told her:

"Aw, Mother, they're only loaded with powder and weeds. I won't get hurt, Mother. I'll be careful, honest." But she made him come away from the cannons.

Two men took the long iron rods from the fire.

Everybody was still, watching. Standing as far behind the cannons as they could, the two men stretched out the rods and touched their red-hot tips to the touchholes. A little flame like a candle-flame flickered up from the powder. The little flames stood there burning; nobody breathed. Then—BOOM!

The cannons leaped backward, the air was full of flying grass and weeds. Almanzo ran with all the other boys to feel the warm muzzles of the cannons. Everybody was exclaiming about what a loud noise they had made.

"That's the noise that made the Redcoats run!" Mr. Paddock said to Father.

"Maybe," Father said, tugging his beard. "But it was muskets that won the Revolution. And don't forget it was axes and plows that made this country."

"That's so, come to think of it," Mr. Paddock said.

Independence Day was over. The cannons had been fired, and there was nothing more to do but hitch up the horses and drive home to do the chores.

That night when they were going to the house with the milk, Almanzo asked Father,

"Father, how was it axes and plows that made this country? Didn't we fight England for it?"

"We fought for Independence, son," Father said. "But all the land our forefathers had was a little strip of country, here between the mountains and the ocean. All the way from here west was Indian country, and Spanish and French and English country. It was farmers that took all that country and made it America."

"How?" Almanzo asked.

"Well, son, the Spaniards were soldiers, and high-and-mighty gentlemen that only wanted gold. And the French were fur-traders, wanting to make quick money. And England was busy fighting wars. But we were farmers, son; we wanted the land. It was farmers that went over the mountains, and cleared the land, and settled it, and farmed it, and hung on to their farms.

"This country goes three thousand miles west, now. It goes 'way out beyond Kansas, and beyond the Great American Desert, over mountains bigger than these mountains, and down to the Pacific Ocean. It's the biggest country in the world, and it was farmers who took all that country and made it America, son. Don't you ever forget that."

Realistic Literature and Children

Because this volume concerns itself with realistic stories, the discussion which follows centers around the values of such books in the life of a child. It is not meant to be inclusive but should be read in relationship to the values of realism. However, on occasion, other types of books will be mentioned, since books do not lend themselves to exclusiveness, no matter how hard one tries to keep the field narrowed. The discussion comprises two parts: pages 224-228, somewhat revised, are from the 1961 edition of *Time for True Tales; pages* 228-241 have been written for this revision.

1. TIME AND THE CHILD

Only grownups know the swiftness of time's passing. To children and young people it moves as slowly as a snail, with long intervals when nothing seems to happen. In those intervals between play and routines, a child needs something to feed upon. Food for the body is essential, but there must also be food for the mind and spirit of a child. And what does a child find to feed upon in this modern age! He may turn to soap operas, television cowboys, the comics, or little gilded books with abbreviated content—pacifiers, not food, designed to kill time, not to fill it richly and fully. If he turns to these pacifiers, it is often because many adults have no respect for their child's time. They say, "Don't bother me just now. Go turn on the television." Or they ask, "Where is that pretty book I bought for you at the grocery store?" They don't even remember the title. It doesn't matter. It is just something to keep the child occupied and out of the way. Yet who should know better than adults the touching swiftness with which childhood passes? And who should be more aware than they of its exuberant eagerness, its hungry curiosities? What happens to a child's dreams and his hungers if he is fed only intellectual chaff? And what may happen if his curiosities are met with strong books which feed his young spirit and give him something to grow on?

Clifton Fadiman, in exploring modern books for children, makes this statement:

Consider, though, how little the child actually *does* read. Librarians estimate that about 500 books represent the *maximum* the average child can get through between seven and fourteen. That's about 70 per year. Hence the child simply cannot afford the commonplace.[1]

It has been over fifteen years since Mr. Fadiman made the above observation, and several new factors have entered the picture to make that observation more true today than when it was originally made. Each new year more and more juvenile books are published, at least fifty or more of which are worthy of being considered "must" reading. So while the number of books which can be read in childhood remains constant, or decreases, the number of books to choose from increases. At the same time, middle-class children have less time to read. They are pressured by the new teaching techniques, working harder and longer than any previous school generation; and they are pressured by parents to participate in numerous outside activities. There are scout troops, dancing lessons, tennis lessons, trips to the orthodontist, Little League baseball, *ad infinitum.* What few hours a child has left to be alone become even more precious. For the slum child, beautifully illustrated books shown in classrooms and libraries and well-told stories may provide the only sources of genuine beauty in his life.

All adults—parents, teachers, librarians, camp counselors, scout leaders—who are in a position to offer reading guidance to children should believe that no second-rate book can provide so much enjoyment as a first-rate book. They should also understand that there *is* a right time to read a juvenile book. No adult, however simpatico, finds quite the same level of enjoyment in books like *Henry Huggins* (see Bibliography, p. 247) and *Homer Price* (see p. 104) as eight- and ten-year-olds do. Once we are safely launched into the world of adult reading, it does not matter if we read *War and Peace* at twenty-five or thirty-five. In fact, a good case can be made for delaying such reading on the grounds that the greater the book, the more experience we should bring to it. The point is that both adult and juvenile read-

[1] Clifton Fadiman, "Party of One," *Holiday,* August 1952, p. 6

ing should add something to the reader's life, and not merely take up a period of his time.

In Part One, we introduce children to a variety of good books, not because we think books, like vitamins, are good for them, but because we want to offer children a chance to grow within themselves. In childhood, all the externals of a child's life are controlled; only within his own mind can he begin to grow as an individual. It is our goal as adults in a child's world to inspire an "inner growth" by making available good books; the role of offering good books should not be seen as an adult conspiracy to force something upon children.

2. BOOKS AND CHILDREN'S NEEDS

How can adults learn to know and select the best reading for children from the enormous mass of juvenile books available? First, adults must understand that children should find in reading vicarious satisfaction for their basic needs. In the opening chapter of *Children and Books*[2] there is a full discussion of those needs and the kinds of books which help to meet them. For example, *security*—physical, material, emotional, spiritual, and intellectual—continues to be a basic need, especially in an age of social unrest, wars, and atom bombs. Children and men alike dream of being safe, comfortable, wealthy, and wise. It is the superman dream that persists no matter how far short of the goal individuals and the world may fall. Fairy tale fantasies on the one hand and the biographies of real heroes on the other minister to this dream and keep young spirits soaring.

The *need to achieve*, to do or to be something worthy of admiration, is even more pressing than the need for security. This is fortunate, or the human race would grow too cautious to survive. Stories built around adventure, from *The Tale of Peter Rabbit* to *Treasure Island,* satisfy this need grandly. Stories for the oldest children, along with adventurous action, begin to emphasize moral achievement. Johnny Tremain aban-

dons his plans for revenge in a self-forgetting absorption in the pre-Revolutionary War plots. Achievement has progressed from riding up a glass hill to moral victory over self.

The *need to belong,* to be an accepted and liked member of a group, motivates the child's desire to achieve and is a part of the maturing process. Stories about family life, neighborhood and gang activities, are built around this need to be a part of a social group as well as around the child's *need to love and to be loved.* These latter needs give rise presently to the romance literature of adolescence.

But neither life nor the child is always in earnest, and there seems to be a healthy rhythm of work and play rising out of a basic *need for change.* Humorous verses and stories meet this desire for fun and change, either realistically as in "The Story of Johnny Head-in-Air"[3] and *The Adventures of Tom Sawyer* (see p. 116), or fantastically as in "Alas, Alack!" and in such tall tales as *Pecos Bill.*

And, finally, there is the *need for aesthetic satisfaction.* We know that children are lusty little animals, but we know that they are far more than this. They reach out for beauty as well as for food. They respond to the beauty of the world around them and to the beauty of decent human beings doing the best they can, and to the varied expressions of this beauty and goodness as we find them in the arts. So children need to discover in books this nebulous experience that we call aesthetic satisfaction—a sense of the significance of life in terms so arresting and so beautiful that life takes on richer meaning.

This brief review of children's basic needs omits one important consideration—namely, that no two children bring precisely the same needs and interests to a book. One child may be developing happily and normally in his social relationships but with a tight literalness of mind that knows nothing about imaginative play and brooks no nonsense. Such a child needs imaginative beauty in his reading, a little fantasy and sheer hilarity to keep him flexible. Another child is pampered and, therefore, is socially immature. He needs stories that will help him to see him-

[2] May Hill Arbuthnot, *Children and Books,* Scott, Foresman, 1964, rev. ed., Chapter 1

[3] May Hill Arbuthnot and Shelton L. Root, Jr., *Time for Poetry,* Third General Edition: "The Story of Johnny Head-in-Air," p. 135; "Alas, Alack!" p. 124

self in relation to other people and to develop increasing social responsibility. The withdrawing child, the overly aggressive one, the indecisive or the insensitive youngsters are all victims of maladjustment to the tasks with which they are confronted. Probably books alone cannot cure their maladjustments, but two things are certain: trashy, trivial, or second-rate reading may afford these children temporary entertainment and escape from their problems, but it will give them no insight into dealing with those problems. On the other hand, strong books, worth-while books, even while they entertain young readers, will also supply them with clues to a better understanding of themselves and other people.

3. QUALITIES THAT MAKE A CHILD'S BOOK WORTH WHILE

Probably no two people would agree upon all the qualities that must go into a book for children to make it worth while. But there may be a few qualities, without which, most people would agree, no book can hope to win the approval of both children and critics of literature.

If children were literary analysts, they would probably insist that the first requisite of a good story is lively *action* or *plot*. It is true that children accept and even like gentle, charming stories without plot, especially if they are illustrated, but the prime favorites, the stories that survive for generations, the stories children wear out with rereading or wear out the grownups with rereading or retelling are plot stories. Such favorites as "The Three Little Pigs," *Millions of Cats, The Adventures of Tom Sawyer* (see p. 116), *Caddie Woodlawn* (see p. 212), all have lively plots, with a great deal happening and with the heroes progressing merrily from deed to deed or escapade to escapade. Even the long descriptions in the idyllic *The Wind in the Willows* are endured by children because of the unexpected scrapes Toad gets into and the exciting action involved in getting him out.

The stream of consciousness style of writing, the stories which begin in the middle and end

up in the air, may pass with adults, but they won't with children. They like stories which have a brisk introduction that launches the plot, a development full of action and growing suspense, and a conclusion that settles everything, including the villain.

An interesting *idea* or *theme* is essential to the development of a good plot. The theme is not always easy to define, but one explanation is that it is the motivating idea of the whole story. *Treasure Island,* for example, has a theme clearly indicated in the title and one sufficiently robust to support a thriller whose popularity has never waned in the more than eighty years of its existence. *The Good Master* (see p. 149) is a gentle, juvenile version of Shakespeare's *The Taming of the Shrew* theme. But whether or not a theme can be readily defined, it is the backbone of a story. The absence of a dominant idea results in a lot of the "so what?" type of stories that may be beautifully illustrated and momentarily entertaining but that will soon be forgotten.

Another characteristic of a superior book for children is *unique and memorable characters.* Stereotypes are soon forgotten, but unique, salty, vivid characters capture the imagination and affection of young readers. Rumpelstiltskin, Padre Porko, Br'er Rabbit, Ping, Smoky, Pinocchio, Huck Finn, Heidi and her grandfather, Long John Silver, Young Fu, Hetty and Hank, the Defender, Jerome Kildee—such characters as these are not easily forgotten. They add spice to reading and to life. Young readers are apt to say, "Oh, I wish I could have known"—Kate or Caddie or Tom or Jancsi or whoever the character happens to be. Or, when they are grown up, they still chuckle over the wickedness of Long John Silver or the pranks and cockiness of Br'er Rabbit. Book characters like these broaden children's understandings and deepen their responses to people, animals, and life in general.

The fourth requisite of a first-rate story is that nebulous quality called *style.* Unfortunately, the lack of good prose style is not always noticed, particularly in the field of children's books, but a good style makes itself felt in many ways. The text moves and flows smoothly. Reading is effortless and agreeable, not because of a denuded vocabulary and short sentences, but because words and meaning are compatible and the phrasing is staccato or sonorous, serene or brisk, according to mood and meaning. If the text reads aloud delightfully, it has good prose style. Folk tales are obvious examples of this. Notice their dramatic dialogues, which characterize without descriptions. Sometimes the narrative has a cadenced swing, sometimes it is literally in a minor key. The beginnings often set the mood and tempo of the whole story, and the conclusions are likewise gay or grave or romantic in the mood of the adventure. There are similar virtues in the modern fairy tales. The books of Dr. Seuss or A. A. Milne or Wanda Gág cry out for reading aloud, so delightful is their style. In the field of realism the style is different but may be equally well done. The laconic vernacular of *Smoky* (see p. 26) suits the story. Not a word of *The Adventures of Tom Sawyer* (see p. 116) can be changed to advantage.

There are, of course, other requisites to good fiction[4] such as close unity of interest centered in the theme, a decent economy of incidents, and balanced proportions in the parts of the story. These contribute, too, but for a child's story, the essentials are *plot* growing out of a worth-while *theme, memorable characters,* and *distinguished style.*

4. VALUES FROM BOOKS

Assuming that grownups know something about the basic needs of children in general and the particular needs of individual children, and that they also have adequate criteria for judging the worth of poetry, stories, and biography for children, what may they hope for from a program of exposing children in their early years to good literature? What should fine books do for children?

Insight into living

One virtue of good reading is that it widens the child's limited experience and teaches him more about himself and others. Intensely per-

[4] For a detailed discussion of these, see May Hill Arbuthnot, *Children and Books,* Chapter 2

sonal in his interests, the small child identifies himself with story characters. *He* is the wise, clever pig. No wolf can get him. He would never think of being as foolish as Henny Penny or Budulinek. He would outwit them all, like Br'er Rabbit, or astonish them like Charley. By way of stories, the child discovers that prying curiosity or irresponsibility may get him into hot water. But though these gay, first stories show him the cause and effect of behavior or teach him manners and morals, they do so with a smile.

As the child and his reading mature together, he begins to see himself with ever widening social relationships and social responsibilities. Ellen Tebbits pays dearly and absurdly for an inadvertent misrepresentation. The Wilder boy (see p. 217) learns the meaning of money in terms of human labor. Standards of home life, of loyalty to a friend or a member of the family, family struggles, and family frolics may become part of a child's social concepts as a result of his reading.

As the young reader acquires a widening knowledge of people, he also explores the world of nature, of pets, and of wild animals—especially of animals that exist in a secret world and order of their own. He soon discovers that some people and animals enjoy security while others must face dangerous insecurity, that some people and animals are accepted and others rejected by the group they value. Gradually, from the vicarious experiences of reading, the child's insight into his own personal problems grows and his understanding of people and creatures outside his immediate experience is enormously increased.

Reverence for life

That remarkable and dedicated man, Albert Schweitzer, used the phrase "reverence for life" as the summation of his philosophy of living. In this day of wars, atom bombs, and a growing callousness toward violence and death, "reverence for life . . . all life capable of development" is an ideal to cherish for ourselves and for our children. It is an extension of our own self-respect and self-love to a respect and love for others. Good books reinforce this attitude toward life without sermonizing. *The Blind Colt* (see p. 13) and *Kildee House* (see p. 39), for example, leave children not only with a better understanding of animal life but also with a deep sympathy and tenderness for animals. *The Defender* (see p. 50), with its unforgettable account of the hunted mountain rams, also gives a picture of social injustice which rouses the reader's pity for the misjudged and rejected man. Books which show animals or men suffering from cruelty or misunderstanding, or sacrificing themselves for another's welfare, build in young readers an abiding reverence for the valiant spirit that won't be downed.

Zest for life

Finally, most children come into the world with exuberant energy and a zest for life that is glorious to behold. Before they have reached maturity these may be sadly diminished, which is unfortunate. Life can be tragic or dull, but it can also be triumphant and gay. Sometimes it is downright comic. Also, human beings are endowed with a mechanism denied to animals, namely laughter, and it is good for man to use all of his endowments. So children should discover in their experience with books some reasons for laughter. There are drolls in fairy tales, humor and nonsense in poetry, and delicious absurdities in realistic stories and even in biography. Top off a dull day by reading a selection from this rich store. "Life is real and life is earnest" for most of us most of the time. But the therapy of laughter is a healthy medicine to be administered frequently. Some forgotten philosopher from the teaching profession once said, "Count the day lost in which your children have not laughed." Sometimes a smile or even a sudden twinkle in the eye means as much as a laugh. It means that tensions are broken and the young spirit is relaxed and at ease. A renewed zest for life will soon follow.

These, then, are some of the desirable results of good reading. Supply the child with worthwhile, entertaining reading; share it with him, and he will gain *insight* into his own behavior, his social relationships, and his responsibilities. He will grow in *reverence for life* and in sensitivity to beauty and goodness. And he will keep his *zest for life* and the gift of laughter.

5. TODAY'S CHILD

Not so many years ago the majority of Americans lived their entire lives in or very near the place of their birth. The man who wandered too far from his birthplace was looked upon as suspect; the man who changed his job more than twice in his working life was considered unstable. Social studies teachers made classes memorize the names and capitals of the then forty-eight states, but almost as an exercise; no one was expected to ever put the information to personal use.

All this has changed in recent times. It began with the Depression when families were forced to move in search of work; it was intensified with World War II when vital war industries actively lured people away from the rural areas to work in war plants in or near large cities. With the mechanization of farms, more and more young people have been forced to move to urban areas in order to survive.

These economic factors are, basically, beyond the control of man. Other economic factors have entered the picture, by design, so to speak. Large corporations now have branch offices across the country, and the transferring of personnel is a set policy. For the man on his way up, being transferred is accepted as a way of life. Add to these business families the thousands of armed forces families who are regularly shifted around the country and the globe, and we have millions of Americans on the move.

This mobility is economic in nature. Another factor is added with the advent of jet travel, which has made every section of these United States and foreign lands a matter of mere hours away from each other. Chartered air flights have made air travel within the budgets of millions of families, and so vacations are no longer limited to a trip to the nearby seashore or mountains. The child growing up in the Midwest can reasonably expect to see either or both of the great oceans; the child of the East may well be exposed to the beauty of the Ozark Mountains and the grandeur of the Rockies. Old Faithful and the Grand Canyon are no longer mere names or photographs in a geography book.

Countless thousands of other families have become enamored of the camping craze and they too set out each summer to see America. The great muddy Mississippi ceases to be something one read about in *The Adventures of Tom Sawyer;* Colonial Williamsburg or Sturbridge, Massachusetts, brings alive the way of life lived by *Johnny Tremain;* and as one rides across the Oklahoma-Texas Panhandle or up the mountain passes, a new appreciation is born for the courageous men and women who crossed the country without benefit of high-speed, air-conditioned automobiles. In a way which our forefathers could only dream about, the collection of states has truly become a Union.

This is the physical mobility which permeates our society. But there is another mobility at work: upward (social) mobility. America has long prided itself on the idea that a man born in a log cabin could become President of the United States. However lowly a man's birth, he could go as far as his talents and willingness to work could take him. There was always a measure of truth to this belief; but today, the truth is being broadened. A Roman Catholic has been President; Negroes have been members of the President's cabinet and the United States Supreme Court; and a Jew has represented our country in the United Nations. Barriers fall slowly, but fall they do.

6. TEACHING TODAY'S CHILD TO LIVE IN HIS WORLD

All this places an added burden on teachers, parents, librarians, and all who work with youth. It is no longer enough to try to teach children to live in their current environment, but to prepare them to live wherever and with whomever they find themselves. No adult who really loves children would deliberately or unconsciously limit their knowledge of the many types of people and ways of life which exist throughout our country and the world.

To allow a child to grow up without respect for other people; to burden him with bigotry; to mislead him into thinking that those who differ from himself are automatically of some lower class; to encourage him to believe that his way of life is not only the best way, but the one all people would choose were they given a choice,

is a great injustice to the child. Even if he is not going to leave his immediate environment this year or in the next five or ten years, it is the adult's responsibility to prepare him for that day when he is faced with the wider world.

What is the role of books in all this? Paul Hazard has said it best:

> Yes, children's books keep alive a sense of nationality; but they also keep alive a sense of humanity. They describe their native land lovingly, but they also describe faraway lands where unknown brothers live. They understand the essential quality of their own race; but each of them is a messenger that goes beyond mountains and rivers, beyond the seas, to the very ends of the world in search of new friendships. Every country gives and every country receives—innumerable are the exchanges—and so it comes about that in our first impressionable years the universal republic of childhood is born.[5]

This is a mighty task, one that can be fulfilled only by the very best of books.

7. CHARACTERISTICS OF A GOOD BOOK

The most important characteristic of a good book is that it gives us pleasure while reading it. Pleasure, however, is a strange word in the average American's vocabulary and needs some clarification. In our society, pleasure seems to be reserved for the frivolous; our pragmatic philosophy seems to divide the world into two parts: those things we must do, and those things we like to do. The first are not expected to give us pleasure, and the second are not expected to be genuinely worth while. This is a simplification, but one that could be defended in any lengthy discussion. What concerns us here is the effects this attitude has upon our approach to books.

Pleasure is, of course, a particularly personal reaction. It influences our decisions about the careers we pursue, the way we live, the music

[5] Paul Hazard, *Books, Children and Men,* Horn Book, Inc., 1944, p. 146

we listen to, the art we hang on our walls; and no two people ever have the same tastes in all things.

In discussing the pleasure of reading, we must keep in mind this peculiarly personal nature of the relationship between book and reader. At the same time, we must recognize that a book becomes popular when it gives pleasure to a large number of readers; while another book, equally well written, may provide pleasure for a much more limited audience. Let us look at some of the kinds of enjoyment books give.

There is the from-the-tip-of-the-toes-to-the-top-of-the-head, crinkly feeling-good-all-over joy that comes with a book like *Did You Carry the Flag Today, Charley?* (see p. 65) or *Jennifer, Hecate, Macbeth, William McKinley, and Me, Elizabeth* (see p. 119). There are the unabashed tears shed for Marguerite Henry's horse-heroes; the spell-binding suspense of a Rosemary Sutcliff historical novel; the feeling of being hunted with the Georges' *Vulpes the Red Fox* (see Bibliography, p. 245); and the sense of satisfaction when *Roosevelt Grady* (see p. 93) and *Skinny* (see p. 77) triumph, each in his own way.

Pleasure is not all laughter. It is the act of becoming so involved with the characters in a book that their feelings are our feelings. We laugh, cry, triumph, or fail with them. It is being part of another person for a short time that provides pleasure for most confirmed readers. By being able to lose ourselves in another person we emerge different people, we grow and mature a little each time it happens, and the act of maturing provides us with the ultimate pleasure, although few of us are ever fully conscious of the process.

Almost all the world's great writers and philosophers have written moving testimonials to the power of books, but whether they wrote poems or lengthy philosophical discourses, the idea is always the same: books set us free. We can wander the world at will; we are not confined to our time and place in history. Today we can live in ancient Rome, tomorrow in outer space. We can share the thrills of a sports contest in Decker's *Hit and Run* (see Bibliography, p. 247) and delight in Harriet's testing her wits against her parents. This freedom provides a very special sense of satisfaction, for it enables us to be less concerned with the pettiness of life and to be more involved with its magic.

The confirmed reader may not have fewer problems than the nonreader, but he feels less oppressed by them. It is this sense of enrichment through books which we try to give young people so that they may grow to be happier adults.

Pleasure, then, comes from many types of books and in various forms. But no book, however great, gives pleasure to everyone. The challenge in reading guidance is to find the right book for the reader without trying to impose our own tastes on others—children or adults.

For example, in the one hundred years since its publication, *Little Women* has given millions of girls and some boys untold pleasure. But for some children it is an exasperating book, often begun, never finished, just as some adults never do finish Proust's *Remembrance of Things Past*, despite all good intentions. Determining why one book becomes the favorite of some readers and the bugbear of others would probably require a psychiatrist's analysis.

Not all adults and not all children are going to agree on every book's worth. Some adults will find *Ellen Grae* (see p. 101) a distasteful book; so will some children. However, for some children and some adults, *Ellen Grae* has the magical quality and vitality they find missing in *Little Women*. Certainly, neither Jo March nor Ellen is a paragon of mental health; but just as Jo has vitality for those who like her, so Ellen delights a number of readers, young and old. Isn't there room on library shelves and in classrooms for both heroines? We would hope so, since to attract a wide range of readers we must have a wide range of books, none of which will appeal to everyone, each of which will probably appeal to some reader.

In talking about "good" books, we can almost reduce the discussion to a Parkinson type law: good books are those we like; bad books are those we don't like. Those of us who work daily with books tend to deny the personal factor by establishing criteria for evaluating books. We pretend to ourselves, and others, that book evaluation is—or can be—a reasonably scientific operation.

Certainly, the more books we read the more competent we become in evaluating them, and the less personal our approach becomes. But we make a large mistake if we forget personal appeal when we discuss books. Our tastes are our own; we approve of them or we wouldn't keep them, and we try, consciously or unconsciously, to mold the young people we work with to fit our image of what they ought to be like—namely, like us.

That they have lives of their own, preferences in books as in most other things; that they will accept some of our values and reject others is what the "generation gap" is all about—now, and in times past. By paying attention to the books which give children pleasure, even when we as adults may cringe at their taste, we may not bridge the gap, but we can narrow it. The effort must be ours; it cannot be the children's.

The introductions to each of the sections in this volume (Animal Stories, Life in the United States, Life in Other Lands, and Historical Fiction) have set forth criteria for evaluating specific types of books. "Qualities That Make a Child's Book Worth While" are discussed on pages 226-227. Attention to the criteria plus wide reading should enable the adult user of this anthology to develop his own critical facilities to the point where he will recognize the differences among good, mediocre, and poor books.

However, when an adult recognizes that a particular book is not his cup of tea, he should be willing to accept it if reputable reviewers have commented favorably upon it. He should be willing to let children make the ultimate decision when adults have differing opinions.

8. READING ALOUD TO CHILDREN

The adult who reads aloud regularly to children, whether at home, in the classroom, or in the library, soon discovers that he has hit upon an activity that pays unexpected dividends. Not only does he have the enjoyment that comes from reading fine children's books, but he has the children's enthusiasm to reward him for his efforts.

By sharing books together, children and adults manage to communicate in a way that is unusual in our society. They can share common friends and experiences—something they cannot do un-

der most other circumstances. Annis Duff in *Bequest of Wings*[6] offers numerous examples of those cherished moments when the right quotation from a book sums up the entire situation to everyone's satisfaction. In one delightful example, she tells of the time she read *The Tale of Peter Rabbit* to her four-year-old son and later "found him one morning, crouched down on the rocks by the water, peering anxiously at one of his little boats that had got washed in under a log, and saying, 'I implore you to exert yourself!' "[7]

After reading *The Wind in the Willows* together, both adults and children know what is meant by messing around with boats; and children have a new sympathy for mother when she complains about the senselessness of spring cleaning on a beautiful day. And one can chant with Mole, "Up we go! Up we go!" on almost any occasion when we are fleeing from chores to take time to have fun in the bright, clear air.

Many adults accept the idea that they should read aloud to very young children, but they too often assume that they no longer need to read aloud to a child once he goes to school. This is not true, and many reading specialists, baffled by an intelligent child's inability to learn to read, have, on more than one occasion, made this discovery: the child had unconsciously decided that his learning to read would put an end to home reading aloud, and so he did not learn to read. Bah! says the adult who is unfamiliar with child psychology. The child is simply lazy—or worse, so dependent that he cannot face the world on his own. This reaction overlooks the physical sense of security that a child receives from sitting on his mother's lap, or from having her perched on the edge of his bed reading a story. Too many of us fail to recognize how much courage it takes for the young child to trot off to school and begin learning all those strange tasks at the hands of an unknown adult, surrounded by strange children. Going to school is quite enough change in a child's routine, and even if there weren't other values in reading to children of all ages, the need to keep home

[6] Annis Duff, *Bequest of Wings; A Family's Pleasure with Books*, Viking, rev. ed., 1944
[7] *Ibid.*, p. 55

routines familiar would be quite enough reason to continue the reading aloud period.

Aside from psychological considerations, reading aloud is important because it is one way of stretching children's imaginations. It is obvious that children's aural comprehension exceeds their reading ability for many years. While they struggle with the necessarily simple language of primers, they need the nourishment of great language to spur them on in their efforts. Such books as *The Wind in the Willows, Alice's Adventures in Wonderland, Winnie-the-Pooh,* or *Charlotte's Web* take the child on flights of fancy. If the child's inclinations run toward an interest in real animals and real people, he will listen to the adventures of Jerome Kildee in *Kildee House* (see p. 39) or pull with Justin Morgan's "Little Bub" (see p. 21).

The type of book selected to be read aloud should be based on the child's interests, not determined by what the adult thinks would be good for him to hear, because none of us really listen when we are bored. Because some children will be far more interested in fantasy than realistic stories, and other children will find fantasy less interesting than realism, a range of books is necessary. Satisfying this range of needs is the major purpose of this anthology and its related volumes.

However, adults must take care to see that children do not fall into reading ruts. It is only natural that each of us develops a preference for the type of work we find most satisfying; but we cannot truly know what we prefer until we have had enough exposure to a variety of types of books to make genuine decisions. The man who has never tasted an olive is in no position to claim he doesn't like olives, only that he doesn't know what they taste like. The same is true with books.

Like food, books are best offered without pressure. There is no worse way to turn a child against a particular book or food than by "demanding" that he listen or eat. He may listen or eat at the time because he may have no choice, but the seeds of dislike are planted and may never die.

It should also be noted that some people *never* like to be read aloud to, not at age five or fifty. For them, books are private affairs, to be enjoyed in the exquisite aloneness of book and solitary reader. In the classroom, these children simply "tune out" and, if they do not disrupt the listening pleasure of the other children, should be left alone to think their private thoughts, to gaze out the window and dream. As a member of a group, they may not even be noticeable; at home, they are obvious. But if the parent has tried his best, only to discover that he has a child who does not like being read to, then he should take it in good grace.

9. TECHNIQUES OF READING ALOUD

Whether at home or in school, reading aloud should be a regular part of every week. Almost every selection in this book can be read aloud in fifteen minutes or less, a short time period with long-range consequences. Planning reading aloud time does not require an inflexible schedule, but it does demand a degree of regularity or it loses some of its values.

Reading aloud should not be contingent upon good behavior, and we should not refuse to read as a disciplinary action. To do so creates the impression that reading is frosting on the cake, not an inherent part of education or life. Since giving children a deep appreciation of books as an integral part of life is one of the most important goals of both parents and teachers, anything that makes books appear as frills must be discouraged. The adult who himself loves to read will find little trouble in striking the happy balance between stressing the pleasure and the importance of books without making them seem either frivolous or burdensome necessities.

The reading aloud process demands two things from the adult reader: he must have read the material beforehand, and he must be personally enthusiastic about it. Each is important. Few of us read well aloud when faced with completely strange material. Moreover, we should not suddenly gasp if we come upon the "damn" in *Harriet the Spy* (see p. 123)—if we can't read it without a negative reaction, we shouldn't read it at all. Ease in reading aloud comes when we both know and like the material we are reading. We are also able, usually, to anticipate questions the material will raise with children. Although we should not interrupt the reading aloud process by digressing into a vocabulary lesson, some words may well need further explanation afterwards.

The advantage of beginning with an excerpt from the anthology is that it provides a clue for the adult as to the children's interest in the material. The selections included are simply choice nibbles from the books from which they come, and it is hoped that both adults and children will be stimulated to go on and read the entire book from which the excerpt came. Sometimes, this stimulation will be for private reading; other times, especially in the classroom situation, enough children will be captivated to make reading the complete book a group project. The latter will be particularly true when the material being read aloud is too difficult for the children to read for themselves.

There are a number of ways by which we judge the reaction of children to books. When the fidgeting stops and silence grows within the room, we are made aware that what we are reading is having an effect upon the listeners. Sometimes we receive a second-hand reaction: the school or public librarian says, "Ever since you read X selection to your class, I can't keep the book on the shelf. I'm going to have to buy more copies."

If we watch children as we are reading, we can sometimes see them visibly relax, or watch the corners of their mouths begin to twitch with amusement, or see a sparkle appear in many eyes. And then there are the times when foreheads contract in concentration and deepening thoughts begin to show through clouded eyes. When this happens, we may then see if discussing the book will be the next step in helping children develop literary appreciation.

10. DISCUSSING BOOKS WITH CHILDREN

The astute adult soon begins to gauge the level of reaction and to know when discussion will add meaning to the reading. If we leave our-

selves truly open to hear what children have to say, we can learn much from letting them talk about literature.

How to begin

It takes practice for the average adult to learn how to ask the right questions in a neutral tone of voice, but it can be done if we are willing to work at it. Whether we recognize it or not, most of us simply give orders to children—make the bed, keep quiet, sit down, etc. On the occasions when adults do ask children questions, the questions are either in the form of a quiz in the classroom or they are the meaningless, "What did you do in school today, dear?" types. We tune children out just as often as they tune us out, and genuine conversations between children and adults are rare.[8]

Good book discussions must have a spontaneity about them, with the adult leader willing to let the children go where their thoughts and emotions take them. This demands a kind of neutrality on the part of the adult that is not easily acquired, although it comes naturally to some adults, requiring so little effort that they do not even see the magnitude of their achievement.

Since book discussions usually begin with questions, or at least one initial question, the art the adult needs to develop is to ask the question in a neutral way, not slant it to get the responses he wants to hear. For example, "What do you think it would be like to have *Harriet the Spy* (see p. 123) as a member of our class?" asked in an ordinary tone of voice ought to provoke discussion. "Would we like that horrible Harriet as a classmate?" is a slanted question and will not receive—or deserve—honest responses from the children.

Group discussions, whether in the classroom, in the library, or around a campfire, are easier to get off the ground than the one-to-one discussion between a parent and a child. When a child says, "Mother, you *have* to read this book!" and hands over *Harriet the Spy,* several reactions are possible. The adult may find Harriet an abominable child; the adult may find the book marvelously funny; or the adult may be disturbed,

[8] For a full discussion of this point, see: John Holt, *How Children Fail,* Pitman, 1964

having enjoyed parts of the book, but having been left uneasy by the apparent lack of morals.

What does Mother do in such cases? Well, one sure way to cut off communication is to say, "Thank you for recommending the book, but if this is the kind of thing you're enjoying, you'd better let me see your books before you begin them." We can be sure this child will not make the mistake of recommending a book again.

It would also be a mistake to say, "Thank you, dear, this is the funniest book I've read in ages," unless we know that it *was* funny to the child. (Hearty laughter or chuckles from the bedroom would provide this clue; engrossed silence would warn that whatever the book meant to the child, humor was not it.)

There are a number of words in the English language which can be used effectively in such a situation, for they carry a sense of approval without actually demanding that the speaker express an opinion. "Thank you, I found *Harriet* a fascinating book; she is a most unusual character, isn't she?" is far more neutral than it might appear at first. We can be fascinated by books without approving of them; we can be "intrigued," another fine word for such situations. Even a mundane word such as "interesting" will do for a beginning.

I remember attending a conference where the physical facilities were horrid beyond description. Protocol always demands a statement thanking the management, and we all wondered how the committee assigned to write the thank you would get around the fact that the entire conference had been a disaster as far as physical comfort was concerned. The wording came out this way: "We wish to thank the management of X for a most memorable conference." It was a master stroke— no one who attended would ever forget it—and it carried all the superficial tones of approval to satisfy protocol, without being an outright lie.

A similar courtesy extended to children ought to enable us to get them talking about books unencumbered by knowledge of our attitudes. If we respect the rights of children to differ with us, and if we really want to know what they think, we will find ways to establish the atmosphere in which honest discussion can take place.

How neutral to stay

As any adult knows who has ever attended a Great Books Discussion Group, the leader is under orders never to express an opinion. His role is simply that of moderator: to see that everyone gets a chance to speak, and to keep reasonable order. This role can be defended with adult groups, but when the discussion group is made up of children, the adult will have to step in occasionally and have his say.

The most obvious occasion is when there is an outright erroneous statement made. Unless another child in the group challenges the misstatement, the adult has the responsibility to clear things up. Discussion groups should never be a "sharing of ignorance" occasion. Using *Harriet the Spy* (see p. 123) again, let us suppose a child says, "I don't think it was very nice of Harriet to spy on her friends." Now Harriet does *not* spy on her friends; she merely observes them and records her observations, which is an entirely different situation from her "spy route."

The accuracy with which we read reveals itself in discussion, and adults leading discussion groups will often be amazed at the misstatements made. Some misstatements occur when the material has been too difficult for the reader's maturity; unable to cope with the situation before him, he mentally creates one of his own.

Some misstatements occur because of reader-bias. One of the most chilling stories I have ever heard about reader-bias occurred in a pre-school story program in a public library. The librarian was about to tell Ezra Jack Keats' *The Snowy Day* (see Bibliography, p. 250) when one four-year-old boy, seeing the picture of Peter, shouted, "That's the man who robbed my father's store!" He became hysterical, and the librarian was unable to convince him that this was just a little boy, about his own age. It turned out that the child's father's store had been robbed by a Negro and that the home comments coupled with the naturally upsetting event had combined to instill in him the idea that all Negroes were men who robbed stores.

The librarian to whom this happened and all of us to whom she told the story are still haunted by the event. All adults who undertake to use books with children sooner or later encounter some similar prejudice among one or more of the children, and how it is handled—whether it can, indeed, be handled—is what keeps us on our toes.

Naturally, the younger the group, the more difficult such situations are. This is why we tread carefully with very young children—they are still governed almost completely by emotion rather than reason—and they will generally parrot home attitudes. Children in the intermediate grades will have begun to form their own opinions and will be less susceptible to adult prejudices.

Finally, once we have proved ourselves to the children, we can express opinions of our own without stifling conversation. We can say, "I'm glad so many of you liked *Little Women,* but I found all that preaching too much to swallow." Then some child may well give us a lesson in reading by saying, "Oh, I just skipped those parts!"

And skip they do—quite often the parts adults are secretly hoping the children are most taking to heart. Children skip that which bores them as well as that which is beyond their comprehension; only adults seem to worry about such matters.

11. TYPES OF DISCUSSIONS AND BOOKS TO USE

The type of book selected for discussion depends upon the aims of the discussion group. Although there are numerous gradations, discussion groups basically center around aesthetics —the development of literary appreciation—or concern themselves with issues—the development of values, or a philosophy of life. Some books lend themselves to both types of discussion, but a book is generally better for one or the other.

Literary discussions

One of the best ways to develop literary appreciation is to select two books treating the same subject, one with little literary value, the other with great literary value. By pairing books, it is often possible to make some children see how a book can be engrossing on a surface level without really being a good book. For example, *Black Beauty* and *King of the Wind* make marvelous

contrasts in how a good writer can evoke sympathy without degenerating into the sickening sentimentality of Sewell's portrait. The same type of discussion can be conducted with a *Nancy Drew* mystery and one of Keith Robertson's fine mysteries, *Three Stuffed Owls,* for example. Children ought to develop standards for mysteries as for any other type of book, because such standards provide increased reading pleasure. The child comes to appreciate that reasonable character development helps to create suspense (is there really any fun in knowing from the beginning who is guilty?); that logical plot action and a solution based on a minimum of fortuitous circumstances make for more exciting reading. In pursuing this course of thinking, one eventually realizes that poor authors tell either too much or too little, and the art of good writing is in knowing exactly how much to tell.

By selecting books which demonstrate basic changes in writing techniques, we can also help children develop a sense of historical perspective in what constitutes good literature. Instead of forcing them to read Mary Mapes Dodge's *Hans Brinker* on the grounds that it is considered a "classic" and, therefore, is good for them, why not contrast it with DeJong's *Wheel on the School?* The numerous history lessons and cultural information tossed into the Dodge book are representative of the nineteenth-century idea that juvenile literature should teach children, not merely amuse them. Certainly, Dodge's extraneous interpolations evoke less feeling for the Netherlands than DeJong's superb characterizations of the people inhabiting the land.

An added benefit to such pairings might be to alert adults who cling to sentimental memories of books read in childhood to an appreciation that yesterday's books do not have the same appeal for today's child. Such insight might help reduce the numbers of children who dislike reading because they find little worth in spending time on the nineteenth-century "classics."

However, discussions centering around such titles as *Black Beauty* and *Hans Brinker* would not be entirely devoid of value judgments. Sewell's book should be seen in relationship to the era in which it was produced; a time when horses were a primary form of transportation and source of work power. The mistreatment of horses was serious; the book was written for a purpose and it had some good effects, although it would be possible to make a strong case for the development of the combustion engine as the real force in eliminating the mistreatment of horses.

A discussion of *Hans Brinker* might also point out the strong class system presented in the book. The daughter of the manor is depicted as being far superior to poor Hans and his peers. That is the way things were in those days, and the depiction is accurate, but one can discuss whether Dodge gives any indication of approval or disapproval of the system. One of the most interesting aspects of literary criticism is developing a sensitivity to author approval, disapproval, or neutrality toward the situation he describes.

No one writing in the nineteenth century did a better job of portraying the very worst attitudes toward Negroes than did Mark Twain in his *Adventures of Huckleberry Finn,* but it would be a very insensitive reader who found in the portrait any approval by Twain of the attitudes he was describing. In fact, Huck's decision to "go to hell" for Jim has to be one of the magnificent gestures in all literature. Sydney Carton might die in Dickens' *A Tale of Two Cities,* but death is nothing compared to a willingness to be damned for all eternity. It is this type of insight and sensitivity that comes eventually to many dedicated readers who are blessed with the opportunity to discuss books with other dedicated readers.

But just as few adult readers spend all their time reading the great books, neither should children be expected to spend a majority of their time with the classics. Each era produces its own type of literature, with its special appeals to contemporary readers, and what was best one hundred years ago is not automatically still best for today's readers. The days when there were few children's books, when authors were paid by the word, when there were few competing forms of entertainment, provided the author with leeway to ramble on at great length, often filling his book with incidents that served to inform, but which deterred plot action. Today's fast moving world finds such interruptions annoying. In fact, I will go so far as to say that most of the nineteenth-century classics are of interest only to

adults studying the history of children's literature. The few titles like *Heidi* (see p. 156) which remain meaningful to today's children ought to be allowed to stand out, instead of being buried among the deadwood.

The aesthetics of literary appreciation do not develop automatically or rapidly with most readers. Genuine literary appreciation is a very mature skill and comes only gradually, and is often never developed by many readers. However, the more books are discussed with enthusiasm, the more chance the child has to lay a foundation upon which to build.

Another good starting point is with books of humor. Children who read *Henry Huggins, Homer Price, Harriet the Spy, Henry Reed, Inc.,* and *Jennifer, Hecate, Macbeth, William McKinley, and Me, Elizabeth* may be led to see that the best humorous books center around characters who take themselves very seriously. The humor is for the reader, not the character, and the dead-pan style is most effective in producing humor. Or one might contrast *Homer Price* (see p. 104) with one of the situation comedies on television, analyzing the different techniques used by the two media to produce laughter.

The comparisons and contrasts are unlimited, and it would be possible to write an entire book about developing literary appreciation in children. We can only suggest here a few techniques, knowing that adults will recognize them as mere springboards for developing their own ideas and philosophies of literary book discussions with children.

There are a small number of books which combine literary excellence with thought-provoking ideas. These books are almost always for children in the sixth grade and up, a fact that should not surprise us, since complex ideas do not lend themselves to simplification of style or plot. Two books which are outstanding examples of this superiority are . . . *and now Miguel* (see Bibliography, p. 250) and *Johnny Tremain* (see p. 196). Both Miguel and Johnny start off as self-centered individuals, although Johnny is more obnoxious than Miguel, because his self-centeredness stems from pride while Miguel's comes from his need to belong to the family as "a man" and not as a boy.

By asking children, "What does Johnny want

and what does Miguel want in the beginning of each book?" we can set in action a discussion which can lead children to recognize that pre-occupation with one's self can stem from many sources, some of which are less destructive than others. In pursuing this point, we can suggest that the children look at the obstacles both boys must overcome; and in the process, at least some children will understand that it is the boys' pride that is the biggest obstacle. Because his self-centeredness blurs his vision, neither Johnny nor Miguel is able to see that some people are helping him reach his goals.

This is more obvious in Miguel because the first-person telling of the story enables the reader to see things directly through Miguel's eyes. It takes a discerning reader to recognize all the kindnesses being shown Miguel, and almost no reader, young or old, sees all there is to this book on the first reading. It is a book which withstands numerous re-readings—the sure mark of literary excellence.

Miguel's problem is more personal in nature than Johnny's, which makes *Johnny Tremain* an easier book to discuss. When Johnny's hand is burned he sees his dreams of being a great silversmith ended, and he begins the life of a homeless boy in the teeming city of Boston. As Johnny becomes more involved with the patriots working toward overthrowing British rule, he has less time to feel sorry for himself. He gradually is able to see that service to a great cause is more important than a personal dream. This book must be read the first time around for the sheer excitement of the story and only on subsequent re-readings does the reader have time to admire the writer's craft so ably demonstrated by Esther Forbes.

Perhaps the single most important item to come from literary discussions with children is their eventual recognition that there is very little to say about poor books. They may read them and be momentarily engrossed in them, but when the last page is finished the story is over. With great books, the reader has a heritage of ideas and at least one personal friend to keep him company within his mind and his heart.

Value discussions

Discussions centering around value judgments encompass a wide range of subjects and can be primarily personal or primarily social in nature. Most value discussions are not easily categorized as one type or the other, since the nature of the discussion takes the reader on a twisting pathway, leading this way now, that way a little later.

A discussion centering around *A Dog on Bark-ham Street* (see p. 112) might begin as a personal discussion, or, as the sociologist might say, as inner-directed. The leader would have a number of approaches to this book (a good idea, in general, since one rarely can predict what it is in a book that will capture the interest of youthful readers). For example, the question: "What would you do if you lived next door to someone like Martin Hastings?" might lead to a full discussion about what bullies are like, how they get that way, and what you can do to get along with them. Or the question might evoke little or no response. On the other hand, asking, "Do you think Edward's mother was right in refusing to let him have a dog?" might send the group into a rousing discussion. Do mothers really end up taking care of pets? What are a pet owner's responsibilities? Is owning a pet hard work as well as fun? What are the differences between owning a dog in the country, in the suburbs, and in the city?

Personal approaches to books can be made with any group, but they are especially successful with younger children—those in the third, fourth, and fifth grades. At those ages, what children feel is more important than what they think, and the adult working with them should be concerned with helping them verbalize their feelings. The dangers in this situation are twofold: one, domination of the group by one child; two, that the discussion begins to resemble group therapy sessions. The first problem is present in all group discussions, no matter what the age of the participants, and each discussion leader must develop his own method of shutting people up without shutting them out of the discussion. The one technique which must never be evoked is the use of sarcasm, which is the most destructive weapon in anyone's verbal arsenal. Sarcasm not only devastates the person toward whom it is directed, but creates fear in the minds of the listeners who begin to suspect, rightly, that it is better to keep quiet than to be the subject of attack. This is the fear of the shy child who never volunteers an opinion, and the best way to help such a child is to show him that others do not suffer when they express their opinions.

An important fact to remember when dealing with the loudmouth (or compulsive communicator, as he is called in psychological language) is that while he does not arouse in us the sympathy we are apt to feel for the shy child, he is equally in need of our help. He dominates discussions because he cannot shut himself up; he needs to be the center of attention—just as Martin Hastings, the bully, dominates his world by physical force for the same reasons. Recognition of this makes it harder for the adult to be harsh with the monopolizer, and easier for him to work at finding positive methods to control the child. Most teachers learn the proper methods for dealing with such situations in Educational Psychology courses, but too few of them learn that it is the inner emotions of the adult which determine how successful he will be in coping with problem children. If we become angry, if we lose patience, no formula statements will help, because the emotion, not the words, is conveyed to the children.

Since few of us are trained psychologists or therapists, it is essential that we prevent the book discussion from developing into what is basically a therapy situation. The problem is in foreseeing the trend the discussion is taking and in cutting it off before it develops. This is difficult, because many discussions with younger children bear a strong resemblance to "Show and Tell Time." They begin with, "My mother says," or, "My father said to my mother," and soon one child is trying to top another in sharing personal family matters. Art Linkletter has made a fortune from the things children say, but the teacher, librarian, or group leader must not emulate Mr. Linkletter. If the children are unable to begin to generalize about the topic being discussed, it is better to end the discussion than to let it become uncontrolled.

We encounter both these difficulties, and more, when the discussion centers around value judgments. One way to avoid trouble is to lead up to the real problem discussions. The adult working with children is able to see the progress they make, the maturing they do before his eyes, and to gauge when a book is likely to be appropriate. Unless the children themselves select a book treating an extremely sensitive subject, it is best to leave such books until we have been talking together for some time.

For instance, it might be difficult, if not impossible, to have children whose parents owned large farms and hired migrant workers discuss sympathetically *The Loner* (see Bibliography, p. 249) or *Roosevelt Grady* (see p. 93) when they were just beginning to learn how to talk about books. We know from experience that the closer the subject is to the life of the individual, the harder it is for him to discuss it dispassionately. While we strive to inculcate in children the ability to detach themselves from purely emotional responses to ideas and situations, we must recognize that this is a very mature characteristic, and we may be able to lay only the groundwork for its future development.

To recognize the difficulty of achieving a goal is not to say that we do not make attempts toward achieving it. It simply means that we are cognizant of the nuances apt to be present and we react accordingly. No one really learns anything by having it forced upon him; true learning is an internal assimilation of facts, ideas, and emotional responses which ultimately lead to value judgments, which form the basis of our individual philosophies of life.

With all this in mind, we might begin a comparative discussion of *A Dog on Barkham Street* (see p. 112) and *Roosevelt Grady* (see p. 93) by asking, "If you had a choice, would you rather have Martin Hastings or Roosevelt Grady living next door or down the block?" If the resulting discussion shows that Martin Hastings, despite his being a thoroughly disagreeable boy, is seen as a more "suitable" neighbor by being white, we are made aware of the depth of the children's prejudice. Such a disclosure would indicate a full-fledged attempt by the entire school to counteract the bias; book discussions in isolation will not do the job.

This last point must be stressed. Book discussions are only one means by which we attempt to reach children. They are no panacea, and their limitations must be seen clearly by the adult who uses the technique.

For above-average fifth-graders and alert sixth-graders, *Young Fu of the Upper Yangtze* (see Bibliography, p. 253) might be an interesting book to begin value discussions with since the setting in China removes it from the immediate world of the children and thus reduces personal involvement. This book has numerous possibilities for discussion. For example, take Wang Scholar's comment to Young Fu: "Shall I teach the Ancient Wisdom to one who wishes to use it only for the earning of money? Knowest thou not that the treasure of knowledge is to be revered for itself alone? It has been given that men might learn how to live, not to win fortune. What is fortune without wisdom?"

Isn't this basically the question the hippie dropouts from our society are asking? It is too late to try to discuss issues with young people when they have already dropped out, or are drug addicts, or worse, lying dead in some filthy basement. Adults who consistently put off discussing real issues with children are often forced to face the fact that when adults think it is time for a young person to be able to talk about serious subjects, the young person is lost to us. Sometimes the loss is actual—he has joined the ranks of missing persons; sometimes the loss is figurative—the young person is still physically present, but intellectually and emotionally he wants no part of what the adult world wants to say to him.

We do children a disservice by failing to recognize that they feel, even if they cannot articulate, the intricacies of human relationships and the difficulties of searching for the good life. Adults create the so-called generation gap, not just in this era, but they always have. We cannot allow children to live in the adult world (for good reasons); and yet we steadfastly refuse to see that they have a world of their own. We can enter that world, not completely, but by invitation upon occasion, if we can learn to listen to what children are willing to tell us. The gap could be narrowed considerably if more adults would bring themselves to acknowledge a very simple fact: the world children live in is always different from the one we lived in as children. What those differences are, what they mean to children, is the crux of understanding between the generations.

Some adults may feel that this sounds terribly ponderous, if not downright pedantic, but we can only say that if they will read the entire books from which our selections have been made, and dip into the books listed in the Bibliography, they will find that provocative ideas are not tediously presented in good juvenile books. There is much laughter here, sheer delight, and a joyous pleasure in being alive. The best books do not resemble juvenile medicine—cherry flavored to hide the fact that it is good for children.

12. THE FLEXIBILITY OF BOOKS

By now it should be obvious that books serve many purposes and functions. They are examples of fine writing; they stimulate ideas; they aid both adults and children in better understanding each other. Beyond these uses lie untold other possibilities. For example, a teacher about to introduce long division to a class might well begin by reading the opening chapters of *Roosevelt Grady* (see p. 93), giving the class in story form the basic idea that long division problems can come out evenly or with a "leftover number." Such an introduction can motivate even non-mathematically inclined children to an interest in the subject.

Natural science is another subject which lends itself to a wide use of books. Emil Liers' biographies of animals are both exciting to read and scientifically informing. And the impact of natural phenomena on man's life can be seen in such books as Southall's *Hills End* (see Bibliography, p. 254), the story of a flood; or *Avalanche!* (see p. 168), which shows the reactions of people as the mountain pours down tons of snow on their town.

Historical fiction has always played a role in supplementing textbook accounts of events, and such books as Betty Baker's *Walk the World's Rim* (see Bibliography, p. 255) can help bring alive the America that existed long before the first English settlers arrived at Jamestown and Plymouth. It also offers insight into the attitudes toward slavery that existed prior to the time depicted in *Canalboat to Freedom* (see Bibliography, p. 255) by Thomas Fall. Such insight helps the young person understand that slavery in the

United States was neither new nor peculiar to our country.

All good books have a relationship to life; they do not exist in a vacuum, and the more we work with children and books the more we are made aware of the infinite ways in which the two interact to give meaning to life beyond the immediate experiences of the group or the individual. Hopefully, these few examples make it clear that a good book can fit in anywhere in the curriculum, and that reading aloud should not be seen as time away from a subject, but rather as adding depth and understanding to it. There must always be time for good books, because without them, true education is impossible.

13. ON KEEPING UP

At the time of this writing no one really knows how many juvenile books are in print. Estimates from informed people run from 16,000 to 40,000 and we will have to await the publication of *The Subject Guide to Juvenile Books in Print* by the R. R. Bowker Company for any reasonably accurate figure. Whatever the number, it is huge and growing each year as more books are published than go out of print.

How does one "keep up"? How does one select from among the best of the new books, refusing to fall into the trap of using the same old reading lists every year as poor teachers do?

The most important person in the life of a teacher is the school librarian. She (or he) is constantly available for information about the best of the new books and so is the children's specialist in the public library. Once a parent or a teacher indicates an interest in being informed he will not lack for news about new books, or even for suggestions about older titles which may have escaped notice.

If the adult is in a very small school or community which does not have specialized help in the public library and lacks anything resembling a good school library, the problem can be eased by asking for help from the State Library Agency concerned with such matters. The patterns differ from state to state, but every state in the union

now has some resources to offer the individual who seeks help.

State library personnel will also be helpful in aiding interested adults in developing and improving local services. There are many places to turn to for help, and adults should be working toward the establishment of reasonable library services at the local level if they want to help children have available the materials they need to work and grow in our current complex educational structure.

Where libraries are available and well stocked, the adult who shows an interest in children's literature will find that children happily share their newest discoveries—recommending as many books to the adult as the adult recommends to them. This often lends great insight into individual children, the way their minds work, and how they feel about many things. It is also tremendously satisfying to know that we have been accepted by the children as worthy of reading the books they have become excited about.

Then there are the innumerable magazines and booklists published regularly. For a fuller discussion of some of these tools we suggest you see *An Introduction to Children's Work in Public Libraries.*[9] One word of advice in analyzing review magazines: watch the masthead carefully. Changes in personnel will inevitably produce changes in the tone of the reviews and articles, and what was once a favorite magazine can become one of our pet peeves—or vice versa.

The magazines and booklists listed here are chosen because they offer the interested adult a wider view of the field than just that of reviewing new books. They are not the only ones available, but they do represent quality at a reasonable price. Any school, however small, should be able to afford them for the teacher's professional collection.

Review magazines

Elementary English, National Council of Teachers of English, 508 South Sixth Street, Champaign, Illinois 61820. $7 per year, with membership.

[9] Dorothy M. Broderick, *An Introduction to Children's Work in Public Libraries,* H. W. Wilson Co., 1965, Chapters 2 and 3

Elementary English publishes articles about the use of books in the classroom as well as reviews and offers teachers many helpful hints in the teaching of English to grade school children.

Horn Book, 585 Boylston Street, Boston, Massachusetts 02116. $6 per year.

Besides reviewing books, *The Horn Book* contains articles by and about authors and illustrators which provide the reader with insight into the creative process.

Young Readers Review, Box 137, Wall Street Station, New York, New York 10005. $5 per year.

This is a comparatively new magazine and contains the longest reviews of juvenile books, telling the adult reader much more about specific titles than any other magazine. It also contains articles and a very special feature, its "New Look at Old Books."

Annual booklists

Children's Books, Library of Congress, Washington, D.C. (order from: Superintendent of Documents, U.S. Government Printing Office, Washington, D.C. 20402, 15¢).

An annotated list of 200 or more of the best books published in a specific year.

Growing Up with Books, R. R. Bowker Co.,

1180 Avenue of the Americas, New York, New York 10036. Single copy 25¢; rates for multiple copies upon request.

Contains annotations for 300 of the best children's books in an attractive format which may be used by either children or adults.

Notable Children's Books, American Library Association, 50 East Huron Street, Chicago, Illinois 60611. Single copy free. Also appears in the April issue of the *ALA Bulletin.*

Fifty or more titles selected by a committee of the Children's Services Division as representing the best of the preceding year's children's books.

Standard lists

Arbuthnot, May Hill, et al., *Children's Books Too Good to Miss,* Case Western Reserve University Press, Cleveland, Ohio 44106, rev. ed., 1966. $1.50.

A very attractive introduction to both new and old titles which the compilers feel have great appeal to many children.

Eakin, Mary K., *Good Books for Children,* University of Chicago Press, 3rd edition, 1966. $2.95 in paperback; $6.00 hard cover.

A collection of 1391 reviews of recommended books published between 1950 and 1965 as reviewed in *The Bulletin of the Center for Children's Books.*

Bibliography

All books listed in the Bibliography were in print at the time this volume went to press. The numbers at the end of the entries indicate the age range for the books, the lower number being an age at which children are able to listen to the story being read aloud, the higher number representing the age at which they should be able to read the book easily to themselves. Almost all of the titles with older age ranges, i.e., 12-14, are listed because they lend themselves to exciting reading aloud with fifth- and sixth-graders. Adults using the Bibliography are reminded that there are always individual differences and what is appropriate to one ten-year-old may be too hard or too easy for another.

ANIMAL STORIES

ANDERSON, C. W., *Billy and Blaze*, ill. by author, Macmillan, 1936. 4–8
Blaze and the Forest Fire, ill. by author, Macmillan, 1938. 4–8
Blaze and the Gypsies, ill. by author, Macmillan, 1937. 4–8
Blaze Finds the Trail, ill. by author, Macmillan, 1950. 4–8
Deep Through the Heart, ill. by author, Macmillan, 1940. 10–14
High Courage, ill. by author, Macmillan, 1941. 10–14
Salute, ill. by author, Macmillan, 1940. 7–12
These are excellent horse stories for children, and the drawings that illustrate them are superb.

AVERILL, ESTHER, *Fire Cat*, ill. by author, Harper, 1960. An easy-to-read story about an adventurous cat who wasn't content to be a mere house pet. 6–8

BALCH, GLENN, *Horse in Danger*, ill. by Lee J. Ames, Crowell, 1960. A vigorous, well-told tale of modern horse rustling on the Tack Ranch in Idaho. 10–12

BAUDOUY, MICHEL-AIMÉ, *Old One-Toe*, tr. by Marie Ponshot, ill. by Johannes Troyer, Harcourt, 1959. A French version of the hunted and the hunters with both fox and human characters warmly portrayed. Old One-Toe is a chicken killer and the farmers are justified in hunting him. But after Piet has stalked and studied the rogue he finds himself siding with the fox. 10–12

BEATTY, HETTY BURLINGAME, *Little Wild Horse*, ill. by author, Houghton, 1949. A small boy's dream comes true—a real ranch in the West and the taming of a little wild horse to be his very own. 3–7

BIALK, ELISA, *Taffy's Foal*, ill. by William Moyers, Houghton, 1949. A little girl meets two major problems in one year—her father's second marriage and the death of her adored horse. 9–12
Wild Horse Island, ill. by Paul Brown, Houghton, 1951. Horses, mystery, and good family relationships make this story of life in northwestern Montana unusually interesting. Good character development and lively plot. 9–12

BORG, INGA, *Parrak, the White Reindeer*, ill. by author, Warne, 1959. A reindeer calf grows up to become herd leader. Brilliantly colored pictures of Lapland. 5–9

BRYAN, DOROTHY and MARGUERITE, *Michael Who Missed His Train*, Dodd, Mead, 1932. A delightful story of an unwanted but ingratiating puppy. 4–6

BUFF, MARY and CONRAD, *Dash and Dart, A Story of Two Fawns*, ill. by authors, Viking, 1942. The first year in the life of twin fawns is beautifully told and illustrated. The cadenced prose reads aloud well and the pictures in sepia and full color are exquisite. 5–8
Hurry, Skurry, and Flurry, ill. by Conrad Buff, Viking, 1954. Another beautifully illustrated book, this one about frolicking squirrels. 5–8

BULLA, CLYDE R., *Star of Wild Horse Canyon*, ill. by Grace Paull, Crowell, 1953. An easy-to-read western story. 7–9

CALHOUN, MARY, *Houn' Dog*, ill. by Roger Duvoisin, Morrow, 1959. A warm and humorous tale that will be enjoyed by many young readers. 7–9

CHIPPERFIELD, JOSEPH E., *Wolf of Badenoch*, ill. by C. Gifford Ambler, McKay, 1959. Magnificent descriptions of nature highlight this perceptive story of sheepherding in Scotland. 12–15

CLARK, DENIS, *Black Lightning*, ill. by C. Gifford Ambler, Viking, 1954. Black Lightning, a black leopard, regains his jungle freedom after harsh captivity in a circus. 12–16
Boomer, ill. by C. Gifford Ambler, Viking, 1955. An Australian kangaroo, adopted as a household pet, later returns to the wild and becomes a leader of his kind. 12–16

DE JONG, MEINDERT, *Along Came a Dog*, ill. by Maurice Sendak, Harper, 1958. A sensitive story of a crippled red hen and the stray dog who protects her. 10–13
The Little Cow and the Turtle, ill. by Maurice Sendak, Harper, 1955. Humorous, read-aloud story about a frisky cow and her adventures. 8–12
Smoke above the Lane, Harper, 1951. Here is told an amusing and touching story of a strange friendship. 6–10

DELAFIELD, CLELIA, *Mrs. Mallard's Ducklings*, ill. by Leonard Weisgard, Lothrop, 1946. A beautiful picture book with interesting text of the seasonal cycle of ducks from egg to winter flight. 6–8

DENNIS, MORGAN, *Burlap*, ill. by author, Viking, 1945. A worthless old farm dog suddenly proves himself by helping to capture an escaped circus bear. 6–9

DILLON, EILÍS, A *Family of Foxes*, ill. by Vic Donahue, Funk & Wagnalls, 1965. When four boys find two black foxes washed ashore on the Irish isle of Inishowan they know they must hide them from the adults who hate foxes. How the boys protect the animals, and the cubs who arrive soon after, makes fine reading for boys and girls. 10–12

EARLE, OLIVE L., *Thunder Wings*, ill. by author, Morrow, 1951. This authentic record of the development of the ruffed grouse from the egg to maturity is well told and illustrated. 6–10

FLACK, MARJORIE, *Angus and the Ducks*, ill. by author, Doubleday, 1930.
Story about Ping, ill. by Kurt Wiese, Viking, 1933.
Tim Tadpole and the Great Bullfrog, ill. by author, Doubleday, 1934.
Each story is unique, each has a well-defined plot, delightful style, and just enough suspense or surprise to keep children interested. 5–8

FROST, FRANCES, *Maple Sugar for Windy Foot*, ill. by Lee Townsend, McGraw-Hill, 1950.
Sleigh Bells for Windy Foot, ill. by Lee Townsend, McGraw-Hill, 1948.
Windy Foot at the County Fair, ill. by Lee Townsend, McGraw-Hill, 1947.
The same delightful people and the same little pony lend adventure, warmth, and fun to these choice stories of American life. 9–14

GARBUTT, KATHARINE and BERNARD, *Hodie*, ill. by Bernard

Garbutt, Dutton, 1949. After Hodie was sent to live on a farm, he had to prove to the farmer that he was a real farm dog so that he wouldn't have to be sent back to a city apartment. 6–8

GATES, DORIS, *Little Vic,* ill. by Kate Seredy, Viking, 1951. From the moment Pony Rivers sees Little Vic, he is sure that the horse is a champion. When all others have given up on the horse, Pony's devotion remains—and eventually proves right. 9–12

GEORGE, JOHN L., and JEAN GEORGE, *Masked Prowler: The Story of a Raccoon,* ill. by Jean George, Dutton, 1950. This is a story about Procyon, a young raccoon, and the dangers and joys he encounters in growing up. 11–15

Meph, the Pet Skunk, ill. by Jean George, Dutton, 1952. This is not only the story of a tame skunk but also the story of the reclamation of an eroded farm and its effect on an embittered farmer and his unhappy son. 11–16

Vison, the Mink, ill. by Jean George, Dutton, 1949. The vicious mink is not an appealing hero, but this book is a fine record of its life. 11–15

Vulpes the Red Fox, ill. by Jean George, Dutton, 1948. The fascinating biography of a red fox and the skills he possesses to outwit the hunters. Even in defeat, Vulpes is magnificent. 10–14

GIPSON, FRED, *Old Yeller,* ill. by Carl Burger, Harper, 1956.
Savage Sam, ill. by Carl Burger, Harper, 1962.
Two excellent stories of the importance of hound dogs in the lives of the frontier settlers. For mature readers. 12–16

HENRY, MARGUERITE, *Album of Horses,* ill. by Wesley Dennis, Rand McNally, 1951. 8–14

Brighty of the Grand Canyon, ill. by Wesley Dennis, Rand McNally, 1953. 9–12

King of the Wind, ill. by Wesley Dennis, Rand McNally, 1948. Newbery Medal. 8–14

Misty of Chincoteague, ill. by Wesley Dennis, Rand McNally, 1947. 8–12

Sea Star: Orphan of Chincoteague, ill. by Wesley Dennis, Rand McNally, 1949. 8–12

Stormy, Misty's Foal, ill. by Wesley Dennis, Rand McNally, 1963. 8–12

White Stallion of Lipizza, ill. by Wesley Dennis, Rand McNally, 1964. 8–12

Horse stories by this author are invariably dramatic and exciting but never sensational, and they are written with fidelity to the animal's nature. Most children, having read one, will read them all. Also the author of *Justin Morgan Had a Horse* (p. 21).

HOFF, SYD, *Julius,* ill. by author, Harper, 1959. The humorous account of a gorilla who makes friends with a small boy. A beginning-reading book. 6–7

HOKE, HELEN, *Factory Kitty,* Watts, 1949. A delightful story about a kitten who has definite ideas about where and with whom he wants to live and play. 6–9

JOHNSON, MARGARET, *Snowshoe Paws,* ill. by author, Morrow, 1949. Easy reading story of a cat who loses his adopted home because he can't get along with the dog. 6–8

KJELGAARD, JIM, *Big Red,* ill. by Bob Kuhn, Holiday, 1956. 12–14

Kalak of the Ice, ill. by Bob Kuhn, Holiday, 1949. 10–14

Snow Dog, ill. by Jacob Landau, Holiday, 1948. 12–16

Swamp Cat, Dodd, 1957. 12–16

These stories are justly popular. They are well written, with plenty of action, and both human characters and animals are well drawn. Big Red is an Irish setter, the constant companion of Danny Pickett. Their adventures together climax in tracking down a huge outlaw bear.

Kalak, known to the Eskimos as the "mist bear," is a heroic figure in her struggle to protect her cubs and survive. Snow Dog, part husky and part staghound, is an orphan struggling for survival in the north woods until he is befriended by a lone trapper. In *Swamp Cat* young Andy Gates plants muskrat colonies on his worthless Louisiana swampland heritage only to have them endangered by human and animal enemies. Also the author of *Irish Red* (p. 5).

KNIGHT, ERIC, *Lassie Come Home,* ill. by Marguerite Kirmse, Holt, 1940. A popular story of a collie's faithfulness to her master and her ability to track her way home over a great distance. 10–16

KNIGHT, RUTH ADAMS, *Halfway to Heaven,* ill. by Wesley Dennis, McGraw-Hill, 1952. This is a great story for family reading. It is the story of the dedicated life of one young monk of the St. Bernard Hospice, high in the Alps, and of his love for the magnificent dogs with which he works. 10–14

LATHROP, DOROTHY, *Who Goes There?* ill. by author, Macmillan, 1935. Exquisitely illustrated story about a winter picnic for birds and animals of the forest. 7–9

LIERS, EMIL, *A Beaver's Story,* ill. by Ray Sherin, Viking, 1958.

A Black Bear's Story, ill. by Ray Sherin, Viking, 1962.

An Otter's Story, ill. by Tony Palazzo, Viking, 1953.
Three excellent animal biographies which depict the dangers facing each species from man as well as other animals. Exciting natural history. 9–12

LIPKIND, WILLIAM, and NICOLAS MORDVINOFF, *The Two Reds,* Harcourt, 1950. The two Reds, boy and cat, both city dwellers, were enemies because they both yearned for the same goldfish, but for different reasons. 4–8

LIPPINCOTT, JOSEPH WHARTON, *Gray Squirrel,* ill. by George F. Mason, Lippincott, 1954.

Little Red the Fox, ill. by George F. Mason, Lippincott, 1953.

Long Horn, Leader of the Deer, ill. by George F. Mason, Lippincott, 1955.

Persimmon Jim, the Possum, ill. by George F. Mason, Lippincott, 1955.

Striped Coat, the Skunk, ill. by George F. Mason, Lippincott, 1954.
The preceding list contains additional stories for those who enjoy *The Wahoo Bobcat* (p. 44). 9–11

MC CLOSKEY, ROBERT, *Make Way for Ducklings,* ill. by author, Viking, 1941. Since this episode really happens in Boston each year, it is largely realistic with a few thoughts and words permitted the sagacious Mrs. Duck. Caldecott Medal. 4–8

MC CLUNG, ROBERT M., *Spike, the Story of a Whitetail Deer,* ill. by author, Morrow, 1952. A clear, factual story of the first year in the life of a whitetail deer. 5–10

Stripe, the Story of a Chipmunk, ill. by author, Morrow, 1951. These easy-to-read animal stories by a scientist and artist are well told, interesting to read to five-year-olds, and good reading for slow readers of nine and ten. 5–10

MC MEEKIN, ISABEL MC LENNAN, *Kentucky Derby Winner,* ill. by Corinne B. Dillon, McKay, 1949. A boy-centered horse story of unusual value. It concerns young Jackie Spratt and his passion for "Risty" (Aristides), the horse which eventually won the first Kentucky Derby. Fine people, good horse lore, and considerable humor make this a memorable story. 9–14

MEADER, STEPHEN W., *Red Horse Hill,* ill. by Lee Townsend, Harcourt, 1930. Bud Martin is happy when he wins a chance to work with horses in a New Hampshire village.

In the process, he discovers a great racer. 11–16

MINARIK, ELSE H., *Father Bear Comes Home*, ill. by Maurice Sendak, Harper, 1959.

Little Bear, ill. by Maurice Sendak, Harper, 1957.

Little Bear's Friend, ill. by Maurice Sendak, Harper, 1960.

Little Bear's Visit, ill. by Maurice Sendak, Harper, 1960. Little Bear has become one of the most popular beginning-to-read series ever published. Delightful pictures complement fun texts. 6–7

NEWBERRY, CLARE TURLAY, *April's Kittens*, ill. by author, Harper, 1940.

Babette, ill. by author, Harper, 1937.

Barkis, ill. by author, Harper, 1938.

Marshmallow, ill. by author, Harper, 1942.

Mittens, ill. by author, Harper, 1936.

Percy, Polly and Pete, ill. by author, Harper, 1952. Clare Newberry's drawings of cats are so entrancing that the slight stories do not matter. *Percy, Polly and Pete* is the best story, and the lesson to small cat lovers who hug their kittens too hard is pleasantly administered. 5–8

O'HARA, MARY, *Green Grass of Wyoming*, Lippincott, 1946. 12–adult

My Friend Flicka, Lippincott, 1941. 10–14

Thunderhead, Lippincott, 1943. 10–14

These books are a trilogy about the McLaughlin's horse ranch, where the problems are complicated by a bad wild-horse strain. Exciting reading.

PEARCE, PHILIPPA, *A Dog So Small*, ill. by Antony Maitland, Lippincott, 1963. A special story for sensitive readers who will sympathize with young Ben's desire to have a dog and the eventual compromise he must make. 10–12

PHIPSON, JOAN, *Birkin*, Harcourt, 1965. This is a story about a young calf, Birkin, who grows up into a monstrous steer. He and his owners lead an eventful life, and Birkin almost ends up as steak and roast beef. 10–12

PIATTI, CELESTINO, *The Happy Owls*, ill. by author, Atheneum, 1964. In a stunningly illustrated book, the owls try to explain to the quarreling barnyard animals the secret of being happy, but their wisdom is rejected. 6–8

RAWLINGS, MARJORIE KINNAN, *The Yearling*, ill. by N. C. Wyeth, Scribner's, 1939. This is a poignant story of growing up, when the boy Jody learns to face and accept the tragic necessity of disposing of his pet deer which has become a menace to the family's livelihood. 10–adult

ROBINSON, TOM, *Buttons*, ill. by Peggy Bacon, Viking, 1938. Wonderful picture-story of an alley cat who became a gentleman. 6–10

ROUNDS, GLEN, *Stolen Pony*, ill. by author, Holiday, 1948. A moving story of a pony stolen by horse thieves and abandoned when it was found that he was blind. A faithful dog guides the pony home. 8–12

SCOTT, SALLY, *The Brand New Kitten*, ill. by Beth Krush, Harcourt, 1956. Combination of suspense and humor will delight young readers as they follow Peggy's attempts to acquire a kitten. 6–8

SEREDY, KATE, *Gypsy*, ill. by author, Viking, 1951. Children of any age and all cat-loving adults will enjoy Miss Seredy's magnificent pictures and simple account of a growing kitten. 4–up

STOLZ, MARY, *Emmett's Pig*, ill. by Garth Williams, Harcourt, 1959. A small boy is delighted with the gift of a real pig for a pet. 4–8

STONG, PHIL, *Honk: the Moose*, ill. by Kurt Wiese, Dodd, 1935. This is undoubtedly one of the most amusing animal tales we have. A hard winter drives a hungry moose into the cozy confines of a livery stable, and the problem is to get rid of him. 9–12

WALDECK, THEODORE J., *Jamba the Elephant*, ill. by Kurt Wiese, Viking, 1942.

Lions on the Hunt, ill. by Kurt Wiese, Viking, 1942.

The White Panther, ill. by Kurt Wiese, Viking, 1941. Authentic and exciting stories of wild animals. 10–14

WARD, LYND, *The Biggest Bear*, ill. by author, Houghton, 1952. The Orchard family said, "Better a bear in the orchard than an Orchard in a bear." But Johnny was bound to get a bear and he did. A prize tale with wonderful pictures. 4–8

WHITE, ANNE, *Junket, the Dog Who Liked Everything "Just So,"* ill. by Robert McCloskey, Viking, 1955. A very funny story about what happens when a city family buys a farm and acquires with it a dog who likes everything "just so." 9–12

LIFE IN THE UNITED STATES

Here, There, and Everywhere

ASSOCIATION FOR CHILDHOOD EDUCATION, *Told under the Blue Umbrella*, ill. by Marguerite Dairs, Macmillan, 1933. A collection of realistic stories which can be read aloud to young children; older ones can read them to themselves. 4–10

BELL, THELMA HARRINGTON, *Mountain Boy*, ill. by Corydon Bell, Viking, 1947. Randy, a mountain boy, was good at reading wood lore but was determined not to read reading. How his mother broke down his resistance makes a delightful story in homespun style. 10–12

BENARY, MARGOT, *The Long Way Home*, tr. from the German by Richard and Clara Winston, Harcourt, 1959. Orphaned during World War II, thirteen-year-old Chris leaves his native village in eastern Germany to find a new home in the United States. 12–16

BINNS, ARCHIE, *Sea Pup*, Duell, 1954. Clint Barlow, an only child living with his parents in a remote region of Puget Sound, knows that he wants to be an oceanographer, and uses his wonderful outdoor life for observations which he carefully records. 9–11

BONHAM, FRANK, *Durango Street*, Dutton, 1965. Rufus Henry has two choices: to become involved with a street gang and face being sent back to a home for delinquents or to get himself killed because he lacks gang protection. A realistic portrait of life in the Los Angeles slums. 12–15

BRINK, CAROL RYRIE, *Family Grandstand*, ill. by Jean M. Porter, 1952.

Family Sabbatical, ill. by Susan Foster, Viking, 1956. These delightful stories tell of the activities of a professor's family in a Midwestern college town and during a year's trip to France. Modern stories by the author of *Caddie Woodlawn* (p. 212). 9–12

BULLA, CLYDE, *A Ranch for Danny*, ill. by Grace Paull, Crowell, 1951.

Surprise for a Cowboy, ill. by Grace Paull, Crowell, 1950. Two stories of a city boy's adventures on his uncle's ranch where he learns how to be a cowboy. 7–10

BURCH, ROBERT, *Queenie Peavy*, ill. by Jerry Lazare, Viking, 1966. A tobacco-chewing, rock-throwing tomboy discovers that there are better ways of getting along in the world. A sensitive picture of a young girl bordering on adolescence and surrounded by problems, many of them of her own making. 10–14

Tyler, Wilkin, and Skee, ill. by Don Sibley, Viking, 1963. The three brothers in the title have grand times together; their relationships with each other and their parents are warmly portrayed, sometimes with humor, sometimes with heartbreaking poignancy. Also the author of *Skinny* (p. 77). 8–12

CAUDILL, REBECCA, *A Certain Small Shepherd,* ill. by William Pène DuBois, Holt, 1965. At six, Jamie still cannot speak. Then, on Christmas Eve, his father befriends a man and woman, and the mysterious power of love of one's fellow man goes to work and Jamie can talk. Moving without being overly sentimental. 5–8

A Pocketful of Cricket, ill. by Evaline Ness, Holt, 1964. A tender story of a young boy who takes his pet cricket to school. Also the author of *Did You Carry the Flag Today, Charley?* (p. 65) . 5–8

CLARK, MARGERY, *The Poppy Seed Cakes,* ill. by Maud and Miska Petersham, Doubleday, 1924. A book of realistic, gay, and funny tales, told in a Russian atmosphere. The stories have a warm, human atmosphere, which is enhanced by the Petershams' gay illustrations. 7–11

CLARKE, TOM E., *The Big Road,* Lothrop, 1965. A good book to give to young people who scoff at their parents' tales of the Depression. It should help readers to see that America did not always have an "affluent society." 11–14

CLEARY, BEVERLY, *Henry and Beezus,* ill. by Louis Darling, Morrow, 1952.

Henry and Ribsy, ill. by Louis Darling, Morrow, 1954.

Henry Huggins, ill. by Louis Darling, Morrow, 1950. Three of the many fine stories about one of the most believable young boys in all of fiction. Fun to read aloud to almost any age group, and nine- or ten-year-olds can read these books for themselves. (See also "Ellen Rides Again," from *Ellen Tebbits,* who, like Henry, has typical fourth-grade problems, p. 72). 8–12

CLYMER, ELEANOR, *My Brother Stevie,* Holt, 1967. Stevie is a problem to his older sister Annie. How Annie turns Stevie's energies from delinquent activities to constructive uses is a sensitively told, understated story. 9–12

COOPER, PAGE, *Amigo: Circus Horse,* World, 1955. This is a thrilling story of circus life which is told from the standpoint of the circus performers and which concerns the struggles of three teen-agers who are trying to qualify for the big center ring. 12–15

DAVIS, LAVINIA R., *Roger and the Fox,* Doubleday, 1947. This is a sensitively perceptive story about a little boy's interest in a wild creature and his patient, persistent lookout, which is finally rewarded. 5–9

The Wild Birthday Cake, ill. by Hildegard Woodward, Doubleday, 1949. This is a full-bodied story of a little boy living intensely in his outdoor environment, with minor adventures appropriate to his age. Enchanting pictures add to the beauty and interest of this fine book. 5–9

DECKER, DUANE, *Hit and Run,* Morrow, 1949. This is an exciting baseball story about a young man's coming from a minor to a major league team, the problems he encounters in getting along with his teammates, the way he learns from a Negro teammate that punching people isn't going to solve his problems, and how he also learns from his new friend that he can be a big person despite his small stature. This is only one of many exciting sports stories by Decker. 12–16

DE REGNIERS, BEATRICE, *A Little House of Your Own,* ill. by Irene Haas, Harcourt, 1955. Even a child needs privacy that is respected, and many an odd place becomes a house of his own. 4–7

DU SOE, ROBERT C., *Three Without Fear,* ill. by Ralph Ray, Jr., Longmans, 1947. Dave Rogers, shipwrecked off the coast of California, is rescued by two Indian children. The three children lead a Robinson Crusoe existence of incredible hardship and survive only through the fortitude and ingenuity of the two Indians. 10–14

ENRIGHT, ELIZABETH, *The Four-Story Mistake,* ill. by author, Holt, 1942.

The Saturdays, ill. by author, Holt, 1941.

Then There Were Five, ill. by author, Holt, 1938. One of the trilogy about the Melendy family, *The Saturdays* is set in New York City, where the children evolve a scheme for taking turns in spending their allowances; the other titles are set in the country. 8–12

Thimble Summer, ill. by author, Holt, 1938. A delightful story of the adventures of a little girl on a Wisconsin farm. Newbery Medal. 8–12

ESTES, ELEANOR, *The Middle Moffat,* ill. by Louis Slobodkin, Harcourt, 1942.

The Moffats, ill. by Louis Slobodkin, Harcourt, 1941.

Rufus M., ill. by Louis Slobodkin, Harcourt, 1943. The Moffat family is fatherless and bordering on real poverty, but the spirit is one of good humor and warm relationships. 9–12

Ginger Pye, ill. by author, Harcourt, 1951. The author's Newbery Medal book centers around the theft of a dog and the children's attempts to find the thief. 9–12

The Hundred Dresses, Harcourt, 1944. Children are not likely to forget Wanda, who was rejected by the group, nor the culprits who taunted her. 9–11

ETS, MARIE HALL, *Play with Me,* ill. by author, Viking, 1955. This is a charming picture-story of a little girl and all the little wild things she meets on a walk through the meadow. 2–5

FALL, THOMAS, *Dandy's Mountain,* ill. by Juan Carlos Barberis, Dial, 1967. Between memorizing the dictionary and helping Bruce, her cousin who is trying hard to be a juvenile delinquent, rejoin the human race, Amanda "Dandy" Miller spends a memorable summer. This is a very funny but thoughtful book about a likable girl. 9–12

FLACK, MARJORIE, *Wait for William,* Houghton, 1935. This amusing circus story turns upon the most natural conflict in the world—a four-year-old's trouble with his shoelace and the older children's impatience with his slowness. 5–8

FRICK, C. H., *Five Against the Odds,* Harcourt, 1955.

Tourney Team, Harcourt, 1954. Two exciting basketball stories with fine human relationships developed. 11–14

GAGE, WILSON, *Dan and the Miranda,* ill. by Glenn Rounds, World, 1962. Humorous story of Dan's half-hearted attempts to do a project for the fifth-grade science fair. 8–11

GARST, SHANNON, *Cowboy Boots,* ill. by Charles Hargens, Abingdon, 1946. On his uncle's ranch, Bob learns cowboy skills through great persistence, despite many discouragements. 9–12

GATES, DORIS, *Blue Willow,* ill. by Paul Lantz, Viking, 1940. The story of Janey Larkin, daughter of migrant workers, who longed for a real home. 9–12

Sarah's Idea, ill. by Marjorie Torrey, Viking, 1938. A girl's story of California ranch life and a coveted burro. 8–10

GEORGE, JEAN, *Gull Number 737,* Crowell, 1964. When birds cause a fatal plane crash, Dr. Rivers and his son Luke are called upon to help drive the birds from the runways. A natural science detective story with important human values. 12–14

GILBERT, HELEN EARLE, *Dr. Trotter and His Big Gold Watch*, Abingdon, 1948. This is a little story about an amusing device of a wise old doctor for allaying the fears and worries of his small patients. 6–9

GUILFOILE, ELIZABETH, *Nobody Listens to Andrew*, ill. by Mary Stevens, Follett, 1957. A humorous sustained story for beginning readers. The title describes the grownups' reaction when Andrew tells them there is a bear in his bed. 6–7

HARRIS, ISOBEL, *Little Boy Brown*, ill. by André François, Lippincott, 1949. This story concerns a city boy's day in the country and his return to his confined skyscraper life in the city. 5–8

HAYWOOD, CAROLYN, *"B" Is for Betsy*, ill. by author, Harcourt, 1939.
Little Eddie, ill. by author, Morrow, 1947.
Penny and Peter, ill. by author, Harcourt, 1946.
Carolyn Haywood has written over two dozen books about the mild adventures of suburban children at home, at school, or in the community. Eddie has more humor in his life than the others. (See *Eddie and the Fire Engine*, p. 68). 5–9

HOLBERG, RUTH, *Rowena Carey*, ill. by Grace Paull, Doubleday, 1949. A delightful story of a fat, horse-loving girl who never gets a horse but who does receive jodhpurs and an occasional ride. 9–12

HUNT, IRENE, *Up a Road Slowly*, Follett, 1967. Julie Trelling, left motherless at age seven, is sent to live with her Aunt Cordelia and Uncle Haskell, who, between them, provide her with insight into the qualities necessary to become a mature, happy individual. For girls only. Newbery Medal. 12–16

JOHNSON, ANNABEL and E. K., *The Grizzly*, ill. by Gilbert Riswold, Harper, 1964. A sympathetic story of eleven-year-old David, who is caught between an over-protective mother and an over-athletic father. Realistic portrait of how David comes to accept the best of each parent. 9–12

KINGMAN, LEE, *Peter's Long Walk*, ill. by Barbara Cooney, Doubleday, 1953. There is a childlike spontaneity in this story of a five-year-old boy who goes in search of a new playmate and returns to his old animal friends. 5–7

KRASILOVSKY, PHYLLIS, *Benny's Flag*, ill. by W. T. Mars, World, 1960. The true story of how an Indian boy's entry in a flag contest came to be chosen as the official flag of Alaska. Striking illustrations of Alaska. 7–9

KRUMGOLD, JOSEPH, *Henry 3*, ill. by Alvin Smith, Atheneum, 1967. See the introduction to "Life in the United States" for discussion of this and other Krumgold titles. *. . . and now Miguel* is listed under Minority Groups in the United States since his Spanish-American heritage is central to the story. Newbery Medal.
Onion John, ill. by Symeon Shimin, Crowell, 1959. Andy Rusch, Jr., is a typical American boy growing up in a small town, devoted to his father who is his hero, but fascinated by Onion John, an eccentric town character. There is a father-son conflict which is more happily resolved than Onion John's problems when the town tries to civilize him. Amusing, and skillfully told. Newbery Medal. 10–14

LAWRENCE, MILDRED, *Peachtree Island*, ill. by Mary Stevens, Harcourt, 1948. Orphaned Cissie spends a year on an island in Lake Erie with Uncle Eben, who finds her so helpful that he decides to keep her forever. Good adult-child relationship. 8–11

LENSKI, LOIS, *Cowboy Small*, ill. by author, Walck, 1949.

The Little Airplane, ill. by author, Walck, 1938.
The Little Auto, ill. by author, Walck, 1934.
The Little Sail Boat, ill. by author, Walck, 1937.
The Little Train, ill. by author, Walck, 1940.
Papa Small, ill. by author, Walck, 1951.
It is hard to overestimate the appeal of Lenski's "little" books. Indeed, the Small Family has become a tradition for untold numbers of small children. 3–7

LIPKIND, WILLIAM, and NICOLAS MORDVINOFF, *Even Steven*, Harcourt, 1952. If this is not rock-bottom realism, it is the kind of ranch, cowboy, crooks, and heroism that children dream about. 4–6

MC CLOSKEY, ROBERT, *Blueberries for Sal*, ill. by author, Viking, 1948. A picture story about Sal and her mother, who tangle with a bear and her cub. Eventually each mother—human and animal—gets her own child and blueberries, too. 3–7
Lentil, ill. by author, Viking, 1940. Amusing story of a boy living in a small Midwestern town who saves the day with his harmonica. 6–9
One Morning in Maine, ill. by author, Viking, 1952. Another Sal story with glorious pictures of Maine woods and water. This time Sal has lost her first tooth, but after the initial shock, life goes on serenely. 3–7
Time of Wonder, ill. by author, Viking, 1957. In full color, McCloskey captures both the fun of a vacation in Maine and the power of a hurricane. Caldecott Medal. 6–9

MC GINLEY, PHYLLIS, *The Most Wonderful Doll in the World*, ill. by Helen Stone, Lippincott, 1950. A small girl cannot distinguish between things as they are and as she dreams they might be. A lost doll becomes more and more remarkable until the real doll is a shock when it is found. Gentle, humorous treatment of a common ailment. 7–9

NEVILLE, EMILY, *Berries Goodman*, Harper, 1965. Sharply written story of the effects of anti-Semitism on the friendship of two suburban boys. 10–14
It's Like This, Cat, Harper, 1963. Dave Mitchell is an average fourteen-year-old trying to come to grips with himself and his family. This Newbery Medal book has depth and subtlety, humor and realism. 9–13
Seventeenth Street Gang, ill. by Emily McCully, Harper, 1966. Good picture of ordinary city life and how a new boy on the block wins acceptance. 9–12

PETERSHAM, MAUD and MISKA, *The Box with Red Wheels*, ill. by authors, Macmillan, 1949. This entrancing picture book is the Petershams at their colorful best. The mysterious "box" which so attracts the animals contains a delightful baby, who is as charmed by the barnyard animals as they are with her. 4–7

RENICK, MARION, *Nicky's Football Team*, ill. by Marian Honigman, Scribner's, 1951.
Peter's Home Run, ill. by Pru Herric, Scribner's, 1952.
These stories have few literary qualities, but they do introduce children successfully to football, baseball, and good sportsmanship. 7–9

ROBERTSON, KEITH, *Henry Reed, Inc.*, ill. by Robert McCloskey, Viking, 1958.
Henry Reed's Baby-Sitting Service, ill. by Robert McCloskey, Viking, 1966.
Henry Reed's Journey, ill. by Robert McCloskey, Viking, 1963.
Three very funny stories about a literal-minded boy who provides laughter for everyone but himself. 10–12

ROBINSON, THOMAS PENDLETON, *Trigger John's Son*, ill. by Robert McCloskey, Viking, 1949. Trigger is an orphan in the process of being adopted when he decides to inspect his future parents. He gets off the train prematurely, falls in with a boys' gang and a blind hermit, and the action begins. Boys delight in Trigger's scrapes and good intentions, and Robert McCloskey's sensitive drawings add to the fun. 10–14

SAUER, JULIA, *The Light at Tern Rock,* ill. by Georges Schreiber, Viking, 1951. A Christmas story set against the wild beauty and isolation of a lonely seagirt lighthouse. The story is beautifully told and illustrated, and the moral problem involved makes it unusual. 9–12

SCHAEFER, JACK, *Old Ramon,* ill. by Harold West, Houghton, 1960. A convincing character study of an old shepherd who is wise not only in the ways of sheep but also in the ways of young boys. An effective read-aloud story. 10–14

SCHNEIDER, NINA, *While Susie Sleeps,* ill. by Dagmar Wilson, W. R. Scott, 1948. Pleasantly cadenced text tells about the creatures that sleep the darkness through and those that wake and work at night. 4–7

SORENSON, VIRGINIA, *Miracles on Maple Hill,* ill. by Beth and Joe Krush, Harcourt, 1956. A warm story of a family's experiencing the wonder of woods and fields at all seasons. Newbery Medal. 9–12

SPYKMAN, E. C., *A Lemon and a Star,* Harcourt, 1955. The amusing adventures of four motherless Cares youngsters. For superior readers. 11–14

STOLZ, MARY, *Noonday Friends,* ill. by Louis S. Glanzman, Harper, 1965. Being poor, wearing old clothes, and having a free lunch pass given to needy children eats at eleven-year-old Franny Davis. Despite the very real problem of poverty, this is an inspiring book—sometimes funny, always perceptive in its sensitivity. 9–12

TRESSELT, ALVIN, *Follow the Wind,* ill. by Roger Duvoisin, Lothrop, 1950.
Hi, Mister Robin!, ill. by Roger Duvoisin, Lothrop, 1950.
Hide and Seek Fog, ill. by Roger Duvoisin, Lothrop, 1965.
I Saw the Sea Come In, ill. by Roger Duvoisin, Lothrop, 1954.
Rain Drop Splash, ill. by Leonard Weisgard, Lothrop, 1946.
Sun Up, ill. by Roger Duvoisin, Lothrop, 1949.
White Snow, Bright Snow, ill. by Roger Duvoisin, Lothrop, 1947. Caldecott Medal.
These picture-stories are little dramas of weather and seasonal changes. 4–6

TUDOR, TASHA, *Pumpkin Moonshine,* ill. by author, Walck, 1938. This Halloween story makes a good introduction to the small, beautifully illustrated books of Tasha Tudor. 4–7

TUNIS, JOHN R., *All-American,* Harcourt, 1942. No one writes better sports stories than John R. Tunis. In addition to sports, his books center on the problems of adolescents resulting from religious and racial prejudices. 12–14

UDRY, JANICE, *The Moon Jumpers,* ill. by Maurice Sendak, Harper, 1959. The delight of playing in the moonlight out-of-doors is caught in the artist's luminous drawings. A rare book. 4–7

WIER, ESTER, *The Loner,* McKay, 1963. Boy has no family to help him survive the problems of being a migrant worker. He has had to learn to depend on himself and no one else, a kind of independence which enables him to survive while following the crops, but which causes trouble when he finds himself "adopted" by Boss, a tough old lady with a rigorous way of life and set standards. 10–12

WILSON, HAZEL, *Herbert,* ill. by John Barron, Knopf, 1950.
Herbert Again, ill. by John Barron, Knopf, 1951.
More Fun with Herbert, ill. by John Barron, Knopf, 1954.
Herbert is a younger Homer Price (p. 104), and his adventures and vicissitudes are equally funny. 8–12

YASHIMA, TARO, pseud. (Jun Iwanatsu), *Umbrella,* ill. by author, Viking, 1958. Day after day small Momo waited and hoped for rain so that she might use her bright red birthday boots and new umbrella. Stunning illustrations. 5–8

YATES, ELIZABETH, *Mountain Born,* ill. by Nora Unwin, Coward, 1943.
A Place for Peter, ill. by Nora Unwin, Coward, 1952. Peter is a little boy in the first book, growing into farm activities and enjoying the companionship of a pet lamb. Through his pet, Peter comes to know birth, death, and the continuity of life. In the second book, Peter is a sturdy thirteen-year-old who is in unhappy conflict with his father. Again, farm animals and activities help both Peter and his father. 10–14

Minority Groups[1]

ANGELO, VALENTI, *The Bells of Bleecker Street,* ill. by author, Viking, 1949.
Hill of Little Miracles, ill. by author, Viking, 1942.
In *The Bells of Bleecker Street* twelve-year-old Joey finds himself the accidental possessor of a toe from the statue of St. John. His struggles to return the toe, his adventures with his gang, and his father's return from the war make an amusing story and bring this Italian neighborhood vividly to life. *Hill of Little Miracles* shows Ricco, who was born with one leg too short, starting on the road to normalcy. This book abounds with the good nature and gaiety of the Italians on Telegraph Hill. 10–14

ASSOCIATION FOR CHILDHOOD EDUCATION, *Told Under Spacious Skies,* ill. by William Moyers, Macmillan, 1952.
Told Under the Stars and Stripes, ill. by Nedda Walker, Macmillan, 1945.
The first book is made up of regional stories; the second book is an anthology of short stories about various minority groups in our cities throughout the country. 8–12

BEIM, LORRAINE and JERROLD, *Two Is a Team,* ill. by Ernest Crichlow, Harcourt, 1945. Two little boys find that they get more done as a team than singly. That they are of two different races makes no difference; it's the team that is important. 5–8

[1] This section has been edited from the previous edition, but not expanded. Books about Negroes have been incorporated here. However, recent publications in the area of inter-group relationships are now listed in the "Life in the United States" section of the Bibliography because of the shifting focus found in the books. Teachers wishing comprehensive lists on inter-group relations are advised to consult the following publications:

Baker, Augusta, *Books about Negro Life for Children,* The New York Public Library, revised at regular intervals

Crosby, Muriel, editor, *Reading Ladders for Human Relations,* American Council on Education, 4th rev. ed., 1963

Rollins, Charlemae, *We Build Together,* National Council of Teachers of English, 1967

CARROLL, RUTH and LATROBE, *Beanie,* ill. by authors, Walck, 1953. This story is followed by several others about Beanie and his family, the Tatums. Magnificent sketches of the Smoky Mountains. 7–9

DE ANGELI, MARGUERITE, *Henner's Lydia,* ill. by author, Doubleday, 1936.

Skippack School, ill. by author, Doubleday, 1939.

Two stories of life in a Mennonite community in Pennsylvania. 8–10

Yonie Wondernose, ill. by author, Doubleday, 1944. A favorite, especially when his "wondering" pays off and he proves his courage as well. There could hardly be a more appealing introduction to the Pennsylvania Dutch than Yonie. 6–9

FAULKNER, GEORGENE, and JOHN BECKER, *Melindy's Medal,* ill. by C. E. Fox, Messner, 1945. A humorous and tender story of a little girl's achievement. 8–11

HUNT, MABEL LEIGH, *Ladycake Farm,* ill. by Clotilde Embree Funk, Lippincott, 1952. This joyous story of a Negro family beginning a new life on a farm has its tragic moments, too. A delightful family group by any standard, and a first-rate story. 9–12

JACKSON, JESSE, *Call Me Charley,* ill. by Doris Spiegal, Harper, 1945. The story of the ups and downs in a young Negro's friendship with a white boy in a white community. 9–12

KEATS, EZRA JACK, *Peter's Chair,* ill. by author, Harper, 1967.

The Snowy Day, ill. by author, Viking, 1964. Caldecott Medal.

Whistle for Willie, ill. by author, Viking, 1964.

Three beautifully illustrated stories about a little boy's adventures in the first snow; how, when he is a little older, he learns to whistle for his dog; and his final acceptance of his new little sister. 4–7

KINGMAN, LEE, *The Best Christmas,* ill. by Barbara Cooney, Doubleday, 1949. A simple, moving story of a Finnish-American family's Christmas. 8–11

KRUMGOLD, JOSEPH, *...and now Miguel,* ill. by Jean Charlot, Crowell, 1953. The story of twelve-year-old Miguel, who wishes to be accepted as a man, is told with humor and tenderness. Fine picture of sheepherding in New Mexico. Newbery Medal. 10–14

LENSKI, LOIS, *Bayou Suzette,* ill. by author, Lippincott, 1948.

Blue Ridge Billy, ill. by author, Lippincott, 1946.

Boom Town Boy, ill. by author, Lippincott, 1948.

Judy's Journey, ill. by author, Lippincott, 1947.

Prairie School, ill. by author, Lippincott, 1951.

Strawberry Girl, ill. by author, Lippincott, 1945.

These regional stories are a remarkable contribution to a child's understanding of the people, work, and conditions in different sections of this country. The titles indicate locale or work. 8–12

Prairie School is the story of the courage and resourcefulness with which a teacher and children met the Dakota blizzard of 1949, which marooned them in their schoolhouse. Every book is a good story with lively characters. (See also "Home," from *Cotton in My Sack,* p. 83). 8–12

LINDQUIST, JENNIE D., *The Golden Name Day,* ill. by Garth Williams, Harper, 1955. The delightful quest of a Swedish name day for a little American girl in the midst of her loving Swedish relatives. 8–10

The Little Silver House, ill. by Garth Williams, Harper, 1959. The mystery of a little silver house and a festive Swedish Christmas will please young readers in this sequel to *The Golden Name Day.* 8–10

LOWNSBERY, ELOISE, *Marta the Doll,* ill. by Marya Werten, McKay, 1946. Hanka, a little Polish girl, longs for a soft, cuddly doll such as her American cousins have. Her sister Marysia gives up a new skirt to buy the doll. Hanka and her doll Marta are inseparable and share the pleasant adventures of everyday living. 7–10

MEANS, FLORENCE CRANNELL, *Great Day in the Morning,* Houghton, 1946. In this book a lovable Negro girl experiences the bitterness of racial prejudice but has the courage to go on. At Tuskegee she comes to know Dr. Carver and decides to become a nurse. 12–14

MILHOUS, KATHERINE, *The Egg Tree,* ill. by author, Scribner's, 1950. This beautifully illustrated book of an Easter egg tree in rural Pennsylvania has started egg trees blooming all over this country. Authentic folk art and bright colors made it a Caldecott Medal winner. 6–8

NEWELL, HOPE, *A Cap for Mary Ellis,* Harper, 1953. Two young nursing students enter as the first Negro trainees in a New York State hospital. Their story is told with warmth and humor. 11–14

OAKES, VANYA, *Willy Wong: American,* ill. by Weda Yap, Messner, 1951. Here is the old struggle of a little Chinese boy to be accepted as a one hundred per cent American. A good family story. 10–up

POLITI, LEO, *A Boat for Peppe,* ill. by author, Scribner's, 1950.

Juanita, ill. by author, Scribner's, 1948.

Little Leo, ill. by author, Scribner's, 1951.

Moy Moy, ill. by author, Scribner's, 1960.

Pedro, the Angel of Olvera Street, ill. by author, Scribner's, 1946.

Song of the Swallows, ill. by author, Scribner's, 1949. Caldecott Medal.

These appealing picture-stories have slight plots but a tender beauty that is unique. Pedro and Juanita show the Christmas and Easter customs of the Mexican colony on Olvera Street in Los Angeles. The swallows are the famous birds of San Capistrano Mission. Peppe takes part in the blessing of the fishing boats at Monterey, but Little Leo journeys to Italy and converts a whole village of children to the charms of playing Indian. And Moy Moy, the little sister of three brothers in Chinatown, finds the New Year's festivities wonderful. 5–8

SEREDY, KATE, *A Tree for Peter,* ill. by author, Viking, 1941. A story of shanty town, complicated by rather confusing symbolism, but a beautiful story with some of Seredy's finest pictures. 8–12

STERLING, DOROTHY, *Mary Jane,* ill. by Ernest Crichlow, Doubleday, 1959. A young Negro girl enrolls in a newly integrated junior high school where she is lonely and has problems to solve in winning friendship and understanding. 12–14

TAYLOR, SYDNEY, *All-of-a-Kind Family,* Follett, 1951. This is a heart-warming story of an affectionate Jewish family, living in the early 1900's, that will be enjoyed by all children. 9–12

More All-of-a-Kind Family, ill. by Mary Stevens, Follett, 1954. Further heart-warming adventures of the affectionate family. 9–12

UCHIDA, YOSHIKO, *The Promised Year,* ill. by William M. Hutchinson, Harcourt, 1959. A little Japanese girl and her black cat learn to adjust to their new home and friends in California. 8–12

WILSON, LEON, *This Boy Cody,* ill. by Ursula Koering, Watts, 1950.

This Boy Cody and His Friends, ill. by Ursula Koering, Watts, 1952.

Joyous stories of Cody Capshaw, his family, friends, and neighbors in the Cumberland Mountain region. House building, fiddle making, berrying, riddles, tall tales, livestock, pets, and a tagalong small sister add interest, complications, and fun to Cody's adventures. 9–12

North American Indian Stories

ARMER, LAURA ADAMS, *Waterless Mountain*, ill. by Sidney and Laura Adams Armer, McKay, 1931. A poetic story of Navaho life containing little action and much mysticism. For the special reader. 12–14

BAKER, BETTY, *Little Runner of the Longhouse*, ill. by Arnold Lobel, Harper, 1962. Easy-to-read story of an Iroquois boy and his New Year celebration. 6–7
Shaman's Last Raid, ill. by Leonard Shortall, Harper, 1963. Very funny account of what happens when Great-Grandfather, who rode with Geronimo, tries to teach the old ways to two modern Indian children. 8–12

BLEEKER, SONIA, *American Indian Tribes*, ill. by Althea Karr, Morrow, 1950.
The Apache Indians; Raiders of the Southwest, ill. by Althea Karr, Morrow, 1951.
The Aztec Indians of Mexico, ill. by Kisa Sasaki, Morrow, 1963.
The Cherokee; Indians of the Mountains, ill. by Althea Karr, Morrow, 1952.
Indians of the Longhouse, ill. by Althea Karr, Morrow, 1950.
The Sioux Indians; Hunters and Warriors of the Plains, ill. by Kisa Sasaki, Morrow, 1962.
This prolific anthropologist-author has written about almost every Indian tribe inhabiting North America. The books are factual narratives with good story interest and they give children authentic information about the family life, work and play, customs, and history of each tribe. 8–12

BRONSON, WILFRID S., *Pinto's Journey*, Messner, 1948. A fine adventure story about a Navaho Indian boy of modern times. Brilliant colored pictures. 8–10

BUFF, MARY, *Dancing Cloud, the Navajo Boy*, rev. ed., ill. by Conrad Buff, Viking, 1957. 9–10
Hah-Nee of the Cliff Dwellers, ill. by Conrad Buff, Houghton, 1956. 8–10
Magic Maize, ill. by Conrad Buff, Houghton, 1953. 9–12
Three fine Indian stories from the team which produced *Kobi, A Boy of Switzerland* (p. 140).

BULLA, CLYDE, *Eagle Feather*, ill. by Tom Two Arrows, Crowell, 1953.
Indian Hill, ill. by James J. Spanfeller, Crowell, 1963.
Clyde Bulla, author of over thirty books, has a special touch which makes his easy reading books especially appealing to reluctant readers. 7–10

CLARK, ANN NOLAN, *Blue Canyon Horse*, ill. by Allan Houser, Viking, 1954. A beautiful story of a young Indian boy and his horse. 8–10
In My Mother's House, ill. by Velino Herrera, Viking, 1941. This is a fine story written with simplicity and beauty about the Tewa Indian children. 8–12
Little Navaho Bluebird, ill. by Velino Herrera, Viking, 1943. The story of a little Navaho girl who loves her home and the old ways of life, but who learns to accept going to the white man's school. 8–12

DAVIS, RUSSELL G., and BRENT K. ASHABRANNER, *The Choctaw Code*, McGraw-Hill, 1961. The Choctaws granted a year of freedom to a man under the death sentence, trusting him to appear and accept his punishment. This moving

story recounts how youthful Tom Baxter learned to accept the inevitability of his friend's death. 10–14

LAURITZEN, JONREED, *The Ordeal of the Young Hunter*, ill. by Hoke Denetsosie, Little, 1954. A distinguished story of a twelve-year-old Navaho boy who grows to appreciate what is good in the cultures of the white man and the Indian. 11–14

MC GRAW, ELOISE JARVIS, *Moccasin Trail*, Coward, 1952. Although this story centers on a white boy's decision to return to his own people after being rescued and raised by the Crow Indians, it tells much about the Indians, their ideals, customs, and limitations. 12–16

MC NICKLE, D'ARCY, *Runner in the Sun*, ill. by Allan Houser, Holt, 1954. Before the coming of the white men to the Southwest, a young Indian lad makes a hazardous journey to find a hardier maize. 12–14

SANDOZ, MARI, *The Horsecatcher*, Westminster, 1957. Compelling story of Young Elk, a Cheyenne, who faces disapproval because he would rather capture horses than kill men. 11–14

LIFE IN OTHER LANDS

England, Ireland, Scotland

ARDIZZONE, EDWARD, *Little Tim and the Brave Sea Captain*, ill. by author, Walck, 1936. A picture-story book about life at sea with five-year-old Tim as the hero. 6–8
Tim All Alone, ill. by author, Walck. This is a story about a young seafaring lad who is the personification of achievement. 6–8

DILLON, EILÍS, *The Coriander*, ill. by Vic Donahue, Funk, 1964. Set on the Irish island of Inishgillan (see Dillon's *A Family of Foxes*, Bibliography, p. 244), this story of a kidnaped doctor who reluctantly is pressed into service offers more than just an exciting plot. 11–14

MC LEAN, ALLAN CAMPBELL, *Master of Morgana*, Harcourt, 1959.
Storm over Skye, Harcourt, 1957.
Two suspense-mystery stories which capture the fascination of the Isle of Skye. For better readers. 12–15

MAC PHERSON, MARGARET M., *The Shinty Boys*, ill. by Shirley Hughes, Harcourt, 1963. Earning money on the Isle of Skye is not easy, and the boys must earn fifty pounds over the summer if they are to keep their shinty team. 10–12

RANSOME, ARTHUR, *Swallows and Amazons*, ill. by Helene Carter, Lippincott, 1931. This is the only title in a seven-volume series which is still in print. It is the story of a summer vacation spent on an island by a group of children. They are far enough from home to feel independent, but close enough to feel secure. A satisfying book for special readers. 10–12

STREATFEILD, NOEL, *Ballet Shoes*, ill. by Richard Floethe, Random, 1937.
Circus Shoes, ill. by Richard Floethe, Random, 1939.
Theater Shoes, ill. by Richard Floethe, Random, 1945.
The "Shoes" books are a series of gay tales with vocational themes. 10–14

TOWNSEND, JOHN ROWE, *Good-Bye to the Jungle*, Lippincott, 1967. This fine novel about English slums is a sometimes amusing, sometimes sad, story of what happens to six people when they move into a new neighborhood. 12–15

TUNIS, JOHN R., *Silence Over Dunkerque*, Morrow, 1962.

This is a moving account of the events leading up to the evacuation of thousands of troops across the English Channel during World War II. The horrors of war as they touch the lives of young and old, people and animals, are recounted in quiet understatement. 12–15

TURNER, PHILIP, *Colonel Sheperton's Clock*, ill. by Philip Gough, World, 1966.

The Grange at High Force, ill. by W. T. Mars, World, 1967.

Although both books contain a slight element of mystery, it is the relationships among the three boys and between the boys and the adults which lend flavor to these pictures of small village English life. 12–14

VAN STOCKUM, HILDA, *The Cottage at Bantry Bay*, ill. by author, Viking, 1938. The escapades of the O'Sullivan children—Michael, Brigid, and the twins Francie and Liam—make a lively tale. 10–12

Pegeen, ill. by author, Viking, 1941. This tells of the scrapes and misdeeds of Pegeen, a mischievous orphan, who has come to live with the O'Sullivans. 10–12

France

BEMELMANS, LUDWIG, *Madeline*, Simon and Schuster, 1939. Madeline inhabits a French boarding school with "twelve little girls in two straight lines" doing everything in two straight lines, except the appendix that only Madeline had to have removed. The other *Madeline* books are equally as much fun as this one. 5–8

BERNA, PAUL, *The Horse Without a Head*, tr. from the French by John Buchanan-Brown, ill. by Richard Kennedy, Pantheon, 1958. The right combination of an exciting mystery and the French *joie de vivre* in a picture of lower-class children in France. 9–12

BISHOP, CLAIRE HUCHET, *Pancakes Paris*, ill. by Georges Schreiber, Viking, 1947. A half-starved postwar French child receives a miraculous package of American pancake mix. How he meets two American soldiers and gets the directions for the pancakes translated makes a heart-warming tale. 8–12

Twenty and Ten, ill. by William Pène DuBois, Viking, 1952. During the Nazi occupation of France, nineteen French children with their teacher were asked to feed and hide ten Jewish children. How these fifth-graders shared their food and managed with their teacher held in jail is a moving and satisfying story. 9–12

CARLSON, NATALIE SAVAGE, *The Happy Orpheline*, ill. by Garth Williams, Harper, 1957. An imaginative and amusing story of twenty orphans, happy in their home outside of Paris, afraid only of being adopted. 8–10

A Brother for the Orphelines, ill. by Garth Williams, Harper, 1959. A delightful sequel to *The Happy Orpheline*, this tells of the efforts of the orphans to keep a baby boy foundling left on their doorstep. 8–10

FRANÇOISE, pseud. (Françoise Seignebosc), *Jeanne-Marie at the Fair*, Scribner's, 1959.

Jeanne-Marie Counts Her Sheep, Scribner's, 1951.

Jeanne-Marie in Gay Paris, Scribner's, 1956.

Noël for Jeanne-Marie, Scribner's, 1956.

Springtime for Jeanne-Marie, Scribner's, 1955.

Popular picture-story book series about a sunny little French girl and her adventures. 5–7

Holland

DE JONG, MEINDERT, *Dirk's Dog Bello*, ill. by Kurt Wiese, Harper, 1939. The story of a boy's love for his much too large and hungry dog. A fine picture of present-day Dutch life. 10–12

Far Out the Long Canal, ill. by Nancy Grossman, Harper, 1964. At nine, Moona alone among his classmates cannot skate and his only dream is to learn. 10–12

The Wheel on the School, ill. by Maurice Sendak, Harper, 1954. A tenderly told, warmly humorous story of how a Dutch fishing village brings back the storks to settle there again. Newbery Medal. 9–12

DODGE, MARY MAPES, *Hans Brinker; or the Silver Skates*, ill. by Hilda Van Stockum, World Publishing, 1946. Although still considered a classic, this lengthy story of Hans should not be a first choice for books about Holland. 10–12

KRASILOVSKY, PHYLLIS, *The Cow Who Fell in the Canal*, ill. by Peter Spier, Doubleday, 1957. Stunning picture book which combines humor with an accurate look at Dutch life. 5–8

Italy

ANGELO, VALENTI, *The Honey Boat*, ill. by author, Viking, 1959. Friendly picture of an Italian family at work and play. 10–12

BETTINA, pseud. (Bettina Errlich), *Pantaloni*, ill. by author, Harper, 1957. This author-artist has never created more beautiful pictures than those for this appealing picture-story of an Italian boy's search for his dog. 5–9

Mexico and South America

BEHN, HARRY, *The Two Uncles of Pablo*, ill. by Mel Silverman, Harcourt, 1959. The contrast between Pablo's two uncles creates a real problem for him. How he reunites the family is sensitively told. Fine reading aloud. 9–12

BEIM, LORRAINE and JERROLD, *The Burro That Had a Name*, ill. by Howard Simon, Harcourt, 1939. An amusing story of a boy's attachment to a burro. 6–9

CLARK, ANN NOLAN, *Secret of the Andes*, ill. by Jean Charlot, Viking, 1952. In this Newbery Medal book, Cusi lives among the great peaks of the Andes Mountains, guarding a hidden herd of royal llamas and learning from old Chuto the sacred traditions of his Incan ancestors. Even after his journey to the world of men, Cusi knows that his destiny lies in the remote heights cherishing the flock. 10–14

DESMOND, ALICE CURTIS, *The Lucky Llama*, ill. by William Bronson, Macmillan, 1939. A charming tale of a boy and a llama. 10–12

ETS, MARIE HALL, and AURORA LA BASTIDA, *Nine Days to Christmas*, ill. by Marie Hall Ets, Viking, 1959. Small Ceci enjoys her first posada in this Caldecott Medal book of present-day Mexico. 5–8

GARRETT, HELEN, *Angelo the Naughty One*, ill. by Leo Politi, Viking, 1944. The amusing reform of a small Mexican boy who did not like to take baths. 6–9

KALNAY, FRANCIS, *Chúcaro: Wild Pony of the Pampa*, ill. by Julian de Miskey, Harcourt, 1957. Excellent depiction of life on the Argentine pampas with a story that leaves the reader with much to think about. 9–12

PARISH, HELEN RAND, *At the Palace Gates*, ill. by Leo Politi, Viking, 1949. Appealing adventure story of a small Peruvian living on his own in Lima. 9–12

RITCHIE, BARBARA, *Ramón Makes a Trade* (Los Cambios de Ramón), ill. by Earl Thollander, Parnassus, 1959. A picture-story with English and Spanish text which tells of an enterprising Mexican boy who succeeds in trading his pottery jar for a much-desired green parakeet. 9–10

SOMMERFELT, AIMÉE, *My Name Is Pablo,* ill. by Hans Norman Dahl, Criterion, 1965. Portrait of modern Mexico's poverty problem as seen through the eyes of Pablo, who is befriended by a Norwegian family. 10–12

TARSHIS, ELIZABETH K., *The Village That Learned to Read,* ill. by Harold Hayden, Houghton, 1941. A robust story with humor and an amusing moral. Important for its focus on the national drive for literacy in Mexico. 10–12

WEIL, ANN, *The Silver Fawn,* Bobbs-Merrill, 1939. This book presents an excellent picture of the skillful craftsmen of Mexico and the beautiful things they make. It is also a moving story of one boy's achievement. 8–12

The Orient[2]

AYER, JACQUELINE, *NuDang and His Kite,* ill. by author, Harcourt, 1959.
A Wish for Little Sister, ill. by author, Harcourt, 1960. Colorful picture-stories of Thailand. 5–8

BUCK, PEARL, *The Big Wave,* prints by Hiroshige and Hokusai, Day, 1948. Significant story built around the theme that "life is stronger than death." Two Japanese boys adventure together, survive a terrible catastrophe, and begin life anew. 9–12

DE JONG, MEINDERT, *The House of Sixty Fathers,* ill. by Maurice Sendak, Harper, 1956. Set in China during World War II, this is the story of how Tien Pao and his pig, Glory of the Republic, were finally able to rejoin Tien Pao's family. 10–12

HANDFORTH, THOMAS, *Mei Li,* ill. by author, Doubleday, 1938. The pleasant adventures of a little Chinese girl at the Fair. A picture book which won the 1939 Caldecott Medal. 5–8

KIM, YONG-IK, *The Happy Days,* ill. by Artur Marokvia, Little, 1960. Modern-day Korea is a mixture of disappointments and happiness for orphaned Sang Chun. 10–12

LATTIMORE, ELEANOR FRANCES, *Little Pear,* ill. by author, Harcourt, 1931. 6–9
Little Pear and His Friends, ill. by author, Harcourt, 1939. 6–9
Little Pear and the Rabbits, ill. by author, Morrow, 1956. 6–9
Three adventure stories of a likable little Chinese boy.
Three Little Chinese Girls, ill. by author, Morrow, 1948. Similar to *Little Pear,* but with a feminine appeal. 7–9

LEWIS, ELIZABETH FOREMAN, *Ho-Ming, Girl of New China,* ill. by Kurt Wiese, Holt, 1934. A moving story of China in transition. Ho-Ming learns to read and offers to help the American doctor combat disease. The need for change is balanced against values of the old ways of doing things. 12–16
To Beat a Tiger, ill. by John Heubnergarth, Holt, 1956. A devastating picture of the effects of poverty upon people. Although it has its hopeful side, it is for mature readers. 12–16
Young Fu of the Upper Yangtze, Holt, 1932. This Newbery Medal book gives us a graphic picture of the inner strife and conflict in the life of a young Chinese boy. The details are Chinese, but Fu is any boy of any country trying to make his way in the world. 10–14

LINDQUIST, WILLIS, *Burma Boy,* ill. by Nicolas Mordvinoff,

[2] Included in this section are stories of China, India, Japan, Thailand, Tibet, etc. Most of the stories capture some facet of the Oriental mysticism which dominates existence in the Far East.

McGraw, 1953. An absorbing story of a boy's search for a lost elephant. 9–11

MARTIN, PATRICIA MILES, *The Pointed Brush,* ill. by Roger Duvoisin, Lothrop, 1959. Story of Chung Wee, small sixth son of the House of Chung, who goes to school only because he is least needed in the rice fields, and who convinces his family that "the man who knows the written word has strength." 6–8

MERRILL, JEAN, *The Superlative Horse,* ill. by Ronnie Solbert, 1961. When Po Lo, Chief Groom in Duke Mu's court, grows too old to retain his position, he recommends Han Kan, son of a fuel hawker, as his successor. Han Kan's test is to select one horse for the Duke's stable of already magnificent horses. 8–11

MUHLENWEG, FRITZ, *Big Tiger and Christian,* ill. by Rafaello Busoni, Pantheon, 1952. Here are nearly six hundred pages packed with adventure, people, and strange places in a story so unusual that no one who reads the first chapter will want to put it down. An English and a Chinese boy carry through a dangerous mission for General Wao in wartime China. They travel by truck, ponies, and camel, encounter kindly people and villains, but come through it all competently and with their sense of humor intact. 12–adult

RANKIN, LOUISE S., *Daughter of the Mountains,* ill. by Kurt Wiese, Viking, 1948. A little Tibetan girl undertakes a long and perilous journey alone to retrieve her beloved dog. She is sustained by a deep religious faith. 9–12

SOMMERFELT, AIMÉE, *The Road to Agra,* ill. by Ulf Aas, Phillips, 1961. Thirteen-year-old Lalu's younger sister Maya is going blind, and he decides to take her to the UNICEF hospital in Agra. The trip is long and hazardous, and events depict the poverty of India's small villages and its effects upon people. 9–12

TREFFINGER, CAROLYN, *Li-Lun, Lad of Courage,* ill. by Kurt Wiese, Abingdon, 1947. Li-Lun compensates for his fear of the sea by spending four months alone on a mountain. He learns a way of life for himself and his people. 9–12

UCHIDA, YOSHIKO, *Takao and Grandfather's Sword,* ill. by William M. Hutchinson, Harcourt, 1958. One of a number of good stories by this author which depicts both modern Japan and its rich heritage. 8–10

WIESE, KURT, *Fish in the Air,* ill. by author, Viking, 1948. An amusing account of what happens to a small Chinese boy when he buys the largest kite in the market. Lovely, bright pictures. 6–8

YASHIMA, TARO, pseud. (Jun Iwanatsu), *Crow Boy,* ill. by author, Viking, 1955. This story of a small outcast Japanese boy has unusual social values as well as great pictorial beauty. 6–8

YASHIMA, TARO, and HATOJU MUKU, *The Golden Footprints,* ill. by author, World, 1960. A beautiful story of the devotion of two foxes to their captured cub and how it affects a young Japanese boy. Excellent reading aloud. 8–11

Pacific Islands

OTTLEY, REGINALD, *Roan Colt,* ill. by Clyde Pearson, Harcourt, 1967. A very fine sequel to *Boy Alone* (p.176). 10–13

PHIPSON, JOAN, *The Boundary Riders,* ill. by Margaret Horder, Harcourt, 1963.
The Family Conspiracy, ill. by Margaret Horder, Harcourt, 1964.
Threat to the Barkers, ill. by Margaret Horder, Harcourt, 1965.
These three fine stories are set in the back country of

Australia and show how rugged life is in the wilds.
10–12

SOUTHALL, IVAN, *Ash Road,* ill. by Clem Seale, St. Martins, 1965.
Hills End, St. Martins, 1963.
Two unforgettable stories from Australia about people under pressure from a disastrous fire and a flood. High drama at its best.
10–14

SPERRY, ARMSTRONG, *Call It Courage,* ill. by author, Macmillan, 1940. This Newbery Medal book is an exciting adventure story and also the tale of one boy's conquest of fear. Beautifully illustrated and poetic text.
10–12

Scandinavian Countries

ANCKARSVÄRD, KARIN, *The Mysterious Schoolmaster,* tr. from the Swedish by Annabelle Macmillan, ill. by Paul Galdone, Harcourt, 1959. A coastal village in Sweden provides the background for this captivating tale of two children who outwit an international spy.
10–12
Robber Ghost, tr. from the Swedish by Annabelle Macmillan, ill. by Paul Galdone, Harcourt, 1961. A sequel to the above, with numerous escapades.
10–12

BESKOW, ELSA, *Pelle's New Suit,* ill. by author, Harper, 1929. This beautifully illustrated picture book of how Pelle works for his new suit has acquired the status of a classic.
4–7

LINDGREN, ASTRID, *Rasmus and the Vagabond,* tr. from the Swedish by Gerry Bothmer, ill. by Eric Palmquist, Viking, 1960. Nine-year-old Rasmus runs away from the Swedish orphanage and meets Paradise Oscar, a lovable tramp, with whom he has many adventures. How he finds a home and happiness is well told in this touching tale.
10–12

LINDMAN, MAJ, *Snipp, Snapp, Snurr and the Red Shoes,* ill. by author, Whitman, 1932. This story of Swedish triplets has a gaiety about it that matches the colorful illustrations of the original book.
5–7

UNNERSTAD, EDITH, *The Spettecake Holiday,* tr. from the Swedish by Inger Boye, ill. by Iben Clante, Macmillan, 1958. A warm, humorous story of a little boy's summer on a Swedish farm.
8–10

Switzerland

CHONZ, SELINA, *A Bell for Ursli,* ill. by Alois Carigiet, Walck, 1950. One of the most beautiful picture-stories to come out of Europe, this is also an exciting adventure story of a small Swiss boy's determination to have the largest bell to ring in the spring processional.
5–7

ULLMAN, JAMES RAMSEY, *Banner in the Sky,* Lippincott, 1954. A dramatic and exciting story of young Rudi's determination to become a mountain climber and one day conquer the Citadel, the mountain that dominates his life. Captures, as no other book does, the fascination of mountain climbing.
12–16

Eskimo Stories

FREUCHEN, PIPALUK, *Eskimo Boy,* ill. by Ingrid Vang Nyman, Lothrop, 1951. This epic tale, translated from the Danish, is the grimmest, most terrifying picture of Eskimo life we have had. It is the story of a boy's fight to save his family from starvation. The realistic details make it unsuitable for young children, but the heroism of the boy and his deeds are good for older children to read about.
10–12

LIPKIND, WILLIAM, *Boy with a Harpoon,* ill. by Nicolas Mordvinoff, Harcourt, 1952. This is a substantial story of Eskimo life for younger children, but it, as well as Freuchen's book, should banish forever the igloo stereotype of Arctic life. An absorbing story of a boy's attempts to rid himself of a derogatory nickname and win a respected place in the community of men.
7–10

Other Countries

BENARY, MARGOT, *The Ark,* Harcourt, 1953.
12–14
Castle on the Border, tr. from the German by Richard and Clara Winston, Harcourt, 1956.
12–15
Rowan Farm, tr. from the German by Richard and Clara Winston, Harcourt, 1954.
12–15
Three stories of life in postwar Germany and the problems encountered in rebuilding a normal life out of the ruins of World War II.

BLOCH, MARIE H., *Aunt America,* ill. by Joan Berg, Atheneum, 1963. Without moralizing, Bloch makes clear the meaning of freedom by depicting the lives of those who live in the Communist-dominated Ukraine.
9–12

BROWN, MARCIA, *Henry-Fisherman,* ill. by author, Scribner's, 1959. Small Henry of the Virgin Islands yearns for the day when he can go fishing with his father. When that day comes, he dodges a big shark and comes home in triumph, "a fisherman for true." Lithe, brown bodies against the clear, brilliant colors of islands and sea add to the beauty and grace of this brief tale.
6–9

CATHERALL, ARTHUR, *Yugoslav Mystery,* Lothrop, 1964. Within the framework of an exciting suspense story is an excellent portrait of an Iron Curtain country. 12–14

CLAIR, ANDREÉ, *Bemba: An African Adventure,* tr. from the French by Marie Ponsot, ill. by Harper Johnson, Harcourt, 1962. A mystery story involving an evil witch doctor and the three children who solve the mystery.
8–12

GEBHARDT, HERTHA VON, *The Girl from Nowhere,* tr. from the German by James Kirkup, ill. by Helen Brun, Phillips, 1959. An absorbing story of Magdalene, a nine-year-old girl from nowhere, who arouses wonder and suspicion among the children of a small German town. When she finally leaves them they find they are strangely lost without her.
10–12

HÁMORI, LÁSZLÓ, *Dangerous Journey,* tr. from the Swedish by Annabelle Macmillan, ill. by W. T. Mars, Harcourt, 1962. The dramatic, but believable, story of two Hungarian boys who make their escape to freedom in Vienna.
10–12

HOLM, ANNE S., *North to Freedom,* tr. from the Danish by L. W. Kingsland, Harcourt, 1965. A tremendously moving story of young David's trip from a concentration camp to Denmark and freedom. Contrasts between the camp and life in the free world are excellently drawn and David's experiences arouse in the reader a new appreciation of a way of life we often take for granted. A unique book.
10–14

KINGMAN, LEE, *Pierre Pidgeon,* Houghton. Pierre is French Canadian, and this Christmas story is about a Finnish-American family. Kingman's books (*The Best Christmas, Year of the Raccoon*) are marked by a convincing realism and warmth which many children find deeply satisfying.
10–12

KUSAN, IVAN, *The Mystery of Green Hill,* tr. from the Yugoslavian by Michael B. Petrovich, ill. by Kermit Adler, Harcourt, 1962. A well-paced mystery set in war-weary Yugoslavia.
9–12

MIRSKY, REBA P., *Seven Grandmothers*, ill. by W. T. Mars, Follett, 1955.

Thirty-one Brothers and Sisters, ill. by W. T. Mars, Follett, 1952.

Two stories of Nomusa, a young Zulu girl. Warmly drawn picture of life in a Zulu kraal. 8–10

SEREDY, KATE, *Chestry Oak*, ill. by author, Viking, 1948. An involved and difficult story with a deeply significant theme—the fall of an ancient house and its rebirth in a new land. The boy Michael and his great horse Midnight are the central figures in the tale. By the author of *The Good Master* (p. 149). 10–14

SERRAILLIER, IAN, *The Silver Sword*, ill. by C. Walther Hodges, Phillips, 1959. An inspiring narrative of four courageous children of Warsaw after World War II. The three who have been separated from their parents set off to find them and are joined by a fourth child. Their journey covers three hard years, but their spirit never falters. 10–14

STINETORF, LOUISE A., *Musa, the Shoemaker*, ill. by Harper Johnson, Lippincott, 1959. A lame Algerian boy, apprenticed to a shoemaker, grows up in a village of acrobats but achieves success with another skill. 9–11

WEIL, ANN, *Red Sails to Capri*, ill. by C. B. Falls, Viking, 1952. An unusual story about the discovery of the Blue Grotto on Capri, told almost entirely in dialogue. Considerable suspense and delightful people. 9–12

HISTORICAL FICTION[3]

American

ALCOTT, LOUISA MAY, *Little Women*, ill. by Jessie Willcox Smith, Little, 1934 (1868). Although this forerunner of modern realism for children and young people is chiefly a story of family life, it is also a story of life in Civil War times. There are numerous attractive editions available; but it remains basically a girl's book. 10–14

BAILEY, JEAN, *Cherokee Bill, Oklahoma Pacer*, ill. by Pers Crowell, Abingdon, 1952. A fine story of a boy and his horse. The setting is on the Kansas-Oklahoma border at the time of the opening of the Cherokee strip. 10–14

BAKER, BETTY, *Walk the World's Rim*, Harper, 1965. Chakoh, a young Indian, went to Mexico City with four Spanish survivors of a force of six hundred which had set out to search for gold in the sixteenth-century land of America. "Readers will learn much about colonial Mexico and the hard conditions of primitive Indian life . . ." from this book. 10–12

BERRY, ERIC, pseud. (Allena Best), *Hay-Foot, Straw-Foot*, ill. by author, Viking, 1954. Tale of a little drummer boy in the French and Indian Wars who inspired the tune of "Yankee Doodle." 9–12

BULLA, CLYDE ROBERT, *Down the Mississippi*, ill. by Peter Burchard, Crowell, 1954. 8–10

The Secret Valley, ill. by Grace Paull, Crowell, 1949. Just two of the more than thirty titles this author has produced for young readers. All of them are readable and all capture the atmosphere of times past. 8–10

CARR, MARY JANE, *Children of the Covered Wagon; A Story of the Old Oregon Trail*, ill. by Bob Kuhn, Crowell, new ed., 1957. An excellent story of a pioneer

[3] Those wishing comprehensive lists on historical fiction are advised to consult the following bibliography:

Sutherland, Zena, compiler, *History in Children's Books*, McKinley, 1967

family on a journey from Missouri to the Willamette Valley, Oregon, in 1844. 9–12

Young Mac of Fort Vancouver, ill. by Richard Holberg, Crowell, 1940. Outstanding for fine characterizations and authentic historical background, this is a story of a thirteen-year-old Scotch-Indian boy who accompanies a group of French fur traders on a trip down the Columbia River to Fort Vancouver, Washington. 12–14

CAUDILL, REBECCA, *Tree of Freedom*, ill. by Dorothy B. Morse, Viking, 1949. An outstanding pioneer story which gives a detailed picture of life in 1770, near Louisville, Kentucky. The story involves some stormy family relationships and appealing characters. 12–14

COATSWORTH, ELIZABETH, *Five Bushel Farm*, ill. by Helen Sewell, Macmillan, 1939. Companion volume to *Away Goes Sally* (p. 184), this is the story of Andy, who lives near Sally. 8–10

CONSTANT, ALBERTA W., *Miss Charity Comes to Stay*, ill. by Louise Darling, Crowell, 1959. Lively, imaginative story of a young teacher in the Oklahoma Territory in 1893. 10–12

CRAWFORD, PHYLLIS, *"Hello, the Boat!"* ill. by Edward Laning, Holt, 1938. A resourceful family journeys from Pittsburgh to Cincinnati in 1916 aboard a steamboat fitted out as a store. 9–11

DALGLIESH, ALICE, *Adam and the Golden Cock*, ill. by Leonard Weisgard, Scribner's, 1959. A small boy faces a personal problem of divided loyalty when General Rochambeau's army comes to his Connecticut town during the Revolution. 7–9

The Bears on Hemlock Moutain, ill. by Helen Sewell, Scribner's, 1952. This adventure story is based on a historical episode. There weren't supposed to be any bears on Hemlock Mountain, but there *were*, as poor Jonathan proved. Jonathan's ingenuity in hiding from the bears will delight every young reader. 7–9

The Courage of Sarah Noble, ill. by Leonard Weisgard, Scribner's, 1954. "Keep your courage up, Sarah Noble," her mother had told her as she set off to the Connecticut wilderness to take care of Papa. A wonderfully warm story of courage. 7–9

DE ANGELI, MARGUERITE, *Thee, Hannah!* ill. by author, Doubleday, 1940. A vivid picture of Quaker life in old Philadelphia is given in this story of lively Quaker Hannah. Beautiful illustrations in color and black and white. 8–10

DOUGLAS, EMILY, *Appleseed Farm*, ill. by Anne Vaughan, Abingdon, 1958. Ten-year-old Penny hears about a visit Johnny Appleseed once made to her family's Indiana farm. 8–10

EDMONDS, WALTER D., *Cadmus Henry*, ill. by Manning de V. Lee, Dodd, 1949. The Civil War from the Confederate side is the scene of this humorous and appealing tale of a young soldier's misadventures. 12–14

The Matchlock Gun, ill. by Paul Lantz, Dodd, 1941. This Newbery Medal winner is a thrilling story of young Edward's courage in defending his home while his father is away fighting the Indians during the French and Indian Wars. Stunning illustrations capture the drama. 8–10

FALL, THOMAS, *Canalboat to Freedom*, Dial, 1966. Benjamin Lown, a young Scotch boy, is apprenticed as a hoggee (a towpath driver) to Captain Roach, a hard-bitten canalboat captain on the Hudson and Delaware canals. On the boat Ben works side by side with a freed Negro, Lundius, learns about the Underground Railway for slaves, and encounters a tragedy involving Lundius, which teaches him that there are principles for which a man dies. 12–15

FRITZ, JEAN, *Brady*, ill. by Lynd Ward, Coward, 1960. The Underground Railroad station in a small Pennsylvania town is endangered because Brady can't keep his mouth shut. A fine story of how a boy becomes a man when he learns that there are more important things in the world than his own well-being. 10–12

The Cabin Faced West, ill. by Feodor Rojankovsky, Coward, 1958. Appealing story of frontier life and of a little girl who learns to like being a pioneer. 9–12

GENDRON, VAL, *The Fork in the Trail*, ill. by Sidney Quinn, McKay, 1952. A young boy sets up a trading post on the route to the West during the Gold Rush days. A good picture of the period. 12–14

GRAY, ELIZABETH JANET, *Beppy Marlowe of Charlestown* (1715), ill. by Loren Barton, Viking, 1936.

The Fair Adventure (modern), ill. by Alice K. Reischer, Viking, 1940.

Jane Hope (1860), Viking, 1933.

Meggy MacIntosh (1775), ill. by Marguerite De Angeli, Viking, 1930.

This is Elizabeth Gray's fine series about North Carolina. The period of each book is indicated. The series shows the changes in manners, customs, and problems of one region. 12–14

HALL, ANNA G., *Cyrus Holt and the Civil War*, ill. by Dorothy Bayley Morse, Viking, 1964. At first, life in the upstate New York small town goes on much as it had before the War. Slowly, the effects are felt: wounded men come home, others never return; the glory is dulled, and Cyrus Holt ceases to think of war as a joyful time. 8–12

HODGES, C. WALTER, *Columbus Sailed*, ill. by author, Coward, 1939. Fiction, but based on facts, and tremendously moving. This is a popular book. 12–14

HOLLING, HOLLING C., *Paddle-to-the-Sea*, ill. by author, Houghton, 1941.

Seabird, ill. by author, Houghton, 1948.

Tree in the Trail, ill. by author, Houghton, 1942.

Perhaps the first book is more geography than history, for it is the account of an Indian boy's toy canoe which follows the Great Lakes to the sea. *Seabird* is a story of American ships in terms of one family of shipbuilders. In *Tree in the Trail*, a cottonwood tree on the Santa Fe Trail was a landmark for Indians and white men. All three books are superbly illustrated. 10–12

HUNT, IRENE, *Across Five Aprils*, Follett, 1964. Jethro is nine when the Civil War begins and he sees it in terms of parades and dashing soldiers marching in bright uniforms. When the war is over, Jethro knows better. While similar to *Cyrus Holt* (see above), this is a more mature book and, despite its male central character, is basically a girl's book. 12–14

JOHNSON, ANNABEL and EDGAR, *Torrie*, Harper, 1960. Fourteen-year-old Torrie Anders travels by covered wagon from St. Louis to California in 1846. In the excitement of the adventure, she gains a new understanding of and admiration for her family. 12–16

Wilderness Bride, Harper, 1962. A realistic picture of the persecution of the Mormons, built around a moving love story. 12–16

KEITH, HAROLD, *Rifles for Watie*, Crowell, 1957. Jeff Bussey, Union volunteer at sixteen, gains insight into and sympathy for the problems and ideals of both the North and the South in this powerful Civil War story. Newbery Medal. 12–16

LAMPMAN, EVELYN, *Tree Wagon*, ill. by Robert Frankenberg, Doubleday, 1953. This journey to Oregon is a happy one for all concerned, including potential readers. 10–13

LENSKI, LOIS, *Puritan Adventure*, ill. by author, Lippincott, 1944. Massachusetts is the scene of this vivid tale of Colonial times when a cheerful young aunt from England visits a strict Puritan family, bringing gaiety and laughter with her. 12–14

MC MEEKIN, ISABEL, *Journey Cake*, Messner, 1942. Six motherless children, in the care of an intrepid old free Negro woman, journey through the wilderness to join their father in Boone's Kentucky. This book is followed by *Juba's New Moon*. Both books have good historical details. 10–12

MASON, MIRIAM, *Caroline and Her Kettle Named Maude*, ill. by Kathleen Voute, Macmillan, 1951. An amusing story of a little pioneer girl who asked for a gun but was given a kettle. How she uses this kettle as a weapon will delight young readers. 8–10

The Middle Sister, ill. by Grace Paull, Macmillan, 1947. Early Minnesota provides the background for the story of Sarah Samantha, who took an apple tree with her to her new home. 8–10

MEADER, STEPHEN W., *The Buckboard Stranger*, ill. by Paul Caile, Harcourt, 1954.

The Fish Hawk's Nest, ill. by Edward Shenton, Harcourt, 1952.

Jonathan Goes West, ill. by Edward Shenton, Harcourt, 1946.

Red Horse Hill, ill. by Lee Townsend, Harcourt, 1930.

River of the Wolves, ill. by Lee Townsend, Harcourt, 1948.

Who Rides in the Dark? ill. by James MacDonald, Harcourt, 1937.

Exciting stories with historical background and usually an element of mystery, these and other books by this author are well written and exceedingly popular. 10–14

MEANS, FLORENCE CRANNELL, *A Candle in the Mist*, ill. by Marguerite de Angeli, Houghton, 1931. Pioneer life in a Minnesota settlement in the 1870's is difficult, but fifteen-year-old Janey faces it with high courage. 12–14

MEIGS, CORNELIA, *Covered Bridge*, ill. by Marguerite de Angeli, Macmillan, 1936.

Master Simon's Garden, ill. by John Rae, Macmillan, 1929.

Willow Whistle, ill. by E. B. Smith, Macmillan, 1931.

These well-written stories of other days and ways are not easy reading, but they are rewarding books for the able child. Action and theme carry the interest. 10–14

O'DELL, SCOTT, *Island of the Blue Dolphins*, Houghton, 1960. An Indian girl shows remarkable courage and resourcefulness in living alone on an island off the coast of Southern California for eighteen years. An outstanding historical episode. Newbery Medal. 10–14

The King's Fifth, Houghton, 1966. A remarkable story of the power of gold to corrupt men. It is basically the story of Esteban, a young man, who accompanies the Spanish adventurers in their search for the golden cities of Cibola. 12–16

STEELE, WILLIAM O., *The Buffalo Knife*, ill. by Paul Galdone, Harcourt, 1952.

The Far Frontier, ill. by Paul Galdone, Harcourt, 1959.

The Lone Hunt, ill. by Paul Galdone, Harcourt, 1956.

Tomahawks and Trouble, ill. by Paul Galdone, Harcourt, 1955.

Wilderness Journey, ill. by Paul Galdone, Harcourt, 1953.

Winter Danger, ill. by Paul Galdone, Harcourt, 1954. Fantastically realistic stories of life on the frontier in which the heroes must learn that all goals are achieved at a price—sometimes more than one is willing to pay. 9–12

Perilous Road, ill. by Paul Galdone, Harcourt, 1958. A Civil War story in which youthful Chris learns that there is nothing simple about war. By the author of *Flaming Arrows* (p. 191). 9–12

WIBBERLEY, LEONARD, *Peter Treegate's War*, Farrar, 1960. American Revolutionary days are vividly re-created as the background for the hero, a high-spirited sixteen-year-old boy, who attempts to resolve conflicting loyalties between his real and foster fathers. (Sequel to *John Treegate's Musket*, Farrar, 1959; followed by *Treegate's Raiders*, Farrar, 1962.) 11–14

WILDER, LAURA INGALLS, *By the Shores of Silver Lake*, ill. by Garth Williams, Harper, 1953.
Little House in the Big Woods, ill. by Garth Williams, Harper, 1953.
Little House on the Prairie, ill. by Garth Williams, Harper, 1953.
The Long Winter, ill. by Garth Williams, Harper, 1953.
On the Banks of Plum Creek, ill. by Garth Williams, Harper, 1953.
These Happy Golden Years, ill. by Garth Williams, Harper, 1953.
Originally published in the 1930's and reissued with completely new illustrations in 1953, these seven books cover the saga of a pioneer family and the childhood of the author to the time of her marriage. This is the family invincible, able to stand up to misfortunes and tragedies because it is strong in love and in loyalty. For most children the books are a totally satisfying reading experience. By the author of *Farmer Boy* (p. 217). 9–14

European

BUFF, MARY, *Apple and the Arrow*, ill. by Conrad Buff, Houghton, 1951. The stirring story of William Tell and his son Walter, with many dramatic illustrations by Swiss-born Conrad Buff. 8–11

CHUTE, MARCHETTE, *The Innocent Wayfaring*, ill. by author, Dutton, 1955. Fourteenth-century England brought vividly and authentically to life. 11–14
The Wonderful Winter, Dutton, 1954. In 1596 Sir Robert Wakefield ran away to London to find work. His adventures included finding himself a happy part of an actor's family and, eventually, one of the boy actors in Will Shakespeare's own theater. A vivid picture of the Elizabethan theater. 11–14

DE ANGELI, MARGUERITE, *Door in the Wall*, ill. by author, 1949. When Robin, son of Sir John de Bureford, is stricken with an illness that leaves his legs paralyzed and his back bent, it is brother Luke who helps him to find a "door in the wall" and nurses him back to strength and courage. This tender and beautiful book is not only a valuable addition to children's literature of the medieval period, but it should bring courage to handicapped children everywhere. Newbery Medal. 8–10

GRAY, ELIZABETH JANET, *Adam of the Road*, ill. by Robert Lawson, Viking, 1942. When Adam, by mischance, loses both his father and his dog, he seeks them on the highways and byways of thirteenth-century England. Newbery Medal. 10–14

HARNETT, CYNTHIA, *Caxton's Challenge*, ill. by author, World, 1960. The scriveners of England saw the printing press as a manner of depriving them of a living, and they fought by fair means and foul to keep William Caxton from successfully operating his business. Exciting storytelling, excellent history. 11–14

KELLY, ERIC P., *The Trumpeter of Krakow*, ill. by Janina Domanska, Macmillan, new ed., 1966. Medieval Poland comes vividly alive in this tale of the youthful trumpeter who finishes the Heynal and prevents tragedy. 11–14

KENT, LOUISE, *He Went with Christopher Columbus*, ill. by Paul Quinn, Houghton, 1940. 12–14
He Went with Marco Polo, ill. by C. LeRoy Baldridge, Houghton, 1935. 12–14
He Went with Vasco da Gama, ill. by Paul Quinn, Houghton, 1938. 12–14
The adventures of boys who accompanied the three great explorers of the Middle Ages.

LEIGHTON, MARGARET, *Judith of France*, ill. by Henry C. Pitz, Houghton, 1948. Teen-age girls will enjoy this romantic novel about Charlemagne's spirited granddaughter. The pathetic pawn of kings, she comes into her own at last. 12–16

LEWIS, HILDA, *Here Comes Harry*, ill. by William Stobbs, Criterion, 1960. Henvy VI became King of England at the age of nine months and was thus deprived of anything resembling a normal childhood. Intrigues and power-manipulations surrounded him. All told through the eyes of Harry Rushden, a goldsmith apprentice and devoted follower. 12–15

PARKER, RICHARD, *The Sword of Ganelon*, ill. by William Ferguson, McKay, 1958. A remarkable and stirring tale of ninth-century England invaded by the Danes. 11–16

PICARD, BARBARA L., *Ransom for a Knight*, ill. by C. Walter Hodges, Walck, 1956. After the English loss to the Scots at Bannockburn, young Alys sets forth to try and ransom her father and brother. Excellent picture of the times, combined with a fast moving plot. 12–15

PYLE, HOWARD, *Men of Iron*, ill. by author, Harper, 1891. The training of knights, the clash of battle, and all the glamor of feudal England under Henry IV. 12–14
Otto of the Silver Hand, ill. by author, Scribner's, 1888. The appealing story of a boy whose father, a German robber baron, places him in a medieval monastery to assure his safety. 10–12

SUTCLIFF, ROSEMARY, *Eagle of the Ninth*, ill. by C. Walter Hodges, Walck, 1954. 12–15
Lantern Bearers, ill. by Charles Keeping, Walck, 1959. 12–15
Silver Branch, ill. by Charles Keeping, Walck, 1957. 12–15
Three magnificent novels about the Roman impact upon England, and the influence of England upon the conquerors.
Warrior Scarlet, Walck, 1958. This is a story about a young handicapped boy's long, painful struggle to become a great warrior, told in heroic language that captures the harshness and discipline needed to survive as a Bronze Age inhabitant of England. 12–15

TREECE, HENRY, *Perilous Pilgrimage*, ill. by Christine Price, Phillips, 1959. The Children's Crusade portrayed through exciting incidents and vivid prose. 11–14

Ancient Times

BEHN, HARRY, *Faraway Lurs*, World, 1963. A tenderly told story of tragic yet inspiring dimensions, of a girl of the Forest People who made the mistake of falling in love with a boy of the Sun People. 12–14

BRUCKNER, KARL, *The Golden Pharoah*, tr. from the German

by Frances Lobb, ill. by Hans Thomas, Pantheon, 1959. An excellent introduction to one of the most sensational archaeological discoveries of our time, the tomb of Tutankhamen, Egyptian Pharaoh. 11–14

JONES, RUTH FOSDICK, *Boy of the Pyramids; a Mystery of Ancient Egypt*, ill. by Dorothy Bayley Morse, Random, 1952. Kaffe, a ten-year-old Egyptian boy whose home is near the ancient city of Memphis, watches the building of a pyramid on the desert, sees the Nile in flood, and helps capture a robber. 10–12

KJELGAARD, JIM, *Fire-Hunter*, ill. by Ralph Ray, Holiday, 1951. The adventures of a prehistoric boy with saber-toothed tigers, mammoths, and cave bears. By the author of *Irish Red* (p. 5). 12–14

LAWRENCE, ISABELLE, *The Gift of the Golden Cup*, ill. by Charles V. John, Bobbs, 1960.
Niko: Sculptor's Apprentice, Viking, 1956. *Niko* is an adventure tale about a young Athenian and his friends. *The Theft of the Golden Cup*, ill. by Charles V. John, Bobbs, 1960. Twelve-year-old Atia and seven-year-old Gaius are two of Julius Caesar's relatives, and their adventures present a vivid picture of Roman life. 11–14

MC GRAW, ELOISE JARVIS, *Mara, Daughter of the Nile*, Coward, 1953. Mara, a slave of the Egyptians, is promised every luxury and eventual freedom if she will spy for the Queen, the Pharaoh, Hatshepsut. But Mara also sells her services to the rival political faction which is trying to put the rightful heir, Thutmose, on the throne. Her decision to play both ends against the middle, as she puts it, leads to greater peril than she had expected. 13–17

MEADOWCROFT, ENID, *The Gift of the River, a History of Ancient Egypt*, illustrations adapted from Egyptian sources by Katherine Dewey, Crowell, 1937. Adapted from source material in both text and pictures, this is a useful book for children studying ancient history. 9–12

MORRISON, LUCILE, *The Lost Queen of Egypt*, ill. by Franz Geritz, Lippincott, 1937. This story of ancient Egypt solves the mystery of the disappearance of the young queen when her husband Tutankhamen, king of Egypt, dies. 12–14

RIENOW, LEONA, *The Dark Pool*, ill. by Allen Pope, Scribner's, 1949. A revealing picture of the harshness of primitive man's existence at a time when a moral code was gradually being developed. 9–12

SHORE, MAXINE, *The Captive Princess*, ill. by Kreigh Collins, McKay, 1952. Story of the Roman conquest of Britain in which a Druid princess falls in love with a Roman soldier. 12–14

SNEDEKER, CAROLINE DALE, *The Forgotten Daughter*, ill. by Dorothy Lathrop, Doubleday, 1933. When Chloe's Greek mother died, she suffered many hardships until her Roman father remembered her and made a home for her in Rome. 12–14
A Triumph for Flavius, ill. by Cedric Rogers, Lothrop, 1955. The story of a young Roman boy who, in compassion for his Greek slave and teacher, works to secure his freedom. Interesting background of ancient Rome and early Christian days. 8–11

TREASE, GEOFFREY, *Message to Hadrian*, Vanguard, 1955. Young Paul must journey from England to Rome with a message for Emperor Hadrian if his friend Severus is to stay alive. Paul's trip is one headlong dash, reading like a modern spy thriller for all its historical accuracy. Boys should love it. 11–14

INDEX OF TITLES AND AUTHORS